MONEY AND THE CHURCH IN MEDIEVAL EUROPE, 1000–1200

Religion and Money in the Middle Ages

Edited by

Svein H. Gullbekk, Museum of Cultural History, University of Oslo, Norway
Giles E. M. Gasper, Department of History, Durham University, UK

Religion and Money in the Middle Ages explores the connections between two of the most dominant aspects of medieval society and culture: religion and money. Recognising the importance of both multi- and single-disciplinary perspectives on the issues and questions connected to religion and money, the series accepts joint as well as individual authorship and editorship. All disciplinary perspectives are welcome, particularly from archaeology, history (social, ecclesiastical, intellectual and economic), theology, anthropology and numismatics. The series operates with a broad chronological range: in western European terms from late Antiquity to the Reformation. While the geographical and cultural focus lies in western Christendom, the series will be open to cross-cultural comparative studies, and to treatments of money and religion in all religious communities within the period, within Christendom and without.

Of especial interest are studies which explore issues on the theory and practice of money within religious contexts, and those that further reveal the interconnections and contrasts, overlaps and distinctions, between these attitudes and practices are particularly encouraged. How differences between theory and practice emerge, how they are reconciled, or how they remain unresolved, are further questions the series is keen to explore. The range of source material available, and the centrality of both subjects to medieval life, culture, belief and activity, allow for breadth and depth of investigation and insight into the medieval past at its most intimate and in its largest institutions and social structures.

Money and the Church in Medieval Europe, 1000–1200

Practice, Morality and Thought

Edited by

GILES E. M. GASPER
Department of History, Durham University, UK

and

SVEIN H. GULLBEKK
Museum of Cultural History, University of Oslo, Norway

Routledge
Taylor & Francis Group
LONDON AND NEW YORK

First published 2015 by Ashgate Publishing

2 Park Square, Milton Park, Abingdon, Oxfordshire OX14 4RN
52 Vanderbilt Avenue, New York, NY 10017

Routledge is an imprint of the Taylor & Francis Group, an informa business

First issued in paperback 2019

British Library Cataloguing in Publication Data
A catalogue record for this book is available from the British Library

The Library of Congress has cataloged the printed edition as follows:
Money and the Church in Medieval Europe, 1000–1200: Practice, Morality and Thought /
edited by Svein H. Gullbekk and Giles E.M. Gasper.
pages cm – (Religion and Money in the Middle Ages)
Includes bibliographical references and index.
1. Catholic Church--Europe--Finance. 2. Money--Europe--Religious aspects. 3. Church history--Middle Ages, 600-1500. 4. Catholic Church--Customs and practices. I. Gullbekk, Svein H., editor of compilation. II. Gasper, Giles E. M. (Giles Edward Murray), 1975- editor of compilation.
BX1950.M664 2015
261.8'5--dc23 2014037428

ISBN 978-1-4724-2099-2 (hbk)
ISBN 978-0-367-88229-7 (pbk)

Contents

Prefatory Remarks

Money and the Church in Northern Europe 1000–1200: Practice, Morality and Thought emerges from an extended collaboration between Svein H. Gullbekk and Giles E. M. Gasper, on the subjects encompassed by the title. We have found our particular disciplinary areas, of medieval numismatics and medieval cultural and intellectual history, increasingly in dialogue, and the volume that follows flows from that dialogue, set in a broader and deeper series of contexts. This has developed subsequently into a wide spectrum of research activities under the aegis of a project funded by the Norwegian Research Council, *Religion and Money: the Economy of Salvation in the Middle Ages* (2013–2016) with Svein H. Gullbekk as principal investigator. The papers of which the present volume consists originally formed part of an international conference organised by the Museum of Cultural History, University of Oslo, and the then Institute of Medieval and Renaissance Studies (now Institute of Medieval and Early Modern Studies), Durham University. The conference, 'Church and Money c. 1060–c. 1160' took place between 23 and 25 November, 2011, in Oslo, with the financial assistance of the two institutions, and the Samlerhuset Group Foundation.

The conference was the starting point for a longer process of collective and individual expansion of the papers, on a longer chronological scope and with a focus on north-western Europe. What results is a collection of case studies and surveys, from a wide range of disciplinary perspectives, exploring the many dimensions to an understanding of money and how it was perceived and experienced in the High Middle Ages. The contributions centre on the many roles of the church within those perceptions and experiences, in its institutions, its members both clerical and lay, and as the major repository of documentary record. We hope to put the subjects of the church and money together in ways that will provide new and exciting insights into monetary history and the history of the church. The High Middle Ages marks a period of dynamic growth and change in both histories and in terms of spiritual as well as material aspects. In its case-studies this collection provides particular examples of how the church and money might be investigated, the variety of approaches that can be adopted and the different scholarly directions that can be taken and from which inspiration can be drawn. The result, we hope, will be to provoke more questions, more interest and more engagement in this field.

The editors would like to thank the contributors for their patience and willingness to pour their expertise into this enterprise, jointly and singly. To

Håkon Roland, Anette Sættem, Johnny Kreutz, Timo Stingl, Eileen Sweeney, and Rachael Matthews we owe particular debts for help and advice.

GEMG and SHG

List of Illustrations

The plate section falls between pages 244 and 245.

Church-Building (*Holzkirche*). Source: Auction Fritz Rudolf Künker 130, Osnabrück 2007, no. 1541.

11 Stavelot, Abbey. Anonymous, eleventh century. Penny. 1.03 g. S REMACLVS EPS Bust of Saint Remaclus r. with crosier// STABVLAVS Building. Source: Auction Fritz Rudolf Künker 205, Osnabrück 2012, no. 2435.

12 Marsberg, Mint of the Corvey Abbey. Saracho (1065–71). Penny. 1.38 g. +SCS PETRVS Bust of Saint Petrus//+HERESBVRG Wall with three towers. Source: Auction Fritz Rudolf Künker 152, Osnabrück 2009, no. 6235.

13 Normandy, penny, Rouen, c. 940, 1.24 g, type Dumas XV, 16, with the name of Saint-Ouen. Source: Musée départemental des Antiquités de la Seine-Maritime, inv. 93.4.1 (Ó cg76 – Musée départemental des Antiquités – Rouen, cliché Yohann Deslandes).

14 Normandy, penny, Rouen, c. 965/975, 1.24 g, type Dumas XV, 19/Fécamp 6042 with the name of Saint-Romain. Maybe from the Fécamp hoard. Source: Musée départemental des Antiquités de la Seine-Maritime, inv. 92.13.2 (Ó cg76 – Musée départemental des Antiquités – Rouen, cliché Yohann Deslandes).

15 Normandy, penny, Rouen, c. 965/975, 1.14 g, type Dumas XV, 20/Fécamp 6044, with the name of Saint-Romain. Probably found Place du Vieux-Marché, Rouen, 1867. Source: Musée départemental des Antiquités de la Seine-Maritime, inv. R.93.104.1 (Ó cg76 – Musée départemental des Antiquités – Rouen, cliché Yohann Deslandes).

16 Normandy, penny, Rouen, c. 980, 1.02 g, type Dumas XV, 23–24/Fécamp 4147, with a monogram HGT that has been interpreted as Hugh, archbishop of Rouen. Probably from the Fécamp hoard. Source: Musée départemental des Antiquités de la Seine-Maritime, inv. 79.1.2 (Ó cg76 – Musée départemental des Antiquités – Rouen, cliché Yohann Deslandes).

17 Engraving showing (with some imagination) the grave of St Francis of Assisi at the moment of its discovery in 1818; coins are visible under the right arm. Image from *Compendio della vita del serafico Patriarca Francesco di Assisi con un distinto ragguaglio sul reperimento e verificazione delle sue sagre spoglie rinvenute sotto l'altar maggiore della Chiesa Patriarcale dei MM.RR. PP. Minori Conventuali della stessa Città l'anno 1818,* Assisi 1820 (anastatic reprint, no date).

18 County of Anhalt, Albert the Bear margrave of Brandenburg (1157–70); bracteate (silver, 0.74 g). ADELBERTS MARCHI

Figures

Tables

Introduction

Chapter 1
Money and the Church: Definitions, Disciplines and Directions

Giles E. M. Gasper[1]

In the 1020s an exceptional coin was issued from the Danish Slagelse mint (see Plate 1).[2] Its legend, which runs across both faces of the coin, consists of the opening lines of the Gospel of St John: 'In principio erat verbum, et verbum erat apud Deum, et Deus erat verbum [In the beginning was the word, and the word was with God, and the word was God]'. The Slagelse coin represents not only the oldest gospel quotation from Denmark, and indeed, Scandinavia, but also the earliest coin in Europe to carry a full quotation from the Bible. Why this particular coin was struck is not clear. It does, however, indicate a very specific instruction to a die-cutter at the disposal of Cnut the Great (1018–35), and a die-cutter who was accurate, within reasonable expectation, in his reproduction of the biblical text.

---

1 With bibliographical and subject-specific assistance from Svein H. Gullbekk.

2 P. Hauberg, *Myntforhold og udmyntninger i Danmark indtil 1146*, Det kgl. Danske Videnskabernes Selskabs Skrifter, 6. Række, historisk og filosofisk afdeling, vol. 1 (Copenhagen, 1900), *Knud den Store, Slagelse*, no. 38. Three examples of this issue are known, one in the collection of Stockholm and two in the Royal Collection of Coins and Medals in Copenhagen, of which one was a gift from A. Benzon's collections in 1888/89 (Royal Collection of Coins and Medals, Gaveprotokol [Accession Protocol] 982). Only one of these coins has an identifiable provenance, that from the Enner hoard, Jutland, where 1,315 coins (557 German, 677 Anglo-Saxon, 24 Danish and 14 Irish) were deposited after c. 1030/1. The hoard was deposited close to a Viking Age farm house (Anne Mette Kristiansen, 'Enner-skatten – ny viden om et gammelt fund', *Nordisk Numismatisk Unions Medlemsblad* (2006): 63–71, att. xx). The coin is die-linked with another coin issued at the Slagelse mint by the contemporary moneyer Brihtric, presumably of Anglo-Saxon origin, see J. Jensen et al., *Danish Coins from the 11th Century in the Royal Collection of Coins and Medals* [*Tusindtallets Danske Mønter fra Den Kongelige Mønt- og Medaillesamling*] (Copenhagen, 1995), p. 40. Of all Danish mints in the eleventh century, the use of Christian legends occurs most often at the Slagelse Mint, see Jens Christian Moesgaard, 'Møntprægning i Ringsted og Slagelse i 1000-tallet', Årbog *for Historisk Samfund for Sorø Amt*, 87 (2000): 40–49, at 44. For a general discussion of ecclesiastical coinage in eleventh-century Denmark, see Gert Posselt, 'Nogle danske mønter med gejstelige fremstillinger før ca. 1150', *Hikuin*, 11 *Festschrift to Brita Malmer* (1985): 207–14.

The remarkable features of the Slagelse coin help to pose a number of questions about the relationship between religion and money in the High Middle Ages, between Christian belief and practice and the evolution and development of monetary regimes and systems. That the two should not be held apart as separate spheres is one principal contention of this discussion and this volume. The church and money, however they are defined, were intimately interconnected in this period, connections which are complex, sometimes contradictory, and pervasive throughout the evidence which survives from their contemporary society.

The Slagelse coin reifies the connections and the questions: a Gospel citation, engraved on a coin die in a mint belonging to a king, who in the 1020s ruled a people still in a formative phase of Christianisation. That the coin exists is demonstrable. Why it should have been struck is much more difficult to establish. The numismatic biblical message may be explicable in the context of Cnut's reign, a period in which the political and religious climates were undergoing serious change.[3] The coin may be seen as part of an attempt to articulate Christian underpinnings for lordship. What the Gospel citation means in a mostly illiterate society is difficult to gauge; that the symbolism of the legend was as important as the text would seem reasonable, but serves to indicate how many more questions are prompted than can be definitively or even suggestively answered.

As such, the Slagelse coin stands as an intriguing and tantalizing introduction to the relationship between money and the church in this period. The coin itself is passive, but its very production implies a nexus of conceptual frameworks revolving around the mechanics of minting and Christian thought. The relationships which are largely implicit in the case of the Slagelse coin become possible to explicate in the century or so which followed: and these relationships, in their various articulations, in their various media and with their interweaving of different sources form the subject of the contributions which follow.

The volume as a whole addresses two of the larger subjects of the Middle Ages: the church and money. In so doing, its first purpose is to raise wide-ranging questions, as well as, and in the context of, smaller ones; as with the Slagelse coin, the microcosm is illustrative of the macrocosm, and reflective in many cases of the evidence available. Counter-posing the intimate to the common experience, and the individual to the general, emerges as a guiding methodology throughout the contributions. Second, the volume takes ideas and perspectives which focus on the two subjects and discusses them with reference to a diverse body of evidence: from theological texts to chronicles and charters, from account rolls to saints' lives, from the physical fabric of ecclesiastical buildings to the coins

[3] See T. Bolton, *The Empire of Cnut the Great: Conquest and Consolidation of Power in Northern Europe in the Early Eleventh Century* (Leiden, 2009).

which circulated within society and were dropped or deposited within its built environment. The subject in its constituent sections is not new: neither money, nor the church, nor the late eleventh and early twelfth centuries, are subjects or a period that have been understudied. However, the contributions all suggest that 'money' and the 'church' in this period are related to each other in different, challenging and insightful ways. The theme of the volume has been designedly chosen to seek both fault-lines and bridges between the cultural and intellectual frameworks of the eleventh and twelfth centuries, generated to a great extent by church reform and what is generally known as the rise of a money-economy and the commercial revolution, its use, and perception within the secular world.[4]

Providing any sort of definition of the church in any period of its existence is a complex task. In all periods of Christian history all Christian communities engage, to one extent or another, with a series of relationships: between themselves and their communities, between communities sharing the same devotional ends and the particular circumstances of how that devotion is expressed, and between local and time-bound experience and the universal and cosmic claims of Christianity.

The foundational narratives of the early church, the Acts of the Apostles and the Epistles, especially those attributed to St Paul, speak to these relationships and tensions, and subsequent Christian thinking incorporates many traditions of ecclesiological reflection. One of the many legacies of Augustine of Hippo, the most influential of the Latin authorities of the early church to the church of the High Middle Ages, was the question not merely of predestination, but to which city an individual belonged: the city of God or the city of Man. The answer, for Augustine, was eschatological: only at the final judgement is the identity revealed.[5] How individual Christians interacted with the world, and

[4] The classic study of church reform in the period remains, amongst a vast and growing literature, G. Tellenbach, *Church, State and Christian Society at the Time of the Investiture Contest*, R. F. Bennett (trans.) (Toronto, 1991), originally published as *Libertas: Kirche und Weltordnung im Zeitalter des Investiturstreites* (Stuttgart, 1936). Amongst recent literature see *The Cambridge History of Christianity Volume 3: Early Medieval Christianities c. 600–c. 1100*, Thomas F. X. Noble and Julia M. H. Smith (eds) (Cambridge, 2008) and *The Cambridge History of Christianity Volume 4: Christianity in Western Europe c. 1100–c. 1500*, Miri Rubin and W. Simons (eds) (Cambridge, 2009). On the economic side, R. S. Lopez, *The Commercial Revolution of the Middle Ages* (Englewood Cliffs, NJ, 1971), remains significant, as does the still magisterial account by P. Spufford, *Money and its Use in Medieval Europe* (Cambridge, 1988); for more recent discussion see R. H. Britnell, *The Commercialistion of English Society 1000–1500* (Cambridge, 2009).

[5] Augustine, *De civitate Dei*, Bernard Dombart and Alfons Kalb, (ed.), Corpus Christianorum Series Latina, 47–8 (Turnhout, 1955); *The City of God*, W. Babcock (trans.) (New York, 2012). R. A. Markus, *Saeculum: History and Society in the Theology of St Augustine* (Cambridge, 1970) is still wholly pertinent to this question.

how the church, as the collective and as individual institutions, interacted with the world, were questions of central significance throughout the period under scrutiny. The questions are easy to pose, but complex to address. The church was many things: a human institution with divine sanction, the historical link to the incarnate Christ and the Apostolic community, allegorically the bride to Christ's bridegroom, civic, urban, rural, monastic, a building both physically and metaphorically, a collection of institutions and individuals. The philosophical challenges of how to deal with unity and diversity are echoed in the practical diversity of Christianity alongside its claims to universality.

These themes are keenly observable for the period covered by this book, and are the focus for the contributions which follow. It was a period in which the institutions of the church and their purpose were scrutinised and debated across several generations, and in which the expression of Christian doctrine and identity were affected profoundly by developments in theology and canon law. Speculative and pastoral theology both informed and were themselves informed by the institutional changes which shaped the western medieval church from the eleventh century onwards, and had particular effect in the northern regions converted to Christianity only relatively recently. In this way, the theological interest in creation, time, the consequences of sin, and the humanity of Christ played out in the daily life of northern Christendom. It was a period also of church building on a scale sufficient to transform the landscape, from the stave churches of northern Norway to the soaring cathedrals of northern France and England, exhibiting complete re-building as well as layered re-use of the past. These buildings played their ideological role too, in state-formation and in the inter-twined relationship of secular authority to the territorial and temporal authority of churches from the parish to the metropolitan.

To all of these themes the contributors of the volume address themselves: many different faces and aspects of the church in the regions covered are explored, and many different sorts of material are used from which to construct the lives and experiences of the past. In the period and regions encountered – England, Normandy, Angevin France, Denmark, Norway – evidential coverage varies. In all cases, however, the dominance of a clerical voice within the documentary sources, and to some extent also the material sources, is apparent. This affects distinctly the interpretation of the church and the activity of clerical officers, and the role and emphasis to be placed on the activity of laymen, in all parts of society. An ideal image of the church, in its mediatory role between the world and the world to come, as the body of Christ, as the Gregorian model of a church for the world but unaffected by secular politics, behaviour and other threats to its purity, remained, for the most part, an ideal. Indeed, given that the high medieval period operated with an ecclesiology so heavy on eschatology, the ideal church was predicated on remaining as such. That said, the ideal was preached and expounded in the midst of social and political realities, from acts of grand and sweeping policy, to the quotidian and individual. An episode in the *Lais Le Fresne* by Marie de France, which dates from the end of the period of this book, the 1180s or so, and written in the vernacular Old French, illustrates the way in which the ideal could be gently mocked, testament to the strength of the social message churchmen and monastic chroniclers put forward, and a powerful reminder of the all too often silent laity.

The story concerns twin sisters, Le Fresne (Ash) and La Codre (Hazel). Separated by their mother ashamed of having given birth to twins having previously denounced another woman's twin-bearing as the product of adultery, Le Fresne is brought up at a nunnery. Unaware of her identity or status, she grows up and attracts a young man, for whom she leaves the monastic house and with whom she goes to live. Despite loving Le Fresne the young man becomes betrothed to and marries La Codre: the identity of the two women is revealed when Le Fresne leaves her richest possession, the cloth in which she was wrapped as a baby, as a gift for the husband to be. The cloth is identified by the women's mother, and all ends well, with Le Fresne married to the man she loves.[6] The episode in question concerns Le Fresne's attendance in the nunnery and her young man's craft and guile in gaining unimpeachable access to the community. Le Fresne's beauty was remarkable:

> When she reached the age when Nature forms beauty, there was no fairer, no more courtly girl in Brittany, for she was noble, cultivated, both in appearance and in speech. No one who had seen her would have failed to love and admire her greatly.

Having engineered, successfully, one visit, the protagonist pondered his next move:

---

[6] The resolution to the *Lais* also provides commentary on developing positions on marriage during the twelfth century. Having married Gurun to Le Fresne's sister La Codre on the previous evening, at a point where their relationship as twin sisters was not known, and Gurun's evident affection for Le Fresne had been over-ruled by La Codre's apparent higher social standing, the archbishop of Dol, in response to the discovery of Le Fresne as the equal of La Codre, 'recommended that things be left as they were that night; the next day he would unjoin those he had married. Thus they agreed and the following day the two were separated. Gurun then married his beloved and her father gave her to him as a mark of affection': Marie de France, *The Lais of Marie de France*, G. Burgess and K. Busby (trans), 2nd edition (London, 1999), p. 67. On medieval marriage see Christopher Brooke, *The Medieval Idea of Marriage* (Oxford, 1989), Neil Cartlidge, *Medieval Marriage: Literary Approaches 1100–1300* (Cambridge, 1997), *Medieval Families, Perspectives on Marriage, Household and Children*, Carol Neel (ed.) (Toronto, 2004), and David D'Avray, *Medieval Marriage: Symbolism and Society* (Oxford, 2008).

> He was distraught and did not know what to do, for if he were to return too often the abbess would notice and he would never see the girl again. He thought of a solution: he would increase the wealth of the abbey and give a great deal of his land, thereby enriching it for all time, for he wanted to have a lord's rights to a dwelling-place and residence. In order to join their community he gave them a generous portion of his wealth, but his motive was other than remission for his sins. He went there often to talk to the girl, and begged her and promised her so much that she granted what he sought.[7]

The story of *Le Fresne* provides an alternative interpretative framework for pious donation, and the interaction of church, lay society and money, here in the form of landed wealth. While it is true that this framework is one of literary construction and for entertainment, it serves as a reminder that other frameworks are no less constructed. The episode in question also highlights another question, which lies at the heart of the investigations in this volume: how the people of the high medieval period experienced the church.

Individual experience of church was, naturally enough, bound up with life-cycle, from cradle to grave, from this world to that which is to come. It is the duality of temporal location on the one hand, and the anticipation of eternity on the other, that makes the experience challenging to interpret and express. The notion of the church was grounded on the contingency of creation upon its creator, and the time-bound qualities of existence: what had a beginning will have an end. This applied to individuals as to communities and to the very world itself. This journey was made in hope, a hope sharpened in a society in which the effects of original sin create an inherent imperfection, dependent on divine grace, fuelled by a strong sense of eschatological presence; judgment was real but postponed until the fulfilment of time. In the duality of experience of responsibilities of life in a Christian community both temporal and spiritual, money has a significant role to play, as sign and signifier, and as agent, of those experiences. Money and the church are intimately connected in this period: the chapters in this volume attempt to show how widely and deeply this connection can be made. What

---

7 Marie de France, *The Lais of Marie de France*, Burgess and Busby (trans), p. 64. *Les lais de Marie de France,* (ed.) J. Rychner (Paris: Éditions Champion, 1966): 'Quant ele vint en tel eé / Que Nature furme beuté, / En Bretaine ne fu si bele / Ne tant curteise dameisele; / Franche esteit e de bone escole, / E en semblant e en parole. / Nuls ne la vit que ne l'amast / E merveille ne la preisast'. ll. 231–42, p. 51. 'Esguarez est, ne seit coment, / Kar si il reperiout sovent, / L'abeesse s'aparcevreit; / Jamés des oilz ne la vereit. / D'une chose se purpensa: / L'abeïe crestre vodra; / De sa tere tant i dura / Dunt a tuz jurs l'amendera, / Kar il i voelt aveir retur / E le repaire e le sejur. / Pur aveir lur fraternité, / La ad grantment del soen doné, / Mes il i ad autre acheisun / Que de receivre le pardun! / Soventefeiz i repeira; / A la dameisele parla: / Tant li pria, tant li premist, / Qu'ele otria ceo ke il quist'. ll. 257–74, p. 52.

money was within the period is equally complex, and revealing of the society in which it was produced and whose anxieties and hopes it served.

The classic definition of money stresses its function as a means of exchange, a standard of value and a means to store wealth. Money, it can be argued at a general level, is any object that is generally accepted in payments by sellers of goods and services or by purchasers.[8] The general acceptability of different kinds of money is established when a large proportion of the community accept its existence in particular forms. Part of the universal quality of money derives from this interactivity between supplier and demander: more than the intrinsic value it is the notion of general acceptability which forms money as social convention, and as of universal value.[9] Money facilitates exchange, and does so better than other systems, for example barter, described memorably by W. S. Jevon as a bilateral activity dependent on 'a double coincidence (of wants) that will rarely happen'.[10] With rapid monetisation of value, virtually everything can be expressed in terms of a common denomination: money. Only money, in terms of its pure concept, has attained this final stage; it is nothing, as Georg Simmel puts it, 'but the pure form of exchangeability'.[11]

All of these functions can be found within the period in question: money was used within daily transactions and increasingly as the period went on, in the development of units of value in complex but interchangeable systems and in the deposit of coins to store wealth, for example in hoards, within and without buildings, secular and ecclesiastical. A progressive expansion of monetary affairs occurred with varied underlying reasons for the growth of the monetary economy. Year by year the changes were often imperceptible, but in 200 years their cumulative effect was great.[12] It is important to note that in this process of monetisation, money was certainly not confined to coin: sophisticated monetary

---

8 Fadhel Kaboub, 'Money', in *Encyclopedia of World Trade from Ancient Times to the Present*, vol. 3 of 4, Cynthia Clark Northrup (ed.) (New York, 2005), p. 670.

9 The nature of what becomes designated as money in a given society is culturally constrained, as much as conventions to decide standards of time. The importance lies in the fact that something is chosen as money, not the particularity of choice. Within world history money takes on a wide variety of forms, from the huge stone money from the island of Yap in Oceania, to shells, iron and bronze in other Asian societies, and within Europe at various times tea, pepper, hides, corn, livestock, butter, silver, gold and coins. See, James Tobin, 'Money', in *The New Palgrave Dictionary of Money and Finance* (London, 1992), pp. 770–78).

10 W. S. Jevon, *Money and the Mechanism of Exchange* (London, 1875), p. 3.

11 Georg Simmel, *The Philosophy of Money* (London and New York, 1978), p. 130.

12 Michael Metcalf, *Coinage in South-Eastern Europe 820–1396* (London, 1979), p. 18.

systems could exist without coin.[13] However, coinage retains a pre-eminent hold on the high medieval, as well as the modern conception, of money.

Contemporary writers, which, for the majority of this period, means those from a clerical background, make reference to coin so frequently as for it to be a fundamental aspect of their world-view. The coin becomes a way in which to describe money and economic transaction, but, equally powerfully, becomes a metaphor for spiritual health. Money, and in particular coin, has a capacity in these authors to define and transcend conceptual boundaries. What was money becomes a question with multiple dimensions, kaleidoscopic in its scope. The complexity of this ubiquity is illustrated in the overlapping nature of the source material. Where charters, for example, will, on the whole, discuss money and coin in flat economic terms, other literature, from letters and chronicles to theological treatises and sermons, explores moral issues with reference to money by analogy, by metaphor and by description. The boundaries between these source genres are permeable when it comes to the use of money; money already by the eleventh century is a concept used and explored by churchmen *in re* and *in mens*, in reality and in mentality.

Experience of money, like that of the church, was both individual and communal. What the chapters in this volume address are aspects of those experiences. The authors represent different disciplinary backgrounds, from numismatic and economic history, to theological, historical and literary studies, and from archaeology (with inspiration from anthropological approaches), to art and architectural history. The perspectives of each practitioner, and the interplay between the sources examined and analysed, provide a multi-faceted approach to the question of how money was used, exploited and experienced within the

---

[13] This issue has been the subject of intense debate for Norway, especially between Svein H. Gullbekk and Kåre Lunden. See Gullbekk, 'Medieval Law and Money in Norway', *Numismatic Chronicle*, 158 (1998): 173–84; Lunden, 'Money economy in medieval Norway', *Scandinavian Journal of History*, 24 (1999): 245–65; Gullbekk, *Pengevesenets fremvekst og fall i Norge i middelalderen* (Oslo, 2003), with a revised edition with English summary published by Museum Tusculanum Press in 2009; also his 'Natural or money economy in medieval Norway', *Scandinavian Journal of History*, 30 (2005): 3–19, and 'Lite eller mye mynt i Norge i middelalderen?', *Historisk Tidsskrift*, 84 (2005): 551–72; Lunden, 'Mynt, andre pengar og politisk-økonomisk system i mellomalderen', *Historisk Tidsskrift*, 86 (2007): 7–34; Gullbekk, 'Myntenes omløpshastighet i norsk middelalder', *Historisk Tidsskrift*, 90 (2011): 511–29. Two standard studies of the issue are A. Steinnes, 'Mål, vekt og verderekning i Noreg i millomalderen og ei tid etter', in Sven Aakjær (ed.), *Mål og Vekt* (Oslo-Stockholm-København, 1936) and Lunden, *Korn og kaup. Studiar over prisar og jordbruk på Vestlandet i mellomalderen* (Oslo-Bergen-Tromsø, 1978). Wider discussion on the phenomenon can be found with reference to Iceland in particular, see Gullbekk, 'Money and its Use in the Saga Society: Silver, Coins and Commodity Money', in *Viking Settlements and Viking Society*, Svavar Sigmundsson (ed.), (Reykjavik, 2011), pp. 176–88.

period. The breadth of interpretative arcs allows evidence not often juxtaposed to be so presented: the stave-church coin finds against sermonising metaphors of monk and coin, or the market data from post-conquest England with the money-making activities of the Danish church. In a period where evidence is sometimes limited, or particular rather than general, a collaborative approach serves to stimulate, inform, open and question the investigative paradigms adopted. The complexity of responses to how people used money in the High Middle Ages, the coupling and overlaying, for example, of the pragmatic with the altruistic, the needful and the desirous, the practical and the conceptual, requires concomitant complexity from modern interpretation.

To provide sufficient comparative focus the chapters concentrate on northern Europe, from the northern Holy Roman Empire, Denmark and Norway, to England and Normandy, and within the period bounded flexibly by 1000 and 1200. These parameters allow comparison between regions of shared and dissimilar culture, between established regnal units and those emerging, between regions recently conquered and converted, and between regions of differing documentary traditions, fewer in eleventh- and twelfth-century Scandinavia compared with the richer, principally monastic sources, from further south and west, and differing material remains, such as the coin finds in Scandinavian churches not replicated commonly in northern France or England. The chapters explore continuities and change, and the often intertwined nature of both when applied to particular phenomena. The longevity of the image of the coin for monastic life with its roots within the early texts of monastic history can be held against the considerable extent to which the image was deepened and elaborated within the later eleventh and early twelfth centuries. Numismatic evidence is used in various contributions to investigate market velocity in England, as a measure of Danish kingdom-formation and to pose questions of the nature of church reform in Norway, and of the realities of funding church-building programmes in England and Scandinavia.

The volume is divided into three sections, the first devoted to attitudes towards money within the church, with survey chapters by Naismith and Gasper, exploring these in contexts both secular and monastic, across the greater part of the period in question, with a focus on England and northern France. When, how and why attitudes towards money changed form the basis of these chapters, against the context of church reform in its different manifestations. Detailed studies of the image of the monk as coin by Dinkova-Bruun, and of the writings of Alan of Lille by Langholm, complement and extend the scope of the investigations, showing the variety of responses to money, as concept and as means by which to explore notions of truth, justice and moral goodness.

The second section offers four chapters on the more practical use of money by churches and churchmen. Vroom offers commentary on the mechanisms by which cathedral-building was organised and managed across a broad spectrum of examples. Bolton gives a critical assessment of the English post-conquest church, and the access of its leaders and officers to money in coin. That the period of the later eleventh and twelfth centuries comprised one of the largest building programmes within western history, using huge resource, provides a focal point to the arguments raised. A case-study by Poulsen brings to the fore the different circumstances, in terms of evidence, chronology and institutional experience, of the Danish church, equally involved in property rights, markets and minting concessions, but making an insightful and instructive comparison with the English situation. The nature of monetary exchange and of the post-conquest English economy is taken up in the final chapter of the section by Mayhew and Mayhew. The church here, as in Denmark, is revealed as an agent both passive and active in the processes of monetisation.

A third and final section reflects on the making and the deposit of coins. Steinbach with respect to monastic minting under the Ottonian and Salian imperial houses and Moesgaard with respect to ducal Normandy discuss the challenges in assigning coins to particular places of production, and both, in the course of so doing, open out the question to a consideration of how religious houses expressed their identity and how they interacted with their place within the built environment, and of the mingling of power and politics. The importance of coin deposit within medieval churches is addressed in the final two chapters, by Travaini and Gullbekk. Deposit with or, as is more often the case, without corroborating documentary evidence, involves appreciation of, and acts as a window onto, the ritual practice of countless individuals throughout the period. Both chapters take up the evidential challenges posed by source material which is not only plentiful (and found in some surprising venues, including a cow buried with a coin within the nave of a church, as well as in areas of the church where coin deposit might be expected), but also tactile, and, as a result, beguiling in its proximity to individuals of the past. This is particularly the case in Gullbekk's material, the coins dropped between floorboards in Norwegian stave churches, but set in and related to the wider changes within Norwegian ecclesiastical and secular history. In this way the Norwegian experience may be compared fruitfully with the situation in Denmark discussed by Poulsen. The management and manipulation of money by church authorities, especially episcopal, which is revealed, is given additional and tantalising form in the extraordinary stave-church coin finds.

The period of the eleventh and twelfth centuries witnessed, in the regions under scrutiny, profound change and significance in terms of social bonds and dynamics, military organisation, political life, the church, intellectual matters and economic life, in towns and in the countryside. That these aspects are too often considered within separate historiographical arenas, and rarely used fully to inform each other, is a state of affairs this book seeks to begin to counteract. To examine money and the church in this period is to gain insight into the interconnections between different areas of society at a period of substantial change. Reconstructing and tracing the practical uses of money allows the underpinnings of intellectual exchange, or ecclesiastical politics, to be shown. How building and trade was paid for reveals much about money on the one hand, and about the mechanisms by which society ran on the other. This is not to suggest a materialist over idealist interpretation of the past, or to claim priority for one mode of interpretation. It is merely to recognise that financial transaction of whatever sort (monetary or otherwise) reveals the workings of human society in ways that allow connections to be made between ideologies, institutions and personnel. Money is not constituted of merely coins, as static entities. Money is for transaction; by its nature it is communitarian and interconnected.

The extent to which the church changed its thinking under the influence of an increasingly monetised economy, or how its thinking affected the way in which monetisation was understood and debated, is fertile ground for inquiry. The proper use of money was clearly an on-going concern to various clergy within this period, from parish priests to scholastic thinkers. The relationship of doctrinal change and social behaviour is another problematic question, but there are sources and subjects which can be used to suggest the mutual influence of one on the other. While the ramifications of a full-blown doctrine of purgatory would not be realised fully until the thirteenth century, the economy of the afterlife, built on a concern about the consequence of sin certainly prominent in the period in question, serves to link temporal and spiritual practice, and theory.[14] Money and the church are subjects more than inter-twined, for to study one is to encounter the other, as metaphor, as physical entity, as practical mode and communication of exchange – temporal or spiritual, as the generator of institutions, and as agent with the capacity to bind individuals into communities, and, at the same time, to empower individual experience.

[14] J. Le Goff, *La naissance du purgatoire* (Paris, 1981), translated into English as, *The Birth of Purgatory*, A. Goldhammer (trans.) (Chicago, 1986). See more recently, G. Dameron, 'Purgatory and Modernity', in *Bridging the Medieval-Modern Divide: Medieval Themes in the World of the Reformation*, James Muldoon and Paul Monod (eds) (Farnham, 2013), pp. 87–106.

interconnections between different areas of society in a period of substantial change. Reconstructing and tracing [illegible]

[illegible]

PART I
Attitudes to Money within the Church

Chapter 2

Turpe lucrum? Wealth, Money and Coinage in the Millennial Church

Rory Naismith[1]

One day in 1058, a Flemish monk named Balger was laid up on the Sussex coast in England, and took himself off to a nearby church at Bishopstone.[2] There, he was told, lay the relics of the local saint Lewinna. Balger was suitably awed by her shrine, and had to have not just a souvenir, but a piece of Lewinna herself. He took one of the local clergy by the hand and offered him anything he asked in return for some of the relics. The priest was aghast. He responded: 'Father! Do you not know what you say? Is it proper that a servant of God wishes this, fitting that he utters it, suitable that he does this? Although some fool might wish to commit this crime, you being prudent, you being wise, you a servant of God ought to prevent it!'.[3] The saint's relics, quite clearly, were not the stuff of paltry commerce. Much more suitable was simply to steal the relics during a quiet moment, which is what Balger did, as this meant that the saint herself must have acquiesced to the deed on some level. As the relics ended up at Balger's monastery of St Winnoc in Flanders, this was exactly the argument the author of the text telling of their translation wanted to put forward.

This episode is a classic example of *furtum sacrum*, 'holy theft', in which the successful theft of a saint's remains was justified as having been the result of the saint's own supernatural will.[4] But it also gives one eleventh-century writer's insight into what the clergy should not be doing: buying and selling the relics of the saints. Some things were simply not suitable for commerce, or at least commerce carried out by men of God. But Balger for one readily indulged in this

1 I am grateful to Erik Niblaeus for kindly reading and commenting on a draft of this chapter.

2 G. Thomas, *The Later Anglo-Saxon Settlement at Bishopstone: A Downland Manor in the Making* (York, 2010).

3 'Papæ! scisne quæ loquaris? An decet servum Dei id velle? Convenit dicere, oportet facere? Quamquam quis fatuus id illicitum vellet admittere: tu prudens, tu providus, tu servus Dei deberes tardare?'. Drogo of Saint-Winnoc, *Historia translationis sanctae Lewinnae* I.1 (Acta Sanctorum [AASS] Jul V, col. 615F).

4 P. Geary, *Furta Sacra: Thefts of Relics in the Central Middle Ages* (Princeton, NJ, 1990), esp. pp. 56–128.

and other forms of commerce throughout the story. While returning home by sea with the relics, for example, he went ashore and paid six pennies to be rowed back out to his ship, although in the meantime it sailed off, and shenanigans ensued as he tried desperately to recover the relics.[5]

Balger's experience epitomises broader concerns over how members of the eleventh-century church should engage with money and material wealth in general. Why should the church and its clergy be at the same time so involved with money, and yet have such misgivings about it? To approach an answer, I will concentrate on and draw my examples from the period extending from around 975 to about 1125. These years have often been seen as witnessing profound and interconnected changes in the economic, social, political and spiritual landscape of western Europe; changes sometimes characterised as a 'revolution' or 'transformation'.[6] Territories in Spain, Scandinavia and eastern Europe were brought into the Christian fold. There was growth in agriculture and commerce, and an associated expansion of towns and coinage, arguably associated with a rise in overall population.[7] Even if the pace was slower and more uneven than the terms 'revolution' and 'transformation' might suggest, there is little doubt that much did indeed change,[8] and that one of the principal differences is in source material: the rising tide of evidence in the eleventh century perhaps reveals concerns long present or gestating but hitherto unexposed.[9] For this reason it will be stressed here that many of the developments associated with this time already had a long history behind them, and progressed in fits and starts. Nevertheless, the 'long' eleventh century at various times and places saw existing pressures sharpen to a jagged point. The church, which for better or worse was

---

5 Drogo of Saint-Winnoc, *Historia translationis sancta Lewinnae* I.3 (AASS Jul V, col. 618B–19C).

6 For just a small selection of the voluminous literature see T. N. Bisson, *The Crisis of the Twelfth Century: Power, Lordship and the Origins of European Government* (Princeton, 2009), esp. pp. 1–17; J.-P. Poly and E. Bournazel, *The Feudal Transformation 900–1200*, C. Higgitt (trans.) (New York and London, 1991); G. Bois, *The Transformation of the Year One Thousand*, J. Birrell (trans.) (Manchester, 1992).

7 Bois, *Transformation*, pp. 70–134; but see also C. Wickham, 'Mutations et révolutions aux environs de l'an mil', *Médiévales*, 21 (1991): 27–38. See also R. Bartlett, *The Making of Europe: Conquest, Colonization and Cultural Change 950–1350* (London, 1993), pp. 5–23 and 280–88; A. Murray, *Reason and Society in the Middle Ages* (Oxford, 1978), pp. 50–8.

8 P. Geary, *Phantoms of Remembrance: Memory and Oblivion at the End of the First Millennium* (Princeton, NJ, 1994), pp. 23–6; Wickham, 'Mutations': 33–7.

9 C. West, *Reframing the Feudal Revolution: Political and Social Transformation between Marne and Moselle, c. 800–c. 1100* (Cambridge, 2013), pp. 1–16.

integrated into earthly society, had to face up to evolving social and economic conditions which set the scene for the twelfth century and after.[10]

These shifts played out differently across Christian Europe. Some institutions found themselves presented with new riches that they could use to honour God more dazzlingly than ever before, or were faced with the cure of souls burdened with greater monetary resources. Others rejected the ever-increasing lustre of gold, silver and the marketplace with renewed fervour. The two principal flashpoints for comment and debate were the question of poverty in religious life, and the practice of simony (the acquisition of ecclesiastical office for payment). There could be sharp tensions between clergy who held different views on these points, and between their patrons and supporters.[11] To speak simply of 'the church' as a monolithic entity is, therefore, gravely misleading. When it came to attitudes to wealth there was no single church line. This was a period of adaptation and polarisation: ideas and practices separated, collided and reconverged in kaleidoscopic fashion.[12] Variability in attitudes to wealth was to be expected.

Money and coin was just one component of this, and one which had played a part throughout Christian history thanks to its prominence in the Bible. Currency was above all a tool associated with earthly material resources: as Christ said in the Gospel of Matthew (22:21) when shown a Roman imperial coin, 'render unto Caesar the things which are Caesar's'. This did not necessarily make money in itself bad or sinful. Also in the Gospel of Matthew (20:1–16) the gift of the kingdom of heaven was likened metaphorically to the *denarius diurnus*, the 'daily penny'. Money was, for the Evangelists as for eleventh-century Christians, an accepted part of life and interaction on earth, good or ill: everything depended on the purpose and context of its use.[13] Biblical views on money were therefore tempered by warnings against the temptations of wealth. Paul's First Epistle to Timothy (6:10) famously declared that 'the desire of money (*cupiditas*) is the root of all evils' and advocated humility, while Mark's Gospel (10:25) stated that it was easier for a camel to pass through the eye of a needle than for a rich man to get into heaven. Luke 14:33 stated that 'whosoever he

---

[10] K. L. Jasper, 'The Economics of Reform in the Middle Ages', *History Compass*, 10 (2012): 440–54.

[11] G. Tabacco, *Spiritualità e cultura nel Medioevo: dodici percosi nei territori del potere e della fede* (Naples, 1993), pp. 267–85; H. Leyser, *Hermits and the New Monasticism: A Study of Religious Communities in Western Europe, 1000–1150* (New York, 1984), pp. 83–4.

[12] Giles E. M. Gasper and Svein H. Gullbekk, 'Money and its Use in the Thought and Experience of Anselm, Archbishop of Canterbury (1093–1109)', *Journal of Medieval History*, 38 (2012): 155–82, esp. 158–63.

[13] G. Todeschini, *Ricchezza francescana: dalla povertà volontaria alla società di mercato* (Bologna, 2004), pp. 10–12, and *Il prezzo della salvezza: lessici medievali del pensiero economico* (Rome, 1994), pp. 119–43.

be of you that forsaketh not all that he hath, he cannot be my disciple'. Careful and moderate management of resources could, however, be encouraged, and in the Book of Proverbs (6:6–8) the ant which looked after itself and stored up food at harvest-time was praised as a model to be followed. Readers could and did therefore take a variety of messages away from consideration of wealth in the Bible. But the prevalent view of Benedict of Nursia (d. 546) and other early monastic founders was that hard work and austerity were crucial to a life in the service of God. Property should be held in common, and no giving or receiving was to take place without the abbot's leave. Food was rationed, with the intention that the monks should provide for their own needs as far as possible.[14]

This ideal had metamorphosed considerably by the millennium. Pride had long been considered the principal vice that monks should avoid, but began to give way to avarice as the eleventh century wore on.[15] Labour in the fields had come to be associated with servile status, and the requirement for monks to do manual agricultural work had been reduced by Benedict of Aniane in the early ninth century. It was, by and large, nominal in Benedictine houses of the eleventh century.[16] A parallel and contributing development had been the growth in monasteries' role as 'powerhouses of prayer'. Prayer had always been at the heart of monastic life, but reduced labour requirements freed up mouths to sing in church. As monasteries proliferated and became established, they did so with the support of powerful local patrons. These in return expected to benefit from the prayers of the monastic community; a process which served to develop their liturgical role.[17] The lands and other material goods the monasteries received placed them in a very different position to the humble early churches of the desert fathers, albeit not automatically one of dissolution or corruption.[18] Monetary wealth permitted churches to support the poor through almsgiving on

---

[14] D. W. Witters, 'Pauvres et pauvreté dans les coutumiers monastiques du Moyen Age', in M. Mollat (ed.), *Études sur l'histoire de la pauvreté (Moyen Age–XVI siècle)* (2 vols, Paris, 1974), vol. 1, pp. 177–215.

[15] L. K. Little, 'Pride Goes before Avarice: Social Change and the Vices in Latin Christendom', *American Historical Review*, 76 (1971): 16–59; Richard Newhauser, 'Avarice and the Apocalypse', in R. A. Landes, A. C. Gow and D. C. van Meter (eds), *The Apocalyptic Year 1000: Religious Expectation and Social Chance, 950–1050* (Oxford, 2003), pp. 109–19.

[16] G. Duby, *Hommes et structures du Moyen Age* (Paris, 1973), pp. 384–5; A. J. Gurevich, *Categories of Medieval Culture*, G. L. Campbell (trans.) (London, 1985), pp. 259–61.

[17] Geary, *Phantoms of Remembrance*, pp. 79–80; H. Fichtenau, *Living in the Tenth Century: Mentalities and Social Orders*, P. Geary (trans.) (Chicago, IL, 1991), pp. 74–6; R. I. Moore, 'Property, Marriage, and the Eleventh-Century Revolution: A Context for Early Medieval Communism', in M. Frassetto (ed.), *Medieval Purity and Piety: Essays on Medieval Clerical Celibacy and Religious Reform* (New York, 1998), pp. 179–208, at pp. 186–7.

[18] P. G. Jestice, *Wayward Monks and the Religious Revolution of the Eleventh Century* (Leiden, 1997), esp. pp. 8–15.

a lavish scale, and growth of population, especially in towns, would have served to increase the number of paupers dependent on charity.[19] Material success in the form of gold, silver and new buildings could also be a demonstration of many monasteries' role as effective heavenly intercessors.[20] Nowhere exemplified the liturgical strength of monasticism better than Cluny.[21] This monastery in central France came to house hundreds of monks, and, after the completion of Cluny III in the late eleventh century, included the largest church in Europe. In the words of Hildebert, writing his *vita* of St Hugh, abbot of Cluny (1049–1109), a new basilica could be commanded and planned out in a vision of St Peter, and culminate in an 'ambulatory of angels'.[22] Building was far from empty ostentation. In the eleventh century there was a strong link forged between architectural enterprise and the maintenance of monastic discipline, and even implementation of reform.[23]

Estates held by the church presented difficulties on several levels. Even large monasteries only needed so much food, and so a common practice was to lease land out, or to engage in sale or exchange to acquire more conveniently located estates.[24] Monastic landlords had long been among the most economically 'rational' in Europe,[25] and were at the forefront of developments like the commutation of food rents into specie, and the promotion of towns and markets.[26] Importantly, clergy were charged only with the management of these resources, not their immoderate expansion through taking advantage of others. Good administration within these parameters was stressed by Peter Damian

---

19 M. Mollat, 'Les moines et les pauvres, XIe–XIIe siècles', in *Il monachesimo*, pp. 193–213; Witters, 'Pauvres et pauvreté', p. 206; Jestice, *Wayward Monks*, pp. 35–8; Gurevich, *Categories*, pp. 242–3; I. M. Resnick, 'Odo of Tournai and Peter Damian: Poverty and Crisis in the Eleventh Century', *Revue bénédictine*, 98 (1988): 114–40, at 134–5.

20 L. K. Little, *Religious Poverty and the Profit Economy* (London, 1978), pp. 66–8; Resnick, 'Odo of Tournai': 119 and 129–30; K. G. Cushing, *Reform and Papacy in the Eleventh Century: Spirituality and Social Change* (Manchester, 2005), pp. 91–5.

21 B. H. Rosenwein and L. K. Little, 'Social Meaning in the Monastic and Mendicant Spiritualities', *Past & Present*, 63 (1974): 4–32, at 5–16; Moore, 'Property, Marriage', pp. 189–91.

22 'Deambulatorium angelorum'. Hildebert of Le Mans, *Vita S. Hugonis abbatis Cluniacensis*, ch. 6 (*Patrologia Latina* [*PL*] 159, col. 885A). See J. H. Van Engen, 'The "Crisis of Cenobitism" Reconsidered: Benedictine Monasticism in the Years 1050–1150', *Speculum*, 61 (1986): 269–304, at 285–92.

23 Van Engen, '"Crisis of Cenobitism"': 286–7.

24 Duby, *Hommes et structures*, pp. 382–5.

25 J. P. Devroey, *Puissants et misérables: système social et monde paysan dans l'Europe des Francs (VIe–IXe siècles)* (Brussels, 2006), pp. 591–600; L. Feller, 'Accumuler, redistribuer et échanger durant le haut moyen âge', *Settimane di studio del centro italiano di studi sull'alto medioevo*, 56 (2009): 81–110.

26 Little, *Religious Poverty*, pp. 64–6.

(d. 1072) and Humbert of Silva Candida (d. 1061):[27] ideals of order and lives shaped by routine placed the emphasis in economic matters on structure rather than maximisation of profit.[28] The Benedictine houses which were strictest and most closely managed tended also to be the richest. Raising revenues, like building lavishly, went hand in hand with generosity in giving as a sign of *amplificatio loci*, 'improvement of the place' – in other words, generally effective management on the part of the abbot. Texts such as cartulary chronicles and *gesta abbatum* praised the material wealth and spiritual rigour of a monastery in the same breath.[29]

For Benedictine monasteries, as for other churches, wealth was not therefore in and of itself a bad thing. Nonetheless, many observers were not altogether satisfied with the model of religious devotion presented by mainstream ecclesiastical institutions in the eleventh century. By about 1000 there certainly were plenty of churches and clerics worthy of criticism on account of their attitude towards wealth, which in the eyes of many could slip easily from prosperity into decadence.[30] Bernard of Angers tactfully wrote, when he came to discuss the state of the abbey of Conques in the early eleventh century, that 'for the preservation of a morally upright life nothing is better than a mediocre talent for worldly matters, because then one is neither saddened by harsh poverty nor bloated with immoderate excess ... but I am speaking of an ordinary [i.e. monastic] way of life, because there is a more powerful opinion that judges the highest perfection to belong to those who have absolutely nothing in the world'.[31] The Bible and early Christian history offered other examples of service to God and men, based not least on recognition of Christ's own poverty,[32] and the eleventh century witnessed

27 Todeschini, *Prezzo della salvezza*, pp. 169 and 180–1.

28 Jestice, *Wayward Monks*, pp. 29–35; L. Feller, 'Sur la formation des prix dans l'économie du haut Moyen Âge', *Annales*, 66 (2011): 627–61, at 648–54.

29 Van Engen, '"Crisis of Cenobitism"': 286–90.

30 C. Dereine, 'Odon de Tournai et la crise de cénobitisme au XIe siècle', *Revue du Moyen Age latin*, 4 (1948): 137–54; N. Cantor, 'The Crisis of Western Monasticism, 1050–1130', *American Historical Review*, 66 (1960): 57–67; J. Leclercq, 'The Monastic Crisis of the Eleventh and Twelfth Centuries', in N. Hunt (ed.), *Cluniac Monasticism in the Central Middle Ages* (London, 1971), pp. 217–37; B. K. Lackner, *The Eleventh-Century Background of Cîteaux* (Washington, DC, 1972).

31 'Ad conservandam vite honestatem nihil efficacius mediocritate rerum, qua nec angusta paupertas contristat nec immodica superfluitas extollit ... sed de hac nostra communi vita loquor: de his autem longe potior extat sententia, quorum perfectio etiam nihil prorsus habere in mundo summum esse iudicat'. Bernard of Angers, *Liber miraculorum sanctae Fidis* II.5 (*Liber miraculorum sancte Fidis*, L. Robertini (ed.) (Spoleto, 1994), p. 163; *The Book of Sainte Foy*, P. Sheingorn and R. L. A. Clark (trans) (Philadelphia, PA, 1995), p. 125).

32 P. Jestice, 'A New Fashion in Imitating Christ: Changing Spiritual Perspectives around the Year 1000', in M. Frassetto (ed.), *The Year 1000: Religious and Social Response*

several attempts to take the spiritual life of Christendom in the new directions alluded to by Bernard.[33] Eventually these culminated in the mendicant orders, but key to the early stages of the process were strong personalities eager to essay new lives as canons regular or through different interpretations of monasticism. Among these individuals were Norbert of Xanten, whose new monastery of Prémontré was chosen for its remote location; Bruno of Cologne, who founded Chartreuse and other monasteries which sought to combine the virtues of regulated monastic life with a small, isolated community structure; and Odo of Tournai, who set up a new house of canons which explicitly rejected the rich lifestyle of other Benedictine monasteries and relied on charity.[34] Even Cluny itself, under Peter the Venerable (1122–56), sought to achieve a more austere lifestyle.[35] However, Cluny's model of religious life was explicitly opposed by St Bernard of Clairvaux, who oversaw the expansion of the Cistercian order in the early twelfth century. The latter order's aim was to adhere more closely to the spirit of St Benedict's rule, fleeing the lures of towns and civilisation in favour of remote locations 'since the holy men [the founders of Cîteaux] knew that Saint Benedict built his monasteries not in cities, not in castles, not in villages, but in places remote from the throng, and they promised to emulate this practice'.[36] This austerity was contrasted with the indolence of Cluny, for which St Bernard had nothing but scorn. 'Who', he wrote with reference to Cluniac houses, 'at the dawn of the monastic order, could have believed that monks would sink to such sloth?'; later in the same tract he wryly satirised a line of Persius to challenge the monks of Cluny to 'explain, paupers (if indeed you are paupers), what is

---

to the Turning of the First Millennium (New York, 2002), pp. 165–85, at p. 177; Leyser, *Hermits*, pp. 52–6.

33 Little, *Religious Poverty*, pp. 70–83; Todeschini, *Ricchezza francescana*, pp. 25–39; Rosenwein and Little, 'Social Meaning': 16–18; Poly and Bournazel, *Feudal Transformation*, pp. 170–80.

34 Little, *Religious Poverty*, pp. 87–90; H. E. J. Cowdrey, 'The Gregorian Papacy and Eremitical Monasticism', in P. De Leo (ed.), *San Bruno e la Certosa di Calabria: Atti del convegno internazionale di studi per il IX centenario della Certosa di Serra S. Bruno, Squillace, Serra S. Bruno 15–18 settembre 1991* (Messina, 1991), pp. 33–54, at pp. 43–7; Resnick, 'Odo of Tournai', esp. 121–40.

35 D. Iogna-Prat, *Ordonner et exclure: Cluny et la société chrétienne face à l'hérésie, au judaisme et à l'islam, 1000–1150* (Paris, 2004), pp. 55–60; G. Constable, *The Abbey of Cluny: A Collection of Essays to Mark the Eleven-Hundredth Anniversary of its Foundation* (Münster, 2010), pp. 285–306; Duby, *Hommes et structures*, pp. 390–91.

36 'Quia etiam beatum Benedictum non in civitatibus, nec in castellis aut in villis, sed in locis a frequentia populi semotis coenobia construxisse sancti viri illi sciebant idem se aemulari promittebant'. *Exordium parvum*, ch. 15 (*Les plus anciens textes de Cîteaux: sources, texts et notes historiques*, J. de la C. Bouton and J. B. Van Damme (eds) (Achel, 1974), p. 78).

gold doing in your sanctuary?'.[37] The Cistercians also put a renewed emphasis on the monks' own labour. From the mid-twelfth century, Cistercian houses actually became economic powerhouses in their own right, through the effective development of virgin or underexploited land, and the deployment of *conversi* – adult converts to monastic life – in agricultural work on self-contained farms or granges.[38] Prosperity and expansion necessitated a more pragmatic attitude to economic engagement as the monks grew aware, even from an early stage, that the ideal of isolation and independence was not feasible.[39]

These new monastic initiatives shared a wish to get back to proverbial basics: to retreat into the wilderness like the early desert fathers of monasticism. Some even took steps towards the lifestyle of hermits, and there were many in the eleventh century who followed this path instead of those which led to old or new religious communities.[40] One of them was John Gualbert, who entered a Benedictine monastery in Florence but left in dissatisfaction with the simoniacal and materialistic ways of the city.[41] He wandered with only a few followers, eventually settling at Vallombrosa in 1038. At one point during his journey in the mountains, according to the *vita* written by St Atto early in the twelfth century, Gualbert saw before him a herd of cattle and, lacking anything he might give in alms to the poor, he prayed to St Paul for help. One of the cows promptly dropped dead, and Gualbert had it sent off as food. He prayed again, and another three more cows fell down dead. At this point the local herdsmen took umbrage at the supernatural interference with their herd, and led the remaining cows off to another side of the mountain. But Gualbert and St Paul were not to be defeated so easily: Gualbert prayed, and another five cows were struck down. The distraught herdsmen pleaded with Gualbert to return to his monastery instead of killing their cows. Eventually a compromise was reached whereby the cows' milk was given out in charity, but from this time onwards

---

37 'Quis in principio cum ordo coepit monasticus, ad tantam crederet monachos inertiam devenire?'; 'dicite ... pauperes, si tamen pauperes, in sancto quid facit aurum?'. Bernard of Clairvaux, *Apologia ad Guillelmum Sancti-Theoderici abbatem*, chs 9 and 12 (*PL* 182, col. 909D and 914D).

38 B. Noell, 'Cistercian Monks in the Market: Legal Study, Economic Statutes, and Institutional Evolution in the Twelfth Century', *Cîteaux,* 59 (2008): 169–92, at 169–70; I. Alfonso, 'Cistercians and Feudalism', *Past & Present,* 133 (1991): pp. 3–30; Constable, *Abbey of Cluny*, pp. 381–404.

39 C. B. Bouchard, *Holy Entrepreneurs: Cistercians, Knights, and Economic Exchange in Twelfth-Century Burgundy* (Ithaca, NY, 1991), pp. 185–95.

40 T. Licence, *Hermits and Recluses in English Society, 950–1200* (Oxford, 2011), pp. 1–9 and 27–42.

41 Little, *Religious Poverty*, pp. 75–6; Jestice, *Wayward Monks*, pp. 227–33.

Gualbert relied only on the gifts given to him and his followers rather than on the lethal power of prayer.[42]

Material resources, in this revealing if idealised case, were entirely subordinated to religious needs, and the point was the saint's recognition that God would provide for him without needing to take from others. Other observers saw things in quite different terms; indeed, saw the very fabric of religious life as under threat from worldly demands, above all the taint of simony. Some clergy, or at least writers of their *vitae*, played on the expectation of venality to elicit greater contributions for genuinely good ends. The life of Benno II, bishop of Osnabrück (1068–88), claimed that he was sometimes asked by laymen to commute a fast with a mass, and hinted slyly that he would need some payment, which typically drew a few *denarii*. But he would say this was not nearly enough, and then demand as much as he thought the postulant should be able to afford. Not able to back down, they handed over a lot more money, which Benno would give to a pauper to pray on the rich layman's behalf.[43] A harder line against simony was taken by Peter Damian. He called on his own experience of when, around 1059 or 1060, he had been offered a silver vessel by an abbot while working as a papal emissary in Milan. Peter Damian resisted the gift vigorously, saying that it was improper for a papal emissary to receive *munera* from interested parties, and that it was unnecessary for clergy to demonstrate their affection with material gifts as laymen did. He eventually relented when the abbot suggested he might use the silver to endow a new religious foundation, but remained troubled and eventually returned the cup.[44]

Reformers faced an uphill struggle in the fight against simony.[45] A liberal definition of the abuse, such as that adopted by Peter Damian and the reforming papacy based on the words of Gregory the Great and Matthew 10:8 ('freely have you received, freely give'),[46] included any and all material benefits; but in many places it was acceptable for gifts to change hands as a reflection of goodwill and the acceptability of a commendation.[47] When it was suggested by Pope Leo IX

---

42 Atto of Villombrosa, *Vita sancti Iohannis Gualberti*, ch. 47 (*PL* 146, cols 687A–C). R. I. Moore, 'Family, Community and Cult on the Eve of the Gregorian Reform', *Transactions of the Royal Historical Society* 30 (1980): 49–69, at 54–5.

43 Nortbert, *Vita Bennonis II episcopi Osnaburgensis*, ch. 7 (MGH SS 30.ii (Leipzig, 1934), pp. 875–6).

44 Peter Damian, *De patientia in insectatione improborum*, ch. 4 (PL 145, cols 793D–6B).

45 Leyser, *Hermits*, pp. 69–72; E. Bain, 'Les marchands chassés du temple, entre commentaires et usages sociaux', *Médiévales*, 55 (2008): 53–74, esp. 61–7.

46 Gregory the Great, *Homeliae in evangelia*, I.4.4 and I.17.13 (Corpus Christianorum Series Latina 141, R. Étaix (ed.) (Turnhout, 1999), pp. 30–31 and 126–7).

47 G. Tellenbach, *The Church in Western Europe from the Tenth to the Early Twelfth Century*, T. Reuter (trans.) (Cambridge, 1993), pp. 167–9 and 286–93; J. Cowdrey, *Pope Gregory VII, 1073–1085* (Oxford, 1998), pp. 398–403, 509–10 and 543–6.

(1049–54) that all simoniacal appointments be voided, there was uproar, and the assembled bishops said that this would leave virtually every church in Europe without anyone to say mass.[48] Leo and his successors adopted a slightly more moderate stance which let free and genuine appointments by simoniacs stand, but they did pursue a policy of combating simony, clerical marriage, pluralism and, most famously, lay investiture. To do so the popes had limited material resources and had to develop additional sources of revenue.[49] Papal government therefore acquired a reputation as a financial black hole. One Spanish cleric who visited Rome in 1099 was moved by his experiences to pen a biting satirical tract about the translation to Rome of the bodies of the most blessed martyrs Albinus and Rufinus – 'silvery' and 'goldy'. These worthy saints were gathered from French churches by the archbishop of Toledo, who sought to use them to gain the legateship of Aquitaine. Once in Rome they were brought by a drunk and morbidly obese Pope Urban II (1088–99) to the shrine of St Cupidity, next to that of her sister St Avidissima ('Greedyguts'), and a cardinal read a sermon in praise of Albinus and Rufinus, saying how 'sinners who possess their relics are perpetually justified, made fit for heaven from being earthly, turned from impiety to innocence'.[50]

Where, then, does money and coin fit in? The short answer is that, just as wealth was a temptation to sin rather than evil in itself, so was coin. St Bernard of Clairvaux put it particularly well when he said, writing to Pope Eugenius III (1145–53), that 'in themselves, as regards man's spiritual welfare, [gold and silver] are neither good nor bad, yet the use of them is good, the abuse bad; anxiety about them is worse; the greed of gain still more disgraceful'.[51] Indeed, coined money had a long history in Christian thought as a neutral and ubiquitous phenomenon with which the audiences of sermons might be familiar: Gregory the Great likened scrutiny of the self to the scrutiny of a coin, while Augustine drew a comparison between humanity and currency, with forged coins representing the unfaithful.[52] Peter Damian (among others) used

48 Peter Damian, *Liber gratissimus*, ch. 37 (MGH LdL 1 (Hanover, 1891), p. 70).

49 Cushing, *Reform and Papacy*, pp. 81–5; Cowdrey, *Gregory VII*, pp. 584–607.

50 'Quorum qui habent reliquias, continuo ex peccatoribus iustificantur, ex terrenis coelestes fiunt, ex impiis vertuntur in innocentes'. *Tractatus Garsiae*, ch. 2 (*Tractatus Garsiae, or the Translation of the Relics of SS. Gold and Silver*, R. M. Thompson (ed. and trans.) (Leiden, 1973), pp. 18–19; *La 'Garcineida': estudio y edición crítica con traducción*, M. Pérez González (ed. and trans.) (León, 2001), p. 236).

51 'Ipsa quidem, quod ad animi bonum spectat, nec bona sunt, nec mala: usus tamen horum bonus, abusio mala, sollicitudo pejor, quaestus turpior'. Bernard of Clairvaux, *De consideratione* II.6 (*PL* 182, col. 748A).

52 Gregory the Great, *Moralia in Job* XXXIII.35 (CCSL 143, M. Adriaen (ed.) (3 vols, Turnhout, 1979–85), vol. 2, p. 1725); St Augustine, *Sermo* IX.9 (CCSL 41, C. Lambot (ed.) (Turnhout, 1961), pp. 125–6).

similar monetary metaphors, with the gold *solidi* of antiquity supplanted by silver *denarii*.[53]

Proper use was thus a key issue. Giving money to, or spending money for, religious purposes was positively to be encouraged. But those who brought monetary considerations into inappropriate arenas faced strict condemnation. St Atto claimed, in his *vita* of John Gualbert, that the saint once refused even to speak to a priest who approached bearing the *nummi* he had received in selling all his worldly goods: John would only receive the visitor once all the coins had been given out to the poor, since he 'put God before gold and the poor before the rich'.[54] A story with a similar moral was told by Bernard of Angers, concerning a merchant and the impishly humorous St Foi. The merchant thought that the price being paid for candles at St Foi's church was too low, and saw the opportunity to make a profit. His plan was to buy as much wax as he could, take it home and sell it for four times what he had paid. But St Foi did not take kindly to this, and the last straw came when the merchant could not resist taking one more particularly beautiful candle. Already heavily laden, he had to stuff it inside his shirt. Before long, the candle caught fire through supernatural agency, and the wicked merchant's clothes and beard went up in flames, resulting in comical but educational punishment for an attempt to apply commercial considerations where they were not welcome.[55]

In certain circumstances (especially among laymen) coin could act as a genuine vehicle for goodwill and charity. Coins and alms were particularly closely related. Ralph Glaber, in his *Historiae*, noted how the copious silver spoils taken from the Muslim stronghold of *Fraxinetum* in 995 were melted down and sent to Cluny, where part was used for a chalice and the rest distributed to the poor, 'down to the last coin ... as was only right'.[56] Good laymen, such as the saintly counts Gerald of Aurillac (d. c. 909) and Charles the Good of Flanders (d. 1127), as well as Robert II the Pious, king of France (996–1031), were prodigal in their distribution of coins as alms to the poor, keeping money about them at all times for this purpose, according to hagiographers.[57] But the principle of

---

53 Peter Damian, *Epistolae* 48, 50 (MGH Briefe d. dt. Kaiserzeit 4.2 (Munich, 1988), pp. 57 and 127) and 98 (MGH Briefe d. dt. Kaiserzeit 4.3 (Munich, 1989), p. 95).

54 'Deum auro et inopes divitibus praeponebat'. Atto of Villombrosa, *Vita sancti Iohannis Gualberti*, ch. 56 (*PL* 146, cols 690B–C).

55 Bernard of Angers, *Liber miraculorum sanctae Fidis* I.24 (*Liber miraculorum*, Robertini (ed.), pp. 125–7; *Book of Sainte Foy*, Sheingorn and Clark (trans), pp. 91–2).

56 'Usque ad assem ... ut decebat'. Ralph Glaber, *Historiae* IV.7 (*Rodulfus Glaber: Opera*, J. France, N. Bulst and P. Reynolds (eds and trans) (Oxford, 1989), pp. 206–208).

57 Galbertus notarius, *Vita Caroli boni comitis Flandriae*, ch. 1 (AASS Mar. I D. 2, col. 180E); Odo of Cluny, *Vita s. Geraldi comitis Auriliacensis* I.2 (*PL* 133, col. 652A–B); Helgaud of Fleury, *Vita Roberti regis Francorum*, chs 21 and 27 (*Vie de Robert le Pieux*, R. H. Bautier and G. Labory (eds and trans) (Paris, 1965), pp. 102–105 and 126).

charity (manifested through coin) extended to all levels of society. One letter of Peter Damian's told of a poor householder down to his last *denarius*, who went off to buy some food. En route he met a still poorer pauper, and gave him his one remaining coin. Peter Damian praised this act of kindness, which recalled that of the poor widow who gave her two coins at the temple in the gospels of Mark and Luke, although in this case the poor man was subsequently approached by a mysterious stranger who presented him with a linen sack containing 20 shillings of *denarii*.[58] The emphasis in some cases could be slightly different. Wazo, bishop of Liège (1041–48), during a famine in 1042 took various measures to protect his *familia* and the surrounding populace, including a donation of two *denarii* per week to each *mansionarius*, explicitly so they would not be forced into a life of poverty by having to sell their cattle and give up farming: an unusual policy which protected the interests of both peasants and bishop by preserving the social *status quo*.[59] Another of Peter Damian's letters told the story of a man from Lombardy and his wife who went south on pilgrimage to Rome. On the way they passed lake Bolsena, where the husband went out on a boat to get some food from a fisherman. On returning, he found that he had lost his pouch, which contained 24 shillings of Pavian coin. Despite his wife's complaints they soldiered on, and used six pounds of Lucchese coins to get them through the trip. On the way home the Lombard pilgrim and his wife passed by the same lake, where they decide to stop and mark the earlier loss with a meal. He bought a particularly good-looking fish, initially offering only 12 *denarii* but calmly accepting the fisherman's request to pay 15 *denarii*. Inside the fish's intestines his wife found 24 shillings of Pavian coins. Here the message was moderation: that the man and his wife did not live the high life or drive a hard bargain, but just got by and did good by their fellow men, for which God recouped their losses.[60]

Parables like these presuppose a society in which coin was a standard feature of day-to-day life, and one reason (along with many other changes in society and religious life) for the increased prominence of money in eleventh-century discourse was very probably the resurgence of the monetary economy. Fuelled by discoveries of silver resources in Germany and elsewhere during the tenth and twelfth centuries, the monetised element of exchange grew considerably.[61] In England, the rate of coin-loss reflected in single-finds tripled between the mid-tenth century and the 1060s.[62] The development of one miracle in successive

58 Peter Damian, *Epistolae* 57 (MGH Briefe d. dt. Kaiserzeit 4.2 (Munich, 1988), pp. 177–8).

59 Anselm of Liège, *Gesta episcoporum Leodiensium*, c. 53 (MGH SS 7 (Hanover, 1846), p. 221).

60 Peter Damian, *Epistolae* 169 (MGH Briefe d. dt. Kaiserzeit 4.4 (Munich, 1993), p. 249).

61 P. Spufford, *Money and its Use in Medieval Europe* (Cambridge, 1988), pp. 74–105.

62 R. Naismith, 'The English Monetary Economy c. 973–1100: The Contribution of Single-Finds', *Economic History Review*, 66 (2013): 198–225.

vitae of St Dunstan (d. 988) illustrates how the role of coined money could evolve in the eyes of clerical writers. An anonymous writer who produced a *vita* of Dunstan not too long after his death in the late tenth century said nothing about money or coin.[63] Osbern of Canterbury, writing a new *vita* around 1070, alluded very briefly to how Dunstan passed sentence on counterfeiters before attending Pentecostal services.[64] Finally, Eadmer of Canterbury's early-twelfth-century version of the *vita* developed this episode in detail. Dunstan's concern speaks to his solicitude for justice and the public weal, for the counterfeiters 'ruin, corrupt and cause turmoil throughout the whole country. These men injure the very rich, those with moderate wealth, and the destitute equally, and out of concern for their own interest they lead everyone to shame or poverty or utter devastation'.[65]

Discourse on the nature of money and its use was still, in the eleventh century, not nearly as elaborate as it would become later in the Middle Ages.[66] But coin had already become associated with discourse on, and representations of, avarice;[67] a distaste for usury was also present, and had been for centuries. It stemmed from biblical and patristic opinions that labour, self-sufficiency and moderation were pleasing to God, whereas using surplus wealth to generate more profit without any input of labour was dangerous to a Christian's soul.[68] The Jews' involvement with moneylending, encouraged by their prohibition from many other trades, different religious strictures and by profitable long-distance trading, was one cause of friction with the Christian majority, and the eleventh century (especially the time around the First Crusade) was marred by anti-semitic violence in several places.[69]

For churches, growing involvement with money could be risky, and not only from a spiritual perspective. Commuting rents due in kind into cash, or

---

63 *The Early Lives of St Dunstan*, M. Winterbottom and M. Lapidge (eds and trans) (Oxford, 2012), pp. 1–109.

64 Osbern, *Vita sancti Dunstani*, ch. 31 (*Memorials of Saint Dunstan, Archbishop of Canterbury*, W. Stubbs (ed.) (London, 1874), p. 106).

65 'Totam terram spoliant, seducunt, perturbant. Ipsi diuites, ipsi mediocres, ipsi pauperes in commune laedunt, et omnes, quantum sua interest, aut in opprobrium aut in egestatem aut in nichilum redigunt'. Eadmer, *Vita et miracula sancti Dunstani*, ch. 46 (*Lives and Miracles of Saints Oda, Dunstan, and Oswald*, A. J. Turner and B. J. Muir (eds and trans) (Oxford, 2006), pp. 118–23).

66 D. Wood, *Medieval Economic Thought* (Cambridge, 2002); Todeschini, *Prezzo della salvezza*, pp. 145–85.

67 Newhauser, 'Avarice', pp. 111–12.

68 F. Bougard, 'Le crédit dans l'occident du haut Moyen Âge: documentation et pratique', in J. P. Devroey, L. Feller and R. Le Jan (eds), *Les élites et la richesse au haut Moyen Âge* (Turnhout, 2010), pp. 439–77.

69 Moore, *Persecuting Society*, pp. 26–42; Little, *Religious Poverty*, pp. 42–57.

leasing estates out for a one-off cash payment, for example, made good sense for monastic lands some distance from the church, as food could not be brought back without trouble and expense. Handled judiciously, a policy like this could guarantee a steady supply of money to the church with which to buy specialist goods that could not be grown or made internally. It also helped foster development of markets, as peasant producers needed some way to turn their surpluses into cash. Yet the case of Cluny shows how this process could derail a powerful monastic institution. As charted by Georges Duby, Cluny came (in the later eleventh century) to rely more and more on its cash income, commuting the bulk of its rents in kind into cash. By 1122, only a quarter of Cluny's subsistence came from its estates' produce, while 20,000 shillings per annum was spent on food. Even basic resources were being bought in, and in 1077 a major annual gold tribute sent from Spain was turned to the purchase of grain. This created problems when the number of monks and the cost of the lifestyle they enjoyed continued to rise, and as most of the income was fixed, even a small degree of inflation could have a severe effect. In the twelfth century Cluny started to feel the pinch, and got badly into debt.[70]

Other abbeys and cathedrals took advantage of the monetary economy in different ways. Several indulged in so-called relic quests: fund-raising trips with the remains of saints, which the faithful laity would pay handsomely to get close to. These peregrinations were sometimes provoked by peace movements or an attempt to reach reconciliation with rivals, and on other occasions by financial crisis.[71] The church of St Ursmar in Lobbes suffered losses to its lands during the strife between Emperor Henry III (1039–56) and the count of Flanders, and a new chapel of St Peter begun during those years looked embarrassingly more like a ruin than a new foundation, so in 1060 the abbot chose to send the remains of St Ursmar on tour to raise alms.[72] Trips like these could be very lucrative. St Mary's at Laon was hit by fire during civil unrest in 1112, and sent some of its relics on tour to fund repairs. They eventually made for England, which was often cited as a rich place where alms could be had in plenty. At one point, in Christchurch, Dorset, they even encountered a rival for alms in the form of a local church run by a deacon. This mean soul denied the canons of Laon shelter from a particularly wet dose of English weather, and did everything he could to limit their profit, as he had the welfare of his own – still unfinished – church to think about. Accordingly, the shrine of St Mary was relegated to a dark, remote corner of the church, but it still drew a good crowd because of the relics' formidable reputation. The angry deacon evicted the canons, but a

70 Duby, *Hommes et richesse*, pp. 61–82 and 381–94.

71 R. Kaiser, 'Quêtes itinérantes avec des reliques pour financer la construction des églises (XIe–XIIe siècles)', *Le Moyen Âge*, 101 (1995): 205–25.

72 *Miracula S. Ursmari in itinere per Flandriam facta*, ch. 1 (MGH SS 15.2, pp. 837–42).

lady of the town and her rich husband put them up in a house which became a makeshift chapel, while the town's merchants agreed a five-shilling fine for any of them who went to the rival church.[73]

Money and coin therefore had many uses to churches in the eleventh century, and were an accepted component of their resources. Divine powers regularly intervened in hagiographical texts to protect legitimate ecclesiastical income in cash from negligence or malfeasance. A wealthy woman who failed to fulfil her *promissiones* to give material *gratias* to the Old Minster at Winchester in return for salvation from illness saw her malady flare up again,[74] while another miracle of the canons of Laon centred on the remorse and suicide of a thief who stole coins from them in Devon.[75] Above all, coins were symbolic of dealing with the outside world, as supreme commodities which existed solely to transfer value between individuals regardless of status or relationship. Hermits generally rejected gifts and, above all, money as bringing unwanted obligations to the rest of society; paradoxically, as disinterested and ever-present pillars of morality, they could also provide a primitive banking service.[76] Within a church community monetary transactions were much fewer, though might take place from (for example) laypeople to the clergy during mass. Such gifts or tithes could end up being lost and unretrieved until modern times, as most famously in the case of coins which slipped between the wooden floorboards of churches in Scandinavia or were buried in the vicinity of churches in Ireland.[77]

Another more practical way in which the church was involved with coinage was in minting. In France, the period from about 975 to 1125 saw some 35 bishoprics and abbeys issue coinage; these represented a significant proportion of so-called 'feudal' mints but certainly not a majority.[78] In the Reich ecclesiastical minting was even stronger. By the end of the twelfth century there were some 215 mints in Germany, 106 of which were operated by the church (61 by bishops), and, in contrast, only 28 by the crown.[79] In both France and Germany the origin of ecclesiastical minting goes back to the Carolingian era, when jurisdiction over coinage came into the hands of magnates as delegated representatives of royal or

---

73 Herman of Laon, *Miracula S. Mariae Laudunensis*, II.10 and 22 (*PL* 156, cols 979D–82A and 987A).

74 Lantfred, *Translatio et miracula S. Swithuni*, ch. 9 (*The Cult of St Swithun*, M. Lapidge (ed. and trans.) (Oxford, 2003), pp. 290–93).

75 Herman of Laon, *Miracula S. Mariae Laudunensis*, II.20 (*PL* 156, cols 985A–D).

76 H. Mayr-Harting, 'Functions of a Twelfth-Century Recluse', *History*, 60 (1975): 337–52, at 342–4; Leyser, *Hermits*, pp. 59–62; Licence, *Hermits*, pp. 131–72.

77 See the contribution by Svein H. Gullbekk in the present volume.

78 F. Poey d'Avant, *Monnaies féodales de France* (3 vols, Paris, 1858); F. Dumas, *Le trésor de Fécamp et le monnayage en Francie occidentale pendant la seconde moitié du Xe siècle* (Paris, 1971).

79 J. Barrow, 'German Cathedrals and the Monetary Economy in the Twelfth Century', *Journal of Medieval History*, 16 (1990): 13–38, at 25.

imperial power. Indeed, many churches that gained rights over coin production only did so when they acquired some or all regalian powers formerly vested in the local count.[80] This happened at Rheims in 940 and at Le Puy in 924.[81] In Barcelona the positions were reversed: the bishop had been responsible for the mint since the ninth century but at some stage in the next century the counts came to hold minting rights in fief from the bishop, and granted new minting powers to other secular and ecclesiastical lords in Catalonia.[82] At nearby Cardona, the bishop of Vic challenged the local viscount's right to control of minting, leading to a settlement in 1088 by which the two parties shared the rights and profits.[83] New mints were a slightly different matter, and there were a great many of these in the Reich in the tenth and eleventh centuries. Most were under ecclesiastical control: 63 concessions of minting rights to churches survive from the three Ottos, and over 80 from the period 1002–1105.[84] Minting rights very commonly formed part of a trio of privileges, along with a market and a toll. The aim was to foster their development (or provide formal recognition to what had grown up already), and the local ecclesiastical authority was expected to guarantee good practice as well as derive income.[85] Anxiety over forgery and the hope for a facility geared towards the good of the local community as a whole meant that minting was commonly seen as best assigned to bishops and abbots.[86]

The balance of these motives was very delicate. Profits from minting, at least if later medieval comparanda are considered, were not always a significant proportion of lordly income, and were best preserved in the long run by stability. Indeed, the prestige of holding title to the profits could be just as important

80 R. E. Barton, *Lordship in the County of Maine, c. 890–1160* (Woodbridge, 2004), pp. 51–76 and 140–41.

81 Flodoard, *Historia Remensis ecclesiae*, IV.27 (MGH SS 36 (Hannover, 1998), pp. 418–19); *Recueil des actes de Robert Ier et de Raoul, rois de France*, R. H. Bautier and J. Dufour (eds) (Paris, 1978), no. 4 (pp. 22–5).

82 T. N. Bisson, *Conservation of Coinage: Monetary Exploitation and its Restraint in France, Catalonia, and Aragon (c. A.D. 1000–c. 1225)* (Oxford, 1979), pp. 50–64.

83 J. Botet y Sisó, *Les monedes catalanes* (3 vols, Barcelona, 1908–11), vol. 1, pp. 215–16.

84 B. Kluge, *Deutsche Münzgeschichte von der späten Karolingerzeit bis zum Ende der Salier (ca. 900 bis 1125)* (Sigmaringen, 1991), pp. 101–104.

85 N. Kamp, 'Probleme des Münzrechts und der Münzprägung in salischer Zeit', in B. Diestelkamp (ed.), *Beiträge zum hochmittelalterlichen Städtwesen* (Cologne and Vienna, 1981), pp. 94–110, at p. 106–7; W. Hess, 'Münzstätten, Geldverkehr und Handel am Rhein in ottonischer und salischer Zeit', in Diestelkamp (ed.), *Beiträge*, pp. 111–33, at pp. 125–7; R. Kaiser, *Bischofsherrschaft zwischen Königtum und Fürstenmacht. Studien zur bischöflichen Stadtherrschaft im westfranzösischen Reich im frühen und hohen Mittelalter* (Bonn, 1981), pp. 628–9.

86 Kamp, 'Probleme', pp. 94–7.

as the actual amount that was taken.[87] There are plenty of instances known in Germany especially of monasteries and bishoprics which received minting rights but apparently never made use of them. Likewise in England, Domesday Book notes that by 1086 the bishop of Norwich had the right to one moneyer *si vult* ('if he wishes').[88] Minting rights could thus be as much a manifestation of authority as a source of profit.

Yet bishops and abbots did sometimes indulge in measures which can only be explained as a profit-making exercise. These included debasement or reduction of the weight of the coinage. Guibert of Nogent recounted how moneyers working for Waldric, bishop of Laon (1106–12), took it upon themselves to debase the coinage, in connivance with the bishop.[89] Offences of this sort were frequently seized on in broader accounts of poor morals. In 1104 Otbert, bishop of Liège (1091–1119), was accused of a range of offences by his own clergy. They alleged that he had sold off abbacies and religious services, infringed clerical liberties, despoiled holy treasures, spurned the monks' advice and also – to the detriment of all the churches of the province – changed, diminished and debased the *legitimas monetas*. The text which reports these crimes (the Chronicle of St Hubert, also known as the *Cantatorium*) takes a very dim view of Otbert and his episcopacy, and so the details might be somewhat magnified. But it is nevertheless revealing that corruption of the coinage was seen as damaging to the church community as a whole, and could be mentioned in the same breath as simony and theft.[90]

At the heart of these accusations was an expectation of public concern in running the coinage. Eleventh-century observers may have remembered the words of the Book of Wisdom 11:20: that God had 'ordered all things in measure, number and weight', or known how in England Archbishop Wulfstan (d. 1023), writing in the name of two kings, had equated *feos bot* ('maintenance of the coinage') in the same context as the preservation of peace and the avoidance of sacrilege and homicide.[91] Coinage was an accepted fundament of society,[92] laden with ideals of moderation and stability which could be associated with movements for peace, most famously that of southern France in the eleventh

---

87 N. Kamp, *Moneta regis: königliche Münzstätten und königliche Münzpolitik in der Stauferzeit* (Hannover, 2006), esp. pp. 389–97.

88 Domesday Book, II, fol. 117v (National Archives, UK).

89 Guibert of Nogent, *Monodiae*, III.7 (*Guibert de Nogent: Autobiographie*, E.-R. Labande (ed. and trans.) (Paris, 1981), pp. 324–7).

90 *Cantatorium*, ch. 96 (*La chronique de Saint-Hubert, dite Cantatorium*, K. Hanquet (ed.) (Brussels, 1906), p. 249).

91 *V Æthelred*, ch. 26.1; *VI Æthelred*, ch. 31, 32.1–2; *II Cnut*, ch. 8 (*Die Gesetze der Angelsachsen*, F. Liebermann (ed.) (3 vols, Halle, 1903–16), vol. 1, pp. 242–3, 254–5 and 314–15).

92 Kamp, 'Probleme', p. 89.

century. In Béarn, a coinage at least in part controlled by a Cluniac priory was in the late eleventh century inscribed with the word PAX, as was another from Amiens in the 1030s.[93] In Catalonia, Oliba, bishop of Vich (1018–47), issued a document proclaiming an unbreakable peace at certain times within his diocese. Part of this bid for order and stability was a command that anyone tampering with the bishop's coinage should be excommunicated.[94] The First Lateran Council of 1123 carried the same concerns to the very highest level of the church, when it decreed that counterfeiters and dealers in false coin were excommunicated as oppressors of the poor and disturbers of the peace of the city.[95]

Putting these ideals into practice meant a lord would have to restrict a potential source of revenue, and the eleventh and twelfth centuries saw a number of French magnates extract a payment from their subjects to keep them from devaluing the coinage in any way. Churches might be the agent or recipient of such a promise.[96] One eleventh-century duke of Aquitaine granted to Cluny, in the same way as one might grant land or other privileges, that the coinages in his territory should remain uniform.[97] In this case Cluny's interest in the coinage extended only to the income from production: running the mints was up to the duke, and the design and circulation of the coins were unaffected by the change in revenue allocation.[98]

What control over a mint represented could thus vary tremendously. In England it was very limited. After about 924 there were no coins explicitly inscribed as the product of an ecclesiastical mint as such, but select ecclesiastics enjoyed rights to the profits of one or more moneyers, in the same way as they enjoyed other legal and tributary rights. Even occasional concessions of new minting privileges – such as to Henry I's new foundation of Reading abbey in 1121 – worked in this way, in this case with the moneyer being based in London rather than Reading.[99] This purely financial interest was one extreme. At the other lay a much more hands-on style of management, with power over design and elements of production and sometimes even circulation in the surrounding area. Many German bishops oversaw the establishment of relatively small zones of circulation, within which they operated separate and distinct monetary

93 Bisson, *Conservation*, pp. 54–5; Poey d'Avant, *Monnaies féodales*, nos 6402–7.

94 *Viage literario á las iglesias de España*, J. L. Villanueva (ed.) (22 vols, Madrid, 1803–52), vol. 6, pp. 308–9.

95 *Concilium I Lateranense*, ch. 13 (*Decrees of the Ecumenical Councils*, N. P. Tanner (ed. and trans.) (2 vols, London and Washington, DC, 1990), vol. 1, pp. 192–3).

96 Bisson, *Conservation*.

97 *Recueil des chartes de l'abbaye de Cluny*, A. Bruel (ed.) (6 vols, Paris, 1876–1903), vol. 4, no. 3432.

98 Bisson, *Conservation*, pp. 45–50.

99 M. Allen, *Mints and Money in Medieval England* (Cambridge, 2012), pp. 9–12.

systems.[100] The visual appearance of ecclesiastical coin-issues varied massively. Some were not openly ecclesiastical at all, such as the issues of many French mints which retained immobilised Carolingian royal types. In other cases the church's interest was expressed only through inscriptions, commonly naming the patron saint, the monastery or episcopal centre or, more rarely, the current bishop or abbot. In Germany the initial norm was for the king or emperor to be named and represented as well, but by the reign of Conrad II (1027–39) there were moves to lessen and even suppress the emperor's presence on the coinage, and by the 1070s it was unusual for the king or emperor to be recognised outside those few mints under his own direct control.[101]

There could also be much more expressive images placed on coins to highlight the status and affiliations of their issuing authority. Portrayals of saints and tonsured busts of bishops or abbots were frequently used. Several churches in France with a dedication or other link to St Peter, including Cluny, issued coins with a representation of a key,[102] while German issues frequently carried depictions of ecclesiastical buildings.[103] It should be stressed that ecclesiastical authorities had no monopoly on religious imagery: some of the most dramatic Christian representations on coins were produced by secular rulers, such as the *Agnus Dei* coinages from late Anglo-Saxon England and eleventh-century Scandinavia.[104] A similar design was also used at the mint of Saint-Gilles on the coinage of Alphonse Jourdain, count of Toulouse (1109–48).[105] Moreover, the adoption of overtly ecclesiastical imagery was not always a sign of piety. Guibert of Nogent, lamenting the monetary abuses committed at Laon by Bishop Waldric, mentioned an attempt to make a new issue of highly debased obols more palatable by adding to them the bishop's name and the sign of the crozier.[106]

---

100 W. Hess, 'Pfennigwährungen und Geldumlauf im Reichsgebiet zur Zeit der Ottonen und Salier', in B. Kluge (ed.), *Fernhandel und Geldwirtschaft. Beiträge zum deutschen Münzwesen in sächsischer und salischer Zeit. Ergebnisse des Dannenberg-Kolloquiums 1990* (Sigmaringen, 1993), pp. 17–35.

101 Kamp, 'Probleme', pp. 102–103; and Kluge, *Deutsche Münzgeschichte*, pp. 68–76 and 83–4.

102 Poey d'Avant, *Monnaies féodales*, nos 1542 (Saumur), 5596–9 (Cluny) and 6552–3 (Corbie). Representations of saints include ibid., nos 2165–79 (Souvigny) and 6505–13 (Saint-Médard). Cf. M. Bompaire, A. Clairand and R. Prot, 'La monnaie de Corbie (XIe–XIIe siècles)', *Revue numismatique*, 153 (1998): pp. 297–325.

103 Kluge, *Deutsche Münzgeschichte*, p. 84.

104 S. D. Keynes and R. Naismith, 'The *Agnus Dei* Pennies of King Æthelred the Unready', *Anglo-Saxon England*, 40 (2012): 175–223.

105 E. Cavalié, 'Le type numismatique de Saint-Gilles', *Revue numismatique*, 162 (2005): 417–42.

106 Above, n. 89. See the contribution of Giles E. M. Gasper in the present volume

It is time to conclude this survey of how money and coin were used by the church in the eleventh century. What may have been lost in depth by taking such a broad view is perhaps made up for in breadth: there can be no doubt that very different attitudes co-existed in the plethora of institutions and individuals making up the church at this time. Yet common themes do emerge, among which perhaps the most important is an acceptance that the church needed money. It was, for better or worse, a part of earthly society, and so had to look to earthly as well as spiritual requirements. Wherever coined money was known, it was emblematic of this most basic need to retain some links with the outside world. Revealingly, eleventh-century heretics were singled out for their rejection of the monetary and proprietary norms of society:[107] the French heretic Leutard of Vertus, according to Ralph Glaber, spurned tithes,[108] while Ademar of Chabannes (d. 1034) and a monk of Auxerre named Heribert highlighted that heretics of Périgueux not only refused money, but whatever funds they did have were placed in common.[109] A similar accusation was made against heretics near Milan in 1028.[110] Involvement with money was thus an acceptable – indeed characteristic – part of Christian life, of which the church was a central part. Variation came in how this necessity was handled. Money remained closely bound to the temptation of wealth and worldliness in general, so that many religious preferred to keep as healthy a distance as possible from monetary transactions through voluntary poverty. Yet total rejection of money, and of the goods and resources which even the most devout still required from the rest of society, was not possible, and was one factor in the creation of what have been called 'second-class monks' or *conversi*,[111] who enjoyed affiliation with a monastic or eremitic community but were primarily responsible for its material welfare, leaving the monks or hermits themselves to liturgy, contemplation and study. Another way

107 Moore, 'Property, Marriage'.

108 Ralph Glaber, *Historiae*, II.11 (France, Bulst and Reynolds (eds and trans), p. 88–91).

109 G. Lobrichon, 'The Chiaroscuro of Heresy: Early Eleventh-Century Aquitaine as Seen from Auxerre', in T. F. Head and R. A. Landes (eds), *The Peace of God: Social Violence and Religious Response in France around the Year 1000* (Ithaca, NY, 1992), pp. 80–103, at pp. 90–92; M. Frassetto, 'The Sermons of Ademar of Chabannes and the Letter of Heribert: New Sources concerning the Origins of Medieval Heresy', *Revue bénédictine*, 109 (1999): 324–40, at 330. Compare, J. L. Nelson, 'Society, Theodicy and the Origins of Heresy: Towards a Reassessment of the Medieval Evidence', in D. Baker (ed.), *Schism, Heresy and Religious Protest* (Cambridge, 1972), pp. 65–77; and R. Landes, 'Economic Development and Demotic Religiosity', in R. Fulton and B. W. Holsinger (eds), *History in the Comic Mode: Medieval Communities and the Matter of Person* (New York, 2007), pp. 101–16 and 321–6.

110 Landulf of Milan, *Historia Mediolanensis*, II.27 (MGH SS 8 (Hannover, 1848), pp. 65–6).

111 Little, *Religious Poverty*, pp. 76 and 85–6.

for churches to handle money was to engage more directly with it, but on their own terms. Accumulating wealth was legitimate if done in moderation and put to proper uses such as glorifying God's houses on earth and supporting the poor. Treading this fine line of having wealth but using it with virtue was not easy, especially for institutions with extensive worldly involvements, the leaders of which might even function as secular lords as well as abbots or bishops.[112] Over the course of the eleventh century, it certainly seems that the temptations posed by wealth increased. None of these dangers, or even many of the responses to them, were altogether new, but their quickening tempo sharpened and polarised attitudes. Some institutions, like the papacy and certain greater abbeys and cathedrals, embraced the new opportunities with gusto, and launched ambitious programmes of construction, worship, scholarship and charity. In the process they could become prone to accusations of avarice or simony, and it is no surprise that this period also saw a reinvigoration of the opposite extreme: of religious men and women who advocated austerity, rejected the temptations of wealth and retreated into the wilderness to minimise secular entanglements. There was, in short, no single answer to how the church might best handle its involvement with money and with wealth, but the question of how it would do so in a rapidly changing world was becoming impossible to ignore.

112 See also Barthélemy, *Mutation de l'an mil*, pp. 76–113.

Chapter 3
Contemplating Money and Wealth in Monastic Writing c. 1060–c. 1160

Giles E. M. Gasper

> It is possible to spend money in such a way that it increases; it is an investment which grows, and pouring it out only brings in more. The very sight of sumptuous and exquisite baubles is sufficient to inspire men to make offerings, though not to say their prayers. In this way, riches attract riches, and money produces more money. For some unknown reasons, the richer a place appears, the more freely do offerings pour in. Gold-cased relics catch the gaze and open the purses. If you show someone a beautiful picture of a saint, he comes to the conclusion that the saint is as holy as the picture is brightly coloured. When people rush up to kiss them, they are asked to donate. Beauty they admire, but they do no reverence to holiness. ... Oh, vanity of vanities, whose vanity is rivalled only by its insanity! The walls of the church are aglow, but the poor of the church go hungry. The stones of the church are covered with gold, while its children are left naked. [1]

The famous *Apologia* of Bernard of Clairvaux to Abbot William of St Thierry on the alleged decadence of the Cluniac monastic observance is well known. While Bernard does not makes an unequivocal condemnation of wealth, adornment and money, but rather a series of qualified, if biting, remarks on the subject directed particularly to monastic communities, material prosperity and its

[1] Bernard of Clairvaux, *An Apologia to Abbot William*, M. Casey (trans.) (Kalamazoo, Michigan, 1970), p. 65; *Apologia ad Guillelmum*, in *Bernardi opera*, J. Leclercq and H.M. Rochais (eds) (Rome, 1963), vol. 3, pp. 81–108 'Et ut aperte loquar, an hoc totum facit avaritia, quae est idolorum servitus, et non requirimus fructum, sed datum? Si quaeris: 'Quomodo?' 'Miro', inquam, 'modo'. Tali quadam arte spargitur aes, ut multiplicetur. Expenditur ut augeatur, et effusio copiam parit. Ipso quippe visu sumptuosarum, sed mirandarum vanitatum, accenduntur homines magis ad offerendum quam ad orandum. Sic opes opibus hauriuntur, sic pecunia pecuniam trahit, quia nescio quo pacto, ubi amplius divitiarum cernitur, ibi offertur libentius. Auro tectis reliquiis signantur oculi, et loculi aperiuntur Ostenditur pulcherrima forma Sancti vel Sanctae alicuius, et eo creditur sanctior, quo coloratior Currunt homines ad osculandum, invitantur ad donandum, et magis mirantur pulchra, quam venerantur sacra. O vanitas vanitatum, sed non vanior quam insanior! Fulget ecclesia parietibus et in pauperibus eget. Suos lapides induit auro, et suos filios nudos deserit'.

relation to spiritual health are at the heart of his criticisms. These criticisms were themselves part of a wider polemical landscape within which the newer orders of the twelfth century identified themselves against traditional Benedictine monasticism.[2] While arguments about a 'crisis' in cenobitic monastic life have emphasised the health of these older communities in the period under question, there is little doubt that the fulcrum on which contemporary criticism balanced was the emergence of changing attitudes towards wealth.[3] All of this occurred, as is well established, during a period in which western Christendom experienced major economic expansion and the beginnings of a more integrated process of monetising the local, regional and international economies through which these societies operated.[4] How this expansion occurred in detail and what contemporaries thought about the process, collectively and individually, are less easy to explain or explore.[5]

To a considerable extent these processes involve an evolving understanding of money, in its conceptual role as a means of account and exchange, and in its physical form as coin. Evidence for such evolution is wide-ranging, including

---

2 As John Van Engen expressed it, critical contemporaries in the period 1050–1150, 'knew very well that Benedictine monasticism was a powerful, wealthy, and influential establishment. But the evidence accrued here for "prosperity" or "vitality" largely spelled "bankruptcy" for them ... the strong implication was that material prosperity meant spiritual decadence', 'The "Crisis of Cenobitism" Reconsidered: Benedictine Monasticism in the Years 1050–1150', *Speculum*, 61 (1986): 269–304, at 284–5.

3 On the so-called 'Crisis of Cenobitism' see n. 2 above, with J. Leclerq, 'La crise du monachisme' notable amongst older literature. It is still a term which enjoys invocation, for example, S. Vanderputten, 'Crises of Cenobitism: Abbatial Leadership and Monastic Competition in late Eleventh-Century Flanders', *The English Historical Review*, 127 (2012): 259–84.

4 See Richard H. Britnell, *The Commercialisation of English Society 1000–1500* (Cambridge, 2009). For a more general discussion of economic change see N. J. G. Pound, *An Economic History of Medieval Europe*, 2nd edition (London, 1994), and references within.

5 Studies on the structural changes within the western medieval economy and society from the eleventh century through to the early thirteenth are widespread, and indeed are foundational themes for medieval studies since the emergence of professional historical studies in the late nineteenth century. Peter Spufford's *Money and its Use in Medieval Europe* (Cambridge, 1988) remains seminal on the subject. That said, there are few studies devoted to consideration of the conception of money in a period of monetisation, a notable exception being A. Murray, *Reason and Society in the Middle Ages* (Oxford, 1978). Within case studies, such as Georges Duby's now classic investigation of twelfth-century Cluny 'Économie domaniale et économie monétaire: Le budget de l'abbaye de Cluny entre 1080 et 1155', *Annales*, 7 (1952): 155–71, the focus has tended to be towards the practical responses to economic situations experienced, rather than the mental frameworks in which these experiences were processed.

in an Anglo-Norman context, that of Domesday Book.[6] In terms of how these changes were articulated, evidence from monastic authors plays an extremely important role, although one which requires sensitive use. The dominance of written material from monastic environments in this period cannot be underestimated. As John Van Engen noted, 'Benedictines wrote virtually all the great chronicles and lives extant from the years 850–1150 ... Without the cartularies, chronicles, and lives written by monks historians would know precious little about the European world between 850 and 1100'.[7] The preservation of such documentation is related in great part to the interest these institutions developed in their economic situations, and their mechanisms for navigating market fluctuation and conceptual change. How monastic authors, whether leaders of their communities or the voices of record, write about money and its use can be used as an interpretative thread to illuminate wider responses to systemic economic and cultural change.

As Bernard's remarks above indicate, comments on wealth from within and about monastic houses are common. A particular focus on attitudes to money, however, allows older questions to be re-posed, and re-considered. Central to this re-consideration is money's possession of a dual quality, as both a physical entity, used to practical ends, and as a literary device, used to allusive and metaphorical purpose. The majority of modern scholarship on the subject focuses on the first aspect, the practical production of money and the manner in which it was variously employed within the high medieval period. The prevalence of money as a tool of satire or reforming invective has also been noted.[8] To put the two aspects together, however, is to opens different perspectives on the nature of monetisation in the period, and reflects better the ways in which, especially in monastic hands, the literary and the actual become so tightly woven together that they become difficult to separate. Both aspects speak to a sector of society in which money was becoming ubiquitous (although the partial nature of this process should be stressed), more carefully defined, and patient of multiple interpretations, negative as well as positive.

How monks wrote about money allows a sharper focus on how different monastic communities contemplated worldly wealth. The description of money as it relates to economic practices, within the institution and without, in circumstances quotidian and extraordinary, can be used to explore not

---

6 A vast literature exists on the Domesday Book and Inquest, see D. Roffe, *Decoding Domesday* (Woodbridge, 2007), and recently, S. Baxter, 'The Making of Domesday Book and the Languages of Lordship' in *Conceptualizing Multilingualism in England, c. 800–c. 1250* (Turnhout, 2011), pp. 271–308; for the wider source base, Domesday and beyond, relevant to the expansion and change of English economy in this period see Britnell, *Commercialisation*, pp. 5–75.

7 Van Engen. 'The "Crisis of Cenobitism" Reconsidered': 297–8.

8 Murray, *Reason and Society*, pp. 71–7.

only the articulation of power within religious houses, but also particularities of relationships with their benefactors. However, while the role of monastic communities in the later eleventh and early-twelfth centuries as generators of currency is well known, if still inconsistently explored, what and how they thought about this role is not.[9]

That monks thought about money, in different ways and in different modes, can be established straightforwardly. Money as a subject for monastic authors is found in more than charter or chronicle literature; it takes its place within memorial literature, within letter collections, and within meditative, and, on occasion, theological reflection. The place of money within monastic image-making, in the expression of spiritual value, and as part of a growing articulation of spiritual economy speaks to something of a shift in the underpinnings of the metaphorical language employed. Monastic writing on the subject highlights not only monetisation of the economy, but also of contemporary conceptual frameworks, and as a result can be used to inform interpretation of a society on the cusp or in the first stage of a monetary revolution.[10]

Care must be taken in the interpretation of this language: money, as value and as coin, is a common source of biblical, and especially New Testament, metaphor, from the injunction to 'render unto Caesar' to the parable of the talents.[11] This is an area too where the in-dwelling of high medieval monastic communities with Patristic writing needs to be taken into account, since these authorities wrote also in a society and economy significantly, if far from wholly, monetised.[12] Monastic authors of the later period contribute, for example, to a longer tradition of using the coin, its quality, production and appearance, as an

---

9 See M. Allen, *Mints and Money in Medieval England* (Cambridge, 2012) and *The Durham Mint*, British Numismatic Society Special Publication 4 (London, 2003); Sebastian Steinbach, *Das Geld der Nonnen und Mönche. Münzrecht, Münzprägung und Geldumlauf der ostfränkisch-deutschen Klöster in ottonisch-salischer Zeit (ca. 911–1125)* (Berlin, 2007). See also the contributions of Sebastian Steinbach and Jens Christian Moesgaard to this volume. Giles E. M. Gasper and Svein H. Gullbekk, 'Money and its Use in the Thought and Experience of Anselm of Canterbury', *Journal of Medieval History*, 38 (2012): 155–82 attempts an intepretation of Anselm's experiences in this regard.

10 The most convenient treatment remains P. Spufford, *Money and its Use in Medieval Europe* (Cambridge, 1988).

11 Matthew 22:19–21; Matthew 25:14–30.

12 As a general introduction to the classical background see S. Von Reden, *Money in Classical Antiquity* (Cambridge, 2010), pp. 18–64, and the comments in M. Finlay, *The Ancient Economy*, 2nd edition (London, 1985), esp. 196–8. For the later Roman world and that of late anquity see the contrasting studies of K. Hopkins, 'Taxes and Trade in the Roman Empire (200 B.C.–A.D. 400)', *Journal of Roman Studies*, 70 (1980): 101–24 and Peter Brown, *Through the Eye of a Needle: Wealth, the Fall of Rome, and the Making of Christianity in the West, 350–550 AD* (Princeton, New Jersey, 2012).

analogy for religious life well and badly lived.[13] Interpretation of how monastic authors use money must, therefore, be sensitive to the echoing chamber of the past, especially those texts that informed to a high degree the re-imagining of monastic life in an era of reform.

Taking a conspectus of attitudes towards money across the differing forms of monastic life that emerged in this period allows the range of responses to be considered, and the common themes and conceptual underpinnings to be identified. The period from the later eleventh to the middle of the twelfth century is well known in the medieval west for a remarkable proliferation of monastic orders in the context of wider reform of the church. The vogue for variety in monastic life carried with it those who wished to adopt it themselves, and amongst those who wished to offer support. Different houses, different orders and different communities offered different registers of monastic life and identity, and, presumably, different registers of lay association and engagement.[14] The monastic landscape was one in the process of rapid change in the period 1060–1160; the fact of that change alone speaks to the importance of these communities in society at large.

In seeking a conspectus of monastic opinion attention will be placed on writers who provide an indicative sense of the range of responses to money to be found in monastic communities as well as a guide to the ways in which attitudes changed over the period. The case studies reflect different types of monastic community across the period. Anselm of Canterbury (1033–1109), Guibert of Nogent (c. 1060–1125) and Orderic Vitalis (1075–c. 1142) represent regular Benedictine houses, Ailred of Rievaulx (1110–67) the Cistercians, Guigo I (1083–1132) the Carthusians with the additional testimony on their way of life from William of St Thierry (1085–1148), and finally Stephen of Muret (c. 1047–1124), as founder of the Grandmontines. These individuals and their

[13] See G. Dinkova-Bruun in this volume.

[14] A remarkable example of patronage to a diverse range of religious communities are the foundations made by David I of Scotland in the Border region: Tironensians at Kelso in 1126 (moved from their original foundation of 1113 at Selkirk), Cistercians at Melrose in 1136, Augustinians at Jedburgh in 1138 and Premonstratensians at Dyrburgh in 1150. These foundations are all within 20 miles of each other. Nor was this series of foundations the fulfilment of David's monastic vision, Melrose founded daughter-houses at Newbattle (1140), Dundrennan (1142), Kinloss (1150) within his lifetime, the Tironensians of Kelso established Priories at Lesmahagow, and David settled more Augustinians at Holyrood (1128), Camuskenneth (1147), and was involved in their arrival at Glasgow Cathedral. David also enlarged the Benedictine house at Dunfermline, founded Urqhuat Priory (1124) and introduced Cluniac monks to the Isle of May (1153). See R. Oram, *The King who made Scotland* (Stroud, 2004), and G. W. S. Barrow, 'David I (c. 1085–1153)', *Oxford Dictionary of National Biography*, Oxford University Press, 2004; online edition, Jan 2006, http://www.oxforddnb.com/view/article/7208 (accessed 10 Sept 2012).

communities are also, with the exception of the Carthusians, geographically linked in northern and western France and England, within territories dominated by Norman, Anglo-Norman and Angevin rulers of England, from William the Conqueror to Henry II.

Attitudes towards money will be explored in three thematic areas: I) material and spiritual gain: property and patronage, II) simony and payment: sin and charity, III) ascetic values: debt, poverty and usury. These represent major concerns for the monastic communities represented, and the different opinions expressed are responsive to the prevailing attitudes across the spectrum of monastic experience. From communities whose relationship to money was intricate and nuanced, to those whose existence valorised a more complete rejection of the world, what emerges is a complex articulation of the problems and benefits of monetisation, moving between the intimate circumstances of individual houses, to questions of wider concern. These questions include the notion of change over time in references to money in monastic sources, dealt with, for the most part, in section one, whether and why this change occurs over the eleventh and twelfth centuries, addressed in section two, and the distinction and overlap between metaphorical treatment of money and discussion of the reality of monetary transaction, the focus of section three.

I) Material and Spiritual Gain: Property and Patronage

One of the paramount needs of Benedictine houses of the period from the tenth to the mid-twelfth centuries was the accumulation of sufficient resources to support and sustain their communities, and to do so at more than subsistence levels.[15] Monastic houses needed property, income, and money to function, making interaction with the world and secular society necessary. Explicitly and implicitly money forms part of this wider monastic economy, and in what follows both money and its wider hinterland of monastic wealth will be considered. Attitudes within the cloister towards this necessity provide a touchstone for deeper divisions in attitudes towards wealth and the world.

The importance of patronage was underlined to the community of Bec, in lower Normandy, in 1093 by their recently departed Abbot Anselm, shortly after his promotion to the archbishopric of Canterbury. Anselm's parting injunction to his successor as Abbot, William Bona-Anima, was that he should:

---

[15] See Van Engen 'Crisis of Cenobitism': 278–82 for a summary of the complexities of the economic position of Benedictine houses in the period, and the expansion and contraction of landed wealth in particular.

> Remember too how I always used to gain friends for the church of Bec: follow this example, hasten to gain friends for yourselves from all sides by exercising the good deed of hospitality, dispensing generosity to all men, and when you do not have the opportunity of doing good works, by according at least the gift of a kind word. Never consider that you have enough friends, but whether rich or poor, let all be bound to you by brotherly love. This will be to the advantage of your church and promote the welfare of those who you love.[16]

Anselm presided over a considerable expansion at Bec in terms of personnel and building, triumphantly brought together in the dedication of the new church in 1077. The network of patrons can be drawn together, as a case study of Benedictine survival and then expansion. Herluin, a Norman knight, who would become its first abbot, had founded Bec in the mid-1030s, and its initial properties derived from the lesser aristocracy.[17] Gifts of this order continued to be given, an example being the 120 shillings brought by 'a certain knight' in about 1076.[18] Anselm played a decisive role in attracting this patronage with increased donations after the consecration of the new church and his election as Abbot in 1078. Two diplomas of 1077, one from William the Conqueror, and the other from Philip I of France, confirm the possessions held by Bec.[19] Significant French properties acquired after 1078 include three priories in the

---

[16] Anselm of Canterbury, *Letter* 165, F. S. Schmitt (ed.) *Opera omnia S. Anselmi Cantuariensis archiepiscopi,* 6 vols. [vol. 1 printed at Seckau 1938; vol. 2 at Rome 1940, all reset for the Nelson edition] (Edinburgh, 1946–61), vol. IV, *Ep.* 165: 'Memores etiam estote qua ratione semper ecclesiae Beccensi amicos acquirere consuevi; et hoc exemplo amicos vobis undecumque acquirere festinate, hospitalitatis bonum sectando, benignitatem omnibus impendendo, et, ubi facultas operis defuerit, affabilis sermonis gratiam porrigendo. Nec umquam satis vos habere amicos credatis, sed sive divites sive pauperes, omnes vobis in amore fraternitatis conglutinate, quatenus hoc et ad vestrae ecclesiae utilitatem proficere et ad eorum quos diligitis salute valeat pertingere'. The translation is based, with emendation, on that of W. Fröhlich, *The Letters of Saint Anselm of Canterbury*, 3 vols. (Kalamazoo, Michigan, 1990–94), vol. 2, *Letter* 165.

[17] On Herluin, see Gilbert Crispin, *Vita Herluini*, in *The Works of Gilbert Crispin*, A. S. Abulafia and G. R. Evans (eds) (Oxford, 1986); C. Harper-Bill, 'Herluin, Abbot of Bec and His Biographer' in D. Baker (ed.) *Studies in Church History*, 15 (1978): 15–25.

[18] Anselm *Ep.* 66.

[19] For William's confirmation, M. Fauroux, *Recueil des actes des ducs de Normandie de 911 à 1066 complété d'un index rerum par Lucien Musset* (Paris, 1961), no. 98; For Philip I's M. Prou, *Receuil des actes de Phillipe Ier roi de France* (Paris, 1908), no. 90. Véronique Gazeau has pointed out that although the list of possessions can give the impression of wealth, the property was widely dispersed, and concludes that it was insufficient to support properly the community: 'The Effect of the Conquest of 1066 on Monasticism in Normandy: The Abbeys of the Risle Valley' in *England and Normandy in the Middle Ages*, D. Bates and A. Curry (eds) (London, 1994), pp. 131–42, at p. 135.

Île-de-France, and a church.[20] In this context it may be significant that Anselm was the only Norman prelate present at the signing of agreements at the end of the First Vexin War of 1087.[21] However, in economic terms, less revenue from French properties was paid directly to Bec than to the French priories after 1077.[22] Economic security and expansion relied to a greater extent upon the income from post-conquest English holdings.

The first stages of the accumulation of English endowments for Bec took place under Abbot Anselm.[23] A variety of families made donations, including those of Ralph of Tosny, and Hugh, Earl of Chester, but Bec's principal English patrons were the descendants of Herluin's original overlord Count Gilbert of Brionne, namely Richard fitzGilbert and his son Gilbert fitzRichard whose English lands centred on the honour of Clare, and Baldwin fitzGilbert, and his sons William and Richard.[24] Two priories of the eventual four were established in England before 1093, one at St Neots in about 1079 by Richard fitzGilbert, and one at St John the Baptist, Clare, by Gilbert fitzRichard in about 1090, although this community eventually moved to Stoke-by-Clare in 1124.[25] Alongside these priories came gifts of land and tithes, which directly supported the abbey at Bec. Already in the Domesday assessment Bec held property in England valued at 23 pounds. Of the 21 Norman monasteries recorded as English property holders in the Domesday survey, Bec received the tenth-largest revenue. Only a few houses held property of considerably more value, and in these cases Fécamp, and possibly Mont-St-Michel, had pre-conquest holdings, whilst La Trinité and St Étienne, Caen, and Grestain, had close connexions to the ducal house and were rewarded accordingly.[26]

---

20 V. Gazeau, 'Le domaine continental du Bec; aristocratie et monachisme au temps d'anselme' in *Les mutations socio-culturelles au tournant des Xe–XIIe siècles*, Spicilegium Beccense II, Raymonde Foreville (ed.) (Paris, 1984), pp. 259–71, at p. 262.

21 Prou, *Receuil* 94; J. F. Lemarignier, E. Lamon and V. Gazeau, 'Monachisme et aristocratie autour de St Taurin d'Evreaux et du Bec' in L. Musset (ed.), *Aspects du monachisme* (Paris, 1982), pp. 100–107.

22 Gazeau, 'The Effect of the Conquest of 1066', p. 135.

23 M. Chibnall, 'The English Possessions of Bec in the Time of Anselm' in *Les Mutations*, pp. 273–82, at p. 276. See too her 'The Relations of Saint Anselm with the English Dependencies of the Abbey of Bec, 1079–93' *Spicilegium Beccense* I (Paris, 1959), pp. 521–30. Both of these articles are reprinted in M. Chibnall, *Piety, Power and History in Medieval England and Normandy* (Farnham, 2000). M. Morgan (Chibnall), *The English Lands of the Abbey of Bec* (Oxford, 1968).

24 Morgan (Chibnall), *The English Lands*, p. 278.

25 For this and what follows: Morgan (Chibnall), *The English Lands*.

26 Figures from D. Knowles, *The Monastic Order in England*, 2nd edition (Cambridge, 1963), Appendix VI. La Trinité and St Étienne, Caen, were ducal foundations while Grestain was the burial place of William the Conqueror's mother.

Anselm made three trips to England during his abbacy, in about 1080, about 1086, and 1093, each concerning Bec land and priories. His ability to attract and encourage benefactions and gifts to Bec, and his general skill in running his abbey, emerge from these dealings, although they are not qualities which his chief remembrancer Eadmer, monk of Canterbury, chose to emphasise. Eadmer states quite bluntly that he will pass over the letters Anselm wrote for business reasons [*consilium de negotio*] and although he did describe the first trip to England, which led in all probability to the founding of the priory at St Neots, he places the main focus onto Anselm's visit to Canterbury.[27] Meetings Anselm had with noble families are indicated, but not explored. The good relations Anselm enjoyed with King William do receive attention: the king who 'seemed stiff and terrifying to everyone ... nevertheless unbent and was amiable with Anselm, so that to everyone's surprise he seemed an altogether different man when Anselm was present', but the implications of this and other contacts for Bec's material gain legitimately may be extrapolated.[28]

Eadmer did not record Anselm's second trip to England at all, although since it was probably connected to the Domesday inquiry it held significance for the economic position of Bec.[29] Anselm did, writing from England to the monks at Bec, reporting that:

> Since the king was willing to confirm our charter for the property we have in England, but only in the donors' presence, who were not all in attendance at the Easter Court, he ordered me to wait at court until Pentecost, when everyone would once again convene at the same time.[30]

A generation later, Guibert of Nogent, in his *Monodiae* or memoirs composed in about 1115, was moved to compare the successful support of new orders and houses, such as Bec, in the second half of the eleventh century, with a more negative comparison to his present day. It is possible that Guibert had in mind

27 Eadmer, *Vita Anselmi*, R. W. Southern (ed. and trans.) (London, 1962), i.29. Chibnall questions the date of the first English trip, preferring 1080/1 to 1079/80 which might be imagined from Eadmer's account, 'English dependencies of the Abbey of Bec'. Regarding the foundation of St Neots, Anselm *Epp.* 91, 92 and 93 sought the support of Gundulf, Bishop of Rochester, Baldwin, Abbot of Bury-St-Edmunds and Henry, Prior of Christ Church, Canterbury, and *Ep.* 94 thanked Richard fitzGilbert and his wife, the Lady Rohais, for their sponsorship and gifts.

28 Eadmer, *Vita Anselmi*, i.31. See W. Fröhlich, 'St Anselm's Special Relationship with William the Conqueror', *Anglo Norman Studies*, X (1987): 101–10.

29 Eadmer, *Vita Anselmi*, R. W. Southern (ed. and trans.) (London, 1962), i.20.

30 Anselm *Ep.* 118. H. E Salter, 'Two Deeds about the Abbey of Bec', *English Historical Review*, XL (1925): 74–6 includes a charter of William I confirming Bec property in England, probably dating from 1087.

the circumstances of Bec; he had become acquainted with Anselm during the latter's visits to France, and had studied with him.[31] Guibert praises precisely the acts of patronage that made and secured Benedictine life at Bec:

> The numerous examples all around them aroused a desire in the nobility to accept voluntary poverty. They supported the monasteries they entered with the wealth they now repudiated, and forever exerted themselves in pious pursuits to bring others to this end. ... Men or women who could not completely renounce their possessions supported those who did with frequent offerings from their own wealth. They bestowed gifts of the most welcome sort upon many churches and altars and were eager to match, to the extent they could, those who led a life of prayer and piety; it was a life they could not imitate, but they used their own wealth to help others follow it.[32]

Monastic life flourished, but now, Guibert bewails, the conditions on which that flourishing was based have changed:

> And still today – it pains me to say – sons take back from these holy sites everything their parents had once donated because of their religious desires, or else they never cease in their demands to buy these possessions back, so far have they lapsed from the intentions of their parent'.[33]

Guibert voices an anxiety which would be common to established monastic houses of the twelfth century.

---

[31] Guibert of Nogent, *De vita sua sive monodiae, Autobiographe*, E-R Labande (ed.) (Paris, 1981), 1.17. See also J. Rubenstien, *Guibert of Nogent: Portrait of a Medieval Mind* (New York, 2002).

[32] Guibert de Nogent, *De vita sua sive monodiae, Autobiographe*, E-R Labande (ed.) (Paris, 1981), 1.11: 'Affectabat itaque spontaneam subire pauperim tot exemplis circumcinta nobilitas, et coenobia, quae subibatm rebus a se conemptis inferciens, aliis etiam ad haec ipsa trahendis pia semper venatione tendebat. ... Qui vero, vel quae non poterant rebus ad integrum abrenunciare possessis, eos qui abrenunciaverant crebis substantiarum suarum largitionibus sustentabant, ecclesias et altaria multa jucundissimorum munerum oblatione circundabant, et orationes ac pie vivendi modum, quem tales imitando exequi non poterant, talia facientes propriis ad id faciendum juvando substantiis, inquantum licuerat, exaequare studebant'. Translation from Guibert of Nogent, *Monodies* and *On the Relics of Saints*, J. Rubenstein and J. McAlhaney (trans.) (London, 2011), p. 30.

[33] Guibert de Nogent, *De vita sua*, 1.11: 'Jam nunc enim, proh dolor! quae hujusmodi affectione permoti, locis sacris contulere parentes, aut penitus subtrahunt, aut crebras redemptiones exigere non desinunt filii, a patrum voluntatibus usquequaque degeneres'. Translation from Guibert of Nogent, *Monodies*, p. 30.

These sentiments are echoed, one generation on from Guibert, by Orderic Vitalis. Tradition lay close to his heart. Moving praise is given to the establishment of Benedictine houses in all cases by Orderic, but high amongst them is Shrewsbury, and the encouraging words he puts into the mouth of his own father, Ordelerius of Orléans, to the main patron, Roger of Montgomery. Noting that Roger had found it difficult to find support for the gifts necessary for such an undertaking, Ordelerius stresses the gain assured by foundation:

> Countless benefits are obtained there every day and Christ's garrisons struggle manfully against the devil ... True cenobites are enclosed in royal cloisters as if they were king's daughters ... where the cowled champions may engage in ceaseless combat against Behemoth for your soul.[34]

To this endeavour Orderlerius dedicated the church of St Peter, and, Orderic recounts, 15 pounds sterling for the first stage of the work, half of all his property to demesne, with the remaining half to remain for his son, but under monastic lordship.

In recounting this story Orderic connects himself personally to what he conceives as proper mores regarding monastic property. His own orthodoxy in this respect having been established, Orderic painstakingly records in his *Ecclesiastical History* gifts and donations to St Evroult, his home monastery, in the spirit of a cartulary-chronicle.[35] These include not only the amounts of money given by particular benefactors, but also the mechanisms by which donations were garnered. Amongst these were medical practitioners within the community, whose attendance on lay families often resulted in bequests. One particularly productive practitioner was the doctor Goisbert, who, having joined St Evroult in 1076, was given charge of the Priory of Maule:

> After the renowned physician Goisbert had begun to build the church at Maule, as I have related, he talked seriously with some of his friends and acquaintances about the welfare of his monastery. And since they were all of one mind with him, he urged his abbot to entrust the priory of Maule to another, so that he himself might be freed to set procuring other endowments. His request was granted ... Goisbert the physician then approached a number of French knights, and importuned them for the profit of his brethren. Some he won over with his medical skill and help, others with gifts, all with his eloquent entreaties.[36]

---

[34] Orderic Vitalis, *The Ecclesiastical History*, M. Chibnall (ed. and trans.), 6 vols (Oxford, 1969–80), Book V, vol. III, pp. 142–7.

[35] This is especially the case for Book V.

[36] Orderic Vitalis, *Ecclesiastical History*, Book V, vol. III, pp. 206–9: ' ... Quosdam quidem illexit medicinali cura et subuentu, aliosque muneribus utrosque uero facundis hortatibus'.

None of these behaviours does Orderic condemn; wealth, land, accoutrements and money were all of central importance. Such resources had to be guarded and preserved, an activity described in terms where practical and moral arguments are intertwined institutionally and personally. The contract between donors and monasteries is explored in a deathbed speech of Ansold of Maule, the original benefactor of Maule, in 1118, in a series of admonitions to his son. Orderic puts into Ansold's mouth the clear statement, that his son should honour the monks of his foundation:

> Grant freely that they may enjoy in peace and quiet the goods that my father and I have given them for our salvation. Never try to deprive them of any possessions or revenues, nor allow any of your men to do them wrong. For if you take care to be a true patron to them, they will never cease to pray to God for you.[37]

Numerous examples of the travails of monastic communities beset by offspring unsympathetic to patrons' donations pervade Orderic's text, and stories of their eventual just desserts.[38] How lay patrons behaved towards family endowment forms an important measure of morality for monastic authors.

These values and their betrayal are exemplified, for Orderic, in the character and action of William Rufus, whose multiple offences against monastic property are treated with particular ire, in terms which Guibert would have echoed. Orderic saw as sacrilegious the king's administration of lands originally given to the church:

---

[37] Orderic Vitalis, *Ecclesiastical History*, Book V, vol. III, pp. 194–5: 'Res quas pater meus et ego dedimus eis pro nostra salute ut in pace et quiete habeant libenter concede. De rebus et redditibus suis nunquam uelis eos diminuere nec aliquam eis uiolentiam per subditos tuos patiaris inferre. Ipsi nimirum si fidus eorum fautor studeris esse indesinenter Deum exorabunt pro te'.

[38] Mabel of Bellême is perhaps the best example, Orderic Vitalis, *Ecclesiastical History*, Book III, vol. II, pp. 54–5. Mabel, having attempted to literally eat the monks of St Évroult out of their home, is punished with divine illness. See Lanfranc's letter to Peter, bishop of Chester for his use of similar tactics with respect to the abbey of Coventry, Lanfranc, *Letters*, H. Clover and M. Gibson (eds and trans) (Oxford, 1979), *Letter* 27 (1072–85), pp. 112–13: 'Both the abbot and his monks have lodged a complaint with me that you forced an entry into their dormitory and broke into their strongboxes, and that you have robbed them of their horses and all their goods. Furthermore that you pulled down their houses and ordered the materials of which these were built to be taken to your own residences; finally you remained in that monastery with your retinue for eight days eating up the monks' provisions [Clamorem enim fecerunt ad me tam abbas quam monachi eius quod dormitorium eorum per uim introisti, archas eorum fregisti, et equos et omnes proprietates quas habebant rapuisti; insuper domos eorum destruxisti et materias earum ad tuas uillas asportari precepisti, in ipso quoque coenobio cum familia tua consumens bona monachorum octo dierum moram fecisti]'.

> It is manifestly unjust and contrary to all reason that the things given to God by the generosity of Christian princes, or honourably increased by the care of stewards of the Church's goods, should revert to lay hands and be applied to unholy secular uses. We must believe unquestioningly that just as those who dutifully gave of their wealth to God have received a reward according to their deserts by God's grace, so sacrilegious men who appropriate holy things will be punished by God's vengeance and stripped of their wealth they have unjustly acquired, to their perpetual disgrace.[39]

Both Orderic and Guibert single out concerns for their own monastic houses and, more generally, with the security of income, and the particular problems of benefaction across generations. The novel approach taken to these issues by one of the new orders of the period, mentioned by neither Guibert, nor Orderic, the Grandmontines, illustrates the extent of the concern they engendered.

The Grandmontines were perhaps the strictest and most rigorous of the new orders in the medieval West.[40] The origins of the order are obscure, but the founder, Stephen of Muret, established, probably in the 1070s, a hermitage in the forest of Muret, near Limoges, where others joined him in his solitary life. After his death came the move to Grandmont and by the middle years of the twelfth-century the order was well known (with 39 houses in France in 1167), enjoyed the patronage of Henry II Count of Anjou and King of England, and the approbation of some of the sternest critics of contemporary monasticism. For John of Salisbury, they, and the Carthusians, were remarkable for their resistance to avarice:

> The Carthusians and the new order of Grandmont, firmly planted on the summit of ancient virtues under the guidance of our Saviour, display the greatest caution and conscientiousness in avoiding the name and stigma of hypocrites;

---

[39] Orderic Vitalis, *Ecclesiastical History*, Book VIII, vol. IV, pp. 174–7: 'Iniustum quippe uidetur omnique rationi contrarium, ut quod Deo datum est fidelium liberalitate principium uel sollertia dispensatorum aecclesiasticae rei laudabiliter est auctum, denuo sub laicali manu retrahatur et in nefarios seculi usus distrahatur. Indubitanter credendum est quod sicut illi qui Deo de suis opibus pie dederunt, iam retributionem meritorum donante Deo receperunt sic sacrilegi sacrorum inuasores ultore Deo punientur, opibusque quas iniuste possident cum iugi dedecore spoliabantur'.

[40] C. Hutchison, *The Hermit Monks of Grandmont* (Kalamazoo, Michigan, 1989). The work of Jean Becquet remains central, *Recherches sur les institutions religieuses de l'Ordre de Grandmont au Moyen Age*, École practiques des hautes études (Paris, 1951), and a series of articles in *Revue Mabillon* and the *Bulletin Archaeologique et Historique du Limousin*. See also, E. Hallam, 'Henry II, Richard I and the Order of Grandmont', *Journal of Medieval History*, 1 (1975): 165–86, which is given broader context in her 'Henry II as a Founder of Monasteries', *Journal of Ecclesiastical History*, 28 (1977): 113–32.

> for they have indeed fixed limits to their desires, nay even to their necessities, hold in check avarice with the reins of moderation, and at times even deprive themselves of necessities for fear that avarice under cover of necessity may plot against them ... .They are undoubtedly great men and to be counted among the exceptional since not only few orders but even few individuals in our now aging world with its many passing centuries have been conspicuous for having set limits to their own desires'.[41]

The fervour of the Grandmontines found itself expressed in their *Rule*, finally approved in 1156. On the question of property strict limits were imposed: no land to be held except a smallholding around the individual house and no possession of other churches.[42] More specifically the Grandmontines were strictly enjoined to return gifts to the heirs of donors were they to require them.[43] Title deeds and charters were not to be kept, and there was to be no recourse to law.[44] A position more diametrically opposed to the traditional monastic point of view expressed by Anselm, Guibert and Orderic, would be difficult to find.

While the extreme reaction of the Grandmontines to the issue fits with a wider-ranging critique of Benedictine material prosperity, it is arguable that this was part of a broader response to the questions posed by wealth and money. The differences in ethos aside, both types of community evince a shared sense of how seriously the questions raised by possession of money and wealth had to be taken, and the proper and fitting use of these resources. Outright rejection of both found contemporary approval, but within those communities who did not do so, a serious and complex web of moral positions were adopted to safeguard those who did receive and administer the fiscal support of the secular world.

---

[41] John of Salisbury, *Policraticus*, C. C. J. Webb (ed.) (Oxford, 1909), ch. 23. Translation from John of Salisbury, *Frivolities of Courtiers and Footprints of Philosophers*, J. B. Pike (trans.) (New York, 1972, orig. publ. 1938), pp. 281–6, 281: 'Quod Cartuarienses, dum moderationis habenis auaritiam cohibent, et Magni Montis noua religio, dum omnia mundana contempnens et de crastino non cogitans repellit omnia, auaritiam excludit, ab ypocritarum nota et nomine longius absunt; et qui sint seculares aut religiosi; et quae regula actiuorum et quae otiosorum; et quis sit finis ypocriseos ... .Ypocritarum autem nomen et notam cautissime et fidelissime declinant Cartuarienses et Magni Montis noua professio in antiquae uirtutis culmine, Saluatore praeuio, solidata'.

[42] *Regula Venerabilis Viri Stephani Muretensis*, in *Scriptores Ordinis Grandimontensis*, J. Becquet (ed.), Corpus Christianorum Continuatio Medievalis, 8 (Turnhout, 1968), pp. 61–99.

[43] *Regula Stephani Muretensis*, no. 23, pp. 81–2.

[44] *Regula Stephani Muretensis*, no. 24, p. 82; no. 31, p. 84.

II) Simony and Payment: Sin and Charity

The question how money and gifts were obtained and to what purpose they might be put by monastic communities formed part of a wider debate over simony. This debate touched the core of traditional Benedictine life, not least how monks joined their abbeys. The practice of childhood oblation, giving boys to a particular abbey, has its origins in the early history of monasticism. It features within the *Rule of St Benedict*, where prospective gifts to the monastery, to accompany oblates, are addressed: gifts are allowed for, but are identified as not necessary.[45] The practice of oblation, and of associated gift-giving, became widespread, enduring through the eleventh and earlier twelfth centuries.[46] Orderic Vitalis gives the details of his own oblation, in the course of his father's supposed oration on the foundation of St Mary's Shrewsbury, and the arrangements made for his son:

> I have procured for him a safe place of refuge among the faithful servants of God at Saint-Évroult in Normandy, and have given as my free-will offering for his blessing thirty marks of silver out of my own substance to his future masters and companions.[47]

The benefits to monastic houses of such arrangements in terms of patronage are obvious. However, the practice had all but died out by the end of the twelfth century.[48]

Reform communities did not take forward the practice, using its rejection as a means to distinguish themselves from the older communities for whom it was normative.[49] Furthermore, concerns grew throughout the twelfth century about

---

[45] *Benedict's Rule: A Translation and Commentary*, c. 59, T. Kardong (ed. and trans.) (Collegeville, Minnesota, 1996), pp. 485–6.

[46] See the discussion in J. Clark, *The Benedictines in the Middle Ages* (Woodbridge, 2011), pp. 64–6.

[47] Orderic Vitalis, *Ecclesiastical History*, Book V, vol. III, pp. 146–7: 'eique locum tutae mansionis inter uernulas Dei apud Vticum in Neustria procuraui pro quo eulogias benedictionis xxx scilicet marcos argenti futuris eius magistris et consodalibus de porismate meo libenter erogaui'. Whether Orderic intended any particular New Testament valence in the reference to the 30 marks of silver (Matthew 26:15) is open to question. His feelings of anguish about his exile to St Évroult as an infant come to the fore at the end of his history, Book XIII, vol. VI, pp. 552–5, abandoned, weeping and renounced.

[48] Clark, *Benedictines*, p. 65.

[49] The subject was not one of intensive debate amongst the newer orders, although Bernard of Clairvaux was characteristically direct in his condemnation of the alleged oblation of his nephew Robert to Cluny, in a letter to the same, c. 1119, Bernard of Clairvaux, *Epistolae*, in *Sancti Bernardi Opera*, vii–viii, J. Leclerq and H-M. Rochais (eds), Editiones

the possible implications of simony connected to the practice. The vexatious nature of the issue is indicated by its appearance in canon law collections, especially in Gratian's *Decretum*, composed by the 1150s.[50]

The prologue to *Causa 1* of the *Decretum* sets up the story of an oblate given to a monastery by his father, who paid the sum of 10 pounds demanded by the abbot (see Plate 2). Although the story continues with an outline of the boy's subsequent career as a simoniac, the substance of the first and second questions of the *Causa* was whether the original entry, over which the boy had no control, constituted an act of simony.[51] Gratian decided that the gift should be freely offered; any perceived demand for money rendering the transaction simonaical.[52] This conclusion brought to an end a debate begun in the 1120s with the defence of oblate gifts by Rudolph of St Trond, and was probably a significant factor in the decline of oblate recruitment.[53] That anxiety about simony and entry was expressed in this way in the period c. 1120–c. 1155 speaks to issues of church reform, but bound up within that indicates tensions about the right and proper use of monetary gifts within monastic communities. The harmful or harmonious effects of money are used, by the authors under consideration here, to explore the dynamics of monastic identity, the relation of individuals and the communities they served, and questions of the boundaries of moral behaviour.

Concern over simony emerges as a strong theme for Guibert, who, throughout his *Monodiae*, treats the subject and its practitioners severely, especially, but not exclusively, in a monastic context. Closely connected to this is his evident concern for the sinful consequences of money used in the wrong way, for malign purposes, or with intentions defined as morally dubious. A genuine and growing moral issue with money can be detected within Guibert's text.

Cisterciones (Rome, 1974 and 1977), *Ep. 1*; B. S. James (trans.), *The Letters of St Bernard of Clarivaux* (Stroud, 1998, orig. publ. 1953).

50 Joseph H. Lynch, *Simoniacal Entry into Religious Life from 1000 to 1260: A Social, Economic and Legal Study* (Columbus, Ohio, 1976). See also Lynch's, 'Monastic Recruitment in the Eleventh and Twelfth Centuries: Some Social and Economic Considerations', *American Benedictine Review*, 26 (1975): 425–47.

51 For the text of Gratian, while the standard edition remains Emil Friedberg, *Decretum Magistri Gratiani*, 2 vols (Leipzig, [repr. Graz], 1879 [repr. 1959]), see *Decretum Gratiani*, A. Winroth (ed.): https://sites.google.com/a/yale.edu/decretumgratiani/ (accessed 22/12/13).

52 Gratian, *Decretum*, c. 1 q. 2 d.p.c. 10: 'It is clearer than light by the authority of many, that it is not permitted to demand money from those about to enter a monastery, lest he who demands and he who pays, commit the crime of simony. [Multorum auctoritatibus luce clarius constat, quod ab ingressuris monasterium non licet pecuniam exigere, ne et ille, qui exigit, et ille, qui soluit symoniae crimen incurrat]'.

53 Lynch, *Simoniacal Entry*, p. 95.

By far the most detailed of Guibert's descriptions of money come in his narrative and analysis of the rising of the commune at Laon in 1115. The commune Guibert regarded as an unnatural and evil phenomenon, a lamentable state of affairs brought about by the unhappy leadership of its bishops. The uprising provoked a number of violent episodes, including the murder of bishop Gaudry, and Guibert pays attention to the disruption such events caused within the urban community. He offers particular insight into the dislocation to the systems of coinage which occurred within the city, the consequent effects of bribery and corruption on mintmasters, and the confusion caused by the appearance of different coinages and their impact within not only the city but also its hinterland. As Guibert explains:

> ... the minters, knowing that if they sinned in their duties, they could find salvation through pecuniary redemption, debased the currency with so many counterfeits that a great many people were brought to extreme poverty. They minted coins of the cheapest bronze, and by some crooked technique used a tiny amount of silver to make them shinier.[54]

To combat this, bishop Gaudry decreed that the small coins of Amiens (also heavily debased, according to Guibert) would be legal tender within the city.[55] When that failed to have any effect, he started to mint his own coin:

> ... and had the coins stamped with a bishop's crozier to serve as his symbol. Everyone in private rejected these with such loud guffaws that they had less value than any of the debased currency. In the meantime, to promote every issue of these new coins, decrees were circulated that no one mock the worthless impressions of him, providing numerous opportunities to prosecute the people on the grounds they had insulted the office of the bishop. Enormous revenues could thus be extorted from every possible direction.[56]

---

[54] Guibert of Nogent, *De vita sua*, III.7: ' ... monetae percussores, scientes, si peccarent in suo officio, quod pecuniaria possent redemptione salvari, tanta eandem falsitate corruperunt, ut per hoc ad extremam plurimi indigentiam ducerentur. Nam cum denarios ex aere vilissimo conficerent, quos in momentum pravis quibusdam artibus, argento micantiores facerent ... '; Guibert of Nogent, *Monodies*, p. 128.

[55] On the coinage of Amiens and Laon see Faustin Poey-d'Avant, *Les monnaies féodales de France* (Paris, 1858–62) and A. Dieudonné, *Les monnaies féodales*, Manuel de la numismatique française, tome IV (Paris, 1936). C. Vellet has complete summaries on the coinages of the French provinces (Amiens under Picardy and Laon under Île-de-France) in Michel Amandry *et al*, *Dictionaire de Numismatique* (Paris, 2006). I am indebted to Jens Christian Moesgaard for these references.

[56] Guibert of Nogent, *De vita sua*, III.7: ' ... cui pariter ad suae personae signum ferulam pastoralem imprimi fecit. Quae clam ab omnibus cum tanto cachinno spernebatur,

Gaudry's actions, Guibert contends, were the essential cause of the uprising and, to that extent his misfortunes were a form of divine punishment. Money plays an important role in his articulation of the diabolical nature of the commune and the violence it unleashed. It is important to note, however, that money, as concept and as the reification in coin, is still in itself a bad, but rather something that could, perhaps all too easily, be turned to evil purpose.

The accounts of the Laon commune form part of a larger concern within Guibert's writing on immoral use of money. Two stories told early in his memoirs introduce the theme. The first concerns a simoniac monk: an elderly monk sent to a cell in the Vexin decided to restore a damaged public road. He asked for public contributions, and mended the road, but kept some of the money to himself. Struck down by sickness, he refused to confess, but gave the money to a servant. The monk died but had confessed to his crime and mentioned the servant, who had hidden the money in the straw of his infant daughter's cradle. The baby was tormented by demons whose importuning stopped only when the money was returned. The evil identified by Guibert here is wrongful use of money and the vice of avarice: 'more ruinous to monks, as it is less natural to them, and thus it is difficult to find any other crime where the devil waits in ambush with greater stealth'.[57]

A second story takes a similar subject; a monk received two sous from a noble lady. Soon afterwards he developed dysentery, and died in agonising pain, accompanied by diabolic torments. The monk died unconfessed on account of this cursed money, which was found in a small purse, strapped around his body, and hidden in an armpit. A question arose about where and how the body should be buried most appropriately:

> The abbot took counsel with some wise men and ordered that he be buried in a field, deprived of prayer and psalms, with the money placed on his chest. Yet in their private prayers for him his brothers did not falter, but instead, when they learned that he was in even more need for their support, they pressed on with all the more urgency. As a result of his sudden death, the rest of the monks had more scruples about money.[58]

ut impuriore moneta omnino minus appreciaretur. Interea, cum ad singulas quasque horum novorum nomismatum promotiones ferebantur edicta, ne quis pessimas ipsius caraxaturas cavillaretur, inde creberrimae populum impetendi occasiones, quasi qui calumniam intulissent instituto pontificis: inde largissimorum quocunque fieri poterant censuum extortiones'; Guibert of Nogent, *Monodies*, pp. 128–9.

57 Guibert of Nogent, *De vita sua*, 1.21: ' ... apud monachos perniciosum, utpote minus naturale, ut vix aliquod crimen reperiatur, cui tantopere diabolus surripiendo insidietur'.; Guibert of Nogent, *Monodies*, p. 70.

58 Guibert of Nogent, *De vita sua* 1.22: 'Communicatio itaque abbatis cum viris prudentibus consilio, praecepit agrariam ei fieri sepulturam, et ab oration et psalmis exortem,

This is a less equivocal statement on the evils of money per se, although the private possession of money, which led to the problems in the first place, should be noted. Archaeological evidence confirms the burial of corpses with purses of coin throughout the Middle Ages, within graveyards and without.[59]

The details in Guibert's description provide further evidence for tensions over the improper use of money, tensions which are contextualised around the relationship of the individual monk to his community. To take first the insistence that the monk died unconfessed. Unlike the case for the laity, monastic confession was not uncommon in the early twelfth century.[60] Admonition to confession is included in the Benedictine Rule, where it features as the fifth step of humility.[61] The extent to which such confession was conceptualised as private is a more difficult question, but it did form part of the Benedictine liturgy of death carried out by the community on behalf of their companion in extremis, from which Guibert's unfortunate subject had rendered himself excluded.[62]

Despite the prohibition of prayer and psalms, by which should be understood the death liturgy, Guibert notes that his brethren still offered to their unfortunate companion efficacious private prayers. Private devotion formed an important element in later eleventh-century religiosity among religious communities and the laity, drawing on Carolingian traditions with a strongly liturgical aspect, and incorporating a stronger emphasis on the intercession of the particular saint,

---

et pectori ejus supponi pecuniam. Privata tamen pro eo fratrum non defecit oratio, immo multo amplius institerunt, quo magis noverant eum egere subsidio. Ex hujus igitur morte repentina, caeteri peculium castigatiores redditi'.; Guibert, *Monodies*, p. 71.

59 On this general subject see Lucia Travaini, 'Saints and Sinners: Coins in Medieval Italian Graves', *Numismatic Chronicle*, 164 (2004): 159–81, and her contribution to this volume, including discussion of a quite different example, the deposit of 12 coins in the tomb of St Francis, which appear to have been placed on the chest of the corpse, F. Guadagni, *De invento corpore Divi Francisci Ordinis Minorum Parentis* (Rome, 1819). A striking discovery of a corpse, from about 1190, with a purse of coins, which may or may not have been buried in a graveyard, was recorded from Skännige, Monica Golabiewski Lannby, 'Unikt gravfynd med 1100-talsmynt i Skänninge', *Svensk numismatisk tidskrift*, 5 (2009): 110. I am grateful to Professor Kenneth Jonsson for bringing this example to my attention.

60 A. Murray, 'Confession before 1215', *Transactions of the Royal Historical Society*, sixth series, 3 (1993): 51–81, esp. 70–71.

61 *Benedict's Rule*, c. 7, Kardong (ed. and trans.), pp. 131 and 134.

62 See F. Paxton and I. Cochelin, *The Death Ritual at Cluny in the Central Middle Ages* (Turnhout, 2013). An earlier version of Bernard and Ulrich of Cluny's record of the death ritual at their monastery, from the late 1060s, appeared as F. Paxton, *A Medieval Latin Death Ritual: the Monastic Customaries of Bernard and Ulrich of Cluny* (Missoula, Montana, 1993). Confession at the beginning of the death ritual is recorded in Lanfranc of Canterbury, *Monastic Constitutions*, M. D. Knowles (trans.) (Oxford, 1951), p. 121. Lanfranc's *Constitutions* were presumably based around the customs of his home monastery of Bec, but bear close resemblance to Bernard of Cluny as well.

especially Mary, or Christ.[63] That such private prayers would be appropriate for the occasion Guibert describes is demonstrated by those of Anselm of Canterbury, contemporary to the situation and full of many themes pertinent to an uncertain eternal judgement on the basis of misusing money. In the third *Prayer to Mary*, Anselm addresses theme of forgiveness in all places:

> But, Lady, why do I only speak
> of the benefits with which you fill the earth?
> They go down to hell, they go up to heaven.
> For through the fullness of your grace
> those in hell rejoice that they are delivered,
> and those in heaven are glad at that restoration.[64]

In the *Prayer to Christ*, in a re-imagination of the moments after the crucifixion and resurrection, Anselm reflects on the '... wonder, beyond price and beyond compare' of Christ's redeeming work.[65] The priceless value of salvation is underlined, as are the freedom of Christ's gift and the dependence of fallen humanity on the operation of grace.

Repentance was too late for the monk Guibert describes, whose actions had exemplified sordid sin. The episode, through its juxtaposition of private and public activities, underlines Guibert's consciousness of the moral penalties for wrongful use of money. It is, ultimately, the community who take action in response to the misuse, and who meet a disciplinary challenge provoked by the possession of money.

The threat to community stability by the misappropriation of resources, and inappropriate use of money, underlies Guibert's anxieties about simony, with its stronger implications of sacrilege. These emerge frequently, for example, in an account of a chasuble sought by Guibert's original abbey of Fly from William Rufus of England. Rather than pay for this himself the king ordered the abbot of Battle Abbey to pay his messenger 15 marks; the abbot refused, and Rufus

---

[63] See B. Ward (trans.), *The Prayers and Meditation of Saint Anselm* (London, 1973), pp. 35–43; for a general survey see J-F Cottier. Private prayer in the later Anglo-Saxon period is the subject of the unpublished PhD thesis from the University of York by Kate Thomas, *The Meaning, Practice and Context of Private Prayer in Late Anglo-Saxon England*, 2011.

[64] Anselm of Canterbury, *Prayer to St Mary (3)*, Ward (trans.), *Prayers and Meditations*, p. 119, ll. 141–6; *Opera Omnia*, Schmitt (ed.), *Oratio ad sanctam Mariam pro impetrando eius et Christi amore*, vol. III, p. 21 ll. 76–9: 'Sed cur solum loquor, domina, beneficiis tuis plenum esse mundum? Inferna penetrant, caelos superant. Per plenitudinem enim gratiae tuae et quae in inferno erant se laetantur liberata, et quae supra mundum sunt se gaudent restaurata'.

[65] Anselm of Canterbury, *Prayer to Christ*, Ward (trans.), *Prayers and Meditations*, p. 97, l. 131; *Opera Omnia*, Schmitt (ed.), *Oratio ad Christum*, vol. III, p. 8, l. 66:'Admirabilis, inaestimabilis, incomparabilis'.

responded by looting the abbey and forcing the abbot to buy back the abbey's possessions for 15 marks. Fly received its chasuble, but, reflective of the unhappy circumstances, it was soon after destroyed by lightning. William, Guibert notes, was brought to his end soon after by divine agency.[66] While William Rufus does not provoke the prolonged, fascinated disgust he did for Orderic Vitalis, it is important for Guibert that fraudulent behaviour is highlighted by appropriate punishment.

The tensions provoked by simony on the one hand, and regular, familiar, use of money on the other feature particularly in two contrasting clerics with whom Guibert was connected. The first is his predecessor at Nogent as abbot, Godfrey who: ' ... believing simony to be in both name and deed as accursed as filthy profiteering [lucre], he forbade anything to do with it, whether buying or selling, from happening in the church, and once the market was shut down, only grace was admitted'.[67] Nevertheless, this did not prevent Godfrey being a shrewd businessman, which Guibert pointed out deliberately, a quality that led directly to, but did not pay for, his election as bishop of Amiens in 1104.

Episcopal simony attracts negative commentary, however, regarding the appointment of Hélinand as bishop of Laon, in which diocese Nogent lay, 1052–98. Hélinand had been chaplain to King Edward the Confessor of England, and was often sent on missions to Henry, king of France. Guibert remarks, in a passage worth quoting at length, that:

> 'This king was very greedy, and in the habit of selling bishoprics, so Hélinand would ply him with the most lavish gifts to suggest that upon the death of any of the bishops of France, he ought to take on the episcopal insignia as successor. He had in fact accumulated enormous piles of money, since he had been installed in the chapel of the king and queen at a time when England was brimming with enormous wealth ... Once he was introduced into Laon, he did not think he could obtain influence through respect for his family or his scholarly learning, but had placed his hopes in the riches he held in vast supplies and the acts of generosity he had learned to distribute shrewdly ... By such craftiness, he even attempted to seize the archbishopric of Reims. He did occupy it for two years, after its sizable revenues had fallen into the hands of King Philip, a most venal man in what belonged to God, until he heard from the pope that one who has a wife cannot under any circumstances acquire another. When someone openly asked him why

66 Guibert of Nogent, *De vita sua*, 1. 23; Guibert, *Monodies*, p. 74–5.

67 Guibert of Nogent, *De vita sua* 2.2: 'Simoniacum itaque quippiam in eadem ecclesia aut fieri aut haberi vetuit et, exclusis mercimoniis, solam admisit gratiam, non dissimiliter execrationi ducens lucre turpis et opus et nomen'.; Guibert of Nogent, *Monodies*, p. 90.

> he made such an attempt, he said that he still would not have acted any differently, even if he had been able to become Pope.[68]

Guibert's judgement on Hélinand is worth pausing over. Striking is the reference to pre-conquest England as wealthy, a theme popular amongst monastic observers south of the channel.[69] Orderic Vitalis emphasises the lavish gifts showered on Norman monasteries by Duke William once conqueror and king, and the staggeringly exaggerated report that as king William received a daily income 'in sterling money one thousand and sixty-one pounds, ten shillings and three halfpence from the ordinary revenue of England, not counting royal tribute and judicial fines and many other sources of revenue which daily swelled the royal treasures'.[70]

---

[68] Guibert of Nogent, *De vita sua* 3.2: 'Cum quo rego, quia multum erat cupidus et episcopatuum venditionibus assuetus, largissimis lenocinantibus exeniis egit, ut, si quispiam episcoporum Franciae decederet, pontificalibus infulis ipse succederet. Is enim in capellania regis ac reginae positus, quoniam Anglia infinitis eo tempore florebat opibus, multos pecuniarum montes aggesserat ... Lauduno enim invectus, quia non aestimatione parentum, non scientia literarum se valiturum putabat, in opulentia, quae plurima suppetebat, et quam cautissime, dispensare didicerat, et dapsilitate spes fuerat ... His etiam ipse artibus Rhemensem archiepiscopatum insedit; quem cum dilapidatis penes regem Philippum, hominem in Dei rebus venalissimum, magnis censibus biennio obtinuisset, a domino papa audivit, quia uxorem quis habens, altera superinducere nequaquam possit. Consulenti plane cuidam se cur eo tenderet, dixit quia, si etiam papa fieri possit, haudquaquam dissimularet'. Guibert of Nogent, *Monodies*, p. 108, with emendation.

[69] The subject of the wealth of England before and after the Norman Conquest has occasioned considerable debate. For a positive portrayal see P. Sawyer, 'The Wealth of England in the Eleventh Century', *Transactions of the Royal Historical Society*, 5th series, (1965): 145–64, and expanded in his *The Wealth of Anglo-Saxon England* (Oxford, 2013). Less positive assessments of the capacity of the later eleventh-century English economy include J. L. Bolton, *Money in the Medieval English Economy: 973–1489* (Manchester, 2012). Interpretation of the numismatic evidence especially as marshalled by N. Mayhew, 'Modelling Medieval Monetisation', in *A Commercialising Economy: England 1086 to c. 1300*, (eds) R. Britnell and B. M. S. Campbell (Manchester, 1995), pp. 65–76, and Martin Allen, *Mints and Money in Medieval England* (Cambridge, 2012), is significant in this context. The contributions of Bolton and Mayhew to this volume express the same perspective, and in Bolton's case the same question: by what standard is wealth to be measured? A useful perspective on the effect of high-status commodities in Normandy after the Conquest is provided by D. N. Dumville, 'Anglo-Saxon Books: Treasure in Norman Hands?', *Anglo-Norman Studies*, XVI (1993): 83–99.

[70] Orderic Vitalis, *Ecclesiastical History*, Book IV, vol. II, pp. 196–9 and 266–7: '... mille et LX librae sterilensis monetae, solidique XXX et tres oboli ex iustis redditibus Angliae per singulos dies redduntur exceptis muneribus regiis et reatuum redemptionibus aliisque multiplicibus negociis quae regis aerarium cotidie adaugent'. Orderic is following the tradition of his earlier source, William of Poitiers's, *Gesta Guillelmi*.

More striking, however, is the fact that despite having outlined all of Hélinand's simoniac behaviour Guibert is ultimately unwilling to condemn him. In fact, Hélinand, was, for Guibert, a defender of church liberty, who spent his money enriching his and neighbouring churches:

> he used his enormous wealth to advance his see as well as the churches attached to it, he also protected in splendour the privileged status of the church, and it was fitting for him to have stores of wealth from the outside world, so that he could use it to advance splendidly the lordship of his churches.[71]

In Guibert's opinion this was not only unproblematic, but also, positively creditable, 'it was fitting [ut dignum erat]'. For all of his intensity on the subject of money and the church, Guibert was not fanatical about its intrinsic evil. Money, even unfortunately acquired, could be put to good and praiseworthy use, depending on the circumstances of the individual user and the relation to ecclesiastical lordship.

In this sense, Guibert again represents a view consistent with Benedictine monasticism, which saw material support as necessary, properly defensible and a positive element for spiritual expression. Orderic's description of Ansold of Maule's original bequest to the church of St Mary includes the detail that:

> he gave the quarry for millstones on the wood of Beule to St. Mary, so that twopence should be given towards the lights of the church for every millstone. And if anyone tried to defraud the church he should pay five shillings. Formerly, indeed, the fine for this offence had been sixty shilling; but since the law of the church is milder than the secular law fifty-five shillings are pardoned and five taken.[72]

The moral virtue associated with the fine serves to underline the reasonable monetary gain for the particular church. Respect for the purposes of money, as well as property, directed towards religious use forms the central value Orderic seeks to establish.

---

[71] Guibert of Nogent, *De vita sua* 3.2: ' ... quod et libertatem ecclesiae magnifice tuitus sit, et tam ipsam sedem, quam appendices ejus ecclesias uberrima largitione provexit, et dignum erat, ut externa ei bona suppeterent, quae in dominicarum domuum decore projicerentur'; Guibert of Nogent, *Monodies*, p. 109.

[72] Orderic Vitalis, *Ecclesiastical History*, Book V, vol. III, pp. 184–5: 'Aream quoque molarum in silua Bolæ dedit sanctae Mariae ita ut ex singulis molis duo denarii dentur ad luminaria aecclesiae. Et quisquis inde fraudem fecerit quinque solidos persoluat. Antea nempe pro reatu huiusmodi sexaginta soluebantur solidi. Sed lex aeclesiastica mitior est quam secularis quinquaginta quinque solidi indulgentur, et quinque accipiuntur'.

Moral disbursement of money features especially strongly in the description offered of Archbishop Lanfranc of Canterbury by Orderic's Anglo-Norman contemporary, William of Malmesbury, in his *Deeds of the Bishops of England*, written in the 1120s. William notes alms-giving as one of Lanfranc's particular virtues; he gave generously and judiciously, fulfilling the prognostic at his consecration from Luke 11.41, 'Give alms; and behold, all things are clean unto you'. The fulfilment of worldly transactions in the spiritual gain they brought to the giver is made explicit; Lanfranc was a cheerful giver.[73] He was not, however, indiscriminate with his money. William describes how Lanfranc differentiated his gifts, and what could almost be seen as Dickensian terms for his support of the poor:

> The poor were given bread, shoes, and everything under the head of food and clothing. Cash he did not give, a policy he adopted after mature reflection: ordinary folk of this sort even if they find their pockets full, 'digest hunger dry-mouthed' [Persius, *Satyricon* lxxxii.5]; and he avoided as if it were something sacred the provision of a penny instead of food, for fear of diminishing his pile.[74]

For others, Lanfranc's monetary charity was extended generously, in passages where William reveals a debt to the work which forms the basis for his history of both Lanfranc's and Anselm's archiepiscopates, Eadmer's *Historia novorum in Anglia*. 'On needy clerics and monasteries he lavished large sums of money, frequently encouraging the bashful to make requests'.[75] Lanfranc's gifts of money to monastic houses include Bec and St Évroult, both of whom preserved that memory in Anselm's letters and Orderic's *History*, respectively,

[73] William of Malmesbury, *Gesta Pontificum Anglorum*, M. Winterbottom (ed. and trans.) (Oxford, 2007), i.43.1, pp. 100–101.

[74] William of Malmesbury, *Gesta Pontificum*, i.43.3, pp. 102–103: 'Expendebantur ergo pauperibus panes, calcei, et prorsus quae ad uictum pertinent et amictum. Denarii non dabantur, maturiori tractatu, consilio profundiori, quod huiusmodi uulgus, suffarcinato etiam marsupio, sicco concoquat ore famem. Et quasi aliquid sacrosanctum uitat dare pro uictu nummum, ne debilitet numerum'. I have adopted and adapted the translation of David Preest for the last sentence, which stays closer to the literal meaning, and in this case the resonances of the misuse of money in a clerical context, than Winterbottom's 'he avoided like the plague the provision of money ... '. William of Malmesbury, *The Deeds of the Bishops of England* (Woodbridge, 2002), p. 46.

[75] William of Malmesbury, *Gesta Pontificum*, i.43.3, pp. 102–103: 'Clericis egentibus et monasteriis immensum quantum nummorum cumulabat, plerumque uerecundiores ad rogandum inuitans'.

and there were others as Eadmer states, including St Albans and Rochester, as well as Canterbury.[76]

Lanfranc made similar gestures to individuals, as William of Malmesbury noted: 'He would, without being asked, offer money to young men to help them come to the rescue of needy relatives. If what he gave turned out to have gone astray, he would repeat the gift, telling the recipient to keep it quiet'.[77] Eadmer records in detail Lanfranc's generosity to one of his fellow monks at Canterbury, to whom he gave 30 shillings a year, for the sake of the monk's mother. The monk was astonished that after the accidental loss of one of the instalments, and qualms about the archbishop's response, he simply replaced the five-shilling instalment, and added two more for good measure.[78] The specificity of the references to coin in both Eadmer and Lanfranc is important; this was a facet of Lanfranc's generosity which is commented on, remembered and recalled some 30 to 40 years after his death.

William of Malmesbury's concentration on Lanfranc's use of money is reliant upon its earlier emphasis by Eadmer. Indeed, writing in the 1110s and 1120s, contemporaneously with Guibert, Eadmer displays a similar concern for monetary payment and the moral choices this entailed. Description of money is used to illustrate moral points, and operates as a basic source for metaphorical statements. Like Orderic and Guibert, Eadmer condemned William Rufus's attitude towards monastic property: ' ... he put the Church of Christ up for sale, granting the rights of lordship over it in preference to all others to whoever to the Church's detriment outbid his rival in the price that he offered. With miserable regularity the price was renewed year by year'.[79] When Eadmer came to Henry I money played its part in the rhetorical rehabilitation of the monarch. Critical of Henry's monetary demands fuelled by his, eventually victorious, campaigns in Normandy in 1105, and then 1106, Eadmer used Henry's reform of the coinage in or around 1108 as a counterpoint to his interest in furthering

---

76 Anselm, *Epp*, 89 and 90; Orderic Vitalis, *Ecclesiastical History*, Book III, vol. II, pp. 147–51; Eadmer, *Historia novorum in Anglia*, M. Rule (ed.), Rolls Series (London, 1884), 1, p. 15–18.

77 William of Malmesbury, *Gesta Pontificum*, i.44.4, pp. 104–105: 'Vltroneus iuuenibus offerre denarios, quibus necessitudinum propriarum inopiae occurrerent. Si datum fortuitu excideret, geminare, idque clam aliis esse precipere'.

78 Eadmer, *Historia novorum* 1, pp. 14–15. The episode is discussed in Gasper and Gullbekk, 'Money and Anselm of Canterbury': 162–3.

79 Eadmer, *Historia novorum*, Rule (ed.), p. 26: 'Fecit ergo ecclesiam Christi venalem, jus in ea dominandi prae caeteris illi tribuens, qui ad detrimentum ejus in dando pretium alium superabat. Unde misera successione singulis annis pretium renovabatur', G. Bosanquet (trans.), *Eadmer's History of Recent Events in England*, (London, 1964), p. 27.

church reform, and taking Anselm's advice in this matter seriously.[80] Money and the church are held together tightly by Eadmer: wisely guided by his spiritual leader, Henry I was able to re-make money for the positive good of the Christian community he ruled. Monetisation in this sense reaches to the foreground of concerns expressed by monastic authors about moral well-being and, as they would see it, the intertwined nature of religious and secular society.

III) Ascetic Values: Debt, Poverty and Usury

The intersection between royal and spiritual power drawing on the figure of money is evoked again by the Cistercian abbot Ailred of Rievaulx, writing a generation or so after Guibert, and Eadmer, William and Orderic. Noted for his guide to monastic relations, the *Spiritual Friendship*, written around the 1160s, Ailred was, as abbot of Revesby and then Rievaulx, well acquainted with the practical demands of running a major monastery, even one of the Cistercian order.[81] He had prior experience; before entering the order, Ailred had been an official at the court of David I of Scotland, and, according to the author of his *Life,* Walter Daniel, had been marked as a future bishop.[82] Ailred's discussion

[80] Eadmer, *Historian novorum,* Rule (ed.), pp. 171–2 and 192–5, Bosanquet (trans.), pp. 183–184 and 205–8. Another contemporary Benedictine chronicler, John of Worcester, follows Eadmer's identification of the large sums of money collected by Henry, s.a. 1105, *The Chronicle of John of Worcester*, vol. 3, P. McGurk (ed. and trans.) (Oxford, 1998), pp. 106–7, and then quotes Eadmer directly in a notice of Henry's monetary and ecclesiastical reforms, s.a. 1108, *The Chronicle,* pp. 112–17. On the reform of the coinage see Allen, *Coinage,* p. 370, and Giles E. M. Gasper and Svein H. Gullbekk, 'An Intimate Encounter with English Coinage in the High Middle Ages: The Case of Wulfric of Haselbury' *British Numismatic Journal,* 83 (2013): 112–19. For Henry's campaigns, C. W. Hollister, *Henry I* (New Haven, 2001), pp. 184–91, Tinchebrai, at pp. 198–201.

[81] Walter Daniel, *The Life of Ailred of Rievaulx*, F.M. Powicke (ed. and trans.) (London, 1950). Chapter 30 notes the increase at Rievaulx of resources in personnel, farms, lands, equipment, but makes no specific mention of money.

[82] In the *Genealogy of English Kings* Ailred records his familiarity with Prince Henry of Scotland (d. 1152), King David's son: ' ... a man gentle and devout, a person of sweet spirit and cheerful heart and worthy in every way to be born of such a father. I lived with him from the very cradle. I grew up with him, boys together, and even when we were both adolescents I knew him. To serve Christ I left him while he was stamping out the flowers of youth, as I did his father, whom I loved beyond all mortals, at that time illustrious in the flower of old age. I left them bodily, but never in my mind or my heart'. (25), Ailred of Rievaulx, *The Historical Works*, M. Dutton (ed.) and J. P. Freeland (trans.) (Kalamazoo, Michigan, 2005), p. 121; Aelred of Rievaulx, *Genealogia regum anglorum, Patrologia Latina (PL)*, 195, cols. 736–7: 'virum mansuetum et pium, hominem suavis spiritus et lactei cordis, et dignum per omnia qui de tali patre nasceretur. Cum quo ab ipsis cunabulis vixi et puer cum puero crevi, cujus

of money is limited; the remarks by Bernard of Clairvaux quoted earlier, in the context of his rhetorical dispute with Cluny, emphasise the importance of not acting, in this respect, like the older Benedictine communities. Walter Daniel's *Life* is an epitome of how a Cistercian abbot might be presented: an insistence on the strict adherence to the Benedictine rule, a reminder that the community although expansive remained true to the values of poverty, and the lucent holiness of his subject. Money is not mentioned at all.

The context and purpose of Ailred's use of money within his writings deserves closer examination. A story told in his *Life of St Edward, King and Confessor*, shows his ease in employing money allusively, to emphasise the holiness of Edward's manner of life. He 'scorned money beyond human custom and seemed neither sadder when he lost it, not more cheerful when he gained it'.[83] An extended example follows, and Ailred is explicit that it was a story recorded in English, and well known.[84]

> The king was once lying on his couch to take some rest, but, as often happens thought prevented sleep. A dignitary went to the case in which the royal coin was kept and, for a moment, as it seemed to him, either took something or replaced something. Then, forgetting to close the chest, he left to do some other task. A poor little boy who, they say, had the task of collecting the dishes at table, noticed this. Going over to the chest, he drew out no small number of coins and hid them in his breast; then going out, he put them where he thought they would be safe for a while. Coming back again, he repeated his misdeed as the king watched. Then, when he tried it for a third time, the king observed in spirit, as I believe, that the keeper of the treasure was at that very moment at hand. Wanting to save the thief from danger he said, 'You are overdoing it, young fellow; if you listen to me you will take what you have and run, because, by the Mother of God, if Hugelinus' –

---

etiam adolescentiam adolescens agnovi, quem juventutis flores pulsantem sicut patrem suum quem prae cunctis mortalibus dilexi, jam senili flore fulgentem, ut Christo servirem, corpore quidem, sed nunquam mente vel affectu reliqui'. Ailred would also have been aware of the extent of David's monastic foundations, see n. 14 above.

[83] Ailred, *Life of King Edward*, in *The Historical Works*, Dutton (ed.) and Freeland (trans.), I.6; Aelred of Rievaulx, *Vita S. Edwardi regis et confessoris*, *PL*, 195, col. 746: 'Praeterea supra humanum modum pecuniae contemptor, nec in earum amissione tristior, nec in adeptione videbatur hilarior'.

[84] The story does not appear in the *Vita Aedwardi regis qui apud Westmonasterium requiescit*, F. Barlow (ed. and trans.) (London, 1962) written, possibly by Goscelin of St Bertin, in the 1070s, or in the life by Osbert of St Clare on which Ailred based his own work, M. Bloch, 'La Vie de S. Edouard le Confesseur par Osbert de Clare', *Anelecta Bollandiana*, 41 (1923): 5–131.

> that was the name of the royal chamberlain – 'comes, he will not leave you a single coin'. The boy fled, neither betrayed by the king nor pursued.[85]

Ailred is keen to point out that he had not inserted this story to no end, but to illustrate the greatness of Edward's spirit, in not getting angry and in protecting the thief from discovery. The constructed nature of the episode is clear from the threefold temptation. Part of Ailred's insistence may speak to a consciousness of the risk in using the monetary example within Cistercian quarters; the work seems to have been written for his kinsman Lawrence, Abbot of Westminster, a Benedictine foundation.[86] The setting, a royal chamber, and the king's personal monetary arrangements, may be drawn from Ailred's own experiences at the Scottish royal court.

Ailred did not merely describe money in an hagiographical context, but allowed it to inform some of his most characteristic thinking on friendship. In his celebrated treatise *Spiritual Friendship* he provides a forensic examination of a fundamental concept for monastic community life.[87] Friendship between individuals, within religious communities, and between man and God form the basis of the three dialogues. An important element in the definition of good and bad qualities in friends, and the difficult process of discerning each, the value of friendship is something to which Ailred pays close attention:

---

85 Ailred, *Life of Edward*, I.7; Aelred, *Vita S. Edwardi*, *PL*, 195, col. 746: 'Recumbebat aliquando lectulo rex gratia quiescendi; sed aliqua, ut fieri solet, cogitatio somnum suspenderat. Accessit ad thecam aedituus in qua aes regium servabatur, et aliquid pro tempore sicut ei videbatur aut sustulit aut reposuit. Deinde arcam oblitus claudere, quidpiam operis alias facturus egreditur. Animadvertit hoc puer pauperculus qui, ut dicitur, ad mensas scutellis recolligendis operam daret, et ad thecam accedens, haustum non parvum numismatum numerum in sinu recondit, et exiens, quo tutum interim arbitrabatur reposuit. Reversus denuo, rege inspectante facinus, iteravit. Quod cum tertio attentasset, cernens, ut credo, rex in spiritu jamjamque thesaurorum adesse custodem, et furis volens cavere periculum: "Importune, inquit, agis, o puer. Si mihi credis, tolle quod habes et fuge, quoniam, per Matrem Domini, si venerit Hugelinus (hoc enim erat regii cubicularii nomen), nec unum tibi nummum relinquet". Fugit puer, nec a rege proditus nec fugatus'.

86 Walter Daniel, *Life*, c. 41–2. See M. Dutton, 'Aelred, Historian: Two Portraits in Plantagenet Myth', *Cistercian Studies Quarterly*, 28 (1993): 112–44. On Lawrence of Westminster see Emma Mason, 'Lawrence (d. 1173)', *Oxford Dictionary of National Biography*, Oxford University Press, 2004, http://www.oxforddnb.com/view/article/16168 (accessed 29 Dec 2013).

87 See B. P. McGuire, *Friendship and Community: The Monastic Experience, 350–1250* (Kalamazoo, Michigan, 2000) and Julian Haseldine, 'Monastic Friendship in Theory and in Action in the Twelfth Century', in A. Classen and M. Sandidge (eds), *Friendship in the Middle Ages and Early Modern Age: Explorations of a Fundamental Ethical Discourse* (Berlin, 2010), pp. 349–93.

> Far be it from me to concede that those people know love who put a monetary value on friendship, for they proclaim themselves friends only with their lips, only when they smile in the hope of some temporal gain or lure a friend to become an accomplice in some vile action.[88]

More pointedly, and this time drawing on St Ambrose, Ailred goes on to show the moral limitations of the notions of profit and loss, and the acquisition of money, and to place in counterpoint to such empty desires, the true value of friendship:

> In human affairs many reckon nothing to be good unless it is materially profitable. They love their friends as they love their cattle, *from which they hope to profit. ...* '*For friendship is not taxation*,' as Saint Ambrose says, '*but is full of charm and grace. It is a virtue, not commerce, because it gives birth not to money but kindness, is not a negotiation over value but a concert of good will*.' So the intention of the one chosen must be subtly tested lest he should wish to be linked to you in friendship in the hope of gain, because he calculates friendship as marketable and not voluntary.[89]

Both here, and in the *Life of St Edward*, money when used as an analogy for spiritual value features with respect to secular society, whether royal or quotidian. As Ailred's discussion moves to the society of the religious, so references to money recede. The desire for monastic friendships firmly founded on the grace of love suffuses Ailred's idealised image of the monastic community. Poverty he does not regard as a good in and of itself, rather it is the intention that gives force to the adoption of a poor life. However, Ailred's reaction against the monetisation and commodification of virtues is worth noting. Other contemporary orders reacted far more vigorously, stressing poverty and simplicity above all else; and

---

88 Ailred, *Spiritual Friendship*, M. Dutton (ed.) and L. C. Braceland (trans.) (Kalamazoo, Michigan, 2010), II. 53, p. 82; Aelredus Rieuallensis, *De spiritali amicitia*, Corpus Christianorum Continuatio Mediaevalis, 1, A. Hoste (ed.) (Turnhout, 1971), Liber II: 'absit enim ut eorum quemquam amare concesserim, qui amicitiam quaestum putant; tunc se solis labiis profitentes amicos, cum spes alicuius commodi temporalis arriserit; uel cum amicum cuiuslibet turpitudinis ministrum facere temptauerit'.

89 Ailred, *Spiritual Friendship*, III. 68, 70, pp. 103, 104; Aelredus, *De spiritali amicitia*, Liber III: 'sunt enim plerique qui in rebus humanis nihil bonum norunt, nisi quod temporaliter fructuosum sit. hi sic amicos sicut boues suos diligunt' ... 'non enim, ut ait sanctus ambrosius, uectigalis amicitia est, sed plena decoris, plena gratiae. uirtus est enim, non quaestus; quia pecunia non parturitur, sed gratia; nec licitatione pretiorum, sed concertatione beneuolentiae, eius igitur quem eligisti, subtiliter est probanda intentio, ne secundum spem commodi cuiuslibet tibi uelit in amicitia copulari, mercenariam eam aestimans non gratuitam'. The italicised quotations are from Cicero, *De amicitia*, 21.79 and Ambrose, *De officiis*, 3.134, respectively.

these more extreme ascetic monastic movements offer corresponding judgement on worldly wealth, its mechanisms, tools and modes.

Prominent amongst these movements was the Carthusian Order.[90] The distinctive architecture of Carthusian cloisters, with individual house-like cells, physically inscribes the eremitic within their communities.[91] One of the most important witnesses for the establishment and early development of the order in the 1080s is Guibert of Nogent, and it is an establishment that he ties quite specifically to attitudes to money. The beginning of the order, the retreat of the founder Bruno from the household of Archbishop Manasses of Reims, was catalysed by his mistreatment of money: Manasses occupied his seat simoniacally and broke up a precious chalice for salary payment for his soldiers.[92] Guibert draws attention to Carthusian attitudes towards wealth. No riches were to be kept within the church, no silver vessels for their use; their poverty was very jealously guarded.[93] This sentiment re-occurs repeatedly in Carthusian literature.

William of St Thierry in *The Golden Epistle*, perhaps the most celebrated monastic text of the high medieval period, written for the monks of the Charterhouse of Mont-Dieu, mentions money only once, but significantly. Discoursing on poverty, William praises the simple fashioning of their monastic cells, and, in a similar fashion to Ailred, places this in a discussion about how men can rise from the animal state, to the rational and spiritual. Those in the animal state can be admitted to the company of those who live an ascetic life, but the danger of indulging the animal to the whole community is stressed. This danger is exemplified in the fabric of the community's dwellings:

> For it comes about that with money that does not belong to us the building of costly and, insofar as very shame allows, imposing cells is undertaken ... Banishing from ourselves and from our cells the pattern of poverty and the model of holy simplicity, the true beauty of God's house, bequeathed to us by our Fathers, we build for ourselves by the hands of skilled craftsmen cells which are not so much eremitic as aromatic, each of them costing a hundred *solidi*. They are the delight of our eyes but they come from the alms of the poor ... Take away, Lord, the

---

90 Reference works on the Carthusians are limited, see Gerhard Schlegel and James Hogg (eds.), *Monasticon Cartusiense*, 4 vols in 10, *Analecta Cartusiana* 185, 1–4, (Salzburg, Austria: Institut für Anglistik und Amerikanistik, University of Salzburg, 2004–12), and *Etudes et documents pour l'histoire des Chartreux*, Dom Augustin Devaulx (ed.), *Analecta Cartusiana*, 208 (Salzburg, 2003).

91 For archaeological investigations in Britain see G. Coppack and M. Aston, *Christ's Poor Men: The Carthusians in Britain* (Stroud, 2002) and for wider comparison Ludolphe Jacquemart, Pacome de Falconnet, Bernard-Marie Dubosquet and Gerard Hulsbosch, *Maisons de l'ordre des Chartreux: Vues et notices*, 4 vols (Montreuil-sur-Mer, 1913–19).

92 Guibert, *Mon.* 1.11; pp. 26–7.

93 Guibert, *Mon.*, 1.11; pp. 27–8.

> reproach of these hundred *solidi* from the cells of your poor men. Why not rather a hundred *denarii*? Why not rather nothing at all? Why do not the sons of grace rather build for themselves free of cost?[94]

William, praises the interior over exterior, and extolls the beauty of holy simplicity and poverty.

The same reticence in mentioning money per se, while dwelling at length on poverty and wealth, is to be found in the *Meditations* of Guigo I (1083–1136), the fifth Prior of the Grande Chartreuse, composed 1109–15, which became one of the foundational texts for the Carthusian communities.[95] Guigo's mediations do not mention money often, specifically. His admonitions and allusions tend to revolve around images of fornication more than the evils of money. However, his writing is filled with warnings about the world. Worldly goods are harmful distractions from the true struggle of human life, the transitory should not be preferred to the eternal, no matter how superficially attractive and desirable. Wealth, therefore, is a fundamental element to Guigo's thought, but he does not spend a great deal of time exploring its particularities.

Where money is mentioned the context is, therefore, instructive. Money-lending is condemned, by analogy to a full cellar:

> If you rely on a full cellar, aren't you behaving like money-lenders? And is that not to worship an idol, even though a cellar has no face or eyes? In any case you do not realise how much you rely on a full cellar until it is empty.[96]

---

94 William of St Thierry, *The Golden Epistle*, XXXVI, 147–9, Theodore Berkley (trans.), pp. 59–60, *Epistola ad Fratres de Monte-Dei*, R. Thomas (ed.), 2 vols (Chambarand, 1968): XXXVI 147. 'Inde enim subintrauit iam de aere alieno sumptuosa, et, quantum pudor sinit, ambitiosa cellarum aedificatio ... ' 148. 'Dimissam enim nobis a patribus iure hereditario formam paupertatis, et sanctae simplicitatis speciem, uerum decorem domus Dei, alienantes a nobis et a cellis nostris, per manus artificum exquisitorum, cellas non tam eremiticas quam aromaticas aedificamus nobis, singulas in titulo centum solidorum, concupiscentias oculorum nostrorum, de eleemosynis pauperum'. 149. 'Amputa, Domine, opprobrium centum solidorum a cellis pauperum tuorum. Cur non potius centum denariorum? Cur non potius nullorum? Cur non potius filii gratiae gratis ipsi sibi aedificant?'.

95 D. N. Bell, 'The Carthusian Connection: Guigo I of La Chartreuse and the Origins of Cistercian Spirituality', *Cistercian Studies Quarterly*, 27 (1992): pp. 51–62. See also, Guigues Ier, Prieur de Chartreuse, *Coutumes de Chartreuse. Introduction, texte critique, traduction et notes par un chartreux*, M. Laporte (ed.), Sources chrétiennes, 313 (Paris, 1984).

96 Guigo, *Meditationes*, 116, M. Laporte (ed. and trans.), Sources Chrétiennes, 308 (Paris, 1983): 'Si confidis in pleno cellario, an non usurarii hoc faciunt? An non est hoc, ydolum colere? An quia cellarium non habet faciem et oculos? Non autem nostri quantum confidis pleno, nisi cum depletur'. English translation from *The Meditations of Guigo*, A. Gorden Mursell (trans.) (Kalamazoo, Michigan, 1995), p. 87.

The theme of money, drink and commodification is continued with reference to love:

> Notice how you sell love and the other spiritual affections for half-pennies and smaller coins, like wine in a tavern. And notice too how you buy opinions and loves and other spiritual affections or emotions for half-pennies and smaller coins, like wine in a tavern.[97]

Guigo presents an interesting comment on the fact of small change, presumably half-pennies (probably round given that continental denarii were rarely of a high enough value to cut in two, compared to English coin), which adds to the verisimilitude of the allusion.[98] He also acknowledges wage labour: 'Not only should you accept no salary for doing your duty: you should not even be deterred by any adversities from doing it'.[99] The existence of salaried labour is driven into a different point and is negatively compared to the challenges and virtues of religious life. Guigo is no advocate of mendicancy. Money and wealth exist, are necessary for his community, but are given even less prominence than in Ailred's writing. Attention is focused elsewhere and money is ignored rather than problematised. As Guigo expresses it, an image of dung made in gold is better in substance than image. An image of an angel in gold is better in image.[100] Interior wins out for Guigo over the exterior: the goal of human meditation remains the contemplation of God, and not of the world.

---

[97] Guigo, *Meditationes*, 438: 'Vide quomodo vendis amorem et caeteros affectus animi tui ad obolatus et nummatas, sicut in taberna vinum. Rursus attende qualiter emas opiniones et amores ac caeteros affectus sive motus humanorum animorum, ad obolatas et nummatas, sicut in taberna vinum'; *Meditations*, p. 176. Mursell translates Guigo's reference to coin denominations as 'for pennies and small change', and the sense is that of a phrase such as the American 'nickels and dimes'. The translation has been emended for a more literal reading of the particular coin denominations he references, since obolus generally refers to half of the main denomination.

[98] See in this connection, Thomas J. Sargent and François Velde, *The Big Problem of Small Change* (Princeton, 2002), esp. ch. 4. Gasper and Gullbekk, 'Wulfric of Haselbury': 113–15, discuss the issue with respect to Henry I's coinage. I am very grateful for the comments of the anonymous reviewer of the volume on the issue of Guigo's reference to coin denominations.

[99] Guigo, *Meditationes*, 331: 'Non solum nullum pretium debes suscipere ut facias quod oportet, sed etiam nullis adversis qui facias deterreri'; *Meditations*, p. 139.

[100] Guigo, *Meditationes*, 360: 'Si imago stercoris ex auro fiat, melior est utique substantialiter, quam imaginaliter. Substantialiter namque aurum, imaginaliter vero stercus erit. Si autem angeli imago auro imprimatur, imaginaliter erit melior, quam substantialiter. Imaginaliter enim substantia viva, spiritalis ac rationalis. Substantialiter autem, corpus insensatum et sine vita'; *Meditations*, 149–50.

Excoriation of wealth and money-lending feature powerfully in the writings of Guigo I's Grandmontine contemporary, Stephen of Muret.[101] The main written text associated with Stephen of Muret is the *Maxims* transmitted orally amongst those who gathered around him, and eventually compiled by a second Stephen, he of Liciac, fourth Prior of Grandmont, from 1139. As a text the *Maxims* represent the mores and interests of the 1140s and 1150s as much as they do the vision and experience of the 1070s to early 1120s. They do not offer a coherent treatise on monastic life, but rather, in a series of aphorisms and observations, provide a series of reflections on the values necessary to life in a strict community, and one that had an eremitic bent. Discipline looms large within Stephen of Muret's world, as do the temptations to which his community will be subject. The guiding principle is the imitation of Christ and the attempt to follow the apostolic life: ' ... all such [monastic] Rules are derived from the Common Rule, the Gospel'.[102]

Throughout the *Maxims*, Stephen's pool of imagery, his use of metaphors and similes, as well as his description of real challenges to his lifestyle, draws on the secular world. In particular the market-place and the example and experience of soldiers, including their lust for booty, loom large. The *Maxims* deals with a number of circumstances where money, and wealth, impinge on the life of the community. These include occasions where Stephen's community is distinguished and set apart from other monastic orders, and others where it is the secular world that forms the point of contrast and comparison:

> You may move on to any monastery you wish, where you will find impressive buildings, delicate foods served up according to their seasons. There too you will meet with great expanses of land covered with flocks. Here you will find only poverty and the cross.[103]

Simony is condemned also, with an implicit criticism of the *Rule* of Saint Benedict: 'If anyone entered religious life because of some promise of earthly

101 *Vita venerabilis viri Stephani Muretensis*, in *Scriptores Ordinis Grandimontensis*, pp. 103–37.

102 Stephen of Muret, *Maxims*, D. van Doel (trans.) (Kalamazoo, Michigan, 2002), Prologue, p. 8; *Liber sententiarum uel de doctrina ab Hugone Lacerta et sociis eius collectus*, in *Scriptores Ordinis Grandimontensis*, Initium Libri: 'Attamen, totum sumitur de communi regula, id est de euangelio'.

103 Stephen of Muret, *Maxims*, 1.3; *Liber de doctrina*, 1: '"Tu uero pergere potes ad quodlibet monasteriorum, ubi magna inuenies aedificia, cibos que delicatos suis temporibus constitutos. Illic bestias reperies terrarum que latitudinem, hic tantum crucem et paupertatem"'.

goods, Stephen would have considered him a simoniac'.[104] Moreover, the same theme of the value of love raised by Ailred is addressed, with slightly different force:

> In the marketplace of this world, God pits his own love against the attractions of silver and gold and other earthly things; in this way he makes it dearer and more valuable to those who would possess it. For when they want to covet something, some earthly thing, God is there to confront them with a choice, as if to say, 'Choose now which you would prefer: me your God, or the temporal thing. Should you choose me, I will give you more than you could ever covet: choose the other, and you will lose everything.[105]

Stephen immediately goes to provide a more detailed example of God's gifts, money and need: as long as no harm is caused to one who amasses wealth, and the expenditure is on the good, the accumulation of money is not to be condemned:

> God gives to each according to that person's needs, so you are not ever going to be condemned for making a lot of money, provided you harm neither yourself nor anyone else in the process. In fact this is how God contrives to spend on many the wealth amassed by one. Whoever has made a fortune by cheating and exploiting others, unwittingly has wasted it; the one who gathers wealth, yet spends it too, on doing good, will have God as a business partner.[106]

However, the subject on which Stephen expends most rhetorical effort, the more striking in a genre defined by epigrammatic and gnomic style, is money-lending.

> Whoever has recourse to a money-lender is doing wrong and is, in fact, just as wrong as the money-lender. This is why: if you spend what you cannot afford on

---

[104] Stephen of Muret, *Maxims*, 1.4; *Liber de doctrina*, 1: 'Simoniacum enim eum aestimaret, si cuiuslibet terrenae rei promissione in religionem ueniret'.

[105] Stephen of Muret, *Maxims*, 42.1; *Liber de doctrina*, 42: 'Idcirco Deus amorem immisit in auro et argento ceteris que rebus terrenis, ut suus amor esset inde carior meriti que maioris ipsum habituris. Cum enim aliquis uult concupiscere quodlibet huius saeculi, a Deo sibi datur optio, quasi diceret: "Elige quod malueris, aut me qui sum Deus, aut rem temporalem. Si me elegeris, magis tibi dabo quam concupiscere possis; si aliud elegeris, totum amittes"'.

[106] Stephen of Muret, *Maxims*, 42.3; *Liber de doctrina*, 42: 'Attamen Dominus bene concedit homini quidquid sibi necessarium est, nullus que propter hoc umquam damnabitur, si omnem censum congreget quem acquirere poterit, tali modo ne sibi primum inde faciat iniuriam nec alii. Eo namque modo quo census ab aliquo colligitur Dominus disponit ut expendatur. Quisquis enim peruerse et iniuste congregat, insipienter deuastat; qui uero iuste congerit, Deo cooperante, in bonum expendit'.

> expensive luxuries – fancy foods, clothing, etc. – when you already have enough to live comfortably, you will end up needing the services of a money-lender.[107]

Both the lender and the creditor incur the same guilt before God, wanting for things that they do not have (as Alan of Lille would later observe also).[108] The money-lender is if anything worse however, as a facilitator of this vice. Stephen reserves his most scathing comments for the usurer, as practising a type of money-lending that transcends death:

> The money-lending trade offers many ways to be wicked, but the worst of all its practitioners is the usurer. An end will come to the life of a usurer, and his children will have to inherit the pledges he held. This state of affairs will speak more eloquently than if the man had said, 'My child I am about to die. While I could I fought hard against God, but that is not enough for me; by leaving you these pledges, I will carry on my fight through you'.[109]

In this way even a dead moneyer can go on putting his money out at interest, noting that 'and whatever is received over and above the amount borrowed is usury'.[110] Stephen reminds his community at the end of this disquisition that to claim money or property from borrowers is to inherit a place in Hell. As he puts it:

> But beyond any doubt, this you would never actually do: spend but a second in that place, and you would not wish to repeat the visit – not for all the wealth in the world.[111]

---

107 Stephen of Muret, *Maxims*, 60.1; *Liber de doctrina*, 60: 'Quisquis usuram accipit, delinquit; et qui eam tribuit, similiter; hoc modo: cum aliquis immoderantia sua fecit expensam quam sua nequit tolerare facultas in cibo uel in uestibus, siue ceteris rebus, posset que uitam suam quoquo modo cum re possessa sustentare, postmodum propter illam superfluitatem pergens ad feneratorem, similiter peccat in censu quem illi tribuit, quemadmodum alter qui accipit'.

108 See the contribution by Odd Langholm within this volume.

109 Stephen of Muret, *Maxims*, 60.2; this translation uses 'pawnbroker' in place of 'usurer', the latter is preferred in this context, given the general range of meaning that 'usura' could carry. *Liber de doctrina*, 60: 'Multis modis in usura delinquitur, sed ab eo penitus, a quo pignora capiuntur. Postquam enim ea susceperit circa finem uitae suae filio suo uel cui uult ea relinquere, dicit; hoc uero dicit operibus ualidius sermone loquentibus: "Fili, ego moriar, et Deum impugnaui, quamdiu uixi, nec mihi sufficit, sed te uicarium pro me relinquam, ut illum cum hac eadem usura impugnes"'.

110 Stephen of Muret, *Maxims*, 60.3: 'Quidquid enim recipitur praeter id quod commissum est, usura est'. The translation offers for 'usura es' 'counts as such ill-gotten profit', a literal translation seems more appropriate here.

111 Stephen of Muret, *Maxims*, 60.4; *Liber de doctrina*, 60: 'Sciat autem indubitanter se numquam illic adfuisse; nam si uno tantum momento illic exstitisset, numquam pro uniuerso

In this fear of the usurer's hell the Grandmontine is joined by the Benedictine. At about the same time as Stephen's *Maxims* were composed Orderic was composing the eighth book of his *Ecclesiastical History*, in which he recorded the priest Walchelin's experience of a diabolical cavalcade, made up of the recent dead enduring horror and torture for their sins in life.[112] William of Glos is singled out, tormented for a gamut of worldly crimes but suffering most for usury, receiving a mill in pledge for a monetary loan which he kept on non-payment, disinheriting the legitimate heirs. As punishment William states 'I carry a burning mill-shaft in my mouth, which, believe me, seems heavier than the castle of Rouen', begging that his wife and son should be contacted to restore the mill to its rightful owners.[113]

The vehemence of the warnings against usury, more extreme amongst the more ascetic voices, grow throughout the later eleventh and the first half of the twelfth century. These voices are amongst the most pointed monastic reactions to a gradual monetisation of the economy and of society. Other contemporaries, too, placed, conceptually, the differing expression of monastic values amongst the various orders of the period, alongside and as a moral mirror to contemporary economic and social change. This is the case in John of Salisbury's *Policraticus*. In his praise, and criticism, of monastic orders, it is, as discussed earlier, their resistance to hypocrisy which provides his most important category. While he notes that secular priests, operating within the world, find it challenging to establish discipline needed to engender, nurture and sustain the holy life, regular canonical and other monks do include the holy within their ranks, as do the Cluniac and Cistercians. Pre-eminent amongst the religious orders, for John, are the Carthusians, and at the pinnacle, the Grandmontines. What defines John's discussion of hypocrisy, however, is the attitudes shown towards money.

> Love of money well-nigh conquers nature herself and brings almost impossible things within the realm of possibility. ... As long as one can make money, no region of the world appears inaccessible, and the greater flame of avarice will conquer even its torrid zone.[114]

---

censu mundi illuc redire uellet'.

[112] Orderic Vitalis, *Ecclesiastical History*, Book VIII, vol. IV, pp. 236–49. On Orderic's story as amongst the earliest versions of what became known as Hellequin's hunt see J-C Schmitt, *Ghosts in the Middle Ages: The Living and the Dead in Medieval Society* (Chicago, 1998), pp. 93–100.

[113] Orderic Vitalis, *Ecclesiastical History*, Book VIII, vol. IV, pp. 244–5: 'Ecce candens ferrum molendini gesto in ore quod sine dubio michi uidetur ad ferendum grauius Rotomagensi arce'.

[114] John of Salisbury, *Policraticus*, Book VII, ch. 16: 'Ipsam fere naturam uincit amor pecuniae et res pene impossibiles ad possibilem redigit facultatem ... Dum itaque quaestum

Money, for John is an integral element in the broader vice of avarice, but one whose role may be superseded by that for which it is exchanged.[115]

> One not falling victim to the love of money is at times conquered by greed for its trappings. Horses, apparel, spurred falcons, hunting dogs, numerous herds of cattle and smaller beasts, and the varied furniture of the world (since it exceeds human capacity to enumerate each) are preferred to money by many, and they exhaust the strength of their whole being in acquiring and keeping these possessions. For the frenzy of avarice in the abstract is based upon two considerations: that it covets to excess the possessions of others or guards its own too tenaciously; and that he who seeks to excess what he lacks, makes demands beyond the law of necessity of utility.[116]

Monastic lives of observance, discipline and vigilance against the corruption of money are the main defences John offers for individuals and communities so affected. At the extremes of ascetic lifestyle are lodged deeper criticisms of contemporary society.

Conclusions

Monastic witness to money and that to which it gives value is both complex and variable. How far spiritual values are seen to inflect description of the world, and how far the values of the world inscribe themselves within monastic expression, require constant interpretation. Nevertheless, to describe the retreat from the worldly necessitates acknowledging the world and its practices. Beneath the divisions between authors over time, and from order to order, describing the world outside or the world within the cloister, reactions to economic and social transformation can be detected. The acquisition and management of wealth, lordship, especially kingship, and usury emerge as themes common to

faciat, nulla pars mundi uidetur inaccessibilis et ipsius torridae estum maior auaritiae ignis exuperat', Pike (trans.), pp. 275–6.

115 For a discussion of avarice in this period see A. Murray, *Reason and Society*, pp. 59–80.

116 John of Salisbury, *Policraticus*, Book VII, ch. 16: 'et quem non subigit amor pecuniae, interdum superat cupiditas specierum. Equos, uestes, aues armatas, uenaticos canes, numerosos greges armentorum et pecorum, et uariam mundi supellectilem (quoniam per singula currere uires humanas excedit) plerique pecuniae praeferunt et totius hominis uires exhauriunt in adquirendis his aut tenendis. Nam in his duobus articulis furor totius auaritiae constat quod immoderatius appetit aliena aut sua tenacius seruat; et quidem immoderatius appetit quisquis quod deest, legem necessitatis excedens et usus, exposcit', Pike (trans.), p. 277.

the monastic authors considered. The varied discussions underline the protean quality of money, as physical and real, with tangible benefits, and as symbolic both of temptation and of its rejection. The Gospel injuction, illustrated through coin, to render unto Caesar that which was his, and to God that which was his, may lie at the root of the multi-layered monastic response to money. The invocation, description and debate on the possession of money and the consequences of its use indicate the evolution of money as a conceptual category and of its presence within systems and schema of value and economy. Both deliberately and despite themselves, these authors reveal a great deal about how embedded a monetary economy, and a monetary way of thinking, had become within their lifetimes.

Chapter 4

Nummus falsus: The Perception of Counterfeit Money in the Eleventh and Early Twelfth Century

Greti Dinkova-Bruun

In Book III, Chapter 36 of his *Sententiae*, written in the years just preceding his death in 636, Isidore of Seville states:

> Just as in a coin the metal, image and weight are scrutinized, so in every doctor of the Church one needs to examine what he follows, what he teaches and how he lives. Thus the quality of the metal denotes doctrine, the image – similarity to the fathers, the weight – humility. Indeed, he who deviates from these three (characteristics) will not be metal but earth.[1]

This statement captures precisely the two lines of inquiry that will be followed in this chapter: first, the materiality of the coin, or which of its physical attributes were inspected in establishing its validity; and second, its symbolic value, or how

---

[1] Isidorus Hispalensis, *Sententiae*, P. Cazier (ed.), Corpus Christianorum Series Latina 111 (Turnhout, 1998), Book 3, cap. 36.5, p. 277, ll. 23–8: 'Sicut in numismate metallum, et figura, et pondus inquiritur, ita in omni doctore ecclesiastico, quid sequatur, quid doceat, quomodo uiuat. Per qualitatem igitur metalli doctrina, per figuram similitudo patrum, per pondus humilitas designatur. Qui uero ab his tribus discrepauerit, non metallum, sed terra erit'. Interestingly, a short poem versifying Isidore's text and entitled *Similitudo denarii et doctoris* is found among the epigrams attributed to Hildebert (d. 1133). See, A. B. Scott, Deirdre F. Baker and A. G. Rigg, 'The *Biblical Epigrams* of Hildebert of Le Mans: A Critical Edition', *Mediaeval Studies* 47 (1985): 272–316, at 314, no. 5. The epigram reads:

> Quale metallum sit, quod pondus, cuius imago
> queritur in nummo. Sic in doctore metallum
> sermo, figura patrum sentencia, pondus honestas.

[In a coin one examines of what metal it is made, how much it weighs and whose image it carries. Similarly in the doctor (of the church) the metal denotes his speech, the image the teaching of the fathers, the weight his honesty.]

the material qualities of the specie relate to the moral make-up of the individual who is compared to it. In the process of this discussion also some considerations on vocabulary will be presented.

The earliest author who explores the close connection between the physical aspects of the coin and their spiritual meaning is the early ascetic writer John Cassian (d. 435). In chapters 20, 21 and 22 of the first section of his vast work, entitled *Collationes* (*Conferences*), Cassian explains that every believer has to constantly examine the thoughts that emerge in his heart in order to ascertain their origin and true nature. In this every Christian needs to become a spiritual money-changer by scrutinising his heart in the same way in which a worldly money-changer (*trapezita* from the Greek *trapeza* 'table') determines the value of the coins presented to him. The steps the *trapezita* takes in his examination are outlined as follows by Cassian.[2]

First, he makes sure that the coin (*nomisma* or *numisma*) is made of purest gold (*aurum purissimum* or *obrizum*) and is not a common brass denarius (*aereus uilisque denarius*) which is being passed off as a valuable piece.[3] Spiritually, this first step means that the Christian must establish whether the doctrine learned by him has been purified (like gold) by the divine fire of the Holy Spirit and that no counterfeit currency, namely Jewish superstitions, heretical errors and seductive teachings of secular philosophy, has been accepted in the treasure of his heart. These false doctrines shine like counterfeit money only superficially but their core is vile and base, deceitful and harmful.

The second test performed by Cassian's *trapezita* involves verifying the image on the coin (called *uultus* or *imago*). Here again two possible fraudulent practices can be detected: one, that the coin is stamped not with the face of a true king but with the face of a tyrant (*non ueri regis sed tyranni praeferunt uultus*); and two, even when the image of a true king is seen on it, the specie still has to be deemed a counterfeit if it has not been minted lawfully (*non legitime figurata* or *signata*). This forged currency, naturally, has to be rejected. Spiritually, the coins made of pure gold but stamped with the false image of a tyrant signify the precious words of Sacred Scripture, to which harmful and contrary meaning is ascribed, with the purpose of luring the faithful into error. Even when the coin exhibits the face of a true king, it still has to be rejected, if the image has not been stamped by lawful minters (*legitimi monetarii*) and does

---

2 Iohannes Cassianus, *Collationes XXIIII*, M. Petschenig (ed.), Corpus Scriptorum Ecclesiasticorum Latinorum 13 (Vienna, 1886; repr. curante Gottfried Kreuz, Vienna, 2004), pp. 29–34. For an English translation, see *John Cassian: The Conferences*, Boniface Ramsey (trans. and annotated), Ancient Christian Writers 57 (Mahwah, NJ, 1997), pp. 59–63.

3 The Roman silver denarius ceased to be struck in the third century. After this point, and including the western Middle Ages, the denarius was used both as a generic term for coin, and sometimes (as in English) to denote a specific coin type.

not originate from a legitimate public workshop. The *legitimi monetarii* are none others but the approved Catholic fathers (*probati et Catholici patres*), while the legitimate minting workshop represents their theological discussions. Thus the examination of the image on the coin is concerned with the notion of authority, a concept that shapes medieval theological and literary discourse for centuries.

Cassian uses two terms to denote false coins in this context, namely, *adulterina nomismata* and *paracharaxima* (also called *paracharagmata* in the edition of Cassian's text in the *Patrologia Latina*, volume 49).[4] However, the *adulterina nomismata* should be understood as debased coins in which cheap metals had been mixed with the pure gold or silver, while the *paracharaxima* or *paracharagmata* are the coins stamped with a false *imago* or of illegal provenance.

Finally, the money-changer examines the coin in order to assess whether its proper weight (*legitimum pondus*) has been preserved. Pieces that do not weigh enough have to be refused. Spiritually, this test signifies placing our thoughts on the scale of our hearts and establishing whether they are sufficiently heavy with the fear of God or whether, in contrast, they are too light as a result of human presumption, being diminished by pride and eroded by vanity to the point where they are out of balance with the testimonies of the prophets and the apostles. As for the vocabulary used here, Cassian does not have a particular term for coins whose weight has been tampered with; he simply calls them 'light, condemnable and insufficiently heavy' (*nomismata leuia atque damnosa minusque pensantia*).

In conclusion, from everything discussed to this point it becomes apparent that for Cassian external testing of the coin equates to the internal examination of the soul. The rich imagery of Cassian's text sets the stage for everything that follows. Slowly but surely Cassian's ideas, as well as his vocabulary, will be changed and adapted to new historical realities, which is the focus of the rest of this chapter. This speaks also to the longevity of Cassian's *Collationes* as a core text within western monasticism over the rest of the medieval period. The *Collationes* were a common text to which monastic reformers of all stripes returned, notably in the eleventh and twelfth centuries.

The next example in tracing the spiritual understanding of the *nummus falsus* in the Middle Ages is Gregory the Great who, even though inspired by Cassian, changes the tenor of his coin-related analogy by linking it to the image of the false prophets of the Antichrist. Gregory proposes this imagery in his monumental treatise *Moralia in Job* (*Morals on the Book of Job*), composed between 578 and 595 and consisting of 35 extensive books on various moral issues. The commentary had a powerful influence on later medieval religious thinkers and writers. The passage in question is found in book 33, chapter 35, in a section where Gregory comments on Job 41, a chapter in which God

---

[4] See *Patrologia Latina* (*PL*) 49, col. 519.

describes in apocalyptic terms the dreadful creature Leviathan.[5] 'Out of his mouth proceed lamps as kindled torches of fire', reads verse 10 in this chapter of the Book of Job, and this statement prompts Gregory to talk about the preachers of the Antichrist who will appear at the end of times. Such impostors and hypocrites, however, exist also in our own time, continues Gregory, because are they not preachers of the Antichrist, 'who while they hold the holy orders of God, grasp with all their desires the fleeting world, who boast that all their doings are virtues, but everything they do is sin'.[6] This lamentable behaviour of concealing and pretending with the purpose of deceiving prompts Gregory to compare the false prophets to a coin which has been marred and whose true value needs to be determined by an expert money-changer, called *nummularius*, a term that has replaced Cassian's *trapezita*. It would not be such a strange thing, says Gregory, if we do *spiritaliter* (spiritually) what we see the money-changers doing daily *corporaliter* (physically).

This statement is followed by a summary of Cassian's coin-inspired analogy, which, however, is stripped from its framework of internal self-examination and infused with concerns about how the false prophets are to be recognised by the faithful. Thus, for Gregory the brass concealed under a layer of gold in counterfeit money symbolises both vice that is hiding under the appearance of virtue, and bad intentions that are masquerading as good ones. Similarly to Cassian, the approved minters (*probati monetarii*) or the ones authorised to stamp coins legally are compared to the ancient fathers and their piety, which has to be imitated and preserved, not distorted and perverted. Finally, the full weight of the coin (*integrum pondus*) is linked to the sum of perfection (*summa perfectionis*), which has not been marred by anything being taken away from it. When subjected to this triple examination, the preachers of the Antichrist are easily exposed as counterfeit coinage. Surely they are false prophets, because they seek temporal glory, persecute the just, reject their piety and 'have not only not attained the perfection of humility, but have not even reached its threshold'.[7]

This discussion makes it clear that there is a shift in Gregory the Great's use of the coin-analogy from the ascetic to the pastoral and from the personal to the communal. This shift undoubtedly reflects Gregory's concerns as a pope

5 Gregorius Magnus, *Moralia in Iob*, M. Adriaen (ed.), Corpus Christianorum Series Latina 143B (Turnhout, 1985), Lib. 33, cap. 35.60, pp. 1724–6. For an English translation, see Gregory the Great, *Morals on the Book of Job*, James Bliss and Charles Marriott (trans), 3 vols in 4 (Oxford, 1844–50).

6 Gregorius, *Moralia in Iob*, CCSL 143B, p. 1725, ll. 31–4: 'An praedicatores simulationis illius non sunt, qui cum sacros Dei ordines obtinent, fugientem totis desideriis mundum tenent; qui uirtutes ostendunt esse quae faciunt, sed uitium est omne quod agunt?'

7 Gregorius, *Moralia in Iob*, CCSL 143B, p. 1725, ll. 62–4: 'Quomodo in se integritatis pondus ostendunt, qui non solum humilitatis perfectionem nequaquam assecuti sunt, sed neque ipsam primam eius ianuam contigerunt?'

and leader of the entire flock of Christian believers. The dangers to the faithful are manifold. People can be seduced so easily by the shining gold of falsehood and led into doubt and error. In order to avoid this danger, the faithful have to become a spiritual *nummularius* who possesses the wisdom and the expertise to uncover the true nature of the false preachers and reject their doctrine as counterfeit money that has no right to be preserved in the treasury of his heart.

Gregory the Great's approach of using the examination of a false coin as a cautionary tale against mistaken doctrine and practice is adopted and expanded further by Humbert of Silva Candida who in the middle of the eleventh century (that is in 1057–8, just three years before his death in 1061) wrote a lengthy treatise against the rampant simoniac practices of his contemporary church, entitled *Libri tres aduersus simoniacos.*[8] As one of the most trusted men of Pope Leo IX, Humbert was deeply involved in the reforming efforts of his administration, and remained an influential figure in what is conveniently termed the Gregorian reform. As a cardinal and papal legate, Humbert was the head of the papal mission to Constantinople in 1054, whose purpose was to address the theological differences between the eastern and the western church. In this the mission failed utterly, with Humbert excommunicating the Patriarch of Constantinople, and as a result the year 1054 is traditionally accepted as the beginning of the Great Schism.[9]

In light of his simoniac concerns, it is probably not surprising that Humbert uses the coin-analogy in the *Libri tres aduersus simoniacos.* After all, simony is the practice of paying in order to obtain ecclesiastical offices. Money is, thus, at the heart of this controversy. The coin-analogy is found in Book 1, chapter 6, entitled 'De differentia pseudoepiscoporum et ordinationibus eorum (On the difference between the pseudo-bishops and their ordrinations)' in Robinson's edition. Humbert's text contains elements that are completely new and quite revealing of the new economic and monetary climate of the eleventh century.[10]

---

[8] *Humberti Cardinalis Libri III adversus Simoniacos*, Friedrich Thaner (ed.), Monumenta Germaniae Historica, Libelli de Lite, 3 vols (Hannover 1891–7; repr. 1956), vol. 1, pp. 95–253, at pp. 109–10. The text discussed here is edited also in Elaine Robinson, 'Humbertus de Silua Candida, *Libri tres aduersus simoniacos:* A Critical Edition with an Introductory Essay and Notes', unpubl. PhD Dissertation, Princeton University (1972), Lib. 1, cap. 6, pp. 24–6.

[9] For the most pertinent bibliography on Humbert, see Ute-Renate Blumenthal, *The Investiture Controversy: Church and Monarchy from the Ninth to the Twelfth Century* (Philadelphia, 1988), p. 101. On the Great Schism, see Steven Runciman, *The Eastern Schism: A Study of the Papacy and the Eastern Churches during the XIth and XIIth Centuries* (Oxford, 1955) and more recently Henry Chadwick, *East and West: The Making of a Rift in the Church from Apostolic Times until the Council of Florence* (Oxford, 2003).

[10] For a general discussion of these phenomena, see Alexander Murray, *Reason and Society in the Middle Ages* (Oxford, 1978).

The first book of the treatise expounds on the idea that bishops who have purchased their offices cannot be considered true bishops, because the gifts of the Holy Spirit cannot be bought. The existence of such ecclesiastics has disastrous consequences for the regular believers because, according to Humbert, the simoniac bishops are by definition powerless to dispense valid sacraments, meaning that the Christians who accept sacraments from such priests are in reality deprived of them.

In regard to the coin-analogy, Humbert is the first author to propose that a false thing is deemed false sometimes partially and sometimes in its entirety (*falsum non semper uniformiter dici, sed aliquando ex parte, aliquando ex toto*). From this, Humbert presents a schema in which a coin that is only partially counterfeit will be faulty only in its stamp or in its material or in its weight, whereas the one that is completely false will fail in all three categories. For Humbert the first coin has some value, albeit a diminished one, while the second one is worth absolutely nothing. The partial falsification is a result of human presumption, whereas the total deception is orchestrated by diabolical illusion and lacks any integrity whatsoever.[11] This distinction in the levels of falsity in a coin was completely lacking in Cassian and Gregory.

It is worth mentioning here that Humbert does not talk about the worldly *nummularius* and neither does he ask his reader to imitate him *spiritualiter*. In regard to the remaining vocabulary, the older term *numisma* is replaced by *nummus*, the false coin is simply called *nummus falsus*, and the material of which the coin is made is referred to only as *materies*, without further specification. The most interesting usage is undoubtedly the Greek word *caragma* for the image on the coin instead of the Latin *imago* and *figura*, which we saw before. *Caragma*, meaning 'mark, stamp, engraving', is the mark that the beast from Revelation 13:16 places on the palms and foreheads of his followers. Traditionally, this beast has been interpreted as representing the false prophet, the devil or the Antichrist.[12] It is also significant that Revelation 13:17 continues by stating: 'And no man will be able to buy or sell, save the one who has the mark' (*et ne quis*

---

11 Robinson, 'Humbertus, *Libri tres aduersus simoniacos*', Lib. 1, cap. 6, p. 24, ll. 11–18: 'Dicitur equidem nummus falsus, qui tamen aliter se habet visus a vigilantibus, aliter a dormientibus. Nam ille aut in caragmate aut in materie aut certe tantum in pondere fallit, iste autem in cunctis, quia nec extitit nec existit, sed ex toto se falsum est et nichil. Unum quidem etsi humana praesumptio maximo aut minimo sui tenore fraudat, tamen vel parum aut plurimum eidem dat. Alterum diabolica illusio totius probitatis vacuum fingit nilque illi praeter solam decptionem attribuit'.

12 See for example, Primasius Episcopus Hadrumetinus, *Commentarius in Apocalypsin*, A. W. Adams (ed.), CCSL 92 (Turnhout, 1985), Lib. V, cap. XIX, p. 270, ll. 226–9: '*Et apprehensa est bestia cum illo pseudopropheta,* diabolus et antichristus uel praepositi totumque corpus eius, *qui fecerat signa sub oculis eius, quibus signis seducti erant adorare imaginem bestiae, et qui acceperant caragma illius*'.

possit emere aut vendere nisi qui habet caracter). Hence, a monetary transaction, and a devilish one at that, is clearly associated with the term *caragma*, which is precisely the connection Humbert is trying to establish in relationship to simony. The Greek word *caragma* is translated as *caracter* in the Latin Vulgate. This lexical choice might look surprising, except for the fact that the original meaning of the word *caracter* is 'a sign or mark that is burned or imprinted'. From here the meaning 'character' develops logically. Thus, in the same way God imprints or shapes the character of his followers or marks them as his, the Antichrist brands those who have accepted him as their master. The interplay between the stamping of a design onto a coin and the character of a man is subtle here but unmistakable.

The second difference between Humbert and his predecessors is that Humbert compares directly his targeted group of individuals to a counterfeit coin. By using verbs such as *comparatur* et *assimilatur*, Humbert turns the coin-analogy into a much more explicit comparison. If for Cassian and Gregory the point was to urge the reader to become a spiritual money-changer in order to distinguish between what is fake and what is genuine, be that inclination, doctrine or preaching, for Humbert the examination has already been performed and the falsity established. His concern is, therefore, taken a step further, namely to identifying partial and total fallacy. As a result, Humbert talks of two distinct types of pseudo-bishops, one Catholic and one heretical. Both are counterfeit coins, but differently. The Catholic *pseudoepiscopus*, like a coin made by human skill (*humana ars format*), is imperfect in some of its features and perfect in others. This coin, called *noster nummus*, can still have some value despite being deficient in either weight or material or stamp. Even when two of these three qualities are lacking, there is still one left that can be accepted as true. So, perhaps, the qualities of the Catholic *pseudoepiscopus* have been diminished; still, since he has been approved by God originally, he cannot be thoroughly false. The heretical *pseudoepiscopus* is a different story altogether. He is compared to a coin made by the devil (*diabolica ars format*), possessing nothing genuine in itself and only having the appearance of perfection. The value of this *nummus falsus* is zero. No one should believe it to be money at all; in fact, according to Humbert, the *nummus falsus* has never been a coin and will never be one. It is simply a fallacy and a sacrilege, as is all heresy, simony included. There is no question that in this eleventh-century context the understanding of heresy is much more closely connected to church politics than to doctrinal considerations.

The same approach is found also in the writings of Peter Damian (1007–72), another ardent proponent of the Gregorian movement for church reform of the eleventh century and an associate of the Pope, who attacks the simoniac heresy even more virulently. The passage pertinent to the present discussion is found in the *Actus Mediolani de privilegio Romanae ecclesiae*, a report Peter wrote in December 1059 after his legatine mission to Milan. It is significant that the work is addressed to Cardinal and Archdeacon Hildebrand, the future Pope Gregory VII, who would go on to use parts of it in his campaign to establish the Roman *principatus* over the entire western church.[13] In this letter Peter Damian calls simony an ecclesiastical custom that is reprobate, detestable, hated by God, shameful, perverse, and condemned by the authority of all church rules. Like a lethal and pestiferous leprosy it contaminates the innocent souls and encourages perilous negotiations that lead to paying money for ecclesiastical offices. Peter even quotes the going-rates for the various clerical orders: 12 coins (*nummi*) to become a sub-deacon, 18 to advance to the rank of deacon and 24 to obtain priesthood. Peter ends his invective against the church of Milan by comparing it to a minting workshop, in which Simon Magus, like an unjust *trapezita* or *monetarius iniquitatis*, manufactures danger for all souls.[14] This is a novel element in the coin-analogy, which focuses on the questionable identity of the minter rather than on the faulty quality of his product. The two aspects are, however, closely linked. If the *monetarius* is not to be trusted, neither should be the money that he makes. In another letter from 1065–66 on the Nicolaitan heresy Peter Damian elaborates further on this relationship implying that the most worthless minter of all (*nequissimus trapezita*) is no other than the devil who labours ceaselessly in the smithy of his perversity to forge within the folds of the church coins marked with the stamp of Hell (*tartarae monetae nummos*).[15] These devilish coins are undoubtedly the symbols of the various heretical movements within the Catholic church.

Anselm of Canterbury (1033–1109), the author of an abundant and varied corpus of works, expanded the rich imagery associated with false money even

[13] Ian Stuart Robinson, *Authority and Resistance in the Church Investiture Contest: the Polemical Literature of the Late Eleventh Century* (Manchester, 1978), pp. 24–31.

[14] *Die Briefe des Petrus Damiani*, Kurt Reindel (ed.), Monumenta Germaniae Historica Epistolae 2:4, 4 vols (Munich, 1983–93), vol. 2, Ep. 65, pp. 228–47, esp. 240–41: 'Non ignorat sancta devotio vestra, dilectissimi fratres et filii, quam reproba, quam detestabilis, Deo odibilis, ignominiosa atque perversa, omniumque sanctorum canonum auctoritate damnata consuetudo in hac sancta aecclesia, cui Deo auctore deservio, antiquitus inholeverit, quamque laetalis atque pestiferae leprae animas innocentum contaminatione perfuderit, symoniacae videlicet heresis damnata semperque damnanda venalitas et pernitiosa negotiatio huiusmodi in hac sancta aecclesia consuetudinaliter optinebat, ut quisquis ad clericales ordines provehendus accederet, de subdiaconatu quidem duodecim nummos, de diaconatu vero decem et octo, postremo de presbyteratu suscipiendo viginti quattuor, quasi per praefixam conditionis regulam daret. Hoc itaque modo Symon Magus, heu prodolor, hanc sanctam Ambrosianam aecclesiam perversitatis suae velut officinam fecerat. Follem, malleos et incudem trapezita ac monetarius iniquitatis habebat, nihilque aliud nisi animarum omnium commune periculum fabricabat'.

[15] Reindel, *Die Briefe des Petrus Damiani*, vol. 3, Ep. 129, pp. 431–2: 'Non enim cessat trapezita nequissimus officinam suae perversitatis intra aecclesiae septa construere, non desinit tartareae monetae nummos malleis cudentibus fabricare'.

further. The literature on Anselm is extensive, the historical and theological importance of his legacy undisputable.[16] The focus here, however, is on one of Anselm's lesser-known works, the *De humanis moribus per similitudines* or simply *De moribus*. The textual transmission and the authorship of this treatise are a complex matter. According to Sir Richard Southern who in 1969 examined and edited the text together with Franciscus Salesius Schmitt, the *De moribus* represents quite likely a fragmentary draft of a work, which Anselm had left unfinished when he died in 1109.[17] Soon afterwards the treatise (in its original form) seems to have been 'published' or put into circulation by the Augustinian canons of Llanthony on the Welsh border. In addition, the original text was very quickly (certainly before 1130) revised and expanded with suitable material from the works of Anselm's close associates Alexander and Eadmer. Even though it is not known precisely who was responsible for the revision, it is quite likely that it was done at Canterbury. This enlarged version of the *De moribus* is generally referred to as *De similitudinibus* and this is the text printed among Eadmer's works in volume 159 of the *Patrologia Latina*. The complexities in the textual transmission of Anselm's *De moribus* do not play a decisive role for the argument advanced in this chapter. In both versions of the text, the passage under consideration contains more or less the same text, with only a paragraph added at the end of the enlarged revision that simply presents a general statement on the vices and virtues and does not advance further the main point of the passage.

The text in question is preserved as chapter 90 in Anselm's treatise, bearing the title: 'Similitudo inter monachum et denarium (The similarity between a monk and a penny)'.[18] The coin-analogy in this context contains both familiar and new elements. Known from before are the three features that distinguish a valid coin from a counterfeit one, namely: the purity of the metal, the correct weight, and legitimate mintmark. In addition, Anselm states clearly that, if even one on these three qualities is marred in some way, the coin has no purchasing

---

16 For a more general introduction to the topic, see Giles E. M. Gasper and Ian Logan (eds), *Saint Anselm of Canterbury and His Legacy* (Toronto, 2012); Eileen C. Sweeney, *Anselm of Canterbury and the Desire for the Word* (Washington, DC, 2012).

17 See *Memorials of Anselm*, Richard W. Southern and Franciscus S. Schmitt (eds) (London, 1969), pp. 4–18.

18 Anselm of Canterbury, *De humanis moribus per similitudines*, in *Memorials of Anselm*, Chapter 90, pp. 76–7. For a translation of this *similitudo*, see the Appendix to this chapter. The subject of money as it relates to Anselm is discussed in Giles E. M. Gasper and Svein H. Gullbekk, 'Money and its Use in the Thought and the Experience of Anselm, Archbishop of Canterbury (1093–1109)', *Journal of Medieval History*, 38 (2012): 155–82. The penny is not the only analogy Anselm uses in his treatise; the monks are further compared to angels and gardeners, trees and fire, even medicinal potions. It is clear that this type of symbolism was a beloved literary device employed often by Anselm, as is evident too in the records of his sermons recorded by Eadmer in the *Vita Anselmi*, R. W. Southern (ed. and trans.) (Oxford, 1972).

value (*venalis esse non poterit*). Even though money-changers, bankers and minters were mentioned by previous authors, this is the first time an explicitly commercial context is invoked in relationship to money usage. This should perhaps not come as a surprise in the context of the late eleventh and early twelfth centuries, when the new economic developments in Europe shape a new trading and monetary reality.

Another shift in the coin-analogy is seen in the fact that it is for the first time applied to monks. This change is indeed highly indicative of the spiritual sensibilities of both Anselm and his immediate audience. The monk is truly like a penny, says Anselm, because the pure metal of the coin signifies the monk's obedience (*obedientia*), the accurate weight of the piece shows the steadfastness of monastic purpose (*stabilitas propositi*), while the mintmark on the penny denotes the monk's habit, tonsure, the profound *ante et recto* bowing at the altar during mass[19] and other similar attributes (*habitus monachilis atque tonsura, ante et retro, et consimilia*).

In examining these features, Anselm starts with the one that is immediately apparent, namely, the *moneta* (the mintmark) or what the earlier texts referred to as *imago* and *uultus* (Cassian), *figura* (Gregory the Great and Isidore) and *caragma* (Humbert of Silva Candida). Just as the minting of the coin indicates its place of origin, so the habit of the monk reveals his order. The elderly monks who can no longer bend *ante et retro* are like old coins whose minting has been effaced by the passing of time; and here the *ante et recto* expression brings immediately to mind the obverse and reverse faces of a coin. On the other hand, those who have not yet adopted the monastic habit and the name 'monk' are like blank pieces that have not yet received their official mintmark and therefore possess no commercial value. He who collects coins for his earthly treasure wants them to be minted correctly; God, who wishes to accept all Christians in his heavenly treasure, will admit there only the monk who wears his habit properly. This statement allows Anselm to move to the next feature of the coin, the purity of its metal or, in symbolic terms, the obedience of the monk. It is not enough for a monk to don the habit while carrying disobedience in his heart. Such a monk is similar to a coin that is made of impure metal and is thus, according to Anselm, a counterfeit. Neither the rich man on Earth nor God in Heaven would want such false money in their coffers. However, God is merciful, and he can distinguish between a false coin and an invalid one. This is new terminology, not found in the authors presented above, even though Humbert de Silva Candida used the distinction in his discussion of the Catholic bishop and his heretical colleague, who were called *noster nummus* and *falsus nummus*, respectively.

---

19 See Mackenzie E. C. Walcott, 'Bowing to the Altar', *Notes and Queries*, 5th series, 10 (1978): 437–8.

In Anselm's text the *invalidus denarius* is a coin whose lawful weight has been reduced but which is still made of pure metal and should therefore not be rejected entirely. In difference, the *falsus denarius* pretends to be a valid piece while concealing under a legitimate minting the fact that it is made of alloyed metal; such money is to be refused outright. This is not an idle distinction. In fact, it reflects a larger historical context in addition to its symbolic meaning regarding the nature of the monk. Thus, the invalid penny signifies the weak brother (*debilis monachus*) who is mostly obedient and pure but who commits sin on account of his feeble human nature. The *falsus monachus*, in contrast, wears the habit like a good monk while the falsity of disobedience is hidden deep inside his soul. The weak monk can be forgiven, if he repents; the disobedient one will be rejected by God and will not be allowed in his heavenly treasure:

> As the false penny is different from the invalid one, so the false monk is unlike the weak one. Indeed, the invalid penny weighs less than what it should, but what is left of it consists of pure copper. The false penny pretends to have the same mintmark as the good one, but false copper hides inside it. Similarly, also the false monk wears the same habit as the good one, but the falsity of his disobedience hides underneath. The weak but obedient monk, even though he falters in stability when he falls, still preserves the purity of obedience. For soon he feels remorse for his wrongdoing and does what pure obedience orders him to do. The false monk, as a false penny, is thrown out of the heavenly treasure; the weak one is put there for the measure of his strength. Thus, it is of use to nobody to wear only the external habit of a monk, if he does not strive to obtain also the internal one.[20]

A glimpse of the wider historical reality behind Anselm's discussion of the invalid and the counterfeit coin is afforded in the *Historia novorum in Anglia* written by Anselm's close associate Eadmer towards the end of Anselm's life. The *Historia novorum* covers events from 1066 to 1122, even though originally the work ended at the death of Anselm in 1109. The passage of interest here is found in Book IV, where King Henry I seeks the advice of Anselm and other nobles on how to alleviate the great evils that were oppressing the poor in the realm.

---

[20] Anselm of Canterbury, *De humanis moribus per similitidines*, in *Memorials of Anselm*, ch. 90, pp. 76–7: 'Ut enim ab invalido denarius falsus, sic a debili differt monachus falsus. Invalidus quippe denarius minus habet pondus quam debeat, sed illud quod habet, puro ex aere constat. Falsus vero eandem quam bonus monetam praetendit, sed interius latet falsitas aeris. Sic falsus monachus eundem quem bonus habitum habet, sed inoboedientiae falsitas interius latet. Debilis vero, sed oboediens, licet non tantam quin cadat quandoque habeat stabilitatem, oboedientiae tamen retinet puritatem. Mox etenim paenitet eum quia deliquit; quod ei praecipitur, pura oboedientia facit. Ille ergo ut denarius falsus a caelesti thesauro repellitur, hic vero pro sui modulo vigoris ibi reponitur. Nihil igitur cuiquam prodest habitum monachi exteriorem habere, si non studuerit et interiorem habere'.

This event can be dated to 1108 by the mention in the previous paragraph of the death of Gundulf, the well-known Bishop of Rochester. The text pertinent to the present discussion reads:

> Then again spoiled and false coinage was harming many people in many ways. Which situation the king ordered to be improved through such severe punishment that no one, who was caught making false coins (*falsos denarios*), could save himself with any other compensation than losing his eyes and the lower parts of his body. Moreover, because very often when coins were picked out, they were bent, broken and rejected, he ordered that no penny or halfpenny (*denarius vel obolus*) should be perfect (*integer*). From this deed a great good was achieved at once for the entire kingdom.[21]

The coin that is 'bent, broken and rejected' in Eadmer's account bears a clear resemblance to Anselm's *invalidus denarius*, a penny that is under-weight but still made of pure metal and thus not completely worthless. This connection, in addition to the other unique elements in Anselm's use of the coin-analogy, makes a strong case for Anselm's familiarity with money and its production: from their regional differences to the legitimacy of their designs and proper weight to their commercial value and use. Thus, through the symbolic meaning of the coin Anselm betrays a new awareness of the monetary realities of his contemporary world.

From the texts examined in this chapter it becomes apparent that the coin, as a physical object, possesses a strong symbolic quality. Its tangible standard (weight and metal), its fabric, and its design are features that facilitate an easy allegorical link to morality. Accordingly, the coin-analogy was infused with meaning that best suited the interests of the author who was using it. John Cassian was concerned with the inner thoughts of the Christian soul in an ascetic context, Gregory the Great wanted to expose the false preachers of the Antichrist, Humbert of Silva Candida and Peter Damian were fighting against the corrupted practice of simony, and Anselm of Canterbury was teaching his fellow monks how to be true to their holy vocation. For all these different perspectives the coin proved to be the perfect metaphor in the hands of each of

---

[21] Eadmer, *Historia nouorum in Anglia*, Martin Rule (ed.), Rolls Series, vol. 81 (London, 1884; repr. 1965), p. 193: 'Item moneta corrupta et falsa multis modis multos affligebat. Quam rex sub tanta animadversione corrigi statuit, ut nullus qui posset depraehendi falsos denarios facere aliqua redemptione quin oculos et inferiors corporis partes perderet iuvari valeret. Et quoniam saepissime dum denarii eligebantur, flectebantur, rumpebantur, respuebantur, statuit ut nullus denarius vel obolus integer esset. Ex quo facto magnum bonum ad tempus toti regno creatum est'. For a translation of this text, see *Eadmer's History of Recent Events in England*, Geoffrey Bosanquet (trans.) (London, 1964), p. 206 (slightly revised).

the authors above. A century later, in 1265, it would be used in the treatise *De eruditione principum*, by Guillelmus Peraldus, to denote the difference between a mendacious and a truthful prince,[22] thus demonstrating that it was suited to both religious and secular contexts.

At this point one further observation needs to be presented. It has been established thus far that the coin's metal, weight and design are qualities that possess a strong symbolic meaning. However, there is one additional element that the money-changer could use in his efforts to establish the value of the money presented to him. This is the *tinnitus* or the sound the coin makes. Even though Jerome in his commentary on the Ephesians mentions that the very prudent *trapezita* examines the coin not only by looking at it, but also by checking its weight and sound,[23] almost nobody after Jerome includes the sound-examination in their treatment of the coin-analogy. Only Haimo of Halberstadt, who died in 853, expands in any meaningful way Jerome's brief statement. He does that in his own exposition on the Ephesians, which probably is the explanation for his adopting Jerome's imagery, where he states that as the money-changer inspects the metal of the coin for three features, that is, weight, purity and ringing sound (*tinnitus*), so we have to examine our actions by considering their weight or how great and important they are, their purity or whether we have performed them with good intention, and finally their resonance or whether they occasion the spread of good reputation.[24] This last element represents an important consideration that could have very easily been included in the various accounts of the coin-analogy examined here. Its omission could probably be explained by the fact that Cassian, whose text played the most influential role in the development of the symbolic meaning *of nummus* in the Middle Ages, did not talk about the coin's *tinnitus* and so the later authors did not include it either. However, it is worth asking the question whether a deeper meaning can be attributed to sight

---

[22] This work was printed among the *opera omnia* of Thomas Aquinas. See *Sancti Thomae Aquinatis Opera Omnia* (Parma, 1852–73), vol. 16 (1865), *Opusculum XXXVII*, Lib. 1, cap. 7: 'Quod principi cauendum mendacium', cols 389–477, at 398–9: 'Quae differentia est inter denarium bonum et falsum, est inter principem mendacem et veracem; vilis est denarius falsus respectu boni, centum enim falsi non valent unum bonum, sic princeps mendax parvi valoris est, cum princeps nolit unum de denariis suis falsum esse, quomodo se velit esse falsum et mendacem, videtur se habere viliorem denario uno'.

[23] Hieronymus, *Commentarii in IV epistulas Paulinas*: Ad *Ephesios*, *PL* 26, col. 557AB: 'Ea tantum quae scimus Deo placere, faciamus: in morem prudentissimi trapezitae qui sculptum numisma non solum oculo, sed pondere et tinnitus probat'.

[24] Haymo of Halberstadt, *In Epistolam ad Ephesios*, cap. 5, *PL* 117, cols 699B–734D, at 726D: 'Sicut trapezita, id est monetarius, probat metalla pondere, puritate et tinnitus, ita debemus nos opera nostra probare. Debemus illa probare pondere considerantes quanta et quam magna sint; puritate, utrum puro et simplici animo, bonaque intentione fiant; tinnitu, utrum bonam famam de se reddant'.

being preferred to hearing when a coin and subsequently a human character needed to be judged. It is possible that the authors using the analogy between a man and a penny felt that as the perception of sound depends to a much higher degree on the particular circumstances in which the sound is produced, so also the reputation of a man could be more easily manipulated and not to be trusted to the same degree as when it is possible to judge a man's character by seeing and examining him personally. However, it is hard to imagine that the medieval *nummularii* did not use the coin's *tinnitus* to establish its validity. The fact that this test is almost completely missing in the textual evidence presented here, on the one hand proves the enduring influence of Cassian's imagery, while on the other it presents a cautionary tale of how carefully and soberly the relationship between written sources and material culture needs to be evaluated.

Appendix

Anselm of Canterbury, *On the Similarity Between the Monk and the Penny*. Edition in: Anselm of Canterbury, *De humanis moribus per similitidines*, in *Memorials of Anselm*, Richard W. Southern and Franciscus S. Schmitt (eds) (London, 1969), ch. 90, pp. 76–7.

Again from a similitude we must see how many (qualities) have to exist in the perfect monk. Three are the features that are integral to a good penny, and these have to belong also to the good monk. Indeed, the good penny (*denarius bonus*) has to be of pure copper, accurate weight and legitimate mintmark. Even if one of these qualities is marred, the penny cannot be used for selling and buying. Thus, in order for a penny to have purchasing value, it has to possess all three mentioned qualities equally.

In order for a monk to be truly considered a monk, he also has to have these qualities. Indeed, the purity of the penny's metal is the monk's pure obedience, for no impurity of disobedience must be found in him, only obedience. The penny's accurate weight is the monk's steadiness of purpose, for he must not be deterred easily from what he has set out to do, but should persevere steadily until the end. The penny's mintmark is the monk's habit and tonsure, the bowing *ante et retro*, and other similar attributes; for the order of the monk is recognised by these, as the penny's mintmark denotes the region whence it comes. Moreover, the monk who is so old that he cannot bend *ante et retro* any longer is like a penny whose mintmark has already been deleted by the passing of time. On the other hand, he who has not yet adopted the monastic habit and is not yet called a monk can be likened to a penny which does not yet have a mintmark and thus cannot be used for buying and selling. And as the man, who wishes to amass treasure, wants a penny of the kind that has a mintmark that is done properly, so also God, who desires to accept all of us in his heavenly treasure, will place there a man of the kind who wears the monastic habit in a just manner. The man, whom God sees wearing the habit of a monk but who is disobedient, that is, made of impure copper, this man God will never place in his heavenly treasure precisely as nobody seeks to put in his treasury a false penny. However, the man who is seen to be obedient, even if he sins occasionally on account of his human frailty, this man God will not reject, if he repents readily.

As the false penny (*denarius falsus*) is different from the invalid one, so the false monk is unlike the weak one. Indeed, the invalid penny (*denarius invalidus*) weighs less than what it should, but what is left of it consists of pure copper. The false penny pretends to have the same mintmark as the good one, but false copper hides inside it. Similarly, also the false monk wears the same habit as the good one, but the falsity of his disobedience hides underneath. The weak but obedient monk, even though he falters in stability when he falls, still preserves the purity of obedience. For soon he feels remorse for his wrongdoing and does what pure obedience orders him to do. The false monk, as a false penny, is thrown out of the heavenly treasure; the weak one is put there for the measure of his strength. Thus, it is of use to nobody to wear only the external habit of a monk, if he does not strive to obtain also the internal one.

Chapter 5

A Herald of Scholasticism: Alan of Lille on Economic Virtue

Odd Langholm

In the last quarter of the twelfth century the budding University of Paris attracted a number of scholars who later made their names as authors in the border area of theology and canon law. The person at the centre of this circle was Peter of Paris, Chanter of Notre Dame Cathedral. His students include some, like Robert of Courson and Thomas of Chobham, who took a particular interest in what we now call economic subjects and thereby established the foundation of scholastic economic analysis in theological and philosophical traditions from the early thirteenth century on. The purpose of this study is to examine the economic ideas of Alan of Lille, a contemporary of Peter the Chanter. Alan was not so much a member of the Chanter's circle as a polyhistorian belonging to a number of related and sometimes intersecting circles. Difficult to classify, he looms in the hazy dawn of academic life in Europe. Not unfittingly, Alan was honoured with the title he shared with Albert the Great, that of *doctor universalis*, for, like no other man of his age, he embraced the sum of learning. During his lifetime, the knowledge of Roman law spread in the West, and several important compilations of canon law were issued. The Latin classics were revived, as well as Latin poetic form. At the same time, great advances were made in theology and in Biblical exegesis. Much of this found expression in Alan's work. It may as well be admitted that the search for constructive contributions to economic reasoning brought but meagre results. What permeates his work is a certain simple philosophy of wealth and economic activity. In that sense the 'Renaissance of the Twelfth Century', of whose intellectual life he is the perfect embodiment, was an age of innocence, at least in terms of intellectual responses to the challenges of changing economic circumstances.

What is known with certainty about the man himself is limited to a few dates and places. His birthplace used to be disputed but there is now no doubt that he had his origins in the city of Lille in Flanders. Alan spent the last years of his life as a monk at the abbey of Citeaux where he died in 1202. His grave has been located. The remains were exhumed and found to be those of a man greatly advanced in age; some date his birth as early as 1116. Alan is known to have studied at Chartres and at Paris where he soon became a master. He also had sojourns in the south of France. Much of his phenomenal wealth of learning seems to have been amassed early in life. Examination of his works led one biographer to speculate that his youth was spent in the habit of the Benedictines with access to one of their splendid libraries. Later he may have been expelled from that order, only to join that of the Cistercians much later, perhaps in preparation for death.

Alan of Lille's epitaph at Citeaux describes him as 'Alan ... , who knew the two, who knew the seven, who knew all that could be known'. The two are theology and philosophy; the seven are the liberal arts. Of some 30 works, long or brief, attributable to him, some are devotional, and a large number deal with speculative theology, including a collection of theological maxims and a dictionary of the Bible. In the Middle Ages, however, the relationship between theology and philosophy was permeable and in Alan's case philosophy is brought to bear on theology, either to serve it or to stand in contrast to theology, by which philosophy is infinitely surpassed. A treatise on the virtues and the vices and a book of penance can be classified, from one point of view, as moral philosophy. But the philosophical works for which Alan of Lille is best remembered are literary allegories, with the Virtues and Vices personified. The following is a survey of works having a marginal or better bearing on our subject. Chronological arrangement is not essential. In any case exact dating is a problem in most instances.[1]

De planctu naturae is most likely a relatively early work. The author is already a mature philosopher and poet. The work is a moral allegory, composed alternately in verse and prose, recalling Boethius's *On the Consolation of Philosophy*, on which it is evidently modelled. Just as Philosophy appears before Boethius in the condemned cell, so Alan, despairing of the corruption and perversion rampant in the world, is visited in his sleep by Nature in the shape of a maiden. Her dress and appearance are described at length; yet the poet does not recognise her, and she has to present herself and explain that she has come to Earth in order to rectify the ills wrought by man. Man alone has gone against Nature and caused an ugly rent to disfigure her garment.[2] This occasions, at the poet's request, a detailed account to be given of men's vices. There is an emphasis on sexual morality, but improper behaviour in relation to material wealth is not

---

1 There are several early editions of Alan's *Opera*. Most of the items collected in vol. 210 of *Patrologia Latina* (*PL*) are reprints of the edition of Charles de Visch (Antwerp, 1654). Where a more recent edition is lacking, I have used *PL* 210. Some works included there, as well as some previously unprinted works, have appeared in modern critical editions and these are used when relevant. English translations are available in a few instances only; unless otherwise indicated, the translations are mine.

2 In Boethius the garment of Philosophy is similarly rent by erring sects; see *De consolatione philosophiae*, I, Prose 1: 22–4, H. F. Stewart, E. K. Rand and S. J. Tester (trans), Loeb Classical Library (Cambridge, Mass., 1973).

at all spared either. In a long prose passage, which is a veritable tour de force of classical allusion, Alan condemns avarice. Later on he returns to this theme in some strongly worded metric sequences.[3]

Morality is once more discussed in allegorical form in the epic poem known for short as *Anticlaudianus*, Alan of Lille's best-known work. The title refers to a work by Claudian, the late Roman poet, depicting the completely evil man. In Alan's poem Nature (again taking centre stage) invites all the Virtues to unite their efforts and bring into existence a man who is absolutely perfect and good. With God's help this is achieved. The new creature is immediately set upon by the Vices but eventually triumphs. Among Virtues and Vices taking part in these dramatic proceedings are Generosity and her opposite, Avarice. The former is quoted as she instructs the New Man, the latter is caught by the poet's pen at the moment when she marches into battle with her retinue.[4] In connection with these two fictional works, mention may be made of Alan's *Liber parabolarum*, a series of versified moral maxims, ordered according to subject.[5]

Alan's theological writings consist mainly of brief tracts addressing specific topics. But this group also includes what is by far his most extensive single work, namely, an alphabetical dictionary of the Bible.[6] If it is relevant here, it is because a number of economic terms occur in the Scripture and in scriptural glosses and commentaries. A number of Alan's sermons are extant.[7] Moreover, he wrote an instruction for preachers, *De arte praedicatoria*, which contains specimen sermons and general advice on how to approach various subjects.[8] Some of its chapters, such as 'On the Contempt of the World', 'Against Avarice', and so forth, as well as some of Alan's own sermons in the same vein, bear directly on

3 Nikolaus M. Haring, 'Alan of Lille, *De Planctu naturae*', *Studi medievali*, series 3, 19 (1978): 797–879; Alan of Lille, *The Plaint of Nature*, J. J. Sheridan (trans.) (Toronto, 1980).

4 Alan of Lille, *Anticlaudianus*, R. Bossuat (ed.) (Paris, 1955); Alan of Lille, *Anticlaudianus or the Good and Perfect Man*, J. J. Sheridan (trans.) (Toronto, 1973).

5 Alan of Lille, *Liber parabolarum*, *PL* 210, col. 581–94.

6 Alan of Lille, *Distinctionibus dictionum theologicalium*, *PL* 210, cols 685–1012. It was not a completely alphabetical dictionary, but rather by the beginning letter, so, all words beginning with 'a' are listed under 'a' but not in alphabetical order. See Gilbert Dahan, 'Alain de Lille et l'exégèse de la Bible' in *Alain de Lille, le docteur universel, philosophie, théologie et littérature au XIIe siècle*, J.-L. Solère, A. Vasiliu and A. Galonnier (eds) (Turnhout, 2005), pp. 455–84 and Tuija Ainonen, 'Manuscripts, Editions and Textual Interpretation: Alan of Lille's Distinction Collection *Summa "Quot modis"* and the Meaning of Words', in Marko Lamberg, Jesse Keskiaho, Elina Räsänen and Olga Timofeeva (eds), with Leila Virtanen, *Methods and the Medievalist: Current Approaches in Medieval Studies* (Newcastle, 2008), pp. 12–37.

7 Alan of Lille, *Sermones*, *PL* 210, cols 197–228 and Alanus de Insulis, *Textes inédits*, Marie Thérèse d'Alverny (ed.) (Paris, 1965).

8 Alan of Lille, *De arte praedicatoria*, *PL* 210, cols 109–98.

attitudes to worldly riches. A more formal analysis of these matters is found in Alan's main ethical treatise, *De virtutibus et de vitiis et de donis Spiritus Sancti*.[9]

Alan of Lille's *Liber poenitentialis* marks a decisive step in the historical development of the medieval manual for confessors, that is, the systematic exposition of doctrine and procedure regarding penance.[10] Increasingly conscious of a conflict with temporal authorities, the church had come to realise the crucial part played by the confessor facing the individual as Christ's personal representative. It was in this confrontation in the confessional that the church could best exercise its authority on the individual plane. But the average cleric was ill prepared for this task. Hence the increasing demand for books of instruction, not least in the rapidly developing area of economic activity. The confessor, says Alan of Lille, is a *medicus spiritualis*. In order to prescribe a remedy for his spiritual patient he must establish a certain relationship on human terms which enables him to understand and evaluate the sin committed on the basis of its true circumstances, much like a *physicus materialis* entrusted with the cure of bodily complaints.[11] To this end, Alan provides some sensible yardsticks. For instance, a poor man returning from his labours is less excused for falling victim to lust than a rich man tempted all day. On the other hand, one should consider whether a poor man is more compelled (*magis cogatur*) to a certain sin than a rich man; thus theft is a greater sin in the rich than in the poor who have a more compelling reason to steal.[12]

If there is one economic theme that runs through all these works, it is the condemnation of *avaritia*, one of the seven mortal sins, and the one among the seven that represents all kinds of economic misdeeds. Alan defines it in his treatise on the virtues and vices: 'Avarice is a plague of the soul which consists in a covetous desire to obtain and retain riches'.[13] Avarice can apply to immaterial greed, as in the case of appetite for honours or an exaggerated quest for knowledge, but Alan's main target is the greed for money. In *De planctu naturae*, the poet's heavenly visitor laments the state of the world where 'cash conquers, cash rules, cash gives orders to all':[14]

> When the accursed greed for gold pierces the heart of man, the hungry human mind can feel no fear. It weakens the bonds of friendship, begets hatred, gives rise

[9] A short and a long version (the one used here) were edited by O. Lottin, *De virtutibus et de vitiis et de donis spiritus sancti*, in his *Psychologie et morale aux XIIe et XIIIe siècles*, vol. 6 (Gembloux, 1960), pp. 27–92.

[10] The longer of three versions of Alan's penitential was edited by J. Longère, *Liber poenitentialis*, 2 vols, Analecta Mediaevalia Namurcensia, 17–18 (Louvain, 1965).

[11] Alan of Lille, *Liber poenitentialis*, I.2; Longère (ed.), vol. 1, p. 25.

[12] Alan of Lille, *Liber poenitentialis*, I.2; Longère (ed.), vol.1, pp. 30–31.

[13] Alan of Lille, *De virtutibus et de vitiis*, II.1; Lottin (ed.) p. 72.

[14] Alan of Lille, *The Plaint of Nature*, Sheridan (trans), p. 177.

> to anger, sows the seeds of war, fosters contentions, reknots the severed lines of battle, unties the knots of covenants, stirs up children against their fathers, mothers against their offspring, causes brother to ignore the peaceful intent of brother. This one madness harmfully disunites all whom unity of blood makes one.[15]

Avarice causes a man to lose his reason and worship false gods:

> The rich man does not possess his riches but is possessed by them; he is not the possessor of money, money possesses him and the soul of the miser lies buried in his coins. These are the gods he worships, these are the idols he enriches with the honour of divine worship, and money bestows divine authority. Thus man's reason, trodden under foot by greed, becomes the slave to flesh and is forced to wait upon it as its handmaid.[16]

Like so many other Christian writers before and after him, Alan quotes Ecclesiastes 1:2: 'Vanity of vanities, and all is vanity'. And where is there more vanity than in riches, which 'marry satiety and give birth to hunger', which only increase cupidity rather than reduce it, and which are earned by lies and preserved in fear and suspicion?[17] The theme is a favoured one in his oratory works as well. At least once in his extant sermons, as well as in his instruction for preachers, Alan denounces avarice as the worship of idols, invoking St Paul.[18] True wisdom in economic matters dictates that all this should be renounced:

> Do you wish to be an excellent merchant, an outstanding moneylender and a prudent shopkeeper? Give what you cannot preserve so that you may pursue that which you cannot let slip, give a little so that you pursue a hundredfold gain; give possessions that are not yours, so that you may pursue your eternal heritage.[19]

The Christian ideal of poverty implies the notion that material abnegation provides the straightest path to salvation. Poverty, therefore, is an exalted state. When you preach to the poor, says Alan of Lille, speak of poverty and commend it, taking for your example Christ Himself who was rich in Heaven and was made poor for us on Earth, so that by his poverty we could become rich. And let

---

15 Alan of Lille, *The Plaint of Nature*, Sheridan (trans.), p. 181.

16 Alan of Lille, *The Plaint of Nature*, Sheridan (trans.), p. 183.

17 Alan of Lille, *De arte praedicatoria*, II (*De mundi contemptu*), *PL* 210, cols 114–15.

18 Alan of Lille, *Sermones*, *PL* 210, col. 203, with reference to Ephesians 5:5: 'For know you this and understand: That no fornicator or unclean or covetous person (which is a serving of idols) hath inheritance in the kingdom of Christ and of God'; and *De arte praedicatoria*, VI (*Contra avaritiam*), PL 210, 123, with reference to Galatians 5:20 on the works of the flesh: 'Idolatry, witchcrafts, enmities, contentions, emulations, wraths, quarrels, dissensions, sects'.

19 Alan of Lille, *De arte praedicatoria*, VI (*Contra avaritiam*), PL 210, 124.

the ancient Fathers be your example, who naked followed the naked Christ.[20] At times, however, this Christian ideal of poverty based on dogma seems to change subtly into what may perhaps be called the Stoic ideal of poverty, which is based on a psychological proposition. According to Seneca, whom Alan quotes in *De arte praedicatoria*, cupidity creates poverty because true poverty is not measured by what little one has but by what more one wants: 'It is not he who has too little, but he who desires more, that is poor'.[21] The poor in material riches can judge themselves lucky if they are content with what they have, whereas material wealth carries the germ of cupidity and want because *much* will always have *more*. In *De planctu naturae*, closing a long verse section detailing the ugly aspects of cupidity, Alan adds that he does not condemn wealth as such:

> This discourse does not disparage riches or the rich but rather seeks to sink its teeth into vice. I do not condemn property, riches or the practices of the rich, provided that the mind, with reason as its mistress, is in command, brings this wealth into subjection to itself and treads upon it – in a word, provided that reason, the noble charioteer, shall direct the use of riches.[22]

This is a key statement. It is Nature who speaks, invoking Reason. Man is the only creature equipped with reason. If man alone has torn Nature's dress, it is because he has stopped listening to reason. Accepting the social order, as did nearly all medieval writers, means accepting that some will be rich and some poor. But natural reason ought to suffice to teach the rich a proper attitude to riches or, in behavioural terms, a proper use of riches. Alan's recommendations in this respect will naturally differ in tone in works written for different purposes, but they all convey the impression of a common emphasis which is perhaps at first sight a little surprising. If you preach to the rich, Alan states in *De arte praedicatoria*, rather predictably, induce them to almsgiving, to contempt of riches and to the love of heavenly (rather than earthly) coins.[23] In his other, more philosophical works, in which moral theology still underpins their structure and conclusions, the virtue of giving freely is very much accentuated. In *De planctu naturae* the rich are invited, when the situation asks for it, to 'let the mass of buried treasure arise,

---

[20] Alan of Lille, *De arte praedicatoria*, XXXIX (*Quibus proponenda sit praedicatio*), *PL* 210, cols 184–5.

[21] Alan of Lille, *De arte praedicatoria*, VI (*Contra avaritiam*), *PL* 210, col. 124; quoting Seneca, *Epistulae morales*, R. Gummere (trans.), Loeb Classical Library 75 (Cambridge, Mass., 1917), II, 6: 'Non qui parum habet, sed qui plus cupit, pauper est'.

[22] Alan of Lille, *The Plaint of Nature*, Sheridan (trans.), p. 184.

[23] Alan of Lille, *De arte praedicatoria*, XXXIX (*Quibus proponenda sit praedicatio*), *PL* 210, col. 185.

let the purses completely disgorge their cash'.[24] Similarly in the *Anticlaudianus*, where Generosity in person comes on the stage and offers her instructions:

> Next comes the virtue which takes delight in scattering gifts and pouring out wealth and spreading abroad a mass of riches. She refuses to suckle property and feed cash; neither does she allow treasure to lie idle and inactive in her possession nor glut her purse with coins but compels it to disgorge whatever money it has at any time swallowed. Once she was very frugal, now she is lavish to one person, surpasses herself and outdoes her own powers in regard to him. She urges him to keep his mind aloof from all gifts; drop them from his hands and not succumb to the love of riches; spurning wealth in his soul and triumphing over it in his mind, to trample riches in such a way as to prevent their trampling on him; not to let his hand reach quickly out for bribes, not to let the snare of avarice close with tight grip on the gift in hand, not to send gifts in quest of a corresponding recompense; not to thirst for gain nor let a gift given successfully beg rewards but to pour out gifts far and wide without hope of return and let nobility alone and simple kindness of soul condition the present and season the use of the gift.[25]

The last line here is reminiscent of one in the Sermon of the Mount, as recorded in Luke's Gospel, which reads, in the Vulgate, '*mutuum date, nihil inde sperantes* (and lend, hoping for nothing thereby)'.[26] The canonists understood this statement as referring to any payment in excess of the principal of a loan, that is, as forbidding usury. Since Alan speaks of a *munus* (gift) rather than a *mutuum* (loan), his words in the mouth of Generosity do not warrant this interpretation. His intention seems to be more in accord with the spirit of selfless love, with which Christ's sermon is infused, than with the canonistic reading of this particular line. There is no suggestion to be found, either in these quotations or elsewhere in Alan's works, that possession of wealth entails a duty to put it to *productive* use, nor indeed any mention of moral obligations regarding productive use at all. This fact may seem strange unless one recognises that the world to which Nature returns in the two allegories that feature her is a pre-capitalistic world, and that this frame of reference must be placed on Alan's more overtly theological works as well. For Alan money spells power not only in the sense of purchasing power in the marketplace; it can also be used to buy favour, influence and social position, including ecclesiastical preferment: simony is constantly under attack. To let money be the 'guardian of right' (*custos honoris*),

24 Alan of Lille, *The Plaint of Nature*, Sheridan (trans.), p. 195.

25 Alan of Lille, *Anticlaudianus*, Sheridan (trans.), pp. 185–6.

26 Luke 6:35. Matthew's account of the Sermon on the Mount does not include quite this injunction, although Christ enjoins his listeners to 'Give to him that asketh of thee, and from him that would borrow of thee turn not away [Qui petit a te, da ei: et volenti mutuari a te, ne avertaris]'. (Matthew 5:42).

as it is called in *De planctu naturae*, is presumably partly to spend it in such a way as to further honourable social ends.[27] But judging by all that he says, Alan of Lille's main advice as far as material wealth is concerned simply seems to be for the haves to share with the have-nots in a lavishness of spending which at times seems excessive. Turning this around, his main target of criticism is the *miser* who does not use his riches at all but just keeps them and, whenever possible, seeks to augment them.

An extreme variant of the miser's behaviour is that of the hoarder who loves his riches so much that he cannot even bear to part with what is necessary to lead a decent life. In one of his parables Alan compares his situation with that of King Midas, who committed the ultimate alchemical blunder of wishing to the gods that all he touched be turned into gold:

> Both wretched and rich was once King Midas,
> Rich in gold but wretched in living conditions;
> Thus lives any miser, any guardian of riches,
> For of goods he possesses at once much and nothing.[28]

The mythical Midas had to go hungry because gold cannot be eaten. The miser, Alan seems to say, is prevented by his greed (rather than by material transformation) from spending his wealth sensibly. But albeit the miser may hunger and thirst for consumables which greed prevents him from enjoying, his psychology is such that this counts for less than his craving for ever more wealth. If hoarding is despicable, all the more so is accumulation at the cost of others, be it by robbery or other means. One way of increasing the hoard is to lend some of it at usury. This is the note on which economics proper enters the stage of Alan of Lille's two moral allegories. In *De planctu naturae*, Nature laments the state of the world where

> not tears, not honeyed prayers, not the very poverty itself of a man can succeed by its pleas in deterring the rich man from devouring the poor man by his interest rates, as he reduces the bulk of the unhappy man's little purse.[29]

In the *Anticlaudianus*, Usury personified goes to war against Virtue in the train of Avarice:

> A more evil band of clients accompanies Avarice – constant Worry, greedy Usury, foul Robbery. She, with sleepless care and avid mind, reckons which money is out

---

27 Alan of Lille, *The Plaint of Nature*, Sheridan (trans.), p. 195.

28 *Liber parabolarum*, *PL* 210, col. 585 (author's translation).

29 Alan of Lille, *The Plaint of Nature*, Sheridan (trans.), p. 193.

hunting for wealth, which lies idle in the strongbox and is not serving the interests of its mistress.[30]

The concept of usury was sometimes taken rather loosely by early Christian writers. Gratian in the *Decretum*, referring to St Augustine, reserved the word *usura* for any payment in excess of the principal of a loan.[31] It is clearly in this tradition that we must place Alan of Lille. In his treatise on the virtues and vices he defines usury as 'the keen cupidity which consists in receiving anything above the principal'.[32] His dictionary of the Bible contains the same definition under the word *sors*, for which the alternative term *capitale* is also given.[33] Alan lists other sins pertaining to avarice and often associated with commercial activity, such as theft and robbery, falsehood, fraud and bribery, but usury is singled out for particular denouncement.

Repeatedly usury is associated with robbery (*rapina*). Alan's dictionary of the Bible offers several synonyms to usury. One is 'sin (*peccatus*)', another is 'robbery (*rapina*)'.[34] In the *Anticlaudianus*, as we saw, *Usura* goes to war along with *Rapina*. This association of usury and robbery places Alan of Lille within a patristic tradition. It had recently found expression in standard legal and theological texts. Gratian quotes St Ambrose of Milan saying that he who accepts usury is guilty of robbery.[35] Except for indicating that usury is usually extorted from the poor and resourceless, Alan makes no attempt to explain how the fulfilment of an economic transaction (which after all is what the payment of usury can be said to be) can be associated with robbery (which is an offence suffered by the victim against his will). Nevertheless, the very juxtaposition of these terms as we find them in Alan of Lille is significant because it poses a moral dilemma which could not for long be left alone, and which has indeed come to engage (and often to divide) economic philosophers of all periods since the early scholastics.

---

30 Alan of Lille, *Anticlaudianus*, Sheridan (trans.), p. 200.

31 Gratian, *Decretum Magistri Gratiani*, II, 14, 3 Emil Friedberg (ed.), 2 vols (Leipzig 1879, [repr. Graz, 1959]); Augustine, *Enarratio in Psalmum* 36 (37), 3.6: Augustinus, *Enarrationes in Psalmos I-L*, E. Dekkers and J. Fraipoint (eds), Corpus Christianorum Series Latina (CCSL 38) (Turnhout, 1956, [repr. 1990]). Augustine uses a form of the word *faenus*, which Sheridan renders from Alan as 'interest rate'; but in a medieval context I would prefer 'usury', *interesse* being a technical term designating an extrinsic title to indemnity rather than a payment for the loan of money as such.

32 Alan of Lille, *De virtutibus et de vitiis*, II.1; Lottin (ed.) p. 72.

33 Alan of Lille, *Distinctionibus dictionum theologicalium*, *PL* 210, col. 988.

34 Ibid.

35 Gratian, *Decretum*, II, 14, 4, 10; see Ambrose, *De bono mortis*, 12: Ambrosius, *Hexemaron, De paradiso, De Cain, De Noe, De Abraham, De Isaac, De bono mortis*, C. Schenkl (ed.), Corpus Scriptorum Ecclesiasticorum Latinorum, 32/1 (Vienna, 1896).

Alan's book on penance naturally devotes some space to the restitution of usurious moneys, as did most works of this genre, because, in a frequently quoted phrase of St Augustine's, 'sin is not remitted unless what was taken is returned'.[36] However, Alan is not very explicit. All he says about usury in that connection (using the same phrase in two separate chapters) is that the penitent should be made to restore 'that which he robbed by usury'.[37] In one instance there follows a chapter which concludes similarly in the case of gain from fraudulent business transactions (*negotiationem fraudulentam*).[38] The question of just and unjust terms of exchange is not raised. Neither in his theological and pastoral work nor in his moral treatises and allegories does Alan of Lille mention the 'just price'. If he can be said to have alluded to it at all, it is in one of his parables. Although the parables are allegorical poems, and require some caution in their interpretation, there are some lines there that are highly suggestive and worth quoting as heralds of a future academic theme soon to emerge from the depth of popular wisdom:

> Things are not bought dearly by the laws of markets,
> Seller and buyer are there equal regarding the goods;
> But nothing under the sky is bought more dearly
> Than what long entreaty buys with downcast brow.[39]

Supply and demand establish a just market price which buyer and seller both accept. In individual exchange, on the other hand, a seller can profit unduly from a needy buyer. The translation is literal enough, which should allay any concerns that we give the interpretation of a twelfth-century author such a modern slant. Such, at any rate, is the gist of what the schoolmen were soon to teach about pricing in and out of markets.[40]

The true significance of Alan of Lille, as placed here at the top of a genealogy of medieval authors on economic subjects, must be sought on a deeper level of his moral philosophy. In the topography of early European ethics, economic activity did not occupy a field of its own, requiring and defining its own terms. On the contrary, it was part of a vast field of human activity under the eyes of God and the guidance of the church. As set down formally in his treatise on the virtues

---

36 Augustine, *Epistola CLIII ad Macedonium*, 6.20: Augustinus, *Epistulae 124–84*, A. Goldbacher (ed.), CSEL, 44 (Vienna, 1904).

37 Alan of Lille, *Liber poenitentialis*, II.10, IV.37; Longère (ed.), vol. 1, p. 52, vol. 2, p. 185.

38 Alan of Lille, *Liber poenitentialis*, II.10; Longère (ed.), vol. 1, p. 53.

39 Alan of Lille, *Liber parabolarum*, *PL* 210, col. 584 (author's translation).

40 For further discussion see Odd Langholm, *Price and Value in the Aristotelian Tradition. A Study in Scholastic Economic Sources* (Bergen, 1979) and *Economics in Medieval Schools. Wealth, Exchange, Value, Money and Usury according to the Paris Theological Tradition, 1200–1350* (Leiden, 1992).

and vices, Alan's conception of morality is essentially legalistic, but it is based on the theological premise that while man may possess a natural disposition toward the good, the fall damaged this natural disposition so severely that the only path away from sin is through grace. Virtue consists in the attempt to exercise this inherent disposition, in conformity with the laws and norms of the church, which directs man's actions toward God and encourages the spirit of charity toward his fellow men. It is for the authority of the church on all levels, from the occupant of Peter's throne through the doctor of theology or canon law in his chair at the University to the parish priest in his confessional chair, to make and enforce rules of conduct in economic activity as in other areas, and for man (businessman or not) to obey. But obeying such rules will not go against man's true nature. Nor will it go against the findings of rational analysis, for man is graced with reason precisely in order better to understand the natural world and his duties within it. Allan of Lille's moral allegories are colourful illustrations of this thesis. It is when man abandons reason that Nature must intervene and teach him virtue once more, even though Nature ends up as an inadequate guide.

In short, to apply these arguments to the narrow field which concerns us here: It is natural and rational for merchants and moneylenders to be just and charitable towards their customers, following the rules and regulations taught by the doctors. Avarice and personal enrichment at the cost of others is perverse and irrational. It does not require protracted enquiry into economic realities to understand that this kind of business ethics must run into difficulties, but it was for the savants of the next century to face this problem squarely. Looking about him, Alan of Lille was painfully aware that some of the rent in the garment of Nature was caused by commerce. It finds expression in the moving oration with which he closes his *Sermon on the Lord's Cross*, asking where in this world Christ can take up residence:

> 'But the Son of man hath not where to lay his head' (Luke 9:58). He cannot take lodging in the prelates of the Church, for simony is billeted there; lodging is denied him in soldiers, where pillage dwells; he is given no lodging in burgesses, where usury has placed its tent; he is banished by merchants, where falsehood rules; he finds no room in common people, where theft has established its residence. Where, then, shall Christ take quarter? Only in Christ's poor, of whom it is said: 'Blessed are the poor in spirit, for theirs is the kingdom of heaven' (Matthew 5:3).[41]

When Alan of Lille died, Francesco Bernardone was still a merry young man, but the moment was not far off when Christ was to speak to him from the crucifix and initiate the age of the Poverello. Scholastic economic reasoning, interestingly so often carried forward by Franciscan authors, can only be

---

41 Alanus de Insulis, *Textes inédits*, Marie Thérèse d'Alverny (ed.), p. 238.

understood against the background of a need to teach right and wrong to a generation that had banished the Saviour by pillage and usury, falsehood and theft. But the death of Alan of Lille also coincides with another event. The year 1202 saw the publication of Leonardo Pisano's *Liber abaci*, which introduced oriental algebra to Europe and taught its merchants and bankers the calculus of commercial capitalism. In a period of sustained material growth and prosperity the moralist cannot easily ignore the material benefits created by economic practices such as lending at interest, and the social benefits of allowing peoples to make and keep their profits, nor can he, therefore, summarily condemn the profit incentive, but rather can render a moral judgment in which they and their costs and benefits are considered. Thus the thirteenth century was born with a tension, and it was under that tension, between asceticism and acquisitiveness, that the scholastic moral theologians and philosophers must struggle in their attempt to work out viable norms of economic behaviour.

PART II

Buying, Selling and Building: The Use of Money by the Church

Chapter 6

Financing Cathedral-Building in the Middle Ages: The Eleventh to Thirteenth Centuries[1]

Wim Vroom

> Just before the third year after the millennium, throughout the whole world, but most especially in Italy and Gaul, men began to reconstruct churches, although for the most part the existing ones were properly built and not in the least unworthy. But it seemed as though each Christian community were aiming to surpass all others in the splendour of construction. It was as if the whole world were shaking itself free, shrugging off the burden of the past, and cladding itself everywhere in a white mantle of churches. Almost all the episcopal churches and those of monasteries dedicated to various saints, and little village chapels, were rebuilt better than before by the faithful.[2]

These famous and much quoted lines from the Cluniac monk Raoul Glaber's (965–1047) *Historiarum Libri Quinque*, leaving aside all questions of interpretation, are characteristic of the general sense of release experienced throughout Christendom after the year 1000, an apocalyptic year whose approach he and his contemporaries had awaited with fear and trembling. The wave of church-building that made its way across France, Italy and also the

---

1 This chapter is based on the book by the same author: Wim Vroom, *Financing Cathedral Building in the Middle Ages: The Generosity of the Faithful* (Amsterdam, 2010). The notes provided here are mainly additions to the notes in this book.

2 'Igitur infra supra dictum millesium tercio iam fere imminente anno, contigit in universo pene terrarum orbe, precipue tamen in Italia et in Galliis, innovari ecclesiarum basilicas, licet plereque decenter locate minime indiguissent, emulabatur tamen queque gens christicolarum adversus alteram decentiori frui. Erat enim instar ac si mundus ipse excutiendo semet, reiecta vetustate, passim candidam ecclesiarum vestem indueret. Tunc denique episcopalium sedium ecclesias pene universas ac cetera queque diversorum sanctorum monasteria seu minora villarum oratoria in meliora quique permutavere fideles', Rodulfi Glabri, *Historiarum libri quinque* / Rodulfus Glaber, *The Five Books of the Histories*, John France (ed. and trans.) (Oxford, 1989), pp. 114–17. This work was written between the years 1030 and 1047.

Holy Roman Empire around the year 1000 encompassed abbey and monastery churches, but cathedral churches as well.[3]

The subject of this discussion is the financing of these cathedral churches in particular – that is, the churches that housed a bishop's *cathedra* and were the principal church of the diocese – focusing on the period spanned by this volume, between roughly the eleventh and the thirteenth centuries. What systems were put in place for the management of the church building, and by what means were the resources earmarked for its construction and maintenance brought together? What underlying structural patterns might be identified? Where possible, this discussion will also consider the value and variety of financial resources that individual cathedrals had at their disposal and, thus, the scale of their building works.

Information about how construction was funded during this period is extremely scarce. Glaber himself gives an interesting, albeit atypical, example of how a felicitous stroke of fate might provide the impetus for building a cathedral. Bishop Arnulfus of Orléans (987–1003), 'a man distinguished alike in birth, education and wisdom, and by the revenues of his patrimonial lands very rich' threw himself into building a new cathedral after a fatal fire in 989:

> He was favoured by the clearest divine intervention. One day when the masons were examining the firmness of the earth as they prepared to lay the foundations of the church, they found a hoard of gold. There was so much of it that men believed it would suffice to pay for the rebuilding of the church on however grand a scale it was undertaken. Those who had chanced on the gold took it intact to the bishop. He received it [...] and delivered it to those in charge of the works, '*custodibus operis*', ordering that it should all be faithfully spent on the rebuilding of the church.[4]

[3] Xavier Barral i Altet, 'Les moines, les évêques et l'art', in Dominque Iogna-Prat and Charles Picard (eds), *Religion et culture autour de l'an mil, Actes du colloque 'Hugues Capet 987–1987, la France de l'an mil'* (Paris, 1990), p. 72.

[4] '[...]nimium evidenter prestitum est illi divinitus iuvamentum. Contigit igitur quadam die, dum cementarii fundamina basilice locaturi soliditatem perscrutarentur ipsius telluris, ut repperirent copiosa auri pondera, que scilicet ad totius, quamvis magne, basilice fabricam reformandam certissime crederentur sufficere. Suscipientis ergo qui fortuito invenerant aurum, ex integro episcopo detulerunt. Ipse vero omnipotenti Deo pro collato sibi munere gratias agens, ac suscipiens illud, custodibus operis tradidit totumque fideliter in opus eiusdem ecclesie expendi iussit', Rodulfi Glabri, *Historiarum libri quinque*, pp. 66–7. This is not the only instance of employing a treasure of gold for building a cathedral; other examples include Ely c. 1075; Otto Lehmann-Brockhaus, *Lateinische Schriftquellen zur Kunst in England, Wales und Schottland vom Jahre 901 bis zum Jahre 1305*, vol. 1 (Munich, 1955), n. 1552.

This passage is important for several reasons. First, it recounts a fortunate find not of coins but of gold ingots which, as Glaber relates, had been hidden by the fourth-century bishop of Orléans St Evurtius, with a provident eye to the future. Second, the bishop in Glaber's account is the owner of the treasure, and the decision to spend it on construction is his. Third and finally, the text reveals that even as early as around the year 1000 churches were appointing *custodes operis* to take charge of construction.

As indicated, very little information has come down to us about either the management or the financing of cathedral building works in the period that concerns us here, and there are almost no extant quantitative data. Historical sources grow more numerous as time progresses, however, and, though later in date, these subsequent records can nevertheless help shed light on earlier periods, as we shall see.

Every diocese had to have its own cathedral church. Although not formally established as the basic units of the church's organization until the end of the eleventh century, the episcopal dioceses took shape over the period roughly from late Antiquity until the thirteenth century, at the final count resulting in some 700 dioceses of widely diverging scale and significance spread out across the map of Europe. These were most numerous in the oldest Christianised regions, in Italy and southern France, where every *civitas* was the seat of a bishop, but moving northwards dwindled, only a few lone dioceses stretching across vast expanses of Scandinavia and Eastern Europe.[5] The number of parishes in any single diocese was an indication of its size and importance, and could range from a few dozen to more than a thousand.

Management of the cathedral church initially rested in the hands of the bishop, who exercised full authority over the, as yet, undivided diocesan property. In the fifth century, popes stipulated that bishops were to spend a full quarter of their diocesan income on construction and upkeep of the church buildings within their diocese. But this rule was rarely followed in practice, and certainly not any longer in the tenth and eleventh centuries.[6]

In investigating how the building of cathedrals was managed and paid for, there are three separate but connected developments that must be considered, each unfolding over a long period of time and not crystallising fully until around 1200. The first of these was the development of the cathedral chapter. From as

[5] On the creation of an additional 16 dioceses in southern France under Pope John XXII, see Fabrice Delivré, 'Les diocèses méridionaux d'après le *Provinciale Romanum* (XIIe–XVe siècle)', in *Lieux sacrés et espace ecclésial (IXe–XV siècle)*, Cahiers de Fanjeaux 46 (Toulouse, 2011), pp. 395–419; also in this volume, Dominique Iogna-Prat, 'Conclusion', pp. 543–61.

[6] Regarding canonical aspects of this, see also Wolfgang Schöller, 'Funding the Construction of Gothic Cathedrals: Financial and Legal Realities of the Middle Ages', *Athena Review, Quarterly Journal of Archaeology, History, and Exploration*, 4 (2005): 48–52.

far back as the early Middle Ages, bishops were surrounded by a community of clerics, *clerici*. From this community there slowly evolved what was to become the cathedral chapter, forming a college that eventually cemented into a fixed number of members: the canons. A second development, which began in the tenth century, involved the division of the diocesan property into an endowment reserved for the bishop, the *mensa episcopalis*, and another, separate endowment reserved for the chapter, the *mensa capituli*. The chapter's endowment was broken down again into the individual prebends to which each canon was entitled. Third, and far and away the most important development as far as our enquiry is concerned, was the emergence of a separate funding body within the chapter charged with responsibility for the cathedral building and its liturgical furnishings and known as the *fabrica ecclesie cathedralis*, later occasionally also as the 'third' *mensa*. This new fund resulted neither from a yet further division of the diocesan property nor from a split in the *mensa* of the bishop or chapter. Indeed, most cathedral fabrics had no property of their own at all, or not until much later. Instead, the fabric was funded by earmarked gifts in the form of particular revenues or rights to revenues allocated to it by the bishop and chapter. The nature of this income is a subject to which we shall return.[7]

From their first beginnings at the end of the eleventh century, the development of such building funds steadily progressed until, by the end of the thirteenth century, there was hardly a cathedral in existence without its own fabric. By then, the fund's management had also been more or less uniformly established, with administrative responsibility vested not in the bishop but in the chapter corporate.[8] Though under the provisions of canon law bishops still held final responsibility for the church that housed their *cathedra* and to which they were tied, in the words of Pope Innocent III (1198–1216), in the bonds of spiritual matrimony, gradually they lost authority over their own cathedrals.[9]

Daily management activities came to be delegated to one or two canons appointed to serve in the capacity of *magister* or *procurator fabrice*, normally for a fixed number of years, and it was they who collected the income and made the expenditures for construction and furnishings. Moreover, they also rendered a subsequent account of their acts and deeds during an audit before the chapter, recorded in the account rolls of the fabric. It is these fabric rolls that supply our main source of, chiefly quantitative, information about how cathedral construction was financed. Of the 700 cathedrals known to us, fabric rolls have been preserved at around 80; the oldest, of which there are but a few,

---

[7] Vroom, *Financing Cathedral Building*, pp. 44–54.

[8] In Italy, it was the city that had management of the fabric, or *opera*, going back to the thirteenth century and earlier; for this reason the Italian *duomi* fall outside the scope of the discussion here.

[9] Vroom, *Financing Cathedral Building*, p. 488, n. 65.

date from the end of the thirteenth century.[10] Yet these rolls are of only indirect significance for the period that interests us here, insofar as they occasionally contain elements that hark back to a much earlier period.

Where, then, should we look to discover the source of the initiative, and, in some cases, the monumental vision, to build a new cathedral church in that time before the building works came under the control of the chapter and cathedral fabric? The answer, without question, is the bishop. In Orléans, for example, it was Bishop Arnulf who after the devastating fire of 1000 'took wiser counsel and with great preparation immediately began to rebuild the great church [...]'.[11] Narrative sources are rich with praise for episcopal building patrons.[12] Such praise grows scattered over the course of the thirteenth century, marking the transition of building patronage from the bishop to the body that administered the building fund; that is, the chapter. Bishops gradually relinquished their roles in managing their cathedrals. Rouen is a typical example, where three successive archbishops between 1130 and 1207 gave their patronage to the building works, whilst their followers showed no interest whatsoever. Quite possibly the creation of the cathedral fabric was an underlying factor.[13]

Responsibility for the cathedral building and furnishings was subject to canon law, though these requirements were concerned primarily with the duty to maintain the existing building and did not extend to new building projects. Up through the late Middle Ages, these obligations were mostly laid down in local canon laws such as synodal statutes[14] and it was not until after the Council

---

[10] Vroom, *Financing Cathedral Building*, pp. 631–6, Appendix One: these include only the cathedrals of Exeter, Hereford and Ely in England and Sens, Rodez, Autun, Troyes and Embrun in France.

[11] '[...] potiore usus consilio, magnum colligens apparatum, cepit domum maioris ecclesie [...], jugiter a fundamentis reedificare', Rodulfi Glabri, *Historiarum libri quinque*, pp. 66–7.

[12] Here I shall refer to only a handful of published sources relating to the German Empire and Italy, England and France, respectively: Otto Lehmann-Brockhaus, *Schriftquellen zur Kunstgeschichte des 11.und 12. Jahrhunderts für Deutschland, Lothringen und Italien*, 2 vols (Berlin, 1938); Otto Lehmann-Brockhaus, *Lateinische Schriftquellen zur Kunst in England, Wales und Schottland vom Jahre 901 bis zum Jahre 1305*, 5 vols (Munich, 1955–60); also in particular Victor Mortet and Paul Deschamps, *Recueil de textes relatifs à l'histoire de l'architecture et à la condition des architectes en France au Moyen Âge, XIe–XIIIe siècles*, préface de Léon Pressouyre (Paris, 1995), 2 vols, single binding (first edition 1911 and 1929): in the period between approximately 1000 and 1200 there is mention of bishops as building patrons at Chartres, Cambrai, Coutances, Angers, Maguelone, Le Mans, Aix en Provence, Canterbury, Lyon, Durham, Thérouanne, Amiens, Salisbury, Paris and Auxerre; pp. 147, 152, 156, 169, 173, 177, 187, 247 (n. 4), 248–54, 288–92, 301, 353, 372, 408, 424, 747, 839–40.

[13] *Rouen, La Grâce d'une cathédrale* (Strasbourg, 2012), pp. 31, 32, 385.

[14] Schöller, 'Funding the construction of gothic cathedrals': 49, n. 6.

of Trent that such guidelines were consolidated in practicable form in canonical treatises.[15] These guidelines reflect the tripartite function of the cathedral, which is at once the church of the bishop, the church of the chapter and the church of the diocese, *primitiva mater et domina omnium ecclesiarum*. In them, the existence of a fabric is taken for granted; indeed, the cathedral fabric is cited as holding primary responsibility. Where the fabric's means were insufficient (as was often the case in new building and renovation projects), there followed a chain of accountability, starting with the bishop, continuing with the chapter, and ending with the diocese as a whole, and more particularly, the faithful. This chain of accountability can also provide a good point of reference for structuring the scarce and widely dispersed extant data from the period before the cathedral building works came under capitular control. An important sub-category of donors amongst the faithful that deserves separate mention is secular rulers: in the period up until the thirteenth century, they could often be counted on to provide a large share of the funds for the construction of abbeys and, sometimes, cathedrals, though by the late Middle Ages the systematic character of these contributions had much diminished.[16]

In the period before the emergence of the cathedral fabrics, it was a matter of course that bishops provided funding for the building of their cathedrals.[17] It was the bishop, after all, who was the initiator, the genesis of the new building project. Although there are virtually no extant quantitative data, some narrative sources do provide indications of the sums that bishops donated, whether in coin, precious metal or in kind. From the very fact of their mention we can infer that these sums were comparatively large.[18] In the most characteristically narrative surviving sources such as chronicles, bishops' personal involvement is patently

---

15 Vroom, *Financing Cathedral Building*, p. 505, n. 28.

16 On architecture around the year 1000, see Xavier Barral i Altet, *Le paysage monumental de la France autour de l'an mil, colloque international C.N.R.S. Hugues Capet 987–1987. La France en l'an Mil, June–September 1987* (Paris, 1987), pp. 37–8 ('les conditions de la création architecturale: financement, main-d'oeuvre et matériaux').

17 See the numerous examples in Günther Binding and Susanne Linscheid-Burdich, *Planen und Bauen im frühen und hohen Mittelalter nach den Schriftquellen bis 1250* (Darmstadt, 2002), pp. 25–60.

18 See Lehmann-Brockhaus, *Schriftquellen zur Kunstgeschichte des 11.und 12. Jahrhunderts für Deutschland, Lothringen und Italien*, p. 283, index '*Geld, durch Zahlen ausgedrückte Geldaufwendingen*', approximately 30 cases (including nos 595, 597, 1068, 1069, 1829; also Vroom, 2010, p. 511 n. 107, 108, 109); Lehmann-Brockhaus, *Lateinische Schriftquellen zur Kunst in England, Wales und Schottland*, ns 793, 956, 1583, 2062, 3709, 4698; Mortet and Deschamps, *Recueil de textes relatifs à l'histoire de l'architecture*, p. 354 (the bishop of Lyon c. 1100, 300 solidi); donations of precious metal: the bishop of Chartres in 1024: *bonam partem auri sui et argenti reliquit*, p. 148 n. 1; donations in kind: the bishop of Maguelone (1159–90): 28 *modii grani et vini* (as well as 30,000 solidi), p. 177.

clear: it was the bishop who initiated, who organised and who provided access to monetary resources. For example, the eleventh-century bishop of Cambrai, who lived in fear that death would overtake him before he could complete his work. Or the bishop of Le Mans near that century's end, about whom we are told that he was able, *tanto studio agressus*, to finish the towers begun by his predecessors.[19] In the case of St Peter of Anagni, bishop from 1072 until 1105, it was precisely his boundless efforts, his 'spes restaurationis', to rebuild the cathedral of Anagni that helped lead to his canonisation, according to the *Acta Sanctorum*. During his time as papal ambassador to Constantinople, Peter was able to convince Emperor Michael VII to donate gold and provide craftsmen for its construction. Initially, the emperor refused, having never heard of Anagni. However, when the emperor fell ill and was miraculously cured as a result of Peter's appeal to the holy martyr St Magnus, whose relics were preserved at Anagni, the emperor thought better of his refusal. He even gave the bishop leave to approach him again should the resources provided prove insufficient, as indeed they did. Later, when Peter's enemies accused him of mismanaging the building funds, another miracle served to clear him of all blame.[20] Passionately dedicated bishops like these, and there are many more examples that could be cited, must have provided the financial impetus for such enterprises in the early years as well, even if the sources do not tell us this explicitly. However, building patronage did not automatically entail significant financial backing, and certainly not over longer periods, and these individual contributions, 'propriis sumptibus' or 'suo proprio', were not necessarily what ultimately determined a project's success.[21] As the bishop of Paris from 1160 until his death in 1196, Maurice de Sully immediately became the driving force behind the construction of the new Notre Dame and the radical topographical reorganisation of the cathedral *parvis*. But while, in the words of one thirteenth-century chronicle, the rebuilding of the cathedral was begun 'more at his own expense than that of others', the bequest of *trecentas*

---

[19] Mortet and Deschamps, *Recueil de textes relatifs à l'histoire de l'architecture*, p. 152 (Cambrai); p. 248 (Le Mans).

[20] *Acta Sanctorum, augusti 1*, Antwerp 1733, pp. 230–41. Regarding Emperor Michael VII's donation, see: p. 232 [13] and [14]; p. 233 [17]; p. 237 [16] and [17]; regarding the accusations of mismanagement ('qui [his enemies] dicebant quod censum pro ecclesia reparanda pompose dispersit'), see: p. 237 [19] and p. 238 [25]. St Peter also effected a miracle in connection with the building works, taming a wolf that had devoured one of the cathedral's draught animals and harnessing it to the cart; p. 231 [8]. Peter was canonised in 1110. See also: *The Cathedral of Anagni: Art, History, Legend* (Anagni, 1998), pp. 9–12. Regarding St Peter, see: *Bibliotheca Sanctorum*, vol. 10 (Rome, 1968), col. 663–5.

[21] On the interpretation of '*de proprio*', including many examples, see, Martin Warnke, *Bau und Überbau: Soziologie der mittelalterlichen Architektur nach den Schriftquellen* (Frankfurt am Main, 1979), p. 30.

libras (300 pounds) that he left for the building works was certainly not the largest in his will.[22]

In describing the nature of these contributions, it is crucial that we distinguish between single, possibly sizable, lump sums, and structural contributions made over successive years, as well as combinations of these. An example of the last is a bishop of Laon who donated a lump sum of 100 pounds plus an annual contribution of 20 pounds from the start of work on the new cathedral in the second quarter of the twelfth century. Particularly interesting is the donation made in 1215 by the bishop of Auxerre, specifying an explicit distinction between contributions provided to the building works in his capacity as bishop, including offerings from the faithful and jurisdictional dues, and personal gifts that totalled around 700 pounds *de proprio* in the first year and between 5 and 10 pounds per week thereafter; to these were also added receipts from collections in his own and the neighbouring dioceses from which he drew his episcopal income.[23] Unfortunately, however, it is not possible to make a reliable estimate of the real value of these donations, let alone how much of the total construction costs they covered, since, as indicated, no accounts have been preserved from this period.

Contributions from the chapter were of an entirely different nature, certainly in the period when the college of canons did not yet control the building fund. In the twelfth century we already find steps being taken in some places towards the system of fixed dues that would come to be favoured in the late Middle Ages. In 1196, the archbishop of Arles ordered the chapter to reserve one tenth of the admission dues collected from all new canons for building-related expenditures.[24] In the period between 1161 and 1185, the bishop and chapter of Bayeux earmarked one full year's receipts from the *prebende defunctorum*, the prebends of deceased canons, for the cathedral building works. The fact that this allocation was given papal approval, albeit with some reservations, signals that this was a new policy, although one that would eventually gain widespread usage throughout Europe.[25]

Occasionally, a bishop and chapter joined hands to provide a large portion of their own incomes to fund new building projects for a specific period of usually three, five or seven years. This happened mainly in the twelfth and thirteenth

---

22 Mortet and Deschamps, pp. 747 and 750; on Sully, see Alain Erlande-Brandenburg, 'Le grand dessein de Maurice de Sully (1160)', in Michel Lemoine (ed.), *Notre-Dame de Paris, un manifeste chrétien (1160–1230), colloque organisé à l'Institut de France le vendredi 12 décembre 2003* (Turnhout, 2004), pp. 70–92 and, recently, *Notre Dame de Paris, la grâce d'une cathédrale* (Strasburg, 2012), pp 113–14 (Etienne Hamon).

23 Mortet and Deschamps, *Recueil de textes relatifs à l'histoire de l'architecture*, (n. 9), pp. 839–40; Vroom, *Financing Cathedral Building*, p. 90.

24 Mortet and Deschamps, *Recueil de textes relatifs à l'histoire de l'architecture*, p. 807.

25 Vroom, *Financing Cathedral Building*, p. 105; also p. 108.

centuries, and usually at the initiative of a bishop who had assumed the role of building patron. However, bishops were not always able to persuade their chapters to follow their lead. The sums were usually large, 'pars non modica [...] ex propriis redditibus', as at Chartres after the fire of 1194. In 1233, the bishop of Salisbury had to bend over backwards to get the chapter to agree to renew, again, their joint contribution 'together with you, above what propriety demands', 'una vobiscum ultra quam justitia exegerit'.[26] Where the chapter refused such a renewal for whatever reason, as happened at Chartres, the shortage of funds could become so serious that, 'cum omnis subito pecunia defecisset', the building labourers could no longer be paid.[27] Such contributions could be pledged in the form of specific sums (with the bishop usually giving the largest share) or as fixed shares of the bishop's and chapter's respective revenues over an agreed period.

Third in the chain of accountability, according to the canonical handbooks, was the diocese, which is to say, the faithful. As such, it was to the faithful that the archbishop of Aix appealed on behalf of the cathedral in 1070, the building of which he had begun but could not complete 'sine adjutorio vestro nullo modo'.[28] In Durham, one chronicler tells us, the pace of construction in the early twelfth century rose and fell with the magnitude of the offerings made there.[29]

Bishops and chapters had two options when it came to soliciting offerings from the faithful for the building works. Either they could encourage the faithful to come to them, to visit the cathedral and to offer their money and gifts there, or they could go to the faithful themselves, travelling from parish to parish, and sometimes covering great distances, to collect donations at every church. By the late Middle Ages, both forms, but particularly the latter, had been fairly uniformly systematised in terms of canonical, organisational and devotional structure. Evidence for this can be found in fabric account rolls of the period. But there is ample evidence that even earlier, in the eleventh and twelfth centuries, steps were already being taken in this direction, though it would not be until after the Fourth Lateran Council (1215) that such collections were codified in canonical frameworks.

From the early years of the eleventh century we find parishioners being offered indulgences in return for visiting a church and offering a gift of alms. Even so, it was not until the thirteenth century that bishops began granting indulgences on a large scale, with papal indulgences only gaining significance towards the end of the Middle Ages. Immeasurably more important in soliciting the revenues needed to fund building enterprises were devotions centring on

26 Vroom, *Financing Cathedral Building*, p. 509, n. 69

27 Mortet and Deschamps, *Recueil de textes relatifs à l'histoire de l'architecture*, p. 805.

28 Mortet and Deschamps, *Recueil de textes relatifs à l'histoire de l'architecture*, p. 290.

29 Lehmann-Brockhaus, *Lateinische Schriftquellen zur Kunst in England, Wales und Schottland*, n. 137.

the relics preserved at the cathedral. Raoul Glaber reports several miraculous discoveries of relics shortly after the year 1000, beginning with the cathedral of Sens, which brought the faithful flocking to the cathedral and provided a great boost for the city's economy.[30] Though we lack quantitative data here, too, there are numerous indications that the worship of relics, with the attendant hope and expectation of a miracle, drew countless people to not only abbey churches but cathedral churches as well.[31] From the twelfth century there are preserved compilations of miracles whose occurrence was documented at the cathedrals of Durham, Coutances, Norwich, Paris and Tournai.[32] Sometimes, these miracles were connected with the building works. At Chartres, where all earthly measures had failed to stave off the severe financial crisis that loomed at the end of the three-year term of the bishop's and chapter's donations in 1197, divine intervention by the Virgin Mary produced a series of miracles that brought the faithful to the church in unprecedented numbers.[33] At some cathedrals, the arrangements made for the apportionment of the offerings of the faithful have also been preserved. In Soissons, for example, the bishop determined in 1205 that the offerings which the newly acquired relics of St Stephan were anticipated to attract would be divided up equally between the construction of the cathedral and the construction of its bridge.[34] By contrast, the role that the fascinating phenomenon of voluntary participation by individuals or large groups in cathedral-building played during the eleventh and twelfth centuries, though certainly interesting as a measure of devotional commitment, was of no more than marginal importance economically, being characterised by unskilled labour that lasted only as long as the burst of religious fervour that sparked it.[35]

Another means of reaching the faithful was to visit them in their own parishes throughout the diocese. From the thirteenth century, the organisational and also canonical parameters for this practice were laid down in the form of the *mendicatorium*, or begging letter, drawn up by the bishop and addressing the community of the diocesan clergy and, by extension, all the faithful in his diocese. These letters contained a standard set of components, including directives, guidelines and the promise of spiritual benefits such as indulgences,

---

30 Rodulfi Glabri, *Historiarum libri quinque*, pp. 126–9.

31 Catherine Vincent and Jacques Pycke (eds), *Cathédrale et pèlerinage aux époques médiévales et moderne: reliques, processions et dévotions à l'église-mère du diocese* (Louvain-la-Neuve, 2010); primarily in the later Middle Ages.

32 The earliest such books relate miracles at abbeys and monasteries; Vroom, *Financing Cathedral Building*, pp. 185 and 547.

33 Mortet and Deschamps, *Recueil de textes relatifs à l'histoire de l'architecture*, pp. 805–6.

34 Mortet and Deschamps, *Recueil de textes relatifs à l'histoire de l'architecture*, pp. 835–6.

35 Vroom, *Financing Cathedral Building*, pp. 190–93.

and were composed using equally standard formulations. At least 35 such *mendicatoria* from all over Europe are documented, dating from the second half of the thirteenth up through the sixteenth centuries.[36] The roots of these diocesan collections can already be detected in the twelfth century. One element always included in a *mendicatorium* was the announcement of the arrival of the *nuntii*, or messengers, who would come bearing the relics of the cathedral. The earliest such expeditions with relics had no underlying structure, but were ad hoc events. An example are the journeys made by seven canons and laymen from the cathedral of Laon, who toured northern France for three and a half months in 1112 and a year later even set out on a five-month trip across England.[37] Later on, such collections in foreign dioceses could be held only with special permission.[38]

The earliest *mendicatoria*, albeit still rather rough and rudimentary, date from around 1200. In that year, the bishop of Bayeux established a diocesan building confraternity in which members had to pay annual contributions for a term of at least five years and enjoyed a number of spiritual benefits in return, which was documented by the inscription of their names in the parish registers. Messengers from the cathedral would come round to collect these contributions.[39] In a *mendicatorium* from Strasbourg dating from the same period the bishop informed the collective clergy of the diocese that insofar as the financial support of the city's residents had proved insufficient, the messengers of the cathedral would visit every parish in the diocese (where they were to be given a fitting reception) to collect money; those who gave liberally would earn an indulgence and other spiritual benefits in return for their generosity.[40] Although the actual receipts of diocesan collections are unknown in this period, in the late Middle Ages they would be of instrumental importance in funding many a cathedral building campaign.

Separate from these were the contributions made by secular rules, by emperors, by kings and by lords of all ranks. Their contributions are even less easy to characterise than those of the bishops. Where bishops were committed to and responsible for the cathedral by virtue of their position, secular rules were under no such obligation. Nevertheless, their backing, if sustained, could be of critical importance. A famous inscription carved on the façade of Salerno

---

[36] Vroom, *Financing Cathedral Building*, pp. 213–81, 640–42.

[37] Simon Yarrow, *Saints and Their Communities: Miracle Stories in Twelfth-Century England* (Oxford, 2006), pp. 62–99.

[38] Vroom, *Financing Cathedral Building*, pp. 252–6.

[39] Vroom, *Financing Cathedral Building*, pp. 239, 220–21. The confraternity already existed but had led 'a dormant existence'. Building confraternities are documented as early as c. 1100 in Pamplona and Seo de Urgell, and c. 1175 in London.

[40] Vroom, *Financing Cathedral Building*, pp. 220, 640. The relevant deed is attributed to Conrad II (1190–1202); see also *Strasbourg, La grâce d'une cathédrale* (Strasburg, 2007), p. 29.

Cathedral around 1084/85 memorialises the fact that Robert Guiscard, the Norman conqueror of southern Italy and a papal ally, had had the cathedral built 'de aerario particulari', at his own expense.[41]

A special case in this connection concerns the so-called *Kaiserdome* in cities such as Bamberg, Worms, Mainz and most especially Speyer in the eleventh and twelfth centuries. As the founders of these dioceses with their 'Emperor's cathedrals', the Holy Roman emperors automatically also assumed the role of building patrons. Here, the emperors' ongoing involvement in the cathedral works went beyond mere financing to encompass aspects of management as well. As one *Vita* of Emperor Henry IV (1056–1106) reports, 'imperator vero famosum illud ac laboriosum opus Spirensis monasterii habebat in manibus'.[42] Cathedrals that functioned as both royal coronation church and mausoleum could normally count on structural support. An example is the cathedral of Rouen up until 1204 where, following a fire, the duke of Normandy and King of England, John (1199–1216), not only donated 2,000 pounds on his own account but also provided an impetus for the diocesan collection.[43] Rulers on the Iberian Peninsula, where cathedrals stood as symbols of the Reconquista, very regularly supported cathedral building projects. In 1168, for example, King Ferdinand II pledged to finance the lifelong annual wages of the architects of Santiago and of Ciudad Rodrigo.[44] In the majority of cases, however, secular rulers' involvement in the building of cathedrals was incidental. From the many examples of such ad hoc donations we know that they were never of a determining value.[45]

In conclusion, it can clearly be established that cathedral construction projects were financed from a patchwork of sources. In the period from the eleventh up through the thirteenth centuries, the pace of cathedral-building in France, England, Germany and elsewhere achieved a pitch seldom equalled in the later Middle Ages. Many of the cathedrals initiated during this period

[41] 'M[atthaeo] a[postolo] et evangelistae patrono urbis Robbertus dux R[omani] Imp[erii] maxim[us] triumphator de aerario particulari'; regarding this inscriptions and others like it, see Robert Favreau, 'Commanditaire, auteur, artiste dans les inscriptions médiévales', in Michel Zimmermann (ed.), *Auctor et auctoritas, invention et confirmisme dans l'écriture médiévale, actes du colloque tenu à l'Université de Versailles-Saint-Quentin-en-Yvelines (14–16 juin 1999)* (Paris, 2001), pp. 40–43.

[42] Lehmann-Brockhaus, *Lateinische Schriftquellen zur Kunst in England, Wales und Schottland*, n. 1366.

[43] *Rouen, La Grâce d'une cathédrale*, (Strasburg, 2012), pp. 31 (with illustration), 32, 38.

[44] Jens Rüffer, *Die Kathedrale von Santiago de Compostella (1075–1211), eine Quellenstudie* (Bern, 2010), pp. 181–3.

[45] Vroom, *Financing Cathedral Building*, p. 526, n. 310.

were largely completed within the span of a century.[46] This accelerated pace of building was one that building patrons consciously and proudly aspired to, 'summa celeritate', 'magna celeritate paucis annis'.[47]

The scale of these building enterprises, and specifically their economic impact on regional and wider economies, has engendered considerable discussion, particularly in connection with the provocative hypothesis put forward by Robert S. Lopez in 1952.[48] He pointed out that medieval Italian cities were in the vanguard of economic growth but lagged behind in the size and wealth of their cathedrals, whereas certain French episcopal cities, like Beauvais, were famed for their awesome cathedrals but enjoyed little economic prosperity of any kind. This led him to the question: was cathedral-building a deterrent for economic growth? Could it be that, in France, manpower and capacity were being diverted from economically productive applications to unproductive prestige projects such as the construction of cathedrals?

Based on a calculation of the amount of manpower needed to build a cubic yard and an estimate of the total volume of cubic yards represented by a selected set of cathedrals, some authors have made several estimates of the macroeconomic impact of cathedral-building in England and in France. In England, the available labour capacity estimated to be entailed was 0.5 per cent; in France, by contrast, 2.5 per cent.[49] Although interesting, the unavoidably speculative nature of such a macroeconomic approach can offer no useful insight to advance our enquiry here.

In fact, logically, a *micro*economic approach would appear more useful. An example is the work of the Australian architect John James, who calculated the scale of the building lodge at Chartres Cathedral during the most important phase of its building history, between 1195 and 1223. Combining architectural analyses of the historical building with admittedly anachronistic modern-day prices and production methods, James worked out the cost price of sections of the building completed in each successive year, and plotted the results in a graph to show the distribution of building production over a total of 30 years.

---

46 A handful of examples from France may suffice: Bourges, Chartres, Laon, Meaux, Noyons, Paris, Poitiers, Sens, Senlis, Strasbourg.

47 The bishops of Hildesheim and Worms c. 1050; cited by Warnke, *Bau und Überbau*, p. 23 with additional examples.

48 R. S. Lopez, 'Economie et architecture médiévale: cela aurait-il tué ceci?', in *Annales, économies, sociétés, civilisations*, 7 (1952): 433–9.

49 Virginia Lee Owen, 'The Economic Legacy of Gothic Cathedral Building: France and England Compared', *Journal of Cultural Economics*, 13 (1989): 89–100; also the articles by H. Thomas Johnson cited therein. See also the curious mathematical economic characterisation of 'the economic role of cathedrals in the market for religion as "awe and grandeur" capital' in Brighita Bercea, Robert B. Ekelund Jr and Robert D. Tollison, 'Cathedral Building as an Entry-Deterring Device', *Kyklo*, 58 (2005): 453–65.

Speculative it may be, but this graph of cash flows clearly tracks the changing pace of building in response to events such as the end of the bishop's and chapter's three-year term of support, the influx of offerings sparked by the miracles and their decline after 1209 when the bishop left to join the Albigensian Crusade.[50]

At cathedrals where the fabric rolls survive and provide figures over a period of successive years, we can gain insight into the pace of construction by expressing the sums spent on building and furnishing the cathedral in the standard annual wages of an unskilled labourer (based on a 250-day working year). Fortuitously there is one cathedral in last quarter of the eleventh century where we know how many stonemasons and sculptors (skilled labourers) were employed. This cathedral is Santiago, where construction work began around 1075 with a workforce of approximately 50 skilled labourers.[51] Converted into the lower wages of unskilled labourers, this would have been around 75. Assuming an equally large sum for the costs of building materials, the total investment over the first years of the building campaign at Santiago, which lasted until 1211, amounted to 150 annual wages of an unskilled labourer. Investments this large are also documented in the later Middle Ages, at Exeter in the first quarter of the fourteenth century, for example. At Utrecht Cathedral, expenditures on construction between 1395 and 1527 averaged 81 annual wages, peaking at around 190 in 1505. Periods of extreme activity such as at Milan, where sums climbed to seven- or eightfold the average at Utrecht, were markedly short-lived, in this case probably lasting not more than five years, from 1387 until 1391. By far the largest church building lodge in the Middle Ages was not at a cathedral but that at Westminster Abbey, which employed between six and eight hundred labourers in 1251, but was also a project financed entirely by the king.[52]

Regrettably, the extant sources simply do not permit a reliable estimate of the scale of cathedral building campaigns and how these fluctuated in the period between the eleventh century and the thirteenth century. Nevertheless, they do give us an illuminating general view of the sources of income and therefore of the financial basis of these extraordinary enterprises.

[50] John James, 'What price the cathedrals', in his *In Search of the Unknown in Medieval Architecture* (London, 2007), pp. 503–19.

[51] Rüffer, *Die Kathedrale von Santiago de Compostella*, p. 166.

[52] Vroom, *Financing Cathedral Building*, p. 461.

Chapter 7
The Church and Money in Twelfth-Century England

James L. Bolton

Between the Norman Conquest and the first issue of Magna Carta, the rural and urban landscape of England was transformed by a wave of new building. This chapter will concentrate on the role of the church and its patrons in, first, the reconstruction of existing Anglo-Saxon cathedrals, monasteries and nunneries, and parish churches, which was followed by the foundation of houses for the new monastic orders of the twelfth century and then by yet more rebuilding in the new Gothic style of architecture which reached England in the last decades of that century. What must not be forgotten, however, is that there was a parallel building or rebuilding of castles, manor houses, barns and mills, of new towns and bridges and merchants' houses, and that the two, ecclesiastical and lay, went hand in hand.[1] A new castle, and there were many, would be accompanied by a new priory and a new or rebuilt parish church, often with the same patron for all three. This was a remarkable period of construction and reconstruction, yet it all took place within an economy that was literally strapped for cash, where the money supply, that is, the amount of coin in circulation, was at its lowest medieval levels. The two seem irreconcilable. Major construction in stone was, and still is, expensive. Admittedly, building or rebuilding a cathedral or castle could take years, thus spreading the costs over long periods, but resources still had to be found to finance it, at a time when the endowment of new monastic houses was proceeding apace. The purpose here is to examine the old and some startlingly new evidence for scale of the rebuilding; to discuss the very real

[1] The best general introduction is by Robert Bartlett, *England under the Norman and Angevin Kings: 1075–1225* (Oxford, 2000), pp. 377–476. Janet Burton, *Monastic and Religious Orders in Britain 1000–1300* (Cambridge, 1994) provides the essential background to monastic reform and the introduction of the new orders. C. H. Lawrence, *Medieval Monasticism: Forms of Religious Life in Western Europe in the Middle Ages* (Harlow, 3rd edition, 2001) and R. N. Swanson, *The Twelfth-Century Renaissance* (Manchester, 1999) are good, general guides to the religious and intellectual life of the period whilst R. W. Southern, 'The Place of England in the Twelfth-Century Renaissance', *History*, 45 (1960): 201–16, remains essential reading. The literature on aspects of church life in England is vast and can best be accessed through the Royal Historical Bibliography of British and Irish History, Brepolis, online, http://www.history.ac.uk/projects/bbih.

problem of the twelfth-century money supply; and then to pose, although not necessarily to answer, questions asking how the two might be reconciled.

The transformation of the English church after the Norman Conquest is a well-researched and equally well-told story that will not be re-examined here, but some account of the building and rebuilding programme has to be given. The Conquest brought with it new and aggressive ideas about the government of the church by the papacy and a group of violent and highly motivated laymen, the companions of the Conqueror, all of them imbued with the spirit of monastic reform that characterised religious life in eleventh-century Normandy. The destruction of the existing Anglo-Saxon cathedrals and their replacement by buildings in the Romanesque style began almost immediately after 1066. Lanfranc, the first Norman archbishop of Canterbury, was appointed in 1070 to replace the simoniac Stigand. The cathedral church had been destroyed by a fire in the same year and Lanfranc set in train its rebuilding, which was completed within 10 years. Herbert Losinga, rather ironically, acquired the see of Thetford (Norfolk) by simony in 1090–91, along with the abbacy of Winchester. This allegedly cost him no less than £1,000 and even if that is to be taken as simply representing a large sum, it is still some measure of his individual wealth. The see of Thetford was translated to Norwich in 1094–96 and Herbert immediately put in hand the building of the new cathedral. It was completed by his successor, Bishop Eborard, between 1121 and 1145, but the new cathedral was only part of Herbert Losinga's ecclesiastical patronage. He was also responsible for the foundation of the episcopal palace; St Leonard's, the second monastery within the town; the leper hospital of St Mary Magdalene; the parish church at North Elmham; and cells of the Benedictine cathedral priory at St Nicholas, Great Yarmouth, and St Margaret, Lynn.[2]

The rebuilding at Canterbury and Norwich was part of a much wider programme that was much influenced by those sections in Archbishop Lanfranc's *Decreta* on monastic reform that touched on matters architectural.[3] Table 7.1 shows the chronology of the rebuilding of cathedrals and major monastic houses between 1070 and c. 1130:

2 L. Salzman, *Building in England down to 1540* (Oxford, 1967), pp. 361–2; J. Allerton et al., *Norwich: Cathedral, Church, City, Diocese 1096–1996* (London and Rio Grande, 1996), pp. 22–35, 41–3, 51–2.

3 For these see A. W. Klukas, 'The Architectural Implications of the *Decreta Lanfanci*', *Anglo-Norman Studies*, VI (1984): 136–71.

Table 7.1 Starting dates for the post-Conquest rebuilding of cathedrals and major Benedictine monasteries.

Cathedral/monastery	Starting date
St Augustine, Canterbury	1070
Lincoln	1074–92
Old Sarum	1075–92
Norwich	1076
St Alban's	1077–1115
Rochester	1077–1130
Winchester	1079–93, 1108–20
Hereford	1079–1145
Ely	1083–1130
Worcester	1084–92
Chichester	1088–1108
Gloucester	1089–1100
Carlisle	1090–1123
London, St Paul's	1090–1130
Durham	1092–1133
Canterbury Cathedral	1096–1107
Exeter	1112
Peterborough	1117–55

Source: J. Harvey, *The English Cathedrals* (London, 1961), pp. 77–89.

Anselm, Lanfranc's successor at Canterbury, added the choir and the eastern transepts to the cathedral church between 1096 and 1107, whilst St Augustine's Abbey was completely rebuilt from 1070 onwards. From Carlisle in the north to Winchester in the south and from Peterborough in the east to Worcester in the west, Anglo-Saxon cathedrals and monasteries were torn down and replaced by new buildings in the Romanesque style in the 40 years after the Conquest. Nor was this simply the work of the new bishops and abbots. The lay nobility were deeply involved in this transformation and the patronage of William de Warenne (d. 1088), one of the companions of the Conqueror, serves as a good example of what could be achieved. For his part in the Conquest and his support for both William I and William II, he received extensive lands in 13 English counties, including the Rape of Lewes in Sussex and Castle Acre in Norfolk, which became the caput of his honour. Before 1077 he and his wife Gundred visited the abbey of Cluny. William negotiated with Abbot Hugh, who was initially reluctant to send monks to England to help revitalise the church there but eventually agreed to let six travel across the Channel to found a priory at Lewes for William, by 1077. So, at Lewes, William de Warenne had built a castle, founded a Cluniac priory and established a parish church, a pattern that was copied by his son, William de Warenne II (d. 1138) at Castle Acre and then at Thetford. The powerful Benedictine abbey of La Charité-sur-Loire, Cluny's eldest daughter house, provided yet more monks for England between 1080 and 1108, at Much Wenlock (Shropshire), Bermondsey (Surrey), Daventry (Northants.), Pontefract (Yorks., WR) and Northampton. The founders of these houses were all major Norman nobles, with one exception, and that was Bermondsey, where the wealthy London merchant Alwin Child endowed his new abbey with lands bought from William II.[4]

The magnificence of the achievement of the first 40 years of patronage by church, State and lay aristocracy can still be seen in the cathedrals, parish churches and castles that have survived, and in the ruins of the monastic houses. The motives behind such fervour were mixed. Imposing Norman power on Anglo-Saxon England was one of them and this wave of rebuilding and new building had a serious political purpose. Religious piety and the saving of the patron's soul and the souls of his family, past, present and future, were also important. The Normans brought with them a religiosity born of monastic reform in the Duchy, accompanied by the desire to make their own mark in their new world. As Guitmund of Moulins-la-Marche put it, 'Our Lord Jesus Christ ... who taught us what things are necessary for the good of our souls, admonished us to make gifts for His sake out of our possessions, so that in time we might receive an hundredfold'. He made his donation to the abbey of Saint-Père de Chatres 'to alleviate the heavy burden of our sins and [to] ensure that there shall be no lack of men to pray daily for us'.[5] There were also practical motives. Care in old age and infirmity was available to patrons, as was the chance to retire from the troubles of the world to lead the contemplative life. A new foundation could provide space for family tombs as well as a home for younger sons and daughters without lands or other careers. Status, salvation, commemoration and social care went hand in hand with piety, but the costs of this first wave of building, of furnishing the new cathedrals, monasteries and churches and of providing in the long term for the growing populations of monks, nuns and priests cannot be quantified. Church lands were pillaged after the Conquest by the same men who so piously endowed the new religious houses, and drawing up an account of profits and losses is nigh impossible. Analysis of the Domesday surveys does show that, collectively, the church was the greatest landholder. The total value of land assessed in 1086 was £73,000. Of this, the king, the royal family and their dependents controlled land to the value of £12,600, or 17 per cent of the whole;

4 C. Platt, *The Architecture of Medieval Britain* (London and New Haven, 1990), pp. 4–5, 14, 20, 29, 33, 36–7; Burton, *Monastic and Religious Orders*, pp. 35–9.

5 M. Chibnall, *The World of Orderic Vitalis* (Oxford, 1984), pp. 47, 49–50, quoted in Platt, *Architecture of Medieval Britain*, p. 11.

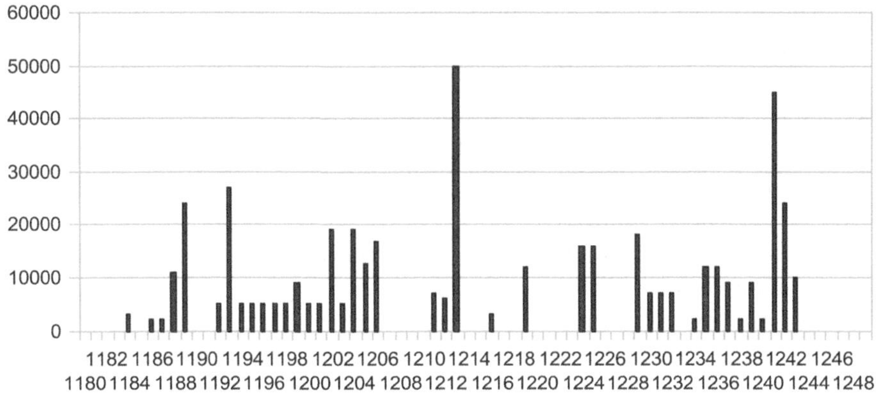

Figure 7.1 Suggested value of coin exports 1180–1250 in £ sterling, year beginning 29 September.

Source: P. Latimer, 'The Quantity of Money in England 1180–1247: A Model', *JEEH*, 32, 2004, table 5, 651.

the wealthiest 100 abbeys, priories, bishoprics and their dependents £19,200, or 26 per cent of the whole; and 170 tenants-in-chief and their men £35,400, or 49 per cent of the whole. Kings alienate lands to buy political support, lay barons come and go, but the church militant here on earth is or was a perpetual institution, at least until the English Reformation, and maintained and increased its share of landed wealth until the third decade of the sixteenth century.[6]

That wealth was unevenly spread. A rich see like Canterbury had an income of £1,750 per annum (and the expenses to go with it), Winchester £1,000, Glastonbury Abbey £840, Ely £790, whilst the bishopric of Selsey/Chichester was valued at only £138.[7] Given the dearth of evidence in the twelfth century, it is difficult to state with any accuracy how the church mobilised its wealth from the land, how much of its income was in labour or in kind, how much money it drew directly from its resources and, if in money, what it did with it. Monastic chroniclers complained loudly about assaults on its wealth in the reigns of William II and Henry I, in the sense of the crown's exercise of its regalian rights over vacant sees and some abbeys, with some justification.[8] Kings did prefer cash to kind, however, and during episcopal and other vacancies this

[6] E. Miller and J. Hatcher, *Medieval England: Rural Society and Economic Change, 1066–1348* (Harlow, 1978), pp. 15–16; for the redistribution of estates see R. J. Faith, *The English Peasantry and the Growth of Lordship* (London, 1997), pp. 178–80.

[7] Miller and Hatcher, *Medieval England*, p. 16.

[8] F. Barlow, *William Rufus* (London, 1983), pp. 181–2; J. A. Green, *The Government of England under Henry I* (Cambridge, 1989), pp. 79–80; C. W. Hollister, *Henry I* (New Haven and London, 2001), pp. 386–90.

may have been hard to find, as will be seen. The church contributed greatly to the First Crusade, according to Tyerman, and to the Second, although here the English contribution went mainly towards the fleet that sacked Lisbon and possibly brought some commercial benefits with it and not towards the much more expensive campaign in the Holy Land for the recovery of the county of Edessa.[9] Everyone in England paid for the Third Crusade and for Richard I's ransom, as Figure 7.1 shows.

Curiously, paying towards the Crusade and the ransom did not drain as much money from England as John's futile campaign in 1214 or Henry III's useless Poitevin campaign in 1242, but by the mid-thirteenth century, with more coin in circulation, shipping a million silver pennies overseas did not have the deflationary consequences that it did in the twelfth century. On the other hand, papal demands on the English church, which could only be paid in cash, were moderate in the twelfth century; Peter's Pence and the census of exempt and protected monasteries did not amount to much, according to Lunt, and direct papal taxation was in its infancy. The civil war during Stephen's reign (1135–54) bore heavily on the church in the south and south-west of England, but its costs in monetary terms cannot be estimated, and the same is true of the consequences of the rebellion of the young king in 1173–74. At the same time, the lure of glorifying God by building and rebuilding in a new architectural style, Gothic, could not be resisted. It was first employed at Roche Abbey, near Maltby (Yorks., WR), from 1147 onwards and then at Canterbury Cathedral, after the destruction of its entire eastern end by fire in 1174. This set in train another great rebuilding across the country, with the new Cistercian orders being the missionaries for the Gothic style in the north. Nor was its use confined to cathedrals and abbeys. It is also to be found in parish churches at Seaton (Leicestershire), Barton-upon-Humber (Lincolnshire), at Youlgreave (Derbyshire), thanks to the patronage of William de Ferrers, fourth earl of Derby (d. 1247) and at Bishop Henry of Blois' last great foundation, St Cross Hospital, Winchester.[10]

Yet even these great rebuildings pale in comparison with the sheer scale of new monastic foundations in twelfth-century England. Medieval monasticism underwent constant waves of reform and renewal. In late Anglo-Saxon England there were 43 houses of Benedictine monks in England and nine Benedictine nunneries, with none of them north of the River Trent.[11] By 1100, this total had reached 84, there having been 32 new foundations after the Conquest, nearly

---

[9] C. J. Tyerman, *England and the Crusades 1095–1588* (Chicago, 1988), pp. 32–3; J. L. Bolton, *Money in the Medieval English Economy 973–1489* (Manchester, 2012), pp. 102–3, 145–52; W. E. Lunt, *Financial Relations of the Papacy with England to 1327* (Cambridge, Mass., 1939), pp. 1–84, 175–6, 240–42, 534–9.

[10] Platt, *Architecture of Medieval Britain*, pp. 59, 61–2.

[11] Burton, *Monastic and Religious Orders*, map 1, p. 6.

all of them influenced by the reformed Benedictine monasticism of Cluny. In 1209 there were 621 monastic houses in England, a more than sevenfold increase which was entirely the result of the arrival of the new orders in England after 1100. The first to arrive were the Augustinians who did not follow the Benedictine rule, but that attributed to St Augustine of Hippo (354–430). Like monks, the canons led a common life according to a timetable but were able to engage with the wider world. They preached, taught, cared for the sick and administered the sacrament according to a rule that emphasised the importance of chastity, obedience and individual poverty. The communities they established served cathedrals, collegiate churches and hospitals, and Augustinian houses were to become the most numerous in the country. Once again, it was royal patronage that helped them expand so rapidly, and particularly that of Matilda, the first wife of Henry I and daughter of St Margaret of Scotland. Her foundation at Holy Trinity, Aldgate (London, c. 1108) acted as a spur to the creation of new communities, particularly in urban settings where the canons could care for the sick and the poor. From then on, successively, other new orders swept into Britain. Most notable among them were, of course, the Cistercians; the Gilbertines, the only English order, who followed the rule of St Gilbert of Sempringham; the Premonstratensians; the Carthusians; and, often overlooked, the crusading monks of the Orders of The Temple and of St John of Jerusalem (Hospitallers), who held substantial estates in the British Isles.[12]

[12] Burton, *Monastic and Religious Orders*, pp. 43–84; Bartlett, *England under the Norman and Angevin Kings*, pp. 417–21, 427–41; some idea of the extent and value of the Templars' lands in England in 1185–95 can be had from B. A. Lees (ed.), *Records of the Templars in England in the Twelfth Century. The Inquest of 1185 with Illustrative Charters and Documents*, Records of the Social and Economic History of England and Wales, IX (Oxford, 1935). For general histories of the military orders see: H. Nicholson, *The Knights Templar: A New History* (Stroud, 2001); M. Barber, *The New Knighthood. A History of the Order of the Temple* (Cambridge, 1994); H. Nicholson, *The Knights Hospitaller* (Woodbridge, 2001); J. Riley-Smith, *The History of the Order of St John* (London, 1999).

Table 7.2 The new orders in twelfth-century England.

Order	Date of first known foundation
Cluniac	1077
Augustinian canons	c. 1100
Tironensian	c. 1120
Canons of the Holy Sepulchre	c. 1120
Savigniac	1124
Cistercian	1128
Knights Templar	1128
Gilbertine	c. 1131
Arronaisian	1133
Victorine	c. 1133
Premonstratensian	1143
Knights Hospitaller	c. 1144
Fontevrault	c. 1154
Carthusian	1178–79
Grandmont	c. 1204

Source: R. Bartlett, *England under the Norman and Angevin Kings: 1075–1225* (Oxford, 2002), table 8, p. 418.

Thanks to the work of the English Monastic Archives Database project at University College London, it is now possible to establish the rate of foundation of these new houses in England over the twelfth century and into the first decade of the thirteenth. Figure 7.2 shows the number of houses in 1000; then the number founded between 1000 and 1100 (almost all of them post-Conquest); and then the number of foundations, by decade, to 1209. Figure 7.3 expresses the numbers slightly differently to show cumulative increase by decade to 1209.[13]

Expansion began in the first decade of the twelfth century, when 43 new houses were added, with 23 between 1110 and 1119, another 40 between 1120 and 1129, and then 77, 65, and 85, respectively, in the next three decades, at a time of disputed succession and civil war when one might least have expected it. The rate of foundation then slowed down but the scale of the increase can be seen quite clearly in Figure 7.3 by comparing the first and last entries on the bar graph. The English Monastic Archives Database also makes it possible to pinpoint the geographic areas of growth. Lincolnshire heads the list, followed by Norfolk and Suffolk, and Yorkshire, North and West Ridings, with Cumbria and Cheshire at the bottom. In purely numerical terms, Augustinian foundations were the

[13] The project was directed by Professor D. D'Avray, assisted by Drs M. Jurkowski, N. Ramsay and S. Renton. The database can be found at http://www.ucl.ac.uk/englishmonasticarchives/.

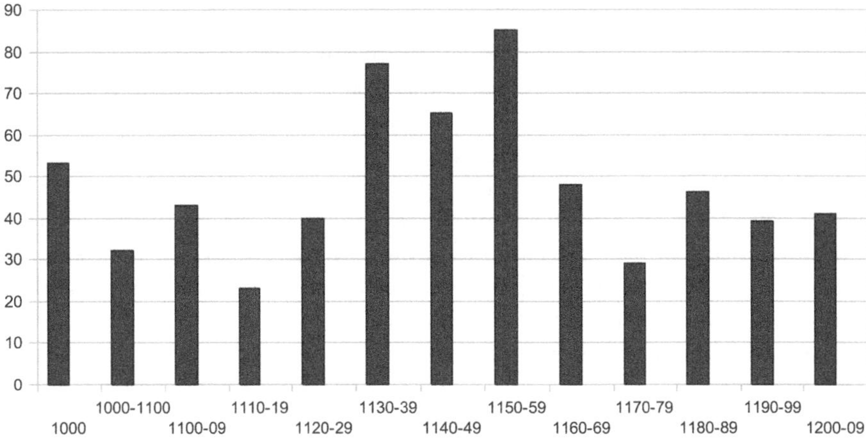

Figure 7.2 Number of monastic foundations in 1000 and 1100 and then new foundations by decade to 1209.

Source: English Monastic Archives Database, University College London.

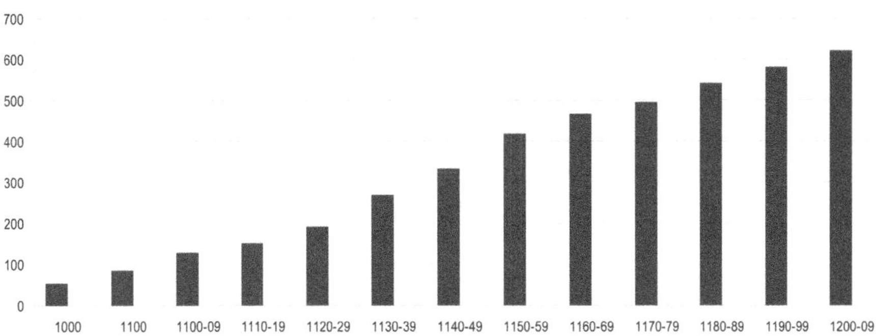

Figure 7.3 Monastic foundations 1000 to 1209: cumulative growth.

Source: English Monastic Archives Database, University College London.

most important since, as R. W. Southern remarked, it took little in the way of resources to establish a small house with a few canons. In terms of stimulating economic development and the use of money, however, the Cistercian houses in North Midland and Northern England probably had the most impact.[14]

[14] R. W. Southern, *Western Society and the Church in the Middle Ages* (Harmondsworth, 1970), p. 245; R. A. Donkin, 'The Cistercian Order and the Settlement of Northern England', *Geographical Review*, 59 (1969): 403–16; J. E. Burton, *The Monastic Orders in Yorkshire,*

The political, religious and social consequences of this century of new monastic foundations are beyond the scope of this chapter which will now focus on the economic implications. The church, after all, lived in the real as well as the spiritual world. Giles Gasper and Svein H. Gullbekk have persuasively argued that Anselm of Bec, Archbishop of Canterbury 1093–1109, was well-versed in the use of money, for making charitable gifts, for his travelling and living expenses in exile, in the administration of the Canterbury estates and of the ecclesiastical mint in the city, and in his moral teachings, where he saw that it could be used to achieve good in the name of God.[15] The difficulty is that there was so little by way of coin in circulation that could be devoted to these ends or towards the foundation of new monastic houses. Recent numismatic research, and principally that undertaken by Dr Martin Allen of the Fitzwilliam Museum, Cambridge, has provided us with a much better idea of the size of the circulating medium in England in the eleventh, twelfth and early thirteenth centuries than we have previously had. He describes the methods used to make the estimates given in Table 7.3, below, in his most recent book, *Money and Mints in Medieval England*. Although some of these estimates have been criticised as being so low as to make it difficult to see how the economy could have functioned at anything beyond a subsistence level, nevertheless, they have been accepted as broadly valid here.[16] In Table 7.3, both his high and low estimates for the size of the circulating medium between 973 and 1205 are given, and the coinage per head of population has been calculated, again using both high and low estimates for the size of the English population. If, for example, the value of the circulating medium was £10,000 or 2,400,00 silver pennies, the only coins in circulation, and the population was 1.5 million, then there would be 1.6d per head. If, however, the value of the circulating medium was £25,000, the upper limit of Allen's estimates, and the population 1.5 million, then there would be 4d per head. Changing the variables in this way produces a range of coinage per head of population between 1.06d and 4d, as shown in column four. The same methodology has been used throughout and the full ranges of estimates expressed in Table 7.3.

1069–1215 (Cambridge, 1999), pp. 98–124, 244–73; J. E. Burton, 'The Cistercians in England' in J. Burton and J. Kerr (eds), *The Cistercians in the Middle Ages* (Woodbridge, 2011), pp. 149–88.

[15] Giles E. M. Gasper and Svein H. Gulbekk, 'Money and its Use in the Thought and Experience of Anselm of Bec, Archbishop of Canterbury (1093–1109)', *Journal of Medieval History*, 38 (2012): 155–82, at 160.

[16] M. Allen, *Money and Mints in Medieval England* (Cambridge, 2012), pp. 318–24; J. L. Bolton, *Money in the Medieval English Economy, 973–1489* (Manchester, 2012), tables 2.1 and 2.2, pp. 25–6.

Table 7.3 Coinage and coinage per head, 973–1205.

Dates	Amount of coin in circulation in £	Range of population estimates in millions	Range of coin per head in pence
973–1016	25,000–30,000	1.5–2	3d–4.8d
1016–1042	15,000–30,000	1.5–2	1.8d–3.6d
1042–1066	20,000–50,000	1.5–2	2.4d–8d
1066–1135	10,000–25,000	1.5–2.25	1.06d–4d
1135–1158	20,000–50,000	1.5–2.5	1.92d–8d
1180	100,000	2.0–3.0	8d–12d
1205a	100,000	2.0–3.0	8d–12d
1205b	250,000	2.0–3.0	20d–30d
1205c	300,000	2.0–3.0	24d–36d

Source: M. Allen, *Mints and Money in Medieval England* (Cambridge, 2012), table 10.12, p. 344.

There are, and there should be, many objections to this crude method of calculating coinage per head in an age when inequality in the distribution of wealth was the norm, but it does provide us with a basic guide to changes in the amount of money available for general use between 973 and 1205. The first steep rise comes between the recoinages of 1158 and 1180, followed by a second between 1180 and 1205, as more and more silver flowed into England from the new mines in Saxony. If coinage per head stood at between 1.06d and 4d between 1066 and 1135, then, by the time of partial recoinage of 1205 it was somewhere between 8d and 36d, but most likely between 20d and 30d. What this shows us is that until its last two decades, twelfth-century England was a cash-starved economy. If we return to Figures 7.2 and 7.3, however, then what we see is that the rate of monastic foundations was at its height precisely when the money supply was at its lowest, between 1066 and 1158, with the peak coming between 1130 and 1159, during years of disputed succession.[17]

The motives behind ecclesiastical patronage have already been discussed and they were no different in the twelfth century than they had been in the eleventh, at the time of the first rebuilding. During Stephen's reign, and notably from 1139 when the Empress Matilda made her own bid for the throne, to the death of Stephen's son and heir Eustace in 1153, the desire to save one's soul and expiate sins may have been stronger than at other times, but perhaps no more so than during the rebellion of the Young King in 1173–74 or the many crises

[17] The reign of King Stephen, 1135–54, is the subject of an extensive literature. The most recent biography of the king is E. King, *King Stephen* (New Haven and London, 2011); on the coinage, see Mark Blackburn, 'Coinage and Currency', in E. King (ed.), *The Anarchy of Stephen's Reign* (Oxford, 1994), pp. 145–205 and Allen, *Mints and Money*, pp. 34–8.

of John's reign, although there was no upsurge in new foundations in either of these periods. It must also be remembered that patronage was not simply a matter of a once-and-for-all donation. The founder or founders of new houses, and their successors, also acquired responsibilities that could be burdensome. Further gifts would be expected and patrons were often called on to provide protection against the encroachments of lay and spiritual rivals, even to the extent of providing defence against physical attacks.[18]

What is beyond doubt, however, is the substantial transfer of land and the income from land from the laity to the church, along with the increasing appropriation of revenues from parishes that were granted to the new orders, and in particular the Augustinians. Some of the new foundations were given extensive lands and rights over lands, which made them comparatively wealthy, whilst others could barely support the few monks or nuns who served in them. Although the evidence drawn from the *Taxatio Ecclesiastica* of 1291 and from the *Valor Ecclesiasticus*, drawn up in 1535 at the time of the dissolution of the monasteries, is imperfect, both give a broad idea of the income of the new houses. The *Taxatio Ecclesiastica* shows 325 churches appropriated to 120 houses of Augustinian canons, besides those where they remained as patrons. Appropriation meant that the house would take all the revenues from the parish church, from the glebe land, the offerings of the parishioners, the tithes and other dues such as mortuary fees. At Cirencester (Gloucestershire), this brought £28 13s 4d to the Augustinian canons of the priory there in 1291, whilst at Leicester the abbey received £8 from the appropriated parish church of St Mary de Castro in the borough. When Newnham Priory (Augustinian, Bedford) was re-founded just outside the borough in 1166 by Simon de Beauchamp, son of Payn, the estates of the pre-existing secular canons were transferred to the new house, along with the tithes of 14 churches in Bedfordshire; the revenues from all the founder's markets, assarts (newly cleared lands) and woods; the castle mill in Bedford and another mill, with lands and water attached; and the free use of the waters belonging to Bedford Castle. The priory's income in 1291 was £164 10s 8d, and of this no less than £92 6s 8d came from spiritualities.[19]

Newnham Priory was probably the Augustinian exception in terms of endowment, rather than the rule, at least in terms of its income. Some of the smaller houses, and especially those for women, had few resources and correspondingly low revenues. The Augustinian priory at Breedon-on-the-Hill (Leicestershire) was a cell of St Oswald's Priory at Nostell (Yorks, NR), founded

[18] Burton, *Monastic and Religious Orders*, pp. 215–24.

[19] Burton, *Monastic and Religious Orders*, p. 246; *Taxatio Ecclesiastica Database*, Humanities Research Institute, University of Sheffield (http://www.hrionline.ac.uk/taxatio/), under Cirencester and Leicester; H. Doubleday (ed.), *The Victoria County History of Bedfordshire, vol. I* (London, 1900), pp. 377–81.

in 1122 by Robert de Ferrers on the site of an old Anglo-Saxon monastery. He gave it the parish church at Breedon and little else so that by 1535 its income was only £24 10s 4d. Even worse off was the priory of Cistercian nuns at Esholt (Yorks., ER), founded by the gift of Esholt to the prioress and nuns of Sinningthwaite (Burton-in-Ainsty, Yorks., NR) by Simon and Maud Ward and their son William not later than 1172. At the time of the *Valor Ecclesiasticus* in 1535 its income was £19 0s 8d gross and £13 5s 4d net, with nothing at all from spiritualities, a sum that can scarcely have kept the small community of 11 nuns in comfort.[20]

There are, of course, inevitable dangers in looking backwards at what was happening in the twelfth century from the standpoints of 1291 and 1535. Both the amount of coin in circulation and its purchasing power had changed radically between 1100 and 1300 and then again between 1300 and 1500. Like is not being compared with like, economically, and no allowance is being made for the church's increasing share of national wealth in the late Middle Ages. The new Orders of Friars had to be endowed in the thirteenth century and grants of lands and revenues to the older monastic houses continued, whatever the statute of Mortmain of 1279 may have said.[21] What cannot be in doubt, however, is that the late eleventh and twelfth centuries saw one of the most significant shifts of wealth to the English church in the Middle Ages. Cathedrals, churches and monasteries were built and rebuilt. Significant sums were spent on their adornment and on sustaining the communities that served foundations old and new. Yet all this was done at a time when the money supply was at its lowest medieval level (1066–1135), with no significant rise in the size of the circulating medium until the 1180s, when the rate of new foundations was beginning to decline.[22]

Even allowing for the fact that many of these foundations were small, the aggregate level of church wealth rose in the twelfth century, a matter to which we shall return. Estimating how much was spent on building is nigh impossible, given the lack of accounts, but it must have been expensive and many payments would have had to be made in cash. Unskilled labour probably came from the locality and could, perhaps, have been paid in kind. Skilled workers, master masons and masons, were both scarce and itinerant and would have expected both regular money wages and payment in kind, and/or a grant of land and the revenues from it, to sustain themselves and their families.[23] Stone had to be

20 *Taxatio Ecclesiastica* sub Breedon-on-the-Hill; *Monastic Archives Database* under Esholt; W. Page (ed.), *The Victoria County History of the County of York, vol. III* (London, 1913), pp. 161–3.

21 See below, pp. 134 and 136.

22 See above, pp. 128–9.

23 Salzman, *Building in England*, p. 68; D. Knoop and G. P. Jones, *The Medieval Mason* (Manchester, 1967), p. 96.

acquired from local quarries, which might be on the lands of the house or its founder, but for more prestigious buildings it came from Caen in Normandy or Barnack in Northamptonshire. Wood was used extensively, for scaffolding and, of course, for the beams that supported roofs great and small. Transporting stone and timber by sea, river or road was expensive, although in some cases peasant carrying services may have been used, as they were for transporting manorial produce to market.[24] There were wall paintings to be commissioned, images of Christ, the Virgin and the saints to be purchased and screens and choir stalls to be erected, all of which, presumably, required some level of payment in cash.[25] Money spent in this way did not vanish into thin air, of course. It passed into general circulation and such spending may have increased the velocity of circulation, which Mayhew argues is a sign of how a cash-poor society copes with the shortage of coin.[26] It has also been argued that the twelfth century saw the wholesale leasing of ecclesiastical demesnes at money rents, accompanied by the commutation of labour services, again for cash. This phenomenon has been explained by the depressed nature of the mid-twelfth-century market, but a more likely explanation may be that it raised the money necessary to fund grandiose ambitions. These do need to be put into perspective, however. In most cases the costs, be they for endowment or building, would have been spread over many years, making them more manageable at a time when coin was in short supply.[27]

Nevertheless, behind this extraordinary story of religious fervour there does lie a much deeper problem. The wholesale alienation of land, and the rights over land to the church, in perpetuity, was creating considerable tensions in lay society, which eventually resulted in the Mortmain legislation of the thirteenth century. The statute of 1279 was not a quick response to an emerging problem. As Raban has shown, it came as the climax to decades of anxiety expressed by vocal landlords. Lay agitation over the disadvantages of Mortmain tenure had become evident by the late twelfth century. A Wells charter granted between 1174 and 1180 stated that the holder of a burgage tenement there was free

---

[24] Salzman, *Building in England*, pp. 119, 263–4; Ref to W. J. Blair and N. L. Ramsay, *English Medieval Industries: Craftsmen, Techniques, Products* (Hambledon, 1991); Lees, *Records of the Templars in England*, pp. lxxx–lxxxi, 1–2.

[25] For Gervase of Canterbury's account of the rebuilding of Canterbury Cathedral after 1174, and its adornment, see Salzman, *Building in England*, pp. 369–75.

[26] N. J. Mayhew, 'Modelling Medieval Monetisation' in R. H. Britnell and B. M. S. Campbell (eds), *A Commercialisng Economy: England 1085 to 1300* (Manchester, 1995), pp. 55–77; N. J. Mayhew, Presidential Addresses to the Royal Numismatic Society on 'The Quantity Theory of Money': 1, 'The Money Supply' *Numismatic Chronicle*, 170 (2010): 525–31; 2, 'Prices', *Numismatic Chronicle*, 171 (2011): 519–24; 3, 'Velocity', *Numismatic Chronicle*, 172 (2012): 397–403.

[27] Bolton, *Money in the Medieval English Economy*, pp. 14–15; for the leasing of estates in the twelfth century, see below, pp. 136–7 and fn. 34.

to mortgage it or give it according to the will of his own disposition, except to religious houses. It became common for private charters of the first half of the thirteenth century to contain clauses stipulating that the land or premises should not in future be alienated to either the church or the Jews, although, as Brand argues, the law at the time did not necessarily respect such restrictions.[28] The increasing concern of lords about the loss of rights over lands held in fee by their tenants and alienated to the church is shown by two clauses added to the second reissue of Magna Carta in 1217. Clause 39 stated that no man was to alienate so large a portion of his tenement that he would be unable to perform the services due from the tenement as a whole from that part of it which he had retained and Clause 43 enacted that in future no man was to alienate land to a religious house on condition that the religious house would grant it back to him, a practice that meant the religious house would enjoy, in perpetuity, the valuable incremental rights arising out of the tenancy.[29]

The law, then as now, focuses on rights, obligations and duties. It offers non-violent means of settling disputes, but such disputes often result from wider changes in society, and that was surely the case here. The loss of income from feudal rights of wardship, relief and marriage was significant, as was the social control over the sub-tenant that went with them, and these were matters that could, ostensibly, be remedied by changes in the law. The movement of land and income from the laity to the church could not, at least, not until the Reformation of the sixteenth century, far into the future, and beyond the realms of anyone's vision in the twelfth and thirteenth centuries, be reversed. No accurate comparisons of the wealth of the church in 1100, 1200 and 1300 can be made, for reasons already explained. In his study of the evidence from the 12 counties covered by the Hundred Roll survey of 1279–80, Kosminsky estimated that it was a third of the whole, which does not seem to be a massive increase compared with the 26 per cent of 1086. Campbell, in his comparative benchmarking of the English, Irish, Scottish and Welsh economies in 1290, gives a figure of £128,372 for the wealth of the English church, excluding tithes, but no figures for lay wealth for comparison.[30] Both may be conservative underestimates, given the continual protests against alienation of land to the church, but we should be equally careful about these. Landlords are always a noisy pressure group and some of the endowment and building costs could be met by the church from

---

28 S. Raban, *Mortmain Legislation and the English Church, 1279–1500* (Cambridge, 1982), pp. 12–13; P. A. Brand, 'The Control of Mortmain Alienation in England, 1200–1300', in J. H. Baker (ed.), *Legal Records and the Historian* (London, 1978), pp. 29–34.

29 Brand, 'Control of Mortmain Alienation', pp. 31–2.

30 E. A. Kosminsky, *Studies in the Agrarian History of England in the Thirteenth Century* (Oxford, 1956), p. 109; B. M. S. Campbell, 'Benchmarking Medieval Economic Development: England, Wales, Scotland, and Ireland, c. 1290', *Economic History Review*, 2nd series, 61 (2008): 901, table 2.

within its own resources. The endowment of new houses was partially achieved by internal transfers, in the sense that lands and revenues could be taken by the laity from one house and given to another. Where parishes were appropriated to provide income for new Augustinian or other foundations, their revenues were essentially being diverted to an alternative recipient within the same organisation, as it were. Appropriations may have had dire consequences for the cure of souls and the religious life of the parish general, but fiscally, in relation to the general wealth of the church, they were neutral. This is also true when one religious house endowed 'sister' houses and granted lands or income to them from their own estates. It was the transfer of wealth in land and over land from all ranks of the laity above the peasantry to the church, in perpetuity, that caused the tensions in society that were only partly eased by the statute of Mortmain.[31]

What were the consequences for an agrarian society with a very limited money supply? Here we begin to enter the realms of speculation by asking questions to which there are not, as yet, entirely satisfactory answers. Lack of coin holds back economic expansion since it makes buying and selling more difficult. In the twelfth century a disproportionate share of the national wealth was being spent on unproductive investment in the economic if not in the religious sense. As has been said, the money that was spent on building did not disappear into thin air but all that this heavy expenditure ultimately achieved was an increase in the velocity of circulation that offered no solution to the underlying problem of an inadequate money supply. This is, of course, something of a counterfactual argument and we cannot know whether investment in rebuilding, new building and the endowment of new houses would have been better employed in other sections of the economy or frittered away in conspicuous consumption by the nobility or foreign wars by the crown. Yet the diversion of wealth to the church may have held back economic expansion and the commercialisation of society.[32] When contemporaries referred to 'the dead hand' of the church, Mortmain, they may well have had an economic point.

This leads to the second question: was the church more efficient or, perhaps, more effective at raising a cash income from its estates and from its rights over new towns, markets and fairs, the implications being that ecclesiastics were harsh landlords? Twelfth-century estate management is a matter of some debate. Was it organised principally to provide food for the household, lay or ecclesiastical, or did landlords try to cope with difficult economic times by leasing out their manorial demesnes for money rents and at the same time commuting peasant labour services for cash payments? The evidence is limited and the conclusions

---

31 The church also bought extensively on the land market and for this see Raban, *Mortmain Legislation*, pp. 130–52; Brand, 'Control of Mortmain alienation', pp. 36–8.

32 These issues are fully discussed in Bolton, *Money in the Medieval English Economy*, chs 4 and 5, pp. 87–135.

drawn from it mixed. Comprehensive surveys that allow management practices to be compared over time exist for only 13 non-royal estates. Some of them show evidence of coherent 'policies' aimed at maximising cash revenues by leasing out demesnes whilst at the same time maintaining or increasing their capital assets, their leasable values and, by implication their profitability, at a time when rising population was increasing the demand for land. Rosamond Faith argues that these were the practices adopted by the managers of the estates of St Paul's cathedral, London, but therein lies the problem, because they were mostly located around the city and the pull of its market would have offered opportunities for profit to potential lessees. The Templars certainly managed their lands for one purpose only, to produce cash revenues to be sent to the Middle East to finance their continual wars against the rising power of Islam.[33] These two estate groups may well be atypical of the rest, and elsewhere Faith has described most ecclesiastical landlords as backward, relying on leasing which had been the customary practice since the eighth century.[34] This hardly seems a fair general judgment. Churchmen lived in the real world. They were deeply involved in the government of the realm at the centre, where rapid advances in accounting (as shown in the pipe roll of 1129) as opposed to listing, which was the main aim of the Domesday surveys, ensured that the crown received all the revenues due to it. What could be done for royal income, with kings much preferring cash to kind, could also be done on their own estates. There is no proof that they did adopt such accounting methods before the first surviving pipe roll of 1208–09 for the Winchester estates. That shows the wholesale adoption of Exchequer practices on the bishop's estates and we should be wary of thinking that others had not followed his example. If what churchmen and laymen required was steady cash income to finance their ambitions, then leasing their estates for money rents was probably the best way of raising it, and not a counsel of despair.[35]

---

[33] P. D. A. Harvey, 'The Manorial Reeve in Twelfth-Century England', in R. Evans (ed.), *Lordship and Learning. Studies in Memory of Trevor Aston* (Woodbridge, 2004), p. 127 and n. 16; R. J. Faith, 'Demesne Resources and Labour Rent on the Manors of St Paul's Cathedral, 1066–1222', *Economic History Review*, 2nd series, 47 (1994): 657; Barber, *The New Knighthood*, p. 243 and chapter 7, *passim*.

[34] R. J. Faith, *The English Peasantry*, pp. 180–93, at p. 186.

[35] The collection of essays edited by R. Britnell, *The Winchester Pipe Rolls and Medieval English Society* (Woodbridge, 2003), admirably illustrates the importance of this source for economic and social historians; for estate management, E. Miller, 'England in the Twelfth and Thirteenth Centuries: An Economic Contrast', *Economic History Review*, 2nd series, 24 (1971): 1–14; C. G. Reed and T. L. Anderson, 'English Agricultural Organisation in the Twelfth and Thirteenth Centuries' *Economic History Review*, 2nd series, 26 (1973): 134–7; E. Miller and J. Hatcher, *Medieval England. Rural Society and Economic Change 1086–1348*, pp. 204–13.

Nor were the regular and secular clergy reluctant to borrow, possibly at interest, either for spending or for paying overdue bills. The church's teaching on usury had been refined over many centuries but the growing use of money in the eleventh and twelfth centuries led to a forcible restatement of its views. So, canon 13 of the Second Lateran Council of 1139 condemned the detestable, disgraceful and insatiable rapacity of usurers, which had been outlawed by divine and human law in the Old and New Testaments. Usury was openly condemned again at the Council of Tours in 1163 and by canon 25 of the Third Lateran Council of 1179, whilst Gratian produced the standard definitions of the practice in his mid-twelfth-century *Decretum*. Lending in the expectation of receiving back more than had been given in the loan was sinful and whatsoever exceeded the principal was usury.[36]

There is a considerable amount of evidence that the church, at least at its highest levels, cathedrals, monasteries and priories and even individual churchmen, borrowed money on quite a large scale from both Christian and Jewish moneylenders, however, whatever the teaching on usury may have been. Mavis Mate's article on the indebtedness of Canterbury Cathedral Priory in the early thirteenth century suggests that the house borrowed extensively to meet the exceptional circumstances of its dealings with Rome, where it had to employ expensive Italian agents at the papal curia. For a loan of 420 marks (£280) from Roman and Sienese merchants in 1220, the monks had to pay 117 ½ marks (£78 6s 8d) interest, and in 1240 a loan of £20 cost the house £2 13s 4d in interest over a year. Circumstances had also changed, since between 1200 and 1250 there had been a substantial increase in the money supply and in liquidity generally, and the Priory was able to borrow extensively from its lay and ecclesiastical neighbours. In fact, there was nothing at all new in this, since borrowing by monastic houses and others was also commonplace in the twelfth century. The abbot of St Augustine's, Canterbury, owed William Cade, the Flemish financier, £100 in 1166, and Richard of Ilchester, Archdeacon of Poitiers and future baron of the Exchequer and bishop of Winchester, £20. Debts to Aaron of Lincoln seized by the Crown in 1191–92 are equally interesting: the Prior of Bullington, founded as a double Gilbertine house in 1148, owed him £304; the Prior and Convent of Belvoir, then in Leicestershire, and a cell of St Alban's abbey, £172; Hamelin the Archdeacon £117 6s 8d; Baldwin, archbishop of Canterbury, £66 13s 4d; and the Cluniac Priory of Prittlewell, Essex, £15 13s 4d.[37] In all this

---

36 The best introduction to this complex subject is D. Wood, *Medieval Economic Thought* (Cambridge, 2002), pp. 159–205.

37 M. Mate, 'The Indebtedness of Canterbury Cathedral Priory 1215–1295', *Economic History Review*, 2nd series, 26 (1973): 183–97; H. Gray, 'Moneylending in Twelfth-Century England', unpubl. London PhD thesis (2007), appendices, pp. 233–315. This thesis replaces all previous published work on William Cade and Aaron of Lincoln; Bolton, *Money in the Medieval English Economy*, pp.196, 205.

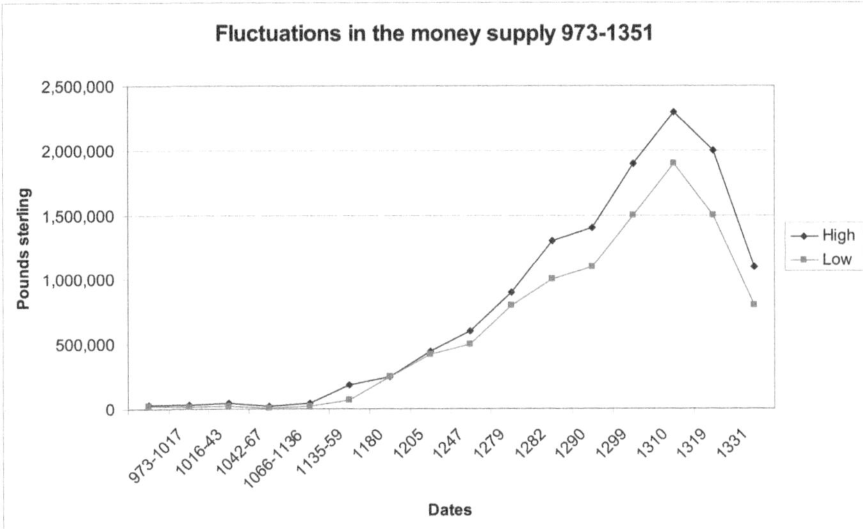

Figure 7.4 Fluctuations in the money supply, 973–1351.
Source: M. Allen, *Money and Mints in Medieval England* (Cambridge, 2012), pp. 318–24.

they were no different from their lay counterparts, the king, the baronage and especially the knightly class. In a cash-starved society, credit, that is, borrowing cash or goods and making deferred repayments when the money or the produce came in, probably after the harvest, was essential. The church had enormous assets. It could afford to borrow and the evidence suggests that it did so, but for purposes that remain unknown.

Speculation is easy but it is conjecture based on limited evidence, and such is the case here. It seems reasonable to assume, however, that the twelfth century saw a significant increase in the church's share of landed wealth and the revenues from it. Coincidentally, the century also saw a literally huge increase in the number of monastic foundations, as the new orders swept into England, and the rebuilding of older houses and cathedrals, all against the background of a very limited money supply, as Figure 7.4 shows.

How was this all accomplished? Costs were spread over long periods, but it is arguable that the church would still have had to extract the most that it could from the lessees and unfree tenants on its estates and borrowed heavily to meet the bill. Its economic activities in estate management, building and town foundation would have made the use of money more common, especially in remoter areas of England, and that in itself was an important step forward towards what was not yet a money-economy. Yet the puzzle remains: how was so much achieved at a time when coin was so scarce? There is, so far, no completely satisfactory answer to that question.

Chapter 8

The Church and Monetisation in Early Medieval Denmark, c. 1060–1160

Bjørn Poulsen

In twelfth-century Denmark it was apparently still inappropriate for a church institution to receive money gifts from merchants. One of the earliest Danish examples of the attitude of the Danish church towards trading communities is a charter from 1161, in which King Valdemar I (r. 1157–82) promised that merchants were allowed to donate gifts to the Premonstratensian monastery of Tommerup (now Tommarp) in Scania 'for the alleviation of their crimes [pro suorum alleuiacione criminum]'.[1] The charter assumes that merchants' capital had been earned dishonestly and that such capital, in principle, should be left untouched. While the church clearly turned itself against avarice, money was vital for its activities. It can be argued that it was the duties demanded, generosity promoted, and values connected to money inculcated by the church which underpinned important aspects of monetisation in this period.[2] Ecclesiastical attitudes were not inimical towards money *per se*, as illustrated by a charter from c. 1160 in which the Danish king negotiates with the Cistercian monks from Esrum and gives land to them in the very room of the mint master Gerhard, 'in stuba Gerardi monetarii'.[3] The presence of coins and mint masters was evidently no problem in itself to churchmen.

1 *Diplomatarium Danicum*, series 1, vol. 2, (Copenhagen, 1938ff), no. 143: 'si eciam mercatorum pro suorum alleuiacione criminum de suis bonis eisdem siue sani morituri aliaqua concesserint ratum ducimus et ne ab aliquot impediantur prohibemus'.

2 Walter Taeuber, *Geld und Kredit im Mittelalter* (Berlin, 1933). Alexander Murray, *Reason and Society in the Middle Ages* (Oxford, 1978). For an earlier period see the arguments advanced in Bettina Emmerich, *Geiz und Gerechtigkeit. Ökonomisches Denken im frühen Mittelalter*, Vierteljahrschrift für Sozial- und Wirtschaftsgeschichte, Beihefte, 168 (Stuttgart, 2004).

3 *Diplomatarium Danicum*, series 1, vol. 2, no. 130.

Denmark in the Late Eleventh Century

The role of the church in the early monetisation of Denmark, from c. 1060 to c. 1160, forms the basic subject for the current discussion. Particular attention will be applied to the role of dioceses in this process, but material from some of the larger monasteries will also be considered.

The late eleventh century has been portrayed as a period of growth across western Christendom. In the words of Georges Duby: 'In the last three decades of the eleventh century we may discern the opening of a fresh phase in European economic history: that of a broad, sustained and rapid development'.[4] This is pre-eminently the case for Denmark. The period from the mid- to late eleventh century was undoubtedly one of intensified trade networks and relationships, especially within urban contexts. This is clearly to be seen in a significant urban centre like Ribe where there is little sign of real town life in the century beforehand, but a great deal afterwards.[5] Already by c. 1060 it would appear, as recently argued by Ingvardson, that the Danish economy was operating at a rather high level of monetisation.[6] A series of monetary developments can be identified before the middle years of the reign of King Sven Estridsen (r. 1047–74). The accumulation of large amounts of silver, through plunder, tribute (*danegeld*), and trade, constituted a necessary precondition for this phenomenon but just as important was the growing circulation of this silver. Coins were used increasingly and in fulfilment of their monetary function, not merely according to silver-value as it is mirrored in stray finds and the occurrence of coin finds with 240 pennies or fractions thereof.[7] Clearly coins were counted

---

[4] Georges Duby, *The Early Growth of the European Economy. Warriors and Peasants from the Seventh to Twelfth Century*, (trans.) Howard B. Clarke (London, 1974), p. 180.

[5] Claus Feveille and Morten Søvsø, 'Ribe genopstår', in Søren Bitsch Christensen (ed.), *Ribe Bys Historie*, vol. 1, 700–1520 (Ribe, 2010), p. 45. The recent finds of five Sven Estridsen pennies found as stray finds in the town of Varde, West Jutland, is also much revealing. Lars C. Bentsen, 'Udgravningerne ved Gl. Jacobi Skole', *Opdatering, Museet for Varde By og Omegns Årbog* (2008): 32–46. Compare also the development of Schleswig. Christian Radtke, 'Schleswig c. 1000–1250. System Theory Sketches for Profiling Urbanization', in Nils Engberg, Anne Nørgaard Jørgensen, Jakob Kieffer-Olsen, Per Kristian Madsen and Christian Radtke (eds), *Archaeology of Medieval Towns in the Baltic and North Sea Area* (Copenhagen, 2009), pp. 51–63.

[6] Gitte Tarnow Ingvardson. *Møntbrug. Fra vikingetid til vendertogter* (Aarhus, 2010). The relatively intensive Viking Age circulation has been stressed for some years: Jens Christian Moesgaard, 'Enkeltfundne mønter fra vikingetiden', in Gillian Fellows-Jensen and Niels Lund (eds), *Beretning fra attende tværfaglige vikingesymposium* (Aarhus,1999), pp. 17–34.

[7] D. M. Metcalf, 'Viking-Age Numismatics, 5, Denmark', *Numismatic Chronicle*, 159 (1999): 398. In the find from Hågerup (c. 1048) there are, amongst other groups of coins, 240 English pennies from 1035–40, making up exactly a mark in coin, and another treasure

according to the system 10 *penninge* = one *ørtug*, three *ørtug* = one *øre*, eight *øre* = one mark, and not weighed.

What was new after c. 1060 was, first, that the coinage used in Denmark was organised on a national scale, expressive of greater royal authority. Danish coins replaced foreign coins; Danish kings and the Danish state monopolised the production and circulation of coin. Second, and in parallel to this process, the church became an increasingly well-organised organisation.[8] The division of Denmark into eight dioceses in 1060 is important in this respect but a growing number of monasteries and parish churches constitute another indicator of a new consolidated vision for the church.[9] The strengthening of both king and church was mutually interdependent and the institutional change, no doubt, manifested itself also in the economic arena.

Securing Money from Town Taxes and Tributes

Danish cathedrals and the emerging monasteries were well endowed, and from an early point in their existence. It is indeed possible, as C. A. Christensen has pointed out, that the Roskilde bishops' large *bona temporalia* had its roots in the reign of King Cnut the Great (r. 1018–35).[10] In the case of Ribe, there is no reason to doubt that bishop Odinkar, who died in 1043, gave his paternal heritage to the diocese.[11] To maintain a chronological approach it is clearly documented that during the reign of Sven Estridsen the *bona spiritualia* of the chapter of Roskilde was founded with a gift of land corresponding to 50 *bol* (similar land units to the English hide), given by Estrid the Queen Mother, sister of King Cnut. Only a little later the bishop of Roskilde, Svein Nordmand,

find from Bonderup, dating from 1065–70, likewise, contains 240 *penninge*, both Danish and English. Jørgen Steen Jensen (ed.), *Danmarks middelalderlige skattefund fra c. 1050–c. 1550, Denmarks mediaeval treasure-hoards c. 1050–c. 1550* (Copenhagen, 1992), pp. 212, 220.

8 Jørgen Steen Jensen, 'Møntfornyelse (renovatio monetae) i Danmark indtil år 1200', *Nordisk Numismatisk Unions Medlemsblad*, 8 (1996): 130–36. Keld Grinder-Hansen, *Kongemagtens krise. Det danske møntvæsen 1241–1340*, (Copenhagen, 2000), pp. 53, 61–3. Svein H. Gullbekk, 'Myntforringelse i Danmark og innføring av monopolmynt under Sven Estridsen (1047–74)', *Nordisk Numismatisk Årsskrift, 1994–96* (2000): 111–29, and see also Gullbekk's contribution to the present volume.

9 Aksel E. Christensen, 'Tiden 1042–1241', in Aksel E. Christensen et al. (eds), *Danmarks historie*, vol. 1 (Copenhagen, 1977), p. 229.

10 C. A. Christensen, 'Roskildekirkens jordegods før år 1200. Fra skibengods til bispegods', *Historisk Tidsskrift*, 14, series 1 (1980): 30–39.

11 *Adam von Bremen. Hamburgische Kirchengeschichte*, Bernhard Schmeidler (ed.), 3rd edition (Hannover and Leipzig, 1917), p. 97: 'ex eius patrimonio narrent episcopatum Ripensem fundatum'.

made significant donations of land to the same church.[12] Before his death Sven Estridsen is also known to have given 2½ *bol* of land to the church in Lund.[13] Land was, as is well known, the economic foundation of medieval institutions.

A number of charters from 1085 onwards reveal, however, that landed wealth was not sufficient to support all of the activities of the church. These charters confirm that the donations they recorded consisted of a mixture of land and other financial sources. The first ever surviving Danish charter is dated 21 May 1085 and records that King Cnut the Holy (r. 1080–86) granted a large amount of land to the Church of St Lawrence at Lund (then part of the Danish Kingdom, since 1658 part of Sweden): 52 *bol* in Scania and Sjælland, as well as 27 marks in annual revenues from the towns of Lomma, Helsingborg and Lund.[14] It is clear from sources which postdate by only a few years this charter that the 27 marks were taken from the sum of money which town dwellers paid annually to the king and which bore the name of *midsommergæld*. This combination of land and an annual cash income, as the following examples make clear, is to be found repeatedly in other sources.

In 1133 the archbishop consecrated the crypt of the cathedral of Lund, and created several prebends which were supplied with land as well 'iii marce de debito ciuitatis et insule', 'three marks from the town taxes and from the tribute from the island of Bornholm'.[15] Later, in 1145, a subsequent archbishop gave donations to his church and created new prebends. Each of the new prebends was given land in addition to a portion of the town taxes and of the Bornholm tribute: 'tribus uidelicet de censu episcopali in Lunda, tribus de Burgundehulm insula [three marks of the bishop's town tax of Lund and three marks of Bornholm]'.[16] When the archbishop made his donations in 1145 also present were the king and an exiled bishop from the Danish border town of Schleswig. The Schleswig bishop had been driven out of his town by a rebellion but was now compensated by the king, receiving a large farm, a mill and 'De mitsumergelt meo in Lunda marcas x singulis annis', 'of my midsommergæld in Lund 10 marks annually'.[17] Moving to Odense, already in c. 1100 the cathedral of the town and its monastery had been given by the king land as well as 20 marks of town tax and 20 marks of a silver tribute paid from the Frisian island of Sylt on the Jutland

---

[12] *Chronicon Roskildense*, M. Cl. Gertz (ed.), *Scriptores Minores Historiæ Danicæ Medii Ævi*, vol. 1 (Copenhagen, 1917), p. 23: '*l mansos*'.

[13] Christensen, 'Tiden 1042–1241', p. 230. According to Saxo, writing around 1200, King Sven Estridsen gave half of the district of Støvnæs herred to the diocese of Roskilde. Saxo Grammaticus, *Gesta Danorum*, J. Olrik and H. Ræder (eds) (Copenhagen, 1931), 314.26.

[14] *Diplomatarium Danicum*, series 1, vol. 2, no. 21.

[15] *Diplomatarium Danicum*, series 1, vol. 1, no. 56.

[16] *Diplomatarium Danicum*, series 1, vol. 1, no. 88.

[17] *Diplomatarium Danicum*, series 1, vol. 1, no. 91.

west coast. The Benedictine monastery in Ringsted was reformed in 1135 by King Erik II 'Emune' (r. 1134–37), who donated to it more than five *bol* of land and 10 marks of the town tax of Ringsted: 'decem marcas ex eiusdem villæ censu, qui dicitur mit sommers gield'.[18]

Several observations can be made from these examples. Most relevant for the present topic, cash was evidently useful in the running of an ecclesiastical institution. It can be strongly argued that early land rent in Denmark seems to have been paid, to some extent, in silver or coin.[19] However, the cash flow from the landed possessions of the ecclesiastical institutions does not seem to have been sufficient to cover their expenses in money. Especially in the late eleventh and early twelfth century there is good evidence that land generated rents in kind and resources which were probably not easily marketable. In this period there were also still a limited number of towns, and within them a limited number of weekly market places, *torve*.[20] Cash, therefore, in the late eleventh and early twelfth century had to be extracted from other sources: primarily from townsmen acting as merchants and out-lying tribute-paying areas. It further becomes evident that access to such revenues was closely connected to royal power, but also, if we take the royal donations cited above as representative, that exactly these two kinds of revenues were by far the most important within the sources of royal income. Apart from fines there do not seem to have been other forms of regular royal cash income that could be made over to others.

Even if the towns were recently established they could provide significant tax and tribute for the king. In Lund, in 1085, the canons already received a quite substantial sum of *midsommergæld*: 'de areis Lunde xx marce et i [from the lands of Lund yearly 21 marks]'.[21] Even if the sum, which the same canons enjoyed in 1231, had grown to 27 marks, in that year the king still took the majority of the tax, namely 33 marks.[22] The Lund town tax seems to have remained remarkably stable and together with the town taxes from all the other towns of the country it secured the king a solid cash income. The tributes paid to the king from out-lying areas were of no lesser importance. The ancient silver tribute from the Frisian *Utland* paid to the king in 1231 amounted to 534 marks of silver, so he could easily spare the part which the cathedral in Odense had received since

[18] *Diplomatarium Danicum*, series 1, vol. 2, no. 65. See further Ebbe Nyborg, 'Kirke og sogn i højmiddelalderens by', in Søren Bitsch Christensen (ed.), *Middelalderbyen* (Aarhus, 2004), pp. 121–2. Ane L. Bysted, *Ringsted Kloster og Skt. Bendts Kirke* (Ringsted, 2010), p. 25.

[19] See in particular, Bjørn Poulsen, *Bondens penge. Studier i sønderjyske regnskaber 1400–1650* (Odense, 1990), p. 17. Niels Hybel and Bjørn Poulsen, *The Danish Resources c. 1000–1550. Growth and Recession* (Leiden, 2007), pp. 340–41.

[20] Hybel and Poulsen, *The Danish Resources*, p. 240.

[21] *Diplomatarium Danicum*, series 1, vol. 2, no. 21.

[22] *Kong Valdemars Jordebog*, Svend Aakjær (ed.), vols 1–3 (Copenhagen, 1926–45, repr. Copenhagen, 1980), vol. 1, p. 23.

1141: 'annuatim xxx marcas de insula Sild [30 marks yearly of the tribute from the island of Sylt]'.[23] Although the amount is unknown there is no reason to underestimate the tribute of Bornholm, which almost certainly dates back to the eleventh century: some of it was donated by the king to the Archbishop of Lund already, at some point before 1123.[24]

Other Sources of Income

The church's income during the late eleventh and early twelfth also derived from other sources of royal revenue. One such source was royal fines which were passed over to the church. For example, around the year 1100 St Cnut's church in Odense received the right of ownership over land belonging to outlaws, and over half the land of those who died without heirs, the king taking the other half. Small royal fines up to 6 øre for settling criminal acts privately could also be collected by the church.[25] In 1145 the exiled bishop of Schleswig was given permission to collect the royal fines of two Sjælland districts, *herreder*.[26] Such income is, however, exceptional in the documentary records.

Bishops of more prominent dioceses began to play a part in minting.[27] A unique Roskilde coin from c. 1080 is the earliest surviving example of this episcopal involvement in minting. The coin shows a full-face portrait of a man who holds a crozier and wears a *pallium*. It bears the inscription SVEIN, whom, it has been strongly suggested, should be identified as Svein Norbagge (d. 1088), bishop of Roskilde.[28] A coin from Lund minted during the reign of King Niels (r. 1104–34) bearing the picture of a bishop has also recently been interpreted as a demonstration of Asser's (d. 1137) new dignity as archbishop, and possibly

---

23 *Diplomatarium Danicum*, series 1, vol. 2, no. 8. Raising the sum given c. 1100 of 20 marks to now 30 marks. *Diplomatarium Danicum*, series 1, vol. 1, no. 35.

24 The list of prebends from Lund from 1123 mentions revenue of 10 marks in money from the 'censu de borrondæholm' / 'de debito ... insule', *Necrologium Lundense. Lunds Domkyrkas Nekrologium*, Lauritz Weibull (ed.) (Lund, 1923), pp. 6–10. For comparison see, *Diplomatarium Danicum*, series 1, vol. 3, no. 56.

25 *Diplomatarium Danicum*, series 1, vol. 1, no. 32, '*aftunc*'. See Niels Skyum-Nielsen, *Kvinde og slave* (Copenhagen, 1971), p. 45.

26 *Diplomatarium Danicum*, series 1, vol. 2, no. 91.

27 Peter Hauberg, *Danmarks Myntvæsen i Tidsrummet 1146–1241* (Copenhagen, 1906), pp. 313, 315. Gert Posselt, 'Nogle danske mønter med gejstlige fremstillinger før ca. 1150', *Hikuin*, vol. 11, Festskrift til Brita Malmer (1985): 207–14. Jørgen Steen Jensen (ed.), *Tusindtallets danske mønter fra den kongelige Mønt- og Medaillesamling* (Copenhagen, 1995), p. 116. Keld Grinder-Hansen, *Kongemagtens krise. Det danske møntvæsen 1241–1340* (Copenhagen, 2000), pp. 54–9.

28 Jensen (ed.), *Tusindtallets danske*, p. 116.

of his rights in minting in 1104.[29] However, beyond these isolated examples, the evidence seems to indicate that it was only from c. 1140 that Danish bishops took part in minting. At this date both the archbishop of Lund and the bishop of Ribe apparently were granted minting rights by the king.[30] Later, c. 1175, a charter of King Valdemar I gave the bishop of Schleswig half the mint workshop in his town: 'dimidium fabrice monetarie eiusdem ciuitatis'.[31] In Ribe there is good reason to assume that the bishop's palace was situated just west of the current cathedral. In 2006, a coin die with the name of bishop Tue (TVVO) (1214–30) was found here, together with several coins apparently struck with the very same die.[32] There is no doubt that mint rights were of the utmost importance to the bishops; both the regular mint duties and those connected to coin renewals (*renovatio monetæ*) when large numbers of coins shifted hands. A hypothetical calculation of the number of *penninge* exchanged in Lund during a *renovatio* shortly before 1201 can be made on the assumption that the 700 marks of 'old money' possessed by one of the archbishop's officials in 1201 represents the archbishop's quarter of the mint profits.[33] If this assumption is correct, 672,000 old *penninge* were exchanged.

Minting was a regalian right which could be settled on bishops. A seemingly more private sort of income was that derived from landed wealth, or ground rent of allodial land. Here it should be borne in mind, however, that duties given for possession of land to lords change dramatically between c. 1100 and c. 1200 when the Law of Scania presents a careful description of the condition of land rent. This development possibly reflects the growing importance of written learned law throughout the twelfth century; a process which can also be observed in Norway and Sweden.[34] In practical terms it may also indicate a shift

---

29 Jørgen Steen Jensen, 'En mindemønt for Assers opnåelse af ærkebispeværdigheden i Lund 1104?', *Nordisk Numismatisk Unions Medlemsblad* (1993): 2–8.

30 *Diplomatarium Danicum*, series 1, vol. 2, no. 98.

31 *Diplomatarium Danicum*, series 1, vol. 3, no. 50.

32 Morten Søvsø, 'Et møntstempel fra Ribe', *Nordisk Numismatisk Unions Medlemsblad* (2007): 117–23.

33 This has been proposed by Michael Andersen, 'Ærkebiskop Absalons testamente – historie og kulturhistorie', in Frank Birkebæk, Tom Christensen and Inge Skovgaard-Petersen (eds), *Absalon. Fædrelandets fader* (Roskilde, 1996), p. 215. The value of the mint right is also indicated when in 1234 it can be seen that the Bishop of Ribe had to be compensated with the income generated by a new plough tax levied in three local country areas and a couple of small towns to give up the revenues he had hitherto received from the mint at Ribe, that is, profit resulting from the renewal of coins.

34 Thomas Lindkvist, *Landborna i Norden under äldre medeltid* (Stockholm, 1979). Tore Iversen, 'Jordeie og jordleie: Eiendomsbegrepet i norske middelalderlover', *Collegium Medievale*, 14 (2002): 79–113. Janken Myrdal, *Jordbruket under feodalismen 1000–1700*, Det svenska jordbrukets historia, 2 (Stockholm, 1999), p. 98.

from the possession of land for military service to ownership of tenant land. This is the argument that Christensen has suggested constitutes the origins of the Roskilde bishop's medieval landholding.[35]

The Lund charter of 1085 reports that King Cnut gave the canons a plot in Lund which had come into the monarch's possession as part of a settlement whereby Øpi, son of Thorbiorn, negotiated the king's peace.[36] From a source dated 1123, it can be seen that this large plot gave its owner six pounds in money each year.[37] Apart from this instance there are no indications of church ownership of urban land plots until after the period considered here.[38] Land possessed by church institutions was therefore presumably mostly rural and it was from this land that annual duties were paid.

Documentation of land rents in Scania and Sjælland has survived from 1123 onwards and the sources indicate that this was a money duty, or at least that it was assessed in money.[39] Also the paraphrase of the Law of Scania by Archbishop Anders Sunesen, which dates from the early thirteenth century, clearly indicates money rents. It states that the tenant (*landbo*) should pay his land rent to his lord in cash before 15 August so that the latter could buy what he needed at

---

35 Christensen, 'Roskildekirkens jordegods før år 1200': 30–39. Niels Lund has rightly criticised this proposal but it remains an interesting thesis. Niels Lund, *Lid, leding og landeværn* (Roskilde, 1996), p. 123. At least the problem of explaining the large tracts of land which must have come into the possession of the Roskilde quite early in the eleventh century exists. The situation probably has some parallels in the early possession of whole districts, *herreder*, by the bishop of Aarhus. Anders Bøgh, 'Bundones regis. Selvejerbøndernes antal og funktion – især i senmiddelalderen', in Agnes Arnórsdóttir, Per Ingesman and Bjørn Poulsen (eds), *Konge, kirke og samfund. De to øvrighedsmagter I senmiddelalderen* (Aarhus, 2007), pp. 117–49. Jens Jeppesen, 'Magnate Farms and Lordship from the Viking Age to the Medieval Period in Eastern Jutland: The Excavations at Lisbjerg and Haldum Churches' in Bjørn Poulsen and Søren Michael Sindbæk (eds), *Settlement and Lordship in Viking and Early Medieval Scandinavia* (Turnhout, 2011), pp. 137–46. Cf. also the case of the famous Swedish runestones erected by Jarlebanke who on one stone says that he owns the settlement of Täby and on another stone that he owns a whole district, a *härad*.

36 'Est igitur terra illam quam Øpi filius Thorbiorn in Lunde pro pace sua emendauit'.

37 *Necrologium Lundense*, p. 6: 'Terra in ciuitate soluens vi libras'. See too Skyum-Nielsen, *Kvinde og Slave*, p. 5. The meaning of the pound used in source ('libras denariorum') is not clear. It is sometimes assumed that it is the same as the mark. The term pound (in money) may have been used because there was a growing difference between the mark in pure silver and the mark in money.

38 See *Diplomatarium Danicum*, series 1, vol. 3, no. 152 (1188).

39 Erik Ulsig, 'Landboer og bryder, skat og landgilde. De danske fæstebønder og deres afgifter i det 12. og 13. Århundrede', in Karsten Fledelius, Niels Lund and Herluf Nielsen (eds), *Middelalder, metode og medier. Festskrift til Niels Skyum-Nielsen på 60-årsdagen den 17. oktober 1981* (Viborg, 1981), pp. 144, 156, 157.

the fish market, that is, at the Scanian markets.[40] It is reasonable to assume that the church secured some ready money from its landed possessions but, as stated above, the fact that the early charters distinguish between payments in cash or kind might suggest a need for caution in stressing the cash contributions from rural land rents during the period discussed here.

Tithes in Denmark are mostly assumed to have been introduced around 1104 in connection with the creation of an archdiocese, and they are documented for the first time in 1135 when the bishop's tenth in Sjælland is mentioned.[41] Although it should perhaps be assumed that tithes by nature were paid in kind, in tenths of the production, this was not always the case. Prior to 1171, tithes to the bishop were paid in cash by the Sjælland *herred* of Ringsted, and in 1201 the people of Scania were also paying their tithes partly in money.[42] Other church levies were paid in money: c. 1177, the monks of Ringsted were given permission to continue 'the old custom' of collecting two payments in cash, ('duos collectas nummorum'), one called '*Knuds skud*', the other '*Marias skud*'.[43]

Amongst ecclesiastical duties, 'Peter's Pence' holds a particular place. The principle of the Peter's Pence was, as it is well known, that each household should pay one *penning* to the Pope. In a letter from Pope Alexander II (1061–73) to King Svein Estridsen written between 1061 and 1073, the Pope orders the king to send the papal tax, *censum*, in the same way as his predecessors had done. From the letter it seems like the Peter's Pence was actually collected but held back by the king.[44] Further, in connection with the creation of the archdiocese in Lund, Pope Paschal II (1099–1118) instructed the archbishop of Lund to send him the yearly tax, *censum*.[45] It is quite feasible that this tax was paid in cash

---

40 *Danmarks gamle Landskabslove med Kirkelovene*, Johannes Brøndum-Nielsen and Poul Johannes Jørgensen (eds), vols 1–8 (Copenhagen, 1933–61), vol. 1, p. 660 (§ 143).

41 *Diplomatarium Danicum*, series 1, vol. 2, no. 64.

42 *Diplomatarium Danicum*, series 1, vol. 3, no. 140 ('silicet tempore quo nummi soluebantur'). See also *Diplomatarium Danicum*, series 1, vol. 4, no. 32. Large amounts of tithe in money was paid to the archbishop around 1257 from parts of Scania. *Acta Processus Litium inter regem danorum et archiepiscopum Lundensem*, A. Krarup and W. Norwin (eds) (Copenhagen, 1932), p. 139. That tithe was worth cash money is also indicated by source from around 1200 in which the bishop of Roskilde sells the tenth of the parish of Benløse to the monastery in Ringsted for a yearly sum of two marks of silver. *Diplomatarium Danicum*, series 1, vol. 3, no. 181.

43 *Diplomatarium Danicum*, series 1, vol. 3, no. 68.

44 *Diplomatarium Danicum*, series 1, vol. 1, no. 3.

45 *Diplomatarium Danicum*, series 1, vol. 1, no. 30. 'De censu etiam quem beato Petri predecessores uestri singulis annis instituerunt'.

in the early twelfth century, but little is known of the actual practices before the thirteenth.[46]

Finally, there were the gifts from all groups in society which are clearly under-documented. One kind of source is pictorial. Two of the donors to a local church are depicted on the walls of the church of Fjenneslev. A fresco also survives from c. 1125–50 showing not only the local nobleman Asser Rig giving a church building to God, but also, behind him his wife Inger, who likewise gives a golden ring away (see Plate 3). One of the few surviving examples in the written documentation of gift-giving is from around 1200 and comes from the monastery in Ringsted, which became consecrated to Duke Cnut ('Holy Cnut') (c. 1096–1131). It is part of the *vita* of this Cnut:

> As a monk from the Ringsted monastery during fishing time sailed to Scania he was told by a man from Halland, that together with 16 neighbours this man had thrown lots between Holy Olav and Holy Cnut in order to stop the death of their cattle. But the lot which was marked with the name of Holy Cnut came out first, and as all had praised him, the cattle death stopped. And he said to the monk: 'See, here are as many coins as we are neighbours'. This money the monk gave to the abbot while we were watching it as a sign of the miracle.[47]

A statute of the Guild of Saint Cnut which must be dated to around 1200 mentions the habit of giving money to the church at funerals. It is stated that when a member had died, then every guild brother and sister should follow the body to the grave and each donate one penny to masses for his soul.[48]

The strongest documentation that such small offerings of money to the church were widespread is supplied by a third kind of source, the archaeological, and consists in the many coins found under church floors, both in the countryside and in towns. Some of the coins are grave gifts, such as a penny from Sven Estridsen, which was minted in Slagelse, and found at the hand of a corpse in the West Jutland church of Trans. Most, however, were presumably lost in the course of offerings made within the church. The majority of the church finds date from the second half of the twelfth century, but there are a limited number from the eleventh century onwards, from the reigns of kings such as Svein Estridsen, Niels and Sven Grathe (r. 1146–57).[49]

---

[46] Ellen Jørgensen, *Fremmed indflydelse under den danske Kirkes tidligste Udvikling* (Copenhagen, 1908), pp. 173–6; Herluf Nielsen, 'Peterspenge', *Kulturhistorisk Leksikon for Nordisk Middelalder*, vol. 13, col. 249–52.

[47] *Vitae Sanctorum Danorum*, M. Gertz (ed.) (Copenhagen 1908), p. 245.

[48] *Danmarks Gilde- og Lavsskråer fra middelalderen*, C. Nyrop (ed.), vol. 1 (Copenhagen, 1899–1900), p. 13, § 45: 'offær en pænning i siælmesse for hans siæl'.

[49] See Kirsten Bendixen, 'Middelaldermønter i de sidste 10 års danske kirkefund', *Nordisk Numismatisk Årsskrift* (1972): 47–70. Keld Grinder-Hansen, 'Mønter som kilde til

Ecclesiastical institutions in Denmark had access to cash money from a number of sources. It must be maintained, nevertheless, that in the period from the late eleventh until the mid-twelfth century, town taxes and tributes donated by the king were fundamental parts of diocesan and monastic income.

Spending the Money

The early Danish charters reveal two important things. First, they document the process whereby reception of town taxes, once granted to the particular church, became prominent sources of cash revenue to the institution, and second they grant an insight into the purposes to which this cash was put. For example, in 1135, when the monastery of Ringsted was given 10 marks of *midsommergæld* annually from the town of Ringsted by the king, it was stated that the money should be used to clothe the monks, 'ad vestituram fratrum'. This was expressly stated in connection with the town tax, not with the gifts of land.[50] The gift was further extended in 1148 when the brothers were granted all of the royal tax on the town of Ringsted to buy clothes, 'totumque censum mithsommers gield eiusdem wille ad vestituram fratrum ibidem'.[51] Cloth and clothes were items to be bought on the market.

Expenditure in an ecclesiastical institution was, perforce, diverse. At the cathedrals a whole staff required food and payment, from the bishop, and dean of the chapter, to the cantor, canons, and many others. There was always building work to be undertaken in addition. Splendid evidence of this is given by twelfth-century buildings of the cathedrals of Lund, Viborg and Ribe, which still survive today. In the case of Roskilde, the chronicle records the deeds in this regard of Bishop Svein (1073–87) who 'built the church of Roskilde nearly from the ground and who decorated it with a splendid crown and marble columns and all sorts of ornaments. It was he who built a monastery of stone to the brethren ... Besides he built a monastery in Ringsted ... and another in Slagelse'.[52] Of Svein's successor Arnold (1088–1124), the same chronicle records that he not only built a wall around the monastery in Roskilde (which now seem to be located archaeologically) but also that he renewed the paintings of this monastery.[53]

middelalderens økonomiske historie – en præsentation af et kildemateriale', *Fortid og Nutid*, 2 (1994): 101–33. Gitte Tarnow Ingvardson, *Møntbrug. Fra vikingetid til vendertogter*, (Aarhus, 2010), p. 48.

50 *Diplomatarium Danicum*, series 1, vol. 2, no. 65

51 *Diplomatarium Danicum*, series 1, vol. 2, no. 101.

52 *Chronicon Roskildense*, p. 23.

53 *Chronicon Roskildense*, p. 25: 'murum tamen lapideum circa monasterium Roskildense constuxit, picturam eciam eiusdem monasterii renouauit'.

After Arnold's death, the chronicle continues, Peder (1124–34) was anointed bishop and he 'decorated his manors with houses of stone and wood'.[54]

Cathedrals were built as well as new monasteries. The chronological distribution of Danish monastic building can be gleaned from various sources.[55] It is clear that the church reform movement is mirrored in, and directly affects, this distribution, but money had to be present to realise the building work. 1151–75 was by far the most important period of foundation, although new monasteries had been founded from the beginning of the twelfth century and, in the case of a few, even earlier.[56]

Alongside these initiatives the building of the many parish churches in the town and in the countryside should certainly be recalled. While only few Danish stone churches date from the eleventh century, between 1100 and 1250 some 1,700 stone churches were built, some of them as early as the first part of the twelfth century. An inscription above the south door of the West Jutland church of Gjellerup thus states that this church was founded in the year of 1140 to the honour of God.[57] In two cases building offerings in the choir walls of other country churches survive; in the church of Østerild seven coins from c. 1160 and in Fensmark church a hoard of 22 coins, dating to c. 1182.[58]

Donations to the many new churches and monasteries were numerous and generous. A striking example occurs in a charter of 1145, which records archbishop Eskil (1137–77) as having placed rich gifts on the altar of the cathedral of Lund: 'costly cloth, chalices and cloth, candelabra, relic gems of amber and ivory, a picture in ivory of the crucified'.[59] Building materials, wages to workers, frescos, baptismal fonts in stone, altars, objects of gold, silver, ivory, including walrus ivory, and many other items must have been paid for by churchmen from the eleventh century.[60] In 1157 the monks of Esrum gave

54 *Chronicon Roskildense*, p. 26: 'Curias suas lapideis et ligneis domibus ornauit'.

55 If we take the period before 1200 and for each 25-year period count the foundation of monasteries, mainly relying on http://www.jggj.dk/KlosterGISkatalog.htm, we get the picture – 1025–50: 1, 1051–75: 0, 1076–1100: 2, 1101–25: 7, 1126–50: 6, 1151–75: 32, 1176–1200: 2.

56 See Jim Bolton's description of the English developments in this sphere in the present volume.

57 'Anno m.c.xl. incarnationis dni est hic fundata sub honore dei domus ista'.

58 Jensen, *Danmarks middelalderlige skattefund fra c. 1050–c. 1550*, pp. 298, 299. Ingvardson, *Møntbrug*, p. 33.

59 *Diplomatarium Danicum*, series 1, vol. 1, no. 88.

60 On the inventory of twelfth-century Danish churches there is a rich literature; see for instance Poul Nørlund, *Gyldne Altre. Jysk Metalkunst fra Valdemarstiden* (Copenhagen, 1968). Henry Petersen, 'St. Kelds Helgenskrin i Viborg Domkirke', *Aarbøger for Nordisk Oldkyndighed og Historie* (1888): 110–14. Else Roesdahl, 'Walrus Ivory – Demand, Supply and Workshops, and Greenland', in A. Mortensen and S. Arge (eds), *Viking and Norse in the*

one gold mark to gild the shrine of the king's father, Cnut, 'ad deaurandum patris nostri Canuti scrinium marcam auri apposuerunt'.[61] To some degree, the material world of the churches is also reflected in treasure hoards. On the small island of Orø a large gold cross from c. 1100, weighing 309 grams, was found, and in the ruins of Haraldsborg castle, outside the town of Roskilde, a chalice and dish of gilded silver were found together with other silverware and more than 629 coins, all deposited c. 1132–33.[62]

Within this period, the church also played an increasingly important role in the land market, to the extent that it can be suggested that this market itself, and the instigation of legal regulation of tenancy, emerged as a direct result of church activity in this sphere. In 1133, a functioning land market is indicated in the charter mentioned above, where the Lund archbishop gave land to several prebends. It is expressly stated in this charter that the land given had been acquired through 'purchase according to law'.[63] It should, however, be noted that other evidence for land purchase mainly is from after c. 1160. There are three cases from c. 1160 where the monastery of Esrum bought land from farmers, *bundones*, for three marks, six marks, and 10 marks of silver, respectively.[64] Later in the twelfth century the monastery of St Peter in Næstved purchased a manor for 16 marks of silver.[65] The first case of church land purchase in a town is seen in c. 1188 when a canon of Viborg bought six plots in the town of Viborg for 40 marks of silver.[66]

Finally, necessary church and ecclesiastical organisation, perhaps especially during an age of reform, was hard, and generated considerable expense. In the period before 1104 when the archbishop of Hamburg-Bremen had supremacy over Scandinavia, Danish bishops regularly went to see him.[67] They could also be ordered to escort the messengers of the archbishop of Hamburg through Denmark.[68] In c. 1100, Danish monks from Odense travelled to Evesham, in

---

North Atlantic. Select Papers from the Proceedings of the Fourteenth Viking Congress Tórshavn 19–30 July 2001 (Tórshavn, 2005), pp. 182–91.

61 *Diplomatarium Danicum*, series 1, vol. 2, no. 122.

62 Jensen, *Danmarks middelalderlige skattefund fra c. 1050–c. 1550*, pp. 259, 282.

63 *Diplomatarium Danicum*, series 1, vol. 1, no. 56.

64 *Diplomatarium Danicum*, series 1, vol. 2, nos 122, 126, 130.

65 *Diplomatarium Danicum*, series 1, vol. 3, no. 259.

66 *Diplomatarium Danicum*, series 1, vol. 3, no. 152. Credit given by church institutions is not documented before 1199 when the monastery of Sorø lent 200 marks to a lord against security in his lands, so that he could go on pilgrimage to Jerusalem. *Diplomatarium Danicum*, series 1, vol. 3, no. 257. Credit given by archbishop Absalon is registered in 1201. *Diplomatarium Danicum*, series 1, vol. 4, no. 32.

67 *Diplomatarium Danicum*, series 1, vol. 2, nos 3, 8.

68 *Diplomatarium Danicum* , series 1, vol. 2, no. 8.

the English midlands, and English monks travelled reciprocally to Odense.[69] In addition, the growing number of church synods and meetings should be included, for example, in the middle of Denmark in 1160, the bishop of Ribe attended a church council in Pavia.[70]

To conclude, money was spent on building, decorating churches, luxuries of all kind, buying land and during travelling. Gold and silver circulated and was constantly transformed as can be shown from the *vita* of a saint, Kjeld of Viborg, (c. 1105–c. 1150), which was composed in Viborg between 1185 and 1187. The *vita* relates that in the 1140s during a journey to the largest town in Denmark, Lund in Scania, he was captured by Slavic people and had to pay ransom to be released. This could exemplify money spent on travels. According to his *vita* he travelled on and reached both the king and archbishop in Lund. Here he was compensated by these lords and, when he left, the archbishop gave him a precious ring and the king gave him much gold. These gifts typify the many donations to churchmen in this period. Finally Kjeld's *vita* states that when he reached a harbour town (Lomma near Lund?) he saw a poor man and gave him the archbishops ring, and, which is more striking in this context, changed the king's gold into money 'pro nummis commutari' and gave this to poor people. Here is, it can be argued, an example of concrete monetisation of the lower levels of Danish society in the twelfth century.[71]

The Result: Greater Ecclesiastical Institutions and the Development of Monetisation

The Danish material clearly suggests that a real tipping point in monetary circulation did not take place before the second half of the twelfth century. An investigation of the numismatic material from the town of Lund made by Peter Carelli showed that if the number of early medieval coins found as stray finds are divided into the regnal periods of the kings under whom the coins found were minted, there is a clear discrepancy between the periods. Measured in this way the period before the mid-twelfth century has a low degree of monetisation in Lund of only 0.2–0.6 coins found per year, whereas in the next 50 years the

69 *Diplomatarium Danicum*, series 1, vol. 2, no. 24.

70 *Diplomatarium Danicum*, series 1, vol. 2, no. 64. See also *Diplomatarium Danicum*, series 1, vol. 2, no. 64. Only a little later we find that money was deposited in safe places in other European places to facilitate foreign payments. Before his death in 1201 archbishop Absalon ordered that half the silver that he had in the monastery of Cluny should be given to this monastery, while the other half should be sent to Clairvaux. *Diplomatarium Danicum*, series 1, vol. 4, no. 32.

71 *Vitae Sanctorum Danorum*, p. 266, https://wikihost.uib.no/medieval/index.php/Sanctus_Ketillus.

amount rises to 1.3–1.8 coins found per year.[72] Gitte Tarnow Ingvardson, in her work on early medieval coin circulation in Sjælland, further demonstrates that a low degree of monetisation in the first part of the twelfth century is observable, compared to a higher degree of monetisation in the period before, c. 1020–80.[73]

A similar picture emerges from the treasure hoards which, from the 1080s onwards, become both fewer and smaller. Gone are the large finds from the preceding years such as the hoards from Hågerup (after 1048, 1,416 coins), Vallø (after 1053, 2,253 coins), Selsø (c. 1060, c. 1,300 coins), Tørring (c. 1060, 2,593 coins), Holsteinborg (c. 1080–86, c. 2,000 coins).[74] From the early twelfth century, there are even hoards without coins but containing jewellery such as the golden crucifix from Orø or the two magnificent brooches of gold and silver (deposited in the 1130s) from the medieval settlement of Østergaard, which may perhaps be seen as sign of a flight from coin use.[75] Peter Spufford's conception of a Europe lacking silver after the Harz mines ran dry in the period from the late eleventh century to c. 1160 most probably explains this phenomenon, perhaps especially considering the relatively new notion of retaining capital in a coinage which was both debased and subject to *renovatio monetae*.[76]

On the other hand, the evidence that large-scale minting was still ongoing in Denmark during the first part of the twelfth century should not be too easily dismissed, as has been pointed out by Kirsten Bendixen and Jørgen Steen Jensen on the basis of die-studies.[77] Source critical considerations are also instructive in any attempt to estimate the genuine number of stray finds from the first part of the twelfth century. The coins are extremely thin and fragile, and accordingly may not have the same chance of recovery as the earlier examples. To some degree the coin circulation also went on in the years after 1080. On Sjælland stray coins

72 Peter Carelli, *En kapitalistisk anda. Kulturella förändringar i 1100-tallets Danmark* (Stockholm, 2001), pp. 188–94.

73 Ingvardson, *Møntbrug* (Aarhus, 2010), p. 61.

74 Jensen, *Danmarks middelalderlige skattefund fra c. 1050–c. 1550*, pp. 209, 224, 237, 238, 245, 252.

75 Jensen, *Danmarks middelalderlige skattefund fra c. 1050–c. 1550*, p. 259. For comparison see also the hoard from Græse, ibid. p. 279. Anne Birgitte Sørensen, Østergaard. *Vikingetid og middelalder* (Haderslev, 2011). The recently discovered hoard from Østermarie, Bornholm, is interesting also in this context.

76 Peter Spufford, *Money and its Use in Medieval Europe* (Cambridge, 1988). In this connection see further the contribution by Bolton in the present volume. Hybel and Poulsen, *The Danish Resources*, p. 330. Ingvardson, *Møntbrug*, p. 96.

77 Kirsten Bendixen, *Skatten fra Lundby Krat. Et himmerlandsk skattefund fra Erik Ejegods tid. De danske mønter* (Copenhagen, 1993). Jørgen Steen Jensen, 'Bårarp-fundet 1932. Et hallandsk møntfund fra Svend Grathes tid', *Numismatiska Meddelanden*, 32 (1983): 101–24. Jørgen Steen Jensen, 'Hvor stor var udmøntningen i Danmark i 1000–og 1100-tallet?', *Fortid og Nutid*, 30 (1983): 19–25.

admittedly disappeared from the rural areas as small trade and craft sites closed down, but coins remained in towns in the vicinity of some large ecclesiastical institutions, or vice versa.[78]

In Lund there are a considerable number of stray finds from the period 1047–1154 at the central market just in front of the cathedral.[79] A similar picture can be drawn from the latest excavations in an area around the cathedral in Roskilde. In the recent excavation at 'Konventhuset' a number of coins were discovered: one Æthelred penny from 991–97, one Cnut the Great (found together with early glazed English pottery of the kind produced in Stamford, Lincolnshire) and one Sven Estridsen. The surroundings of the church in Roskilde were not the only place marked by loss of coins. As noted by Ingvardson, the harbour area of Roskilde also experienced widespread use of coins during the eleventh century.[80] However, a map of the distribution of early coin stray finds inside the medieval area of Roskilde underlines the importance of the cathedral as a centre of monetary transactions (see Plate 4).[81]

In a similar way the recent excavations, from 2008 onwards, just outside the cathedral of Ribe have revealed a considerable number of eleventh- and twelfth-century coins. These include two half-pennies: one of Cnut the Great minted in London 1029–35, and one apparently German. Noteworthy is a penny minted in Emden under Hermann (Billunger), c. 1045–60 (see Plate 5).[82] Danish coins of King Niels and King Sven Grathe have also been found. Not all the coins found in this location are directly connected to the cathedral but they reveal a flourishing coin circulation in its immediate vicinity in the late eleventh and twelfth century.[83] The central parts of the town where the cathedral stood also housed the site of the king's palace and, in Roskilde and Lund, of public functions such as the *thing*.[84] It should not be imagined that cathedrals and monasteries were the only drivers of coin use. These institutions accessed their silver supplies through the donation of royal revenues such as town taxes, they used money as the king and other magnates did, and they were certainly not solely responsible for the concentration of stray finds in the towns of the bishops. King and church

78 Ingvardson, *Møntbrug*, p. 61. On rural 'landing places', see Jens Ulriksen, *Anløbspladser. Besejling og bebyggelse i Danmark mellem 200 og 1100 e. Kr* (Roskilde, 1997).

79 Carelli, En *kapitalistisk* anda, p. 195.

80 Ingvardson, *Møntbrug*, p. 55

81 The map and a detailed personal communication on the excavations in Roskilde have been kindly supplied by Jens Ulriksen, Roskilde Museum.

82 I should like to thank Peter Ilisch, Münster, for kindly pointing out that the coin was minted under Hermann Billunger.

83 I should like to thank Morten Søvsø, Ribe Museum, for a detailed personal communication on the excavations.

84 Peter Carelli, 'Varubytet i medeltidens Lund. Uttryck för handel eller konsumtion?', *Meta. Medeltidsarkeologisk tidskrift*, 3 (1998): 3–27.

were so closely bound together during the period 1060 to 1160 that is difficult to differentiate their role in the process of monetisation.

However, the effect of the church on monetisation is not to be neglected. It might be suggested that church activities in this area magnified the effects of royal power on coin use, by establishing permanent institutions in towns which attracted local and foreign trade. This created urban growth, exchange, and provided a base for increased taxation. Church activities helped to support the process of monetisation through a difficult phase in the history of Danish money from c. 1080 to 1150, a period marked by a distinct lack of silver. In the countryside, a recession in the use of money certainly seems to have occurred. The church, by levying tithes and land rents in money formed part of a process which encouraged a more effective circulation of available coin, the mobilisation of Viking Age silver treasures, and finally, from the mid-twelfth century, large-scale sale of their surplus to markets.

It should be noted that the church collected in coin in rural areas before any regular royal taxes can be identified with certainty in these regions.[85] The many sources of income, including donations from all groups in society, channelled capital to the bishops, making it possible for them to take over part of the minting in their towns by the mid-twelfth century. To return to the example cited in the beginning of this chapter, from Tommerup monastery, the minting rights of bishops together with all other evidence seem to offer a clear indication that there were, in principle, no general ecclesiastical reservations against the use of money. At least in Denmark, quite the opposite seems to have been the case.

[85] The royal military taxes in Denmark, the *leding*, belong to the latest part of the twelfth century. Bjørn Poulsen, *Bondens penge*, p. 17.

Chapter 9

The Church, Markets and Money in Early Medieval England[1]

S. J. and N. J. Mayhew

Historians of medieval England are uniquely fortunate in the survival of the astonishing resource which is the Domesday Book. Whatever the difficulties of interpretation, which are significant, it is an enormous privilege to have so much social and economic evidence from so early a date. However, it is perhaps still true that historians sometimes underestimate the use of money in eleventh-century England, despite the fact that it is writ large on every page of Domesday Book. A hugely distinguished line of English historians from D.C. Douglas, to A.L. Poole, to M.M. Postan, to R. Lennard, to H.R. Loyn have all confirmed the extensive evidence for the use of coin in Anglo-Saxon England and in Domesday Book, alongside other methods of payment and social and economic organisation which might simplistically be grouped together as 'feudal'.[2] In fact the monetary and the 'feudal' are by no means mutually exclusive, but are found in Domesday coexisting easily. Payments in kind, labour or other services are

[1] This chapter concentrates on the tenth to twelfth centuries, but occasionally strays beyond these boundaries when earlier or later evidence seems to have implications for our core period. See for example, Rory Naismith, *Money and Power in Anglo-Saxon England: The Southern English Kingdoms 757–865* (Cambridge, 2012) for a carefully judged assessment of the role of coin in commerce in the earlier period. In a nicely balanced review, which includes a full appreciation of the anthropology of money as gift, Naismith concludes, 'the balance of the surviving written and material evidence suggests that the association of coins with markets and commercial use was much more prominent than has been allowed in some recent literature and could have played an important integrative role in exchanges and society as a whole'. p. 292.

[2] N. Mayhew, 'Modelling medieval monetisation', in Richard H. Britnell and Bruce M. S. Campbell (eds) , *A Commercialising Economy: England 1086 to c. 1300* (Manchester, 1995), p. 75, and the references cited there. For D. C. Douglas, see *The Social Structure of Medieval East Anglia*, Oxford Studies in Social and Legal History, vol. IX, Sir Paul Vinogradoff (ed.) (Oxford, 1927, reprinted New York, 1974), where he writes: 'But in Domesday Book and in the documents nearly contemporary therewith it is possible to watch in many parts of East Anglia the gradual transformation from an economy of natural husbandry to one of money payments ... it is hardly possible to over-emphasise the importance of the cash nexus even in twelfth-century East Anglia ... .', p. 90.

readily commuted to cash or back again. Supposedly self-sufficient peasants raised families on tiny plots but also had to pay taxes, tolls, fines and other dues in cash. The values or rents due from each manor are meticulously recorded in Domesday Book, and they receive confirmation from the contemporary schedule of the archbishop of Canterbury's Kent estates, which shows that money rents were even more prevalent than Domesday Book suggests. Both in turn find further confirmation in surviving twelfth-century rentals from various church estates (for example St Pauls, St Benet of Holme, and the abbeys of Ramsey, Burton, Peterborough and Glastonbury) where Lennard found 'money rents extremely common'.[3] The obligation to pay money rent implies the ability to acquire coin by selling labour or marketing produce, but what does Domesday Book tells us about markets?

Identifying the Markets

Darby notes that

> markets are recorded or implied in Domesday Book in connection with 60 places, of which 19 were boroughs ... Clearly, the record is incomplete. There are entire counties for which no markets are entered; such, for example, are those of Cambridge, Dorset, Shropshire and Sussex, yet they must have had markets, both in their boroughs and elsewhere.[4]

Jones substantiated this argument:

> By ... [975] a significant proportion of output was regularly sold for cash in the emerging network of market towns. London still dominated trade but there were also a sizeable number of provincial and shire towns which, in addition to administrative functions, were involved in more than purely local exchange. More numerous and more significant, however, were the multiplicity of small market towns. Growing in size and number, they constituted tangible evidence of the vitality of the market-based economy that had come to exist during the tenth century.[5]

---

3 Quoted in Mayhew, 'Modelling Medieval Monetisation', p. 75.

4 H. C. Darby, *Domesday England* (Cambridge, 1977), p. 318,

5 S. R. H. Jones, 'Transaction Costs, Institutional Change, and the Emergence of a Market Economy in Later Anglo-Saxon England', *Economic History Review*, New Series, 46 (1993): 673.

Despite the reticence of Domesday Book about towns in general, Chris Dyer is inclined to support J. C. Russell's long-standing contention that perhaps 10 per cent of the population of 1086 lived in towns.[6]

To identify these 'missing market places', which Domesday Book implies but does not mention, we can first nominate King Alfred's *burhs*.[7] The burhs were, essentially, fortified market places: 'in the dooms of Edward and Æthelstan, the borough appears not only as a fortress, but as the official location of a royal mint and of a market, where, before the portreeve or other responsible person, purchases may be authenticated'.[8] The granting of fiscal and commercial privileges to the burhs had important monetary dimensions, for Viking attacks on trading places posed a direct threat to royal income.[9] The strengthened burhs were safe sites for trade and for minting coin, the two processes acting in concert. Winchester is a classic Alfredian burh: it had a market (confirmed by a charter of 1066) on *Ceapstræt* (Market St), five moneyers, the Cathedral, the Priory, and three churches all within 200 metres.[10] Worcester is another ninth-century burh, which was already a cathedral city in the seventh century.[11]

Additionally, David Hill locates 72 pre-Conquest markets which were not Alfredian burhs, but which may also be checked as likely markets omitted by Domesday Book.[12] This number includes the *wics*: coastal trading emporia, provisioned from outside the protected community and characterised by extensive artisanal activity and imports, which have left material traces in excavations. The 'big four' *wics* were Eoforwic (York), Hamwic (Southampton), Gipeswic (Ipswich) and Lundenwic (London). York was described by Alcuin in the eighth century as 'a general seat of commerce by land and sea alike ... a haven for ocean-going ships from the farthest ports', while London was described by Bede as 'an emporium for many nations who come to it by land and sea'.[13]

---

6 C. Dyer, 'The Hidden Trade of the Middle Ages: Evidence from the West Midlands of England', *Journal of Historical Geography*, XVIII (1992): 142, citing J. C. Russell, *British Medieval Population* (Albuquerque, 1948), pp. 45–54, and H. C. Darby, *Domesday England*, pp. 88–9.

7 Anthony Bradshaw's list of burhs from the Burghal Hidage may be found at http://www.ogdoad.force9.co.uk/alfred/alfhidage.htm

8 C. Stephenson, 'The Anglo-Saxon Borough' *English Historical Review*, CLXXVIII (1930): 197.

9 C. Pratt, *The Political Thought of King Alfred the Great* (Cambridge, 2007), p. 104.

10 M. Biddle (ed.), *Winchester in the Eleventh and Twelfth Century* (Oxford, 1976), figure 33 for a map of the town in 1148 in relation to the modern setting.

11 Dyer, 'Hidden trade': 143.

12 D. Hill, *An Atlas of Anglo-Saxon England* (London, 1981), pp. 134–42.

13 P. Godman, (ed. and trans.) *De pontificibus et sanctis Ecclesiae Eboracensis, The Bishops, Kings, and Saints of York* (Oxford, 1982), pp. 4–5 for Alcuin of York (730/740s – 19 May 804): 'emporium terrae commune marisque ... ab extremeo venientibus hospita porta'.

Lundenwic was outside the Roman walls, in the area now called Aldwych, literally, 'the old wic', or market place. There were smaller wics, too, such as Nordwyk and Westwyk (Norwich), Sandwich and Fordwich[14] in Kent, and Dunwich in Suffolk. Hodges saw the prime motivation behind *emporia* as the need of the elite to control power and access prestige items, but he published before the transformation in our knowledge triggered by the explosion of metal detector finds, and Michael Metcalf and most other observers would now argue that at least by the eighth century the numbers and range of sceattas powerfully suggest a use of coin extending far beyond an elite.[15]

Place-names also indicate the sites of markets. The Anglo-Saxons used the word 'port' to describe a market; as in Milborne Port. Wareham, which we know had a market, still has a 'Portland Meadow'. In a Canterbury charter of 956, one of the witnesses is Hlothewig, *portgerefa* – port-reeve – of Canterbury.[16] A successor to this post was one Æthelred (fl. 995 x 1005);[17] Ashburton, Devon, has had a port-reeve since 820 AD, and still has.[18] Port Meadow, Oxford, testifies to that city's status as an Anglo-Saxon market town, as does the road name 'portway' north of Oxford, although Domesday Book does not mention an Oxford market at all.[19] The eccentric nature of Domesday listing of markets is well illustrated by the fact that it does not mention a market in Oxford, but does note one in the much smaller Oxfordshire settlement at Bampton. Wantage, an Anglo-Saxon market town, is linked to Wallingford by the Portway, though neither appear as a market town in Domesday Book, and the name of Newport, Isle of Wight, indicates its Anglo-Saxon market function; it is also a 'productive site' (see below).[20] The road from Warndon to Worcester is identified in its charter

---

Bede, Ecclesiastical History of the English People, Bertram Colgrave and R. A. B. Mynors (eds and trans) (Oxford, 1969), Book 2, chapter 3, pp. 142–3, for Bede's identification of London as an international trading emporium: 'et ipsa multorum emporium populorum terra marique uenientium'; Book 4, chapter 22, pp. 404–5, records the sale, at Lundenwic, of a Northumbrian slave to a Frisian merchant.

14 P. Sawyer, www.esawyer.org.uk, derived from Peter Sawyer's *Anglo-Saxon Charters: an Annotated List and Bibliography*, published by the Royal Historical Society (London, 1968). Charter S 29 remits toll due on two ships at Fordwich, 763 x 764.

15 R. Hodges, *Dark Age Economics* (London, 1982, 1989).

16 S 1215.

17 S 1456.

18 www.ashburton.org/portreeve.htm

19 Eberhard Sauer, 'In Search of the Port-way', see www.oxoniensia.org/volumes/1998/sauer.pdf

20 G. Aston, 'The Towns of Berkshire' in J. Haslam et al., *Anglo-Saxon Towns of Southern England* (Stroud, 1984), pp. 53–86.

boundaries as Port Street, which passes Portefields House.[21] In a tenth-century charter (963 x 975) Chilcomb is described as a 'port': þæs portes.[22] Other charter evidence details further markets: Cirencester,[23] Evesham[24] and, in London, *Hwaetmundes stan*,[25] in a charter of 898 x 899.[26] Billingsgate first appears ca. 1000.[27] A charter of Edgar, dated 975, refers to a 'free market' (*habeant ibidem omni die lune liberum mercatum*) at Bleadon, Somerset.[28] Finberg judges this charter to be spurious, and that post-Domesday particulars have been inserted into what may have been a genuine grant of a five-hide estate, but even a false claim to early market rights remains significant.[29] Bede describes Towcester as a 'market town'.[30] The *Anglo-Saxon Chronicle* records a market-grant to Oundle in 975,[31] and records that in 1052 Harold Godwinson took ship to *Brycgstow* (Bristol) indicating the status of the town as a port.[32] The *Chronicle* also refers to Hereford as a market town in 1056.[33] It seems clear that markets were not

21 D. Hooke and P. Sawyer, *Worcester Anglo-Saxon Charter Bounds* (Woodbridge, 1990), p. 285.

22 S 817.

23 A. Williams, 'An Introduction to the Gloucester Domesday' in *The Gloucestershire Domesday*, Alecto, (London, 1989), p. 9. Cirencester was recognised as a market in 1086 with no indication of burghal status, though burgesses are evident by 1133.

24 W. D. Macray (ed.) *Chronicon Abbatiae de Evesham*, Rolls Series 29 (London, 1863), p. 75.

25 T. Dyson, 'Two Saxon Land Grants for Queenhithe' in J. Bird, H. Chapman and J. Clark (eds), *Collectanea Londoniensia: Studies Presented to Ralph Merrifield* (London, 1978). See also www.archeurope.com

26 Re-named Queenhithe, after William I's queen. In 889, Alfred the Great gave a London enclosure called *Hwaetmundes stan* to the bishop and church of Worcester, to be used as a market. Still known as Queenhithe, three coins of Alfred and one of Edward the Elder have been found in that ward.

27 Ethelred II, Code IV; A. J. Robertson, *The Laws of the Kings of England from Edmund to Henry I* (Cambridge, 1925), p. 71 ff.

28 S 804.

29 H. P. R. Finberg, *Early Charters of Wessex* (Leicester, 1964), no. 519.

30 J. A. Giles, *Bede the Venerable, Saint, 673–735, also, the Anglo-Saxon Chronicle* (London, 1903), p. 210.

31 ibid. p. 382.

32 *Brycgstow* was a major centre for the Anglo-Saxon slave trade. Men, women and children captured in Wales or northern England were traded through Bristol to Dublin as slaves. From there the Viking rulers of Dublin would sell them on throughout the known world. The Anglo-Saxon bishop of Worcester, Wulfstan, whose diocese included Bristol, preached against the trade regularly and eventually it was forbidden by the crown, though it carried on in secret for many years.

33 *Anglo-Saxon Chronicle*, Abingdon Manuscript, AD 1055/6, M. Swanton (trans.) (London, 1996), p. 186.

considered to be the principal object of the Domesday inquiry, but that this deficiency can be remedied by numerous other sources. Consider for example the case of Coventry, presented in Domesday Book as a village, but in 1102 recognised as a fitting location for a bishopric.[34]

The search for potential market sites unrecognised by Domesday Book might also consider the so-called 'productive sites', characterised by large numbers of finds of all kinds. Coins, ferrous and non-ferrous metalwork, including pins, strap-ends and hooked tags, typically identify such sites as well as occasional evidence for industry and production. 'The wide variety of local and foreign issues found at the "productive" sites', writes Katharina Ulmschneider, 'suggests a relatively free movement of coinage to, and probably from, these places of trade and exchange. The economic role of the "productive" sites seems also strengthened by their proximity to important land and water routes, while their siting [primarily] further inland may be a reflection of their function as more localised centres of commerce, such as markets and fairs, not primarily geared towards overseas trade like the more coastal *wics*'.[35]

In this way we can identify some 130 Anglo-Saxon markets. But what was the role of the church in establishing these markets? And what were they worth?

The Role of the Church

In a section on Anglo-Saxon ecclesiastical revenues, tithes and dues, Loyn lists the dues paid to the church: tithes, and church-scot paid to the old minster, in kind, but also dues in cash.[36] The minor dues consisted of light dues three times a year, harvest dues, Peter's Pence (or hearth-penny, paid to Rome) and soul-scot, or burial due, to be paid at the open grave. Loyn comments:

> This list shows well how the Church was involved in the workings of the agricultural year at every stage and with utter regularity from Easter to Easter. The mere recitation of dues is a reminder how used the countryside was to transactions assessed and often paid in hard cash ... Payments must have been formidable in mass, and it is quite understandable why Domesday churches should be treated as property, pure and simple.[37]

---

34 Dyer, 'Hidden trade': 146.

35 K. Ulmschneider, 'Settlement, Economy and the "Productive" Site: Middle Anglo-Saxon Lincolnshire 650–780', *Medieval Archaeology*, 44 (2000): 53–79.

36 H. R. Loyn, *Anglo-Saxon England and the Norman Conquest* (Oxford, 1962), pp. 254–7. For minsters, see now John Blair, *The Church in Anglo-Saxon Society* (Oxford, 2005).

37 Loyn, *Anglo-Saxon England*, p. 257.

It is significant that church-scot was paid direct to the chief minster, for minster churches are thought to represent the first phase of church construction in England, serving as a base from which a group of priests went out to serve the people of an extensive surrounding area. These churches would administer the basic rites of baptism and burial, and took the dues associated with them. Not only did the minsters collect dues; they were also able to market the surpluses generated by the accumulation of tithes. However much the church proclaimed the primacy of spiritual values, its accumulation of material wealth made it a major player in the development of the whole Anglo-Saxon economy.

The church was very often the landlord, too. At Hurstbourne Priors, Hampshire, in 900, the tenants of the Bishop of Winchester had to pay, at the equinox, 40 pence per hide.[38] At Tidenham, Gloucestershire, in 956 the Abbot of Bath held 30 hides, which included 54 yardlands (quarter-hides) of rent-paying land. 'Throughout the whole estate 12 pence is due from every yardland and 4 pence as alms'.[39] And this on top of the labour services and rents in kind, although both of these were increasingly being commuted. Evidence for commutation comes from comparing Anglo-Saxon charters which mention renders in kind with later Domesday records, which refer to cash only. Thus, in a charter no later than 959 one Æthelwyrd will leave his estate at Ickham to his son Eadric, paying £5 'and one day's food-rent'.[40] In Little Domesday Book, however, there is no mention of food-rent, and Ickham is valued at TRE £22 and TRW £32. Similarly, while three of the manors of Bury St Edmund's abbey – Redgrave, Rougham and Barton – supply food-rents in an early eleventh-century charter,[41] by 1087, there is no mention of food-rent.[42] And of the 62 Cambridgeshire manors which had to provide cartage-dues as service, six could pay 8d. per due.[43] Sawyer observes that, in the early eleventh century, 'peasants in all parts of the country were ... expected to pay money to the king, to the church and to their lords. They could not have met their obligations without earning money, and they can only have done that by working for wages or by selling surplus produce'.[44]

There was also money to be made from towns. Beresford and Finberg's[45] analysis of English medieval borough-founding suggests that the church, in all its manifestations, whether abbeys, bishops, or cathedral chapters, was

---

38 A. J. Robertson (ed.), *Anglo-Saxon Charters* (Cambridge, 1956), pp. 204–7.

39 Ibid.

40 Ibid. pp. 58–60.

41 Ibid, pp. 196–7.

42 Domesday Book ii, 360v; 362r; 361v (National Archives, UK).

43 Domesday Book ii, 189v–190v.

44 P. H. Sawyer, 'The Wealth of England in the Eleventh Century', *Transactions of the Royal Historical Society*, 5th series, 15 (1964):155.

45 M. W. Beresford and H. P. R. Finberg, *English Medieval Boroughs: A Handlist* (Newton Abbot, 1973).

responsible for the establishment of just under a quarter of the towns obtaining borough rights of some kind. This seems an under-estimate in the light of Blair's authoritative study of the early role of minsters as precursors of burhs and markets.[46]

The material needs of the great church foundations made them natural economic centres. James Campbell has pointed out that the 600 monks said to have lived at Monkwearmouth-Jarrow will have required a vast network of peasant families to sustain their life of prayer.[47] Something of this is apparent in Domesday Book's assessment of Bury St Edmunds:

> there are altogether thirty priests, deacons and clerks, twenty-eight nuns and poor people who daily utter prayers for the king and all Christian people; eighty less five bakers, ale-brewers, tailors, washerwomen, shoe-makers, robe-makers, cooks, carriers, dispensers altogether. And all those wait daily upon the Saint, the abbot and the brethren. Besides whom there are thirteen reeves over the land who have their houses in the said town and under them five borders. Now thirty-four knights, French and English together, and under them twenty-two bordars. Now altogether there are 342 houses on the demesne of the land of Saint Edmund which was under the plough in the time of King Edward [the Confessor].[48]

Here, then, are clerics, servants, estate managers and knights all located around the great Abbey of St Edmund. Moreover, Douglas was in no doubt about the role of cash in the organisation of this estate. He writes, ' ... the Norman Conquest and the reorganisation of Abbot Baldwin were fatal to the great majority of food rents, which seem to have been commuted, in the lands of one great religious house at least, in the latter half of the eleventh century. By the middle of the twelfth century the Bury economy, except for a few sporadic survivals, depended upon cash payments'.[49] With holdings of 8½ hundreds, the

---

46 Blair, *Anglo-Saxon Church*, p. 336: 'Somewhere around half of all Domesday markets and boroughs can be recognised as minster sites, as can two-thirds of the places where coins were struck during c. 870–1070. ... maybe 50 to 60 per cent of medieval small towns have minster origins'.

47 James Campbell, 'Production and Distribution in Early and Middle Anglo-Saxon England', in Tim Pestell and Katharina Ulmschneider (eds), *Markets in Early Medieval Europe: Trading and 'Productive' Sites, 650–850* (Macclesfield, 2003), p. 18. Duby guessed that 30 peasant families may have been required to maintain one monk. Campbell also speculated on the quantities of cloth, shoes and salt required by a population of perhaps half a million in eighth-century England, and the level of trade implied, given that few households could supply these essentials themselves.

48 Domesday Book ii, 372.

49 D. C. Douglas, (ed.), *Feudal Documents from the Abbey of Bury St Edmunds* (London, 1932), p. cxxxiii.

Abbey of St Edmunds was not merely one of the greatest landlords in England, but a major employer, and all these tradesmen and women needed to be paid at least partly in cash.

Even when servants were paid, in part, by food, their food had to be paid for, as an account of the servants of Peterborough Abbey in 1125 shows:

> the number of monks in the abbey was 60. There was, in addition, a considerable household. In the bakehouse there were two bakers who had the board allotted to one knight; also a winnower, who had the same; two other bakers, who had daily two white loaves and two brown loaves (with beer); two carriers who had four brown loaves and beer; and two grinders who had also the daily supply of four brown loaves and beer. The other food allotted to these nine servants of the bakehouse amounted to 24s. 4d. a year. In the brewhouse there were six servants, whose food, in addition to bread and beer, cost 16s. 4d. a year. In the kitchen there was a master and an under cook, with five other servants, two of whom were wood carriers; their allowance amounted also to 16s. 4d. There were two servants of the church. In the tailory, there were two tailors, two washermen, a wood carrier, and a shoemaker. There were also servants attached to the infirmary, to the lazar house (13 lepers with 3 servants), two carriers of stone for the workers of the abbey, a mason, a curtiler, a swineherd, and a refectorian, making a total of forty servants.[50]

For the 72 monks at Ely,

> £70 was assigned for the clothing of the brethren, and for their food £60 and 200 pigs, as well as all the pigs maintained in the precincts (in curia), all the cheese and butter from their estates, and 7 measures (treias) of wheat and 10 of malt weekly. If there was sufficient wine they should have it for their pittance on Saturdays and feasts of twelve lessons, but if not, half the pittance should be of mead. For their lights were assigned the offerings at the shrine of St. Botolph and burial fees in the town.[51]

Sawyer observed: 'However important wage earning may have been there can be little doubt that there were, in many parts of England, active markets for the sale of produce and that these were patronized by the peasants as well as their

---

[50] W. Ryland, D. Adkins and R. M. Serjeantson (eds), *Victoria County History Northampton*: vol. 2 (1906), pp. 83–95.

[51] L. F. Salzman (ed.), *Victorian County History Cambridge and the Isle of Ely*: vol. 2 (1948), pp. 199–210.

lords'.[52] Evesham Abbey acquired market rights 'just before the Conquest',[53] and there is further evidence for the existence of such markets in Anglo-Saxon laws. Thus, Æthelstan (924–38) decreed that no trading shall take place on Sundays; and if anyone does so he shall lose the goods and pay a fine of 30 shillings. Edward the Elder (900–25) willed that 'every man shall have a warrantor [to his transactions] and that no one shall buy [and sell] except in a market town; but he shall have the witness of the 'portreeve' or of other men of credit, who can be trusted. And if anyone buys outside a market town, he shall forfeit the sum due for insubordination to the king. Echoing Æthelstan, Cnut (1016–35) ordered that 'we admonish that men keep Sunday's festival with all their might, and observe it from Saturday's noon to Monday's dawning; and no man be so bold that he either go to market or seek any court on that holy day'. [54]

It was in the interests of the landholders – whether ecclesiastical or lay – to promote urban growth, for the bigger the resident population served by a market, the greater the profits: through tolls, rents of stalls, charges for the use of distinctive market services, like weighing apparatus, and any fines charged for offences against market rules.[55]

The close connection between the Anglo-Saxon church and markets shows up in church-names. In Cambridge,[56] Bristol,[57] Chichester,[58] Cheapside,[59] Lewes[60] and Lichfield[61] mediaeval church names carry the suffix *[Beate Marie] in Foro* (St Mary le Port: St Mary in the Market). Very often, the long axis of the Anglo-Saxon marketplace was aligned with that of the church – at Worcester,

---

[52] P. Sawyer, 'The Wealth of England':145–64 at 155.

[53] C. Dyer and T. R. Slater, 'The Midlands', in D. M. Palliser (ed.), *The Cambridge Urban History of Britain*, vol. 1 (Cambridge, 2000), p. 616.

[54] John Hudson, *The Oxford History of the Laws of England, II, 871–1216* (Oxford, 2012), p. 153; F. Attenborough, *Laws of the Earliest English Kings* (Cambridge, 1922), p. 115; Dorothy Haines (ed.) *Sunday Observance and the Sunday Letter in Anglo-Saxon England* (Cambridge, 2010), p. 26–7.

[55] R. Britnell, 'The Economy of British towns 600–1300', in Palliser, *The Cambridge Urban History of Britain*, vol. 1, p. 111.

[56] R. Masters, *The History of the College of Corpus Christi, Cambridge* (Cambridge, 1753), Appendix, p. 2.

[57] *Two Compotus Rolls of Saint Augustine's Abbey, Bristol, for 1491–2,* Gwen Beechcroft and Arthur Sabin (eds), Bristol Record Society ([Bristol], 1938)

[58] *Transcript of Sussex Wills,* R. Garraway Rice and Walter H. Godfrey (eds), vol. 1, Sussex Record Society (Lewes, 1935)

[59] *St. Mary Magdalene in foro Londoniarum.*

[60] *Lewes Historic Character Assessment Report*, pp. 28–36, at: www.lewes.gov.uk/Files/plan_Lewes_EUS_reportpg28to36.pdf

[61] T. Harwood, *The History and Antiquities of the Church and City of Lichfield* (London, 1806), p. 457.

Hereford, Coventry and Bury St Edmunds, for example,[62] physically displaying the link between the two functions. The minster church of St Andrew, Wells, founded by 766, fronted directly on to the market place, and at St Albans two churches, the market place, a cross and a major entrance to the town are all aligned. Abbot Wulsin of St Albans is said to have diverted Watling St to pass through a new market-place at his abbey's gate, thereby increasing the number of buyers and sellers. The present street plan of Wantage appears to be Anglo-Saxon in origin, with an ecclesiastical enclosure round the church and an open 'marketing' space nearby.[63]

In some Anglo-Saxon monastic towns, the marketplace evolved as a triangle, with its base across the front of the Abbey 'perhaps because the Abbey gateway could provide an effective architectural display of power'.[64] At Ely, a lay-settlers' market was against the north gate of the Abbey,[65] and in 1189, St Werberg's Abbey, Chester, was granted a fair 'to be kept before their door, and all the traders to pay [the monks] for their standing'.[66] There was money to be made from letting out stalls: in 1206, the kitchener of Evesham Abbey received 5s 6d a week from stall-rents,[67] and by 1250 – admittedly when the thirteenth-century 'commercial revolution' was well under way – a stall, which yielded 9d a week to the High Altar of Coventry Abbey was sold for 2 marks.[68]

As lords, Abbots and Priors could charge a toll on goods which were bought and sold in their markets. In the time of Edward the Confessor, Domesday Book tells us, the market toll at Lewes on the sale of a man was 4d., while that of a horse was 1d. and an ox ½d.[69] In Droitwich, 1086, the toll on salt carts varied with the size of the cart: if drawn by two or more oxen, the toll was 4d., but 2d. only if the trader was from Cheshire. Market tolls stayed curiously static in medieval England; in 1224, the toll at Northampton was 'of every cart or vehicle of another county carrying saleable items to Northampton 1d.; of every horseload of saleable articles, except a load of 1 bushel, ¼d.; of every horse, mare, ox or cow there taken for sale ½d.; of 10 sheep, goats or pigs taken there for sale

62 R. Goddard, *Lordship and Medieval Urbanization: Coventry 1043–1355* (Woodbridge, 2004), p. 45.

63 J. Haslam, (ed.), *Anglo-Saxon Towns* (Chichester, 1984).

64 D. M. Palliser, T. R. Slater and E. Patricia Dennison, 'The Topography of Towns 600–1300' in Palliser (ed.) *The Cambridge Urban History of Britain,* vol. 1, pp. 167–8. Examples survive in Battle, Coventry, St Albans and Evesham.

65 Goddard, *Coventry*, p. 41

66 W. Dugdale, *Monasticon Anglicanum* (London, 1817), vol. 1, p. 115.

67 'vetus villa et forum de Evesham de quibus percipit coquinarius qualibet die sabbati quinque solidos et tres obolos', *Chronicon Abbatiae De Evesham, Ad Annum 1418*, p. 216.

68 P. R. Coss and T. John (eds), *The Early Records of Medieval Coventry* (Oxford, 1986), no. 680.

69 Domesday Book i, f26.

1d.; of 5 sheep, goats or pigs taken there for sale ½d.'.[70] The toll at Meysham in 1272 was 1d for a horse, an ox, eight sheep and four to five pigs, or a cart-load: ¼d. for a man-load. The rates were similar at Ipswich[71] and Bakewell (also on a 'port-way'[72]) at the same date, although a horse-load was charged at ¼d.[73] The fixed and customary nature of these tolls indicates that by the thirteenth century they were already very firmly established at pre-existing levels, which inflation by then was making seem cheap. This is a good example of how moderate inflation could promote commercial enterprise.

Religious foundations could establish markets at any of their vills; for example, Eye Abbey had a market at Orford,[74] Lincoln Abbey had a fair at Newark,[75] and the monks of Ramsey Abbey had a tithe of the profits of their fair at Oakham.[76] Clearly, it was in the interest of the church to maintain their markets; the nuns at St Clements, York, had 20s. yearly from the profits of York market.[77] Such was the value of markets to a religious house that, in 1202, the Abbot of Bury St Edmunds paid 50 marks – £33/6/8d – to remove market-rights at Lakenheath, 16 miles to the north-west. The relationship between the monks and their markets is also revealed in a Glastonbury charter of 1272, for the cellarer and his officers insisted that they be served first in their market there.[78]

Charters also provide evidence of the church's involvement in overseas trade, much of it extremely early in date. Four eighth-century English royal charters describe the remission of tolls on ships owned by ecclesiastics and religious communities. Three such charters benefitted Minster-in-Thanet, which had its own harbour on one of the busiest commercial waterways in Anglo-Saxon England, providing a sheltered haven and safe waterway for ships running between the Thames estuary and the Continent. The large number of sceattas found in this area testifies to its commercial significance particularly during the

---

70 H. Kleineke, *Borough Market Privileges: The Hinterland of Medieval London, c. 1400* (2006), see www.british-history.ac.uk/source.aspx?pubid=345

71 T. Twiss (ed.), *Monumenta Juridica, or the Black Book of the Admiralty* (London, 1875), vol. 2, p. 197.

72 R. Millward and A. Robinson, *The Peak District* (London, 1975), p. 126.

73 J. G. Pease and H. Chitty, *A Treatise on the Law Of Markets and Fairs With The Principal Statutes Relating Thereto* (London, 1899), p. 61, see archive.org/details/treatiseonlawofm00peasiala

74 Dugdale, *Monasticon Anglicanum*, vol. 1, p. 44.

75 Dugdale, *Monasticon Anglicanum*, vol. 3, p. 242.

76 Dugdale, *Monasticon Anglicanum*, vol. 3, p. 34.

77 Dugdale, *Monasticon Anglicanum*, vol. 1, p. 63.

78 Dugdale, *Monasticon Anglicanum*, vol. 1, p. 109.

earliest phase of English sceatta production.[79] A similar charter was granted to St Peter's Minster, Worcester, remitting the toll due on two ships at London.[80]

An example of episcopal temporal wealth is shown by a charter of c. 840 which documents the sale of rights over five places in the west midlands to Bishop Heaberht of Worcester by King Berhtwulf of Mercia[81] for six horses, a gold ring, a dish, two drinking horns and three drinking vessels; the dish alone, probably silver, weighed 11 pounds. In effect, the bishop is here exchanging high status possessions for a steady future money income. Worcester's most famous Anglo-Saxon charter,[82] dating from 884–901, grants:

> At the request of Bishop Waerfirth, their friend, Ealdorman Ethelred and Aethelflaed ordered the borough of Worcester to be built for the protection of all the people ... and they now make it known, with the witness of God, in this Charter, that they will grant to god and St. Peter, and to the Lord of that Church, half of all the rights which belong to their lordship whether in the market or the street, both within the fortifications and outside ... except that the wagon-shilling and load-penny at Droitwich go to the King as they have always done. Otherwise, land-rent, the fine for fighting, or theft, or dishonest trading, and the contribution to the borough wall and all the (fines for) offences which admit compensation, are to belong half to the Lord of the Church.

The wealth of the church was intimately linked with the relics of saints. Relics were 'regarded as points of contact with the supernatural, as objects which would physically rise with the saints in the Last Days, and as the foci of miraculous and thaumaturgic (miracle-working) power'.[83] To visit the relics of a given saint on his or her saint's day was even more powerful. Pilgrims brought an income not only to the church, but also to market booths and inns. Fell uses evidence from contemporary continental miracle-books which give a vivid impression of the attractions of relics and of the great crush of lay-people present at the festivals and translations of the saints.[84] The 'D' version of the Anglo-Saxon Chronicle stresses the royal involvement in the translation of the archbishop St Æthelnoth to Canterbury in 1023:

---

79 D. M. Metcalf, *Thrymsas and Sceattas in the Ashmolean Museum Oxford, I* (London, 1993), p. 89, Map of Single Finds of Series A.

80 www.esawyer.org.uk for S29, S87, S91 and S98.

81 S 192.

82 S 223.

83 D. Rollason, 'Relic-Cults as an Instrument of Royal Policy c. 900–c. 1050', *Anglo-Saxon England*, 15 (1986), p. 96.

84 C. E. Fell, 'Edward King and Martyr and the Anglo-Saxon Hagiographic Tradition', in D. Hill (ed.), *Ethelred the Unready*, British Archaeological Reports (London, 1978), pp. 1–15.

> The illustrious king, and the archbishop and the diocesan bishops, and the earls, and very many ecclesiastics and also lay-folk, conveyed his holy body on a ship across the Thames to Southwark, and there entrusted the holy martyr to the archbishop and his companions. And they then bore him with a distinguished company and happy jubilation to Rochester. Then on the third day Queen Emma came with her royal child Hardacnut, and they then all conveyed the holy archbishop with much glory and joy and songs of praise into Canterbury.[85]

Such was the magnetic power of the relics that Æthelred and Æthelflæd of Mercia used them to bolster their plans for urban growth, transferring relics of St Oswald from Bardney to their newly founded church at Gloucester. 'The movement of relics from eastern to western England, and the building of churches in which to place them, were an important part of Æthelflæd's policy of urbanisation; relics were clearly being used to create a sense of identity for each town.'[86]

Markets, whether or not attached to the relics of a saint, together with church-goers and pilgrims, leave their traces. And this brings us to the role of the numismatic evidence.

The Numismatic Evidence

Our understanding of the use of money in Anglo-Saxon England has been transformed by the systematic accumulation of metal-detector finds data by the Portable Antiquities Scheme and the Fitzwilliam Museum. At its simplest these finds confirm the instincts of Michael Metcalf dating from the 1960s, when he recognised that the size of the Anglo-Saxon coinage was much larger than previously understood.[87] This underlies the fundamental insight that, whatever additional functions they may have had, Anglo-Saxon coins were above all money. The finds evidence also reminds us that the use, or at any rate the loss, of Anglo-Saxon coins was not spread geographically evenly over the whole country, or chronologically over the Anglo-Saxon period. The East of England used/lost

---

[85] Archbishop of Canterbury, 1020–38; previously a monk, and dean of Christ Church, Canterbury.

[86] J. Barrow, 'Churches, Education and Literacy in Towns 600–1300' in Palliser (ed.) *The Cambridge Urban History of Britain*, vol. 1, p. 131. For a map of the principal translations of relics, see D. Rollason, *Saints and Relics in Anglo-Saxon England* (Oxford, 1989), p. 176.

[87] D. M. Metcalf, 'How Large was the Anglo-Saxon Currency?', *Economic History Review*, 18 (1965): 475–82, which prompted Philip Grierson, 'The Volume of Anglo-Saxon Coinage', *Economic History Review*, 20 (1967): 153–60, followed by D. M. Metcalf, 'The Prosperity of North-Western Europe in the Eighth and Ninth Centuries', *Economic History Review*, 20 (1967): 344–57.

more coin than the West, perhaps reflecting the distribution of population or the importance of trade links across the North Sea. Chronologically coin use began gradually with the gold thrymsas (or tremisses), but then exploded with the currency of silver sceattas c. 680–740.[88]

Although early Anglo-Saxon coins sometimes record their mint of origin, English coins do not consistently bear their mint name till the last quarter of the tenth century. However, where mint names are given from the late ninth century it becomes possible to compare mints of origin with known find spots. Michael Metcalf was one of the first to systematically exploit coin find evidence in order to explore patterns of monetary circulation 'by asking how far each [coin] had been carried from its mint of origin before it was accidentally lost'.[89] In a similar way, it is possible to explore the range of individual markets on the basis of the coins from distant mints found there. With the aid of the data from the Fitzwilliam's Medieval Corpus, we have analysed the single finds from each of 162 likely market places operating in 1086. For 27 possible market locations, no single coin finds are recorded, and we may put them to one side for the moment.[90] For each of the remaining relevant market-town findspots, the mints of origin for each find can be plotted, together with the numbers from each mint, and the walking distance from each mint to the market-town findspot can be measured. For example, for Oxford finds, 871–1086, the recorded mints are: London two, Wallingford one, Tamworth one, Frome one, and Oxford one. The Oxford coin is not used in the calculation [which is: 2 × 57 (London) = 104 + 13 (Wallingford) + 70 (Tamworth) + 67 (Frome) = 254 miles].

---

88 Blair, *The Anglo-Saxon Church*, p. 257, citing Metcalf, and Blackburn: 'it is an astonishing fact that the volume of the English currency in these decades was greater than it would ever be again before 1200'. See Blackburn's graph of Single finds of S. England excluding productive sites, recording 3,552 coins from 600 to 1175, in Pestell and Ulmschneider (eds), *Markets in Early Medieval Europe*, p. 32. Figures in Naismith, *Money and Power in Anglo-Saxon England*. We take up the story from the 760s to the conquest, and although losses of the late Anglo-Saxon currency do not reach the sceatta peak, they maintain consistently high levels decade after decade, confirming the impression conveyed by the huge quantities of Anglo-Saxon coin sent to Scandinavia from the last quarter of the tenth century onwards.

89 D. M. Metcalf, 'Continuity and Change in English Monetary History', *British Numismatic Journal*, 50 (1980): 20–49, and *An Atlas of Anglo-Saxon and Norman Coin Finds, c. 973–1086* (London, 1998).

90 They are: Winchcombe, Aylesbury, Old Linslade, Buckingham, Bodmin, Halwell, Totnes, Axminster, Swanage, Christchurch, Berkhamsted, Shrewsbury, Watchet, Lyng, Pilton, Langport, Milverton, Frome, Ilminster, Milborne Port, Eashing, Malmesbury, Wilton, Bradford-on-Avon, Bedwyn, Pershore, and Droitwich. This exercise has not yet included the evidence collected by the Portable Antiquities Scheme at finds.org.uk. We may be confident that by combining both the PAS and the Fitzwilliam evidence, together with that of new finds continually being made, the database will grow. We include any coin recorded as found anywhere in a town believed to be the site of an early medieval market.

These five coins have travelled at least a total of 254 miles, although not necessarily in one single journey. This total is divided by five to give the average 'range' for Oxford, which is 50.8 miles. The same calculation is made for the other 43 market locations for which mint-name data can be found, and the results are shown in Table 9.1.

Table 9.1 Market towns: mean range.

Over 109 miles	76–109 miles	41–75 miles	40 miles and under
London	Norwich	Peterborough	Dover
York	Winchester	Bedford	St Albans
Hamwic	Lewes	Wallingford	Seasalter
Rochester	Cambridge	Oxford	Pershore
Canterbury	Thetford	Southwark	Abingdon
Newark	Northampton	Colchester	Bidford on Avon
	Ipswich	Reculver	Pocklington
	Bristol	Leicester	Bridlington
	Reading	Tamworth	
	Rendlesham	Steyning	
	Guildford	Royston	
	Evesham	Torksey	

At first sight this information is not surprising, and happily so, since, in part, it conforms to established views on Anglo-Saxon monetisation.[91] The coins travelled further to the more important markets, but even smaller markets drew coins from a significant range.

With reference to Table 9.1, three of the four major *wics* are in the group with the largest range, together with the Kentish towns of Canterbury and Rochester, both of which were Mercian mints. Kentish pre-eminence may be attributed both to its key south-east location, and to its very early experience of money. Ever since St Augustine's arrival in 597, Kent was not only a base from which Christianity spread throughout southern and central England, but also the centre of innovation for English monetisation.[92] Both sees were immensely wealthy; for example, around 960, the Bishop of Rochester bought

[91] See R. Britnell, 'Markets and Fairs in Britain and Ireland before 1216', at https://sites.google.com/site/feanbeast/miscellaneous-papers/markets-and-fairs: 'At the time when Domesday Book was compiled in 1086, the regional differences were striking. Southern England (meaning here, and subsequently, England south of the Humber) was one of the most heavily monetised regions of western Europe'.

[92] It owed this status through its proximity to Gaul. The Franks minted their own imitations, mimicking Rome first, and then Byzantium. For Merovingian France, and then

the privileges of Bromley, Kent, for 80 mancuses of gold and six pounds of silver, with a compensatory sum of 30 mancuses of gold to Wulfstan, King Edgar's prefect.[93] At a similar date, Dunstan paid 10 lbs of gold and silver 'for land at Canterbury'.[94] Æthelstan recognised the economic importance of both towns by instituting seven moneyers at Canterbury; only London, with eight moneyers, had more. Rochester, with three, is immediately below Canterbury in this ranking by moneyers.[95]

Certain regional patterns may be observed: while coins from York are found over most of England, all the coins at Pocklington and Bridlington were struck at York, and at York itself, coins minted there outnumber coins from more distant mints five to one. It seems that we are looking at a market somewhat separate from the rest of England, even though the Scandinavian kingdom of York ended in 954. Winchester, too, looks like a regional market centre, for while six of its finds were struck in London, and two in Canterbury, the other coins with a mint name come from Wessex.

The Market Render

We may turn now to consider the value of early medieval markets. Whitelock writes that 'the requirements of a royal estate, as at Reading, Windsor, or Bedwyn or large monastery might cause the congregation of a group of tradesmen and artisans', suggesting that the size of a settlement would influence the value of its market.[96] In only 29 cases, Domesday Book provides both the market render, and the number of tenements.[97] Of these, six list the number of burgesses, messuages, houses and closes, which may be called urban; the remaining 23 list the numbers of peasant households. Correlating the numbers of urban tenements against the market render produces a coefficient of +0.78 – a strong positive correlation associating the value of the market with the size of the settlement. Correlating the peasant tenements with the market render gives an even better correlation: +0.80 as shown in Figure 9.1. This point is not quite so obvious as one might think, because burgesses themselves were excused the payment of market tolls.[98]

---

for Kent, the same sequence prevails: imitation, followed by the independent striking of native coins.

93 S 671.

94 Ibid.

95 F. L. Attenborough, *The Laws of the Earliest English Kings* (Cambridge, 1922), pp. 135, 137.

96 D. Whitelock, *The Beginnings of English Society* (Harmondsworth, 1954), p. 125.

97 Darby, *Domesday Geography*, Appendix 17 lists Domesday Book references to markets, pp. 369–70.

98 Dyer, 'Hidden trade': 144.

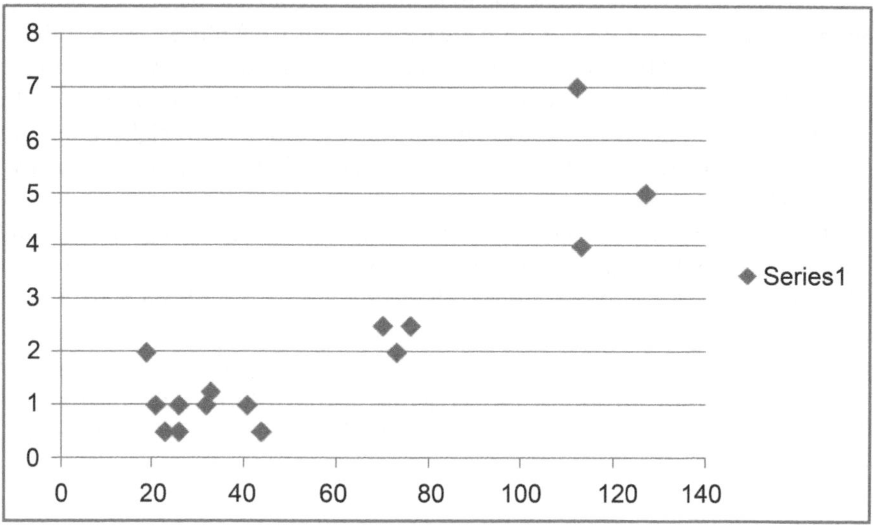

Figure 9.1 Market render and number of tenements (Y = market render; X = number of peasant households).

Based on this apparent relationship between the size of settlements and the value of their markets, it is possible to estimate the likely value of those locations which we have identified as market sites, on the basis of the size of those settlements as indicated in Domesday Book. The results are shown in Table 9.2.

Table 9.2 Forecast market render for 'urban' dwellers; number of households, followed by estimated value of market (£).

		H'holds	Value			H'holds	Value
Kent	Canterbury	378	29	Hampshire	Southampton	89	5.9
	Rochester	49	2.7		Winchester	97	6.5
	Old Romsey	156	11.3	Berkshire	Wallingford	714	55
	Hythe	252	18.9		Reading	60	3.6
	Fordwich	79	5.1	Wiltshire	Malmesbury	82	5.4
Sussex	Lewes	348	26.5		Bedwyn	25	0.8
	Rye	64	3.9		Warminster	30	1.2
	Hastings	131	9.3		Wilton	23	0.7
	Chichester	300	22.7	Dorset	Bridport	80	5.2
	Pevensey	109	7.5		Shaftesbury	66	4.1
	Arundel	15	0.03	Devon	Barnstaple	101	6.8
Wiltshire	Calne	74	4.7		Totnes	95	6.3
	Warminster		1.2		Lydford	21	0.5
	Malmesbury	82	3.6	Hertfordshire	Hertford	42	2.2
	Bedwyn	25	0.82		St Albans	46	2.5
	Warminster	30	1.2		Berkhamsted	52	2.9
				Bucks	Buckingham	26	0.9
Somerset	Bath	200	14.7	Oxon	Oxford	275	20.7

		H'holds	Value			H'holds	Value
Cambs.	Cambridge	319	13.7	Gloucs.	Gloucester	90	6
Cheshire	Chester	487	24.2		Winchcombe	28	1.1
	Rhuddlan	28	1.1	Herefs.	Hereford	64	3.9
Surrey	Guildford	76	4.8		Clifford	16	0.1
	Southwark	53	3	Lincs.	Lincoln	98	6.6
				Leics.	Leicester	333	25.3
	Staines	46	2.5		Torksey	102	6.9
Worcs.	Worcester	170	12.3		Grantham	88	5.8
	Droitwich	109	7.5		Louth	82	5.4
	Pershore	28	1.1		Stamford	300	22.7
Salop	Shrewsbury	201	14.8	Essex	Maldon	181	13.2
Warwicks.	Warwick	256	19		Sudbury	75	4.8
Staffs	Stafford	139	7.3		Colchester	40	2
	Tamworth	22	0.6	Norfolk	Norwich	115	7.9
Hunts	Huntingdon	336	25.6		Yarmouth	70	4.4
Derbs.	Derby	140	9.9		Thetford	735	56.6
Notts.	Nottingham	82	5.4	Suffolk	Ipswich	226	16.7
	Newark	56	3.2		Dunwich	456	35
Yorks.	Pocklington	19	0.3		Eye	25	0.8
	Tanshelf	60	3.6		Bury St E	320	24.3
					Clare	43	2.3

These data for 'urban' settlements indicate a total annual value for the market tolls, etc., of £757 – but are they representative of the reality? In a few cases, we can compare the estimates with later data. Thus, the estimate for Bury St Edmunds is £24.3, that is, £24/6/8d. We know that, in 1202, the Abbot of St Edmunds paid 40 marks, and two palfreys costing 10 marks for a royal charter guaranteeing that no markets or fairs would be established in the liberty of St Edmunds that would damage his revenue.[99] Fifty marks amounts to £33/6/8d., so the Abbot would have covered his costs within two years if the market render was, indeed, around £24. Similarly, in 1189, the receipts of the bishopric of Winchester for a three-day annual fair amounted to £146/8/7d., so that the forecast for the weekly market there of £6/10/- looks modest.[100]

In addition to these markets in towns, described in clearly urban terms in Domesday Book, markets are also recorded in what seem otherwise to be more rural locations. Estimating the likely value of these apparently rural markets, on the basis of the numbers of recorded tenements, yields a figure of £178, to be added to the £757 from the more clearly urban settlements, suggesting that the possible value of renders from all the markets mentioned in Domesday Book might have approached £1,000. Moreover, it needs to be remembered that the market render represents only the sum of dues and tolls owed to the owner of the market; the total turn-over of the market would have been far greater.

[99] D. Whitelock (ed.), *Anglo-Saxon Wills* (Cambridge, 1930), pp. 74, 185.

[100] M. Biddle (ed.), *Winchester in the Eleventh and Twelfth Centuries* (Oxford, 1976), p. 285.

Table 9.3 Forecasts of 'rural' markets.

County	Location	Tenements	Market render	County	Location	Tenements	Market render
Kent	Faversham	70	4	Gloucs.	Cirencester	41	1
	Newenden	29	2		Berkeley	52	2.2
	Lewisham	59	2		Tewkesbury	13	0.58
	Lympne	19	0.5	Worcs.	Evesham	27	3.2
Sussex	Steyning	319	15.3	Warwicks.	Bidford On Avon	43	1.7
Surrey	Southwark	68	2.9	Beds.	Leighton Buzzard	112	7
Hampshire	Neatham	96	2		Luton	127	5
	Basingstoke	39	1.5		Arlesey	23	0.5
	Titchfield	29	2	Northants.	Kings Sutton	21	1
	Christchurch	64	2.7		Oundle	33	1.25
Berkshire	Cookham BE	52	1		Higham Ferrers	26	1
	Wantage	48	1.9		Peterborough	102	4.6
	Windsor	119	5.5	Hunts.	Yaxley	47	1.9

County	Location	Tenements	Market render	County	Location	Tenements	Market render
Somerset	Frome SOM	67	2.3	Lincs.	Bolingbroke	32	1
	Milborne Port	56	3		Spalding	73	2
	Milverton	27	0.4		Partney	44	0.5
	Bruton	65	2.8		Threekingham	19	2
	Crewkerne	113	4		Louth	80	1.45
Devon	Axminster	65	2.8	Wilts.	Tilshead	132	6.1
	Okehampton	4	0.2		Bedwyn	179	8.4
Dorset	Wimborne Minster	160	7.5	Staffs.	Stafford	157	7.3
Bucks	Newport	13	0.2		Lichfield	54	2.3
	Aylesbury	34	1.2	Herefs.	Ewyas Harold	44	1.8
Oxon	Dorchester On Thames	114	5.2	Essex	Horton On The Hill	31	1.1
	Bampton	70	2.5	Norfolk	Caistor-By-Norwich	26.5	0.9
				Suffolk	Hoxne	71	3.1

Conclusion

This chapter has argued that already by the eleventh century England was significantly monetised and that the church actively promoted money payments and benefitted from them. With some 10 per cent of the population urbanised, and commercial activity widespread in town and country, money was a fact of both religious and secular life. The church was a major player in the economic development of early medieval England. Many churchmen were less than comfortable with this situation. For example Gerald of Wales, writing in the 1190s, drew unfavourable comparison between the worldliness of the Llanthony secunda priory in Gloucester compared with the spiritual simplicity of the mother house of Llanthony in rural Wales. Tensions between the two establishments came to a head in 1205 when they formally dissociated from one another. Initially the Welsh house retained its share of property in Gloucester yielding rents worth over £12, but half a century later naivety or profound spirituality induced them to surrender their rights for an annual pension of £3 6s. 8d.[101] On the whole, however, the church managed to reconcile itself to the material foundations on which its spiritual life depended surprisingly easily.

[101] Gerald of Wales, *The Journey through Wales and The Description of Wales*, Lewis Thorpe (trans.) (London, 1988), pp. 97–107. Richard Holt and Nigel Baker, *Urban Growth and the Medieval Church: Gloucester and Worcester* (Aldershot, 2004). For the investment strategies of monastic orders in France see Constance B. Bouchard, *Holy Entrepreneurs: Cistercians, Knights, and Economic Exchange in Twelfth-Century Burgundy* (Ithaca, 1991).

PART III
Money and Power: Coinage, Salvation and Ritual

Chapter 10

From HEINRICVS REX to ROTHARDVS ABBAS – Monastic Coinage under the Ottonians and Salians (c. 911–1125)

Sebastian Steinbach

> Concessimus atque perdonavimus, ut in loco Salsa nominato [...] Faciat et habeat mercatum et monetam publicam imagine et superscriptione utriusque monete Argentinensis et Spirensis praefiguratam, [...] Ut huius imaginis et superscriptionis moneta publica et mercatus habeatur absque contradictione alicuius invide persone et theloneum inde accipiatur sicut in aliis regalibus locis ex monetis publicis.[1]

With these words Emperor Otto III (983–1002) granted the right of coinage on 2 July 993 to the Benedictine monastery of Selz (Alsace, France), which had been founded just two years earlier. The formula for minting is common, but granted economic privilege as well as status to the abbey. In a pre-literate society, the image of the coin was itself a powerful communicative device and instrument and the appearance of commonly accepted coin types often went unchanged for long periods of time. The mass-produced Saxonian *Otto-Adelheid-Pfennige*, for instance, continued to be issued long after the last king named Otto had died.[2]

---

[1] 'We grant and bestow, that Selz should have a market of its own and strike an official coin, its type and legend having been modelled after the Strasbourg and Speyer coins, [...] Furthermore it is our wish that the official coin of this type, bearing this legend, and the market be established there without any objection by envious persons and the duties be collected there the same as at all the other royal places of the public mints'. *Ottonis III. Diplomata*, Theodor von Sickel (ed.), Monumenta Germaniae Historica, Diplomata, Tomus II.2. (Berlin, 1957), no. 130.

[2] For the specific literature focused on the *Otto-Adelheid-Pfennige* see, for the period prior to 1952, Vera Jammer, *Die Anfänge der Münzprägung im Herzogtum Sachsen. 10./11. Jahrhundert* (Hamburg, 1952), pp. 61–4; for the years 1952–90, Gert Hatz, Vera Hatz, Ulrich Zwicker, Noel Gale and Zofia Gale, *Otto-Adelheid-Pfennige. Untersuchungen zu Münzen des 10./11. Jahrhunderts* (Stockholm, 1991), pp. 9–24; for the most recent publications until

Many Westphalian mints in the Ottonian-Salian Empire (919–1125),[3] among them Soest, Münster and Osnabrück, struck the widely accepted Cologne coin type bearing the three-line S-COLONIA-A (*Sancta Colonia Agrippina*) legend. As the Speyer[4] and Strasbourg[5] coin types were the most common currency in the Selz region, the permission to copy them was nothing less than a grant to issue the coins in the same region.[6]

Chronologically speaking, the document granting coinage rights to the Alsatian Selz Abbey is by no means the first in the list of charters pertaining to a right of coinage for monastic communities. The very first bestowal of minting rights on a monastery dates back to the Carolingian period. This first instance is documented in a charter of Emperor Louis the Pious (814–40) from the year 833, granting the right to Abbot Warin (826–56) for Corvey Abbey on the Weser River.[7] From this charter on until the end of the Salians' reign in 1125, there are a total of 49 documented cases in which the right of coinage was

---

2005, see also Bernd Kluge, 'ATHALHET, ATEAHLHT und ADELDEIDA. Das Rätsel der Otto-Adelheid-Pfennige', in Franz Staab and Thorsten Unger, *Kaiserin Adelheid und ihre Klostergründing in Selz* (Speyer, 2005), pp. 91–114.

3 For a general introduction to Ottonian-Salian Coinage see Bernd Kluge, *Deutsche Münzgeschichte von der späten Karolingerzeit bis zum Ende der Salier* (Speyer, 1991) and the catalogue of Hermann Dannenberg, *Die deutschen Münzen der sächsischen und fränkischen Kaiserzeit*, 4 vols (Berlin, 1876–1905). For an introduction to the coinage of Ottonian-Salian monastic communities see Sebastian Steinbach, *Das Geld der Nonnen und Mönche. Münzrecht, Münzprägung und Geldumlauf der ostfränkisch-deutschen Klöster in ottonisch-salischer Zeit (ca. 911–1125)* (Berlin, 2007) and Dorothea Menadier, *Die Münzen und das Münzwesen der deutschen Reichsäbtissinnen im Mittelalter, Zeitschrift für Numismatik*, 32 (1920): 185–291.

4 For the coinage of Speyer see Helfried Ehrend, *Speyrer Münzgeschichte, Teil I: Münzen und Medaillen (um 650–1900)* (Speyer, 2005).

5 For the coinage of Strasbourg see Arthur Engel and Ernest Lehr, *Numismatique Alsace* (Paris, 1887), pp. 145–64; Alain Baron, *Die Münzprägung der Bischöfe, Kaiser und Könige in Straßburg (751–1123)*, unpubl. Dissertation am Institut für Numismatik der Universität Wien (1987).

6 For the coinage of the abbey of Selz see Steinbach, *Das Geld der Nonnen und Mönche*, pp. 174–5; Hermann Dannenberg, *Die deutschen Münzen der sächsischen und fränkischen Kaiserzeit*, vol. IV (Berlin, 1905), pp. 936–7; Franz Xaver Nessel, *Die Münzen der Abtei Selz*, in Frankfurter Münzzeitung 9 (1909), pp. 421–39 and 449–59; Julius Menadier, 'Ein Adelheidspfennig der Abtei Selz im Elsass', *Berliner Münzblätter* 110/111 (1889): 985–90.

7 Wilhelm Jesse, *Quellenbuch zur Münz- und Geldgeschichte des Mittelalters* (Halle/Saale, 1924) pp. 14–15: '[...] Insuper etiam, quia locum mercationis ipsa regio indigebat, monetam nostrae auctoritatis publicam ultra ibi semper inesse Christo militantibus proficuam statuimus, quatenus [...] locus ipse sanctitatis omne inde reditum nostrae auctoritatis publicum possidet [...]'.

granted to a monastic community.[8] Of these, 33 were first-time bestowals and 14 were reaffirmations of existing rights; the preceding charters for the latter, however, have not always survived. Two further charters merely document the existence of a monastic mint, without giving specific information on its status. The number of charters issued by Emperor Otto III is quite remarkable: his reign of only 19 years includes 15 bestowals of a right of coinage on a monastery.

A comparison of this number to the total of surviving charters granting minting rights from the period between 833 and 1125[9] shows monastic charters to make up 29.52 per cent of the total of 166 surviving deeds. In other words, as far as the charters are concerned, monastic minting during the Ottonian-Salian reign by no means constitutes a marginal phenomenon, almost one out of three instances of granting coinage rights involved a monastery as the beneficiary. The only institutions in the empire to receive the right of coinage more often were the episcopal churches, with 48 per cent (107 charters) of the cases. Secular institutions, such as dukes or counts, account for a mere 6 per cent (10 charters) of the total and they thus make up the peripheral group.

An equally interesting picture is painted when analysing the geographic distribution of monasteries receiving the right of coinage. The Ottonians and Salians, for instance, favoured distinctly the parts of the empire that were of great importance to their rule. Fifteen out of 29 coinage right charters in the period from 833 to 1024 went to the Duchy of Saxony. Without exception, the receiving monasteries lay within what has been referred to as the 'politically central areas' of Ottonian rule[10] and, moreover, had familial ties to the dynasty of sovereigns. As Saxony at that time had limited circulation of coins to speak of (compared to the western part of the Empire where minting tradition went partly back to ancient times),[11] the Ottonians might be presumed to have used the imperial abbeys, which were often governed by daughters of the dynasty as abbesses, as centres through which to exercise power and economic control. In this period a comprehensive network of dioceses did not yet cover Saxony, in

---

[8] For a complete list and commentary on coinage rights for monastic communities in the Ottonian-Salian Empire see Steinbach, *Das Geld der Nonnen und Mönche*, pp. 25–46, 391–405 and 446–50.

[9] Kluge, *Deutsche Münzgeschichte*, pp. 101–4.

[10] Eckhard Müller-Mertens, *Die Reichsstruktur im Spiegel der Herrschaftspraxis Ottos des Großen* (Berlin, 1980) and Eckhard Müller-Mertens, *Verfassung des Reiches, Reichsstruktur und Herrschaftspraxis unter Otto dem Großen*, in Matthias Puhle (ed.), *Otto der Große. Magdeburg und Europa*, vol. 1 (Mainz, 2001), pp. 189–98.

[11] In fact, by the beginning of the reign of King Conrad I (911–19) there were only two mints east of the Rhein river: Regensburg and Würzburg. By the end of the Ottonian dynasty there were more than 32. Bernd Kluge, *Otto Rex / Otto Imp. Zur Bestandsaufnahme der ottonischen Münzprägung*, in Bernd Schneidmüller and Stefan Weinfurter (eds), *Ottonische Neuanfänge* (Mainz, 2001), p. 90.

contrast to the west of the empire: the Ottonians needed to employ the abbeys as footholds of their authority.

The reason for the increased density of mints in the Harz area may be found in the heavy mining activities in that region. In the third book, chapter 63 of his *The Three Books of Saxons* or *Three Books of Annals*, Widukind of Corvey recounts the discovery of silver lodes: 'Terra Saxonia venas argenti aperuerit'.[12] Although this particular text is commonly dated back to 968, research by mining archaeologists shows it is safe to assume that the Harz mountains had been mined long before that date.[13] The extent to which the monasteries of the region played a role in the massive striking of anonymous *Otto-Adelheid-Pfennige* can only be guessed at.[14] There were, however, die links to Quedlinburg Abbey among others.[15] Other grants such as those for St Gallen, Trier or Verdun can be explained by their location along important trade routes of the Middle Ages, which at the same time constituted the main travel routes for the itinerant kings.[16] The charter bestowing coinage rights by Otto I (936–73) on Abbot Graloh (942–58) of St Gallen, dated 12 June 947, expounds on the significance of the town for merchants and pilgrims passing through on their way to Italy (Rome in particular) and of their need to have a market with its own coin at their disposal.[17]

---

[12] *Widukini monachi Corbeiensis rerum gestarum Saxonicarum libri tres*, lib. 3, cap. 63, Paul Hirsch (ed.), Monumenta Germaniae Historica, Scriptores rer. Germ 60 (Hannover, 1935).

[13] Christoph Bartels, Michael Fessner, Lothar Klappauf and Friedrich Albert Linke, *Kupfer, Blei und Silber aus dem Goslarer Rammelsberg von den Anfängen bis 1620* (Bochum, 2007), pp. 72–3 with references to older literature on that theme.

[14] For an overview of the studies about the Otto-Adelheid-Pfennige see Kluge, *ATHALHET, ATEAHLHT und ADELDEIDA*: 91–114; Vera Jammer, *Die Anfänge der Münzprägung im Herzogtum Sachsen. 10./11. Jahrhundert*, Numismatische Studien 3–4 (Hamburg, 1952), pp. 61–4; Vera and Gert Hatz, Ulrich Zwicker and Noel and Zofia Gale, *Otto-Adelheid-Pfennige. Untersuchungen zu Münzen des 10./11. Jahrhunderts*, Commentationes de nummis saeculorum IX–XI in suecia repertis. Nova Series 7 (Stockholm, 1991), pp. 9–24.

[15] For the coinage of Quedlinburg see Manfred Mehl, *Die Münzen des Stiftes Quedlinburg* (Hamburg, 2006) and Steinbach, *Das Geld der Nonnen und Mönche*, pp. 141–6.

[16] For the main travel routes in the Ottonian and Salian periods, Eckhard Müller-Mertens, *Verfassung des Reiches, Reichsstruktur und Herrschaftspraxis unter Otto dem Großen*, in Matthias Puhle (ed.), *Otto der Große. Magdeburg und Europa*, vol. 1 (Mainz, 2001), map on p. 194. For the travel routes of the medieval kings in general see Norbert Ohler, *Reisen im Mittelalter* (Zürich / München, 2004), pp. 54–80.

[17] *Conradi I., Heinrici I. et Ottonis I. Diplomata*, Theodor von Sickel (ed.), Monumenta Germaniae Historica, Diplomata (Berlin, 1956), no. 90: '[…] mercatum ibi haberi Italiam profiscentibus vel Romam pergentibus esse commodum'.

The discussion above suggests that abbeys that received coinage rights were either imperially sponsored institutions and as such answerable directly to the king or were bound to the ruling dynasty by the appointment of direct relatives to govern them. Some of them of course were both. There can, therefore, be little doubt that the king used the granting of coinage rights to monasteries as an instrument by which to exercise power and that the privileged towns or regions were 'areas of immediate sovereignty'.

The significance of charters of coinage right for the numismatic study of the Ottonian and Salian imperial period is complex. Previous research often focused on the gap between diplomatic evidence and numismatic findings. On the one hand, there is a dearth of coins that survive from the area indicated amongst some of the surviving charters; on the other, there is a whole series of coin-issues which lack any corroborating documentary evidence. Monastic grants provide a possible explanation for this phenomenon: in 973 Emperor Otto I (936–73) reaffirmed to new abbess Imma (973–92/95) of Herford the right of coinage for the town *Adonhvsa*, modern day Odenhusen, a part of the Radewig district of Herford.[18] The text explicitly points out that the document acknowledges an already existing right of coinage, originally granted by one 'King Louis' (referred to in Latin as *Hlvthvvvici regis* within the text).[19]

The king in question might be in all likelihood Louis 'the Pious' (814–40), who also founded Corvey Abbey and bestowed upon it coinage rights in 833. However, there is no corresponding Carolingian document. In other words, had the Herford certificate of 973 not survived, we would not have known about any Ottonian or even older Carolingian grant of coinage rights and would have classified the Herford coins as mysterious types lacking a right of coinage.

Essen provides another monastic example seen from the coin-side of view. In 1891 a denier bearing the initially mysterious legend ASNIDIA was found in a vegetable garden in the village of D'Emšino, located in the former imperial Russian governorate of Pskow.[20] It was in fact the oldest known coin of Essen Abbey, probably struck under Abbess Sophia (1012–39), a daughter of emperor Otto II (973–83) during the reign of king Conrad II (1024–39), for the writing possibly shows the remnants of a [+ C]O[NRAD]VS [I]MP(erator)

---

18 *Conradi I., Heinrici I. et Ottonis I. Diplomata*, no. 430.

19 'Noverit omnium fidelium nostrorum praesentium scilicet ac futurorum industria, qualiter quaedam venerabilis abbatissa Hefordensi monasterii nomine Imma nobis scripta Hluthuuuici regis de quodam mercato cum omnibus inde exigendi usibus, id est moneta teloneo vel quicquid ad publicum videtur pertinere mercatum, in loco Adonhusa nominato afferens nostramque diletam coniugem nomine Adelheidam haec eadem scripta nos nostri praecepto eius interventu praefato monasterio renovari praecabatur'.

20 For the place name of Essen in the tenth century see among others the document of Otto I from 1 March 966 in which it is called *Astnithe*: *Conradi I., Heinrici I. et Ottonis I. Diplomata*, no. 325.

legend.[21] Without this fortunate find the historical existence of an Essen Abbey coinage under Salian rule would have remained unattested; to date the piece has remained unique. Applying the minimum struck number of 10,000 pieces per die commonly used in die analysis, the survival rate of Essen coins of this type would amount to just about 0.01 per cent.

In contrast, coins and charters stemming from monastic mints show survival rates of close to 35 per cent, because there is diplomatic as well as numismatic evidence for 15 out of the 44 monastic mints mentioned in documents. Many of the mints lacking a charter lay within the Duchy of Lorraine, which can be explained by the fact that their rights might stem from older traditions.[22] Additionally, there is a great amount of anonymous and immobilised coin types that often elude a precise allocation. As the mass medium of the Middle Ages, coins transport images and written information and as such are of great significance when comparing written and material sources. This assertion leads us directly to the monastic coin types.

When considering the geographic distribution of monastic mints documented by coinage in the Ottonian-Salian era, centres of monastic minting are readily recognised (see Plate 6). A corridor running from West to East can be made out, its northern boundary the noble convent of Herford[23] and its southern the monastery of Lorsch.[24] To the south of this corridor only the monastery of St Vitalis in Esslingen[25] and the mints of

---

[21] For the coinage of Essen see Heinz Josef Kramer, *Das Stift Essen. Münzen und Medaillen. Königliche und stiftische Prägungen in und für Essen* (Münster, 1993); Heinrich Buchenau, 'Ein Essener Denar des XI. Jahrhunderts', *Blätter für Münzfreunde*, 7 (1901): 207; Dannenberg, *Deutsche Münzen der sächsischen und fränkischen Kaiserzeit*, vol. II, p. 750 and vol. IV, p. 894; Steinbach, *Das Geld der Nonnen und Mönche*, pp. 125–6 and Kluge, *Deutsche Münzgeschichte*, no. 412.

[22] It is an interesting fact that all the dioceses and abbeys lacking a charter of right to coin in the Lorraine area where founded during the Merovingian and Carolingian periods. Steinbach, *Das Geld der Nonnen und Mönche*, p. 199.

[23] For the coinage of Herford see Steinbach, *Das Geld der Nonnen und Mönche*, pp. 128–32; Dannenberg, *Deutsche Münzen der sächsischen und fränkischen Kaiserzeit*, vol. I, pp. 283–4, vol. II, p. 646, vol. IV, p. 914 and Peter Berghaus, *Münzgeschichte Herfords* (Herford, 1971).

[24] For the coinage of Lorsch see Steinbach, *Das Geld der Nonnen und Mönche*, pp. 169–74; Dannenberg, *Deutsche Münzen der sächsischen und fränkischen Kaiserzeit*, vol. III, pp. 805–6 and Kluge, *Deutsche Münzgeschichte*, nos 505–6.

[25] Ulrich Klein and Albert Raff, *Die Münzen und Medaillen von Esslingen* (Stuttgart, 1997); Steinbach, *Das Geld der Nonnen und Mönche*, pp. 176–9; Dannenberg, *Deutsche Münzen der sächsischen und fränkischen Kaiserzeit*, vol. I, pp. 359–62, vol. II, p. 670 and Kluge, *Deutsche Münzgeschichte*, nos 84, 150, 250, 316 and 508.

Selz[26], St Gallen[27] and Zürich[28] (none of which emanate from a conclusively proven monastic environment) struck coin. It is hard to attribute definitely existing coin to any of these southern mints.

In the Duchy of Bavaria there is no apparent monastery responsible for striking coin. This is a consequence of the special status of Bavarian coinage in the empire, which was marked by the quasi-regal status of the duke, who reigned supreme. The mints were centralised and all coins were modelled after the Regensburg type.[29] The only other places of minting, apart from the ducal mints, were the dioceses of Augsburg, Salzburg, Passau, Freising and Eichstätt,[30] which struck coin mainly during the second half of the eleventh century. When the Bavarian Duke Henry IV (995–1002) acceded to the throne in 1002 as King Henry II (1002–24) the ducal coinage became royal.[31] In the following years the Bavarian bishops became somewhat like the heirs of the ducal coinage rights. It should be borne in mind, however, that even these episcopal portraits on coins seem 'non-clerical', as they largely omit the corresponding attributes and the main difference between the portrait of the king and that of the bishop on one coin is that the second one wears no crown and is bareheaded.[32]

In the north and the east, along the coastlines of Holland, Friesland, Billung March (modern-day Mecklenburg, essentially) and the Northern March (modern-day Brandenburg) there were no monastic mints. However, it should be observed that, for this region, it is hard to find any mint at all that can be proven beyond doubt; monastic mints might well have been in operation.

---

26 For the coinage of Selz see footnote no. 6.

27 For the coinage of St Gallen see Steinbach, *Das Geld der Nonnen und Mönche*, pp. 183–5; Hermann Dannenberg, *Die Münzen der deutschen Schweiz zur Zeit der sächsischen und fränkischen Kaiser* (Genf, 1903), pp. 63–77; Dannenberg, *Deutsche Münzen der sächsischen und fränkischen Kaiserzeit*, vol. II, pp. 674–9, vol. IV, p. 940; Ernst Ziegler, 'Zur Münzgeschichte des Klosters St. Gallen von den Anfängen bis zu Abt Ulrich Rösch (1463–1491)', *Rorschacher Neujahrsblatt*, 77 (1987): 37–52; Hans-Ulrich Geiger, 'Moneta Sancti Galli. Die Münzprägung St. Gallens im Mittelalter', *Schriften des Vereins für Geschichte des Bodensees und seiner Umgebung*, 106 (1988): 131–41.

28 For the coinage of Zürich see Hans Hürlimann, *Zürcher Münzgeschichte* (Zürich, 1966); Dietrich W. H. Schwarz, *Münz- und Geldgeschichte Zürich im Mittelalter* (Aarau, 1940); Steinbach, *Das Geld der Nonnen und Mönche*, pp. 179–83; Dannenberg, *Die Münzen der deutschen Schweiz*, pp. 30–53; Dannenberg, *Deutsche Münzen der sächsischen und fränkischen Kaiserzeit*, vol. I, pp. 372–6, vol. II, pp. 672–3, vol. III, p. 809, vol. IV, pp. 938–40.

29 For the coinage of the Duchy Bavaria see Wolfgang Hahn, *Moneta Radasponensis. Bayerns Münzprägung im 9., 10. und 11. Jahrhundert* (Braunschweig, 1976).

30 Kluge, *Deutsche Münzgeschichte*, pp. 75–6.

31 Kluge, *Deutsche Münzgeschichte*, p. 65.

32 Kluge, *Deutsche Münzgeschichte*, p. 83.

Therefore, a concentration of monastic mints can be established for the area of the Saxon duchy, as well as for Upper and Lower Lorraine. For the eastern part this may be explained by a form of immediate government by the ruling Ottonian kings which were the former Saxonian dukes themselves. In the western part the explanation lies within the long-standing minting tradition in this particular region. First and foremost, mints were granted at the main imperial abbeys of Corvey,[33] Quedlinburg,[34] Fulda[35] or Hersfeld,[36] all of which issued substantial series of coins (see Plates 7 and 8). A closer look at individual issues shows that these monastic mints in matters of weight and style turned to regional standards of coins struck by the regional minting authority, whether clerical or secular; there was no 'uniform monastic coinage' for the whole empire. Monastic coins were always a recognisable part of their particular circulation area.

The majority of right-of-coinage charters date back to the Carolingian and early Ottonian times (30 of 43 charters). The first issues that, by the mention of a mint, prove monastic beyond doubt are from the late Ottonian and, more particularly, Salian periods. Visual similarities and die links suggests that before the year 1000 anonymous imitations of established coin types formed the main activity of monastic minting workshops: Quedlinburg, for instance, which took the *Otto-Adelheid-Pfennige*, current for the region, and began imitating these coins, adding specific symbols (the letter T on either side of the church-building of the reverse) and mentioning the Patron-Saint Servatius in the legend (see Plates 9 and 10).

Not before the reign of the last Ottonian, Henry II (1002–14), do isolated issues emerge that mention the king's name as HEINRICVS REX, among

---

[33] For the coinage of Corvey see Steinbach, *Das Geld der Nonnen und Mönche*, pp. 132–9; Vera Jammer, *Die Anfänge der Münzprägung im Herzogtum Sachsen 10. und 11. Jahrhundert* (Hamburg, 1952), pp. 105–7; Peter Ilisch, *Kleine Corveyer Münzgeschichte* (Paderborn, 1999); Dannenberg, *Deutsche Münzen der sächsischen und fränkischen Kaiserzeit*, vol. I, pp. 284–8, vol. II, pp. 646–7. For the coinage right granted see the extensive study of Heike Bartel, 'Das Münzprivileg Ludwigs des Frommen für Corvey (BM^2 922)', *Archiv für Diplomatik. Schriftgeschichte, Siegel- und Wappenkunde*, 58 (2012): 147–68.

[34] For the coinage of Quedlinburg see footnote no. 15.

[35] For the coinage of Fulda see Richard Gaettens, *Das Geld- und Münzwesen der Abtei Fulda im Hochmittelalter unter Auswertung der Münzen als Quelle der Geschichte und Kunstgeschichte, der Wirtschaftsgeschichte und des Staatsrechts* (Fulda, 1957); Steinbach, *Das Geld der Nonnen und Mönche*, pp. 163–9; Dannenberg, *Deutsche Münzen der sächsischen und fränkischen Kaiserzeit*, vol. I, pp. 332–3, vol. II, p. 745, vol. III, p. 807, vol. IV, pp. 927–9.

[36] For the coinage of Hersfeld see Steinbach, *Das Geld der Nonnen und Mönche*, pp. 159–62; Dannenberg, *Deutsche Münzen der sächsischen und fränkischen Kaiserzeit*, vol. I, pp. 333–4, vol. II, pp. 662–3, vol. III, p. 807 and vol. IV, pp. 929–34.

others from the mints of the Corvey[37] and Esslingen[38] abbeys. These cannot be classified as 'entirely autonomous monastic issues', as the king's presence is still evident, both in the effigy and in the legend.[39]

The only known coins referring to the first Salian monarch Conrad II (1024–39) are the unique Essen example discussed above and a coin from Stablo, also mentioning one IMP(erator) CON(radvs) in its legend.[40] The majority of monastic issues from the first half of the eleventh century do not name individuals, that is, those issuing the coins. Most just mention the name of the mint or the locally venerated saint, the saint as mint-master as it were. As, for instance, in lower-Lotharingian Nivelles,[41] where the local pennies show the legend S GERTRVDIS VIRGO, which is the name of the first abbess to be canonised, Gertrud (626–59), and state the mint to be S / NIVELLA / PRVDENS.[42] In Stablo too, coin was struck anonymously mentioning the founder of the abbey, Saint Remaclus – S REMACLVS EPS – on the obverse and the name of the town STABVLAVS on the reverse[43] (see Plate 11).

Corvey Abbey forms a remarkable exception in this early period of monastic minting, having struck coin as early as the days of its abbot Ruthard (1045–50), whose name this first coin carries. It shows a cross with a long stem and dots in the angles and the name of the ruling sovereign Henry III (1039–56) as

---

37 Steinbach, *Das Geld der Nonnen und Mönche*, no. 53; Dannenberg, *Deutsche Münzen der sächsischen und fränkischen Kaiserzeit*, no. 733 and Kluge, *Deutsche Münzgeschichte*, no. 72.

38 Steinbach, *Das Geld der Nonnen und Mönche*, nos 125–7; Dannenberg, *Deutsche Münzen der sächsischen und fränkischen Kaiserzeit*, nos 951–3, 1272 and Kluge, *Deutsche Münzgeschichte*, nos 84, 316.

39 In case of the Esslingen coins, this type seems to be struck even long after the reign of emperor Heinrich II (1002–24) without changing the image, presumably because it had been widely accepted.

40 For the coinage of Nivelles see Steinbach, *Das Geld der Nonnen und Mönche*, pp. 119–21; Dannenberg, *Deutsche Münzen der sächsischen und fränkischen Kaiserzeit*, vol. I, pp. 134–5, vol. IV, p. 893; Günther Albrecht, *Das Münzwesen im niederlothringischen und friesischen Raum vom 10. bis zum beginnenden 12. Jahrhundert* (Hamburg, 1959), p. 74.

41 For the coinage of Nivelles see Steinbach, *Das Geld der Nonnen und Mönche*, pp. 111–13; Dannenberg, *Deutsche Münzen der sächsischen und fränkischen Kaiserzeit*, vol. I, pp. 102–3; Albrecht, *Das Münzwesen im niederlothringischen und friesischen Raum*, pp. 72–4.

42 Steinbach, *Das Geld der Nonnen und Mönche*, nos 28–31; Dannenberg, *Deutsche Münzen der sächsischen und fränkischen Kaiserzeit*, nos 143–4 and Kluge, *Deutsche Münzgeschichte*, no. 398.

43 Steinbach, *Das Geld der Nonnen und Mönche*, no. 42; Dannenberg, *Deutsche Münzen der sächsischen und fränkischen Kaiserzeit*, no. 271 and Kluge, *Deutsche Münzgeschichte*, no. 400.

HEINRIC REX. The reverse is dedicated to the abbot, whose name ROTHARDVS is positioned in the cross and whose title A-B-A-S appears in the angles.[44]

Ruthard's successors, the abbots Arnold I (1051–55), Saracho (1056–71), Warin (1071–79) and Markward (1082–1106) also have surviving coins to their name, some of them showing impressive effigies.[45] Beginning with the period of Saracho's abbatiate, the legend no longer mentions the name of the king. The abbey appears to have continued striking the anonymous series simultaneously, as can be observed in imitations of the Cologne S-COLONIA-A types[46] from the second half of the eleventh century and issues from Corvey's secondary mint, Marsberg.[47] Why some types mention the abbot as minting lord and others omit him almost at the same time is still something of a mystery (see Plate 12). What is certain is that the middle of the eleventh century constitutes a break in imperial German coinage. On the one hand, the amount of surviving German coins found in Scandinavian and Eastern European hoards substantially declines from that point on, while on the other the production of the royal mints also decreases.[48] Production increasingly shifts toward secular and clerical institutions, such as the ambitious abbeys.

A closer look at coinage charters from the reign of Henry IV (1056–1106) confirms an increase in non-royal minting centres: with 29 charters Henry granted the right of coinage more often than any king before him.[49] Although his 50-year reign exceeds the reigns of all the other kings and emperors of the empire, the majority of coining privileges were granted during Henry's minority.

After the regency ended in 1065, the number of new grants of the right of coinage sharply decreased, not least because the extra effort that had been put into asserting authority no longer needed to be kept up. Significantly, the

---

44 Steinbach, *Das Geld der Nonnen und Mönche*, no. 54 and Dannenberg, *Deutsche Münzen der sächsischen und fränkischen Kaiserzeit*, no. 734.

45 Steinbach, *Das Geld der Nonnen und Mönche*, nos 57–62; Dannenberg, *Deutsche Münzen der sächsischen und fränkischen Kaiserzeit*, nos 736–8, 1620 and Kluge, *Deutsche Münzgeschichte*, no. 409.

46 Steinbach, *Das Geld der Nonnen und Mönche*, no. 64 and Dannenberg, *Deutsche Münzen der sächsischen und fränkischen Kaiserzeit*, no. 739.

47 Steinbach, *Das Geld der Nonnen und Mönche*, no. 65; Dannenberg, *Deutsche Münzen der sächsischen und fränkischen Kaiserzeit*, no. 1622 and Kluge, *Deutsche Münzgeschichte*, no. 411.

48 Gert Hatz, *Handel und Verkehr zwischen dem Deutschen Reich und Schweden in der späten Wikingerzeit. Die deutschen Münzen des 10. und 11. Jahrhunderts in Schweden* (Stockholm / Lund, 1974) and Kluge, *Deutsche Münzgeschichte*, pp. 16–7. For single studies on the coin finds in different European regions with more literature see Bernd Kluge (ed.), *Fernhandel und Geldwirtschaft. Beiträge zum deutschen Münzwesen in sächsischer und salischer Zeit* (Sigmaringen, 1993).

49 Kluge, *Deutsche Münzgeschichte*, pp. 55 and 104.

volatile period of the recently ignited Investiture Controversy and Henry's *Gang nach Canossa* in 1076/77 saw a mere three grants, one of which is even doubted to be genuine.[50] At the same time coinage by non-royal institutions increased, unhindered by lacking legal permission, as it seems.[51]

The main monasteries among those that issued extensive series of coins in the name of the abbot or the abbess of the second half of the eleventh century were Fulda, Hersfeld and the noble convent at Quedlinburg. Coinage by female authorities – the abbesses had issues bear their own effigy – was new as a numismatic phenomenon, unique to imperial East-Francia in the twelfth century and even extremely rare across western Christendom.[52] Close familial ties of the abbesses in office to the ruling dynasty do a lot to explain this phenomenon. For example, in the case of Otto III (983–1002), who, during his Italian campaign of 998, entrusted his aunt Mathilda, Abbess of Quedlinburg, with governing the empire. It is thought that she even waged war against the heathen Slavic people in his name. Thanks to these coins we know about two otherwise undocumented abbesses of the aristocratic convent of Quedlinburg: EILICA and AGNES, who were in office between 1095 and 1125.[53]

However, even the abbeys that struck larger series of coins also varied between anonymous issues and those struck in parallel where the abbot is named as minting lord. Hersfeld and Fulda are good examples of this phenomenon. Of the depicted anonymous coins, Abbot Hartwig (1072–88) in Hersfeld and Abbot Egbert (1048–58) in Fulda issued series that did bear their name, for instance. Generally speaking, monasteries followed the development of the late-Salian dioceses: gradually phasing out the royal effigy and replacing it with the name

---

50 For the Investiture Controversy see, amongst a significant literature the studies of Werner Goez, *Kirchenreform und Investiturstreit 910–1122* (Stuttgart, 2008); Stefan Weinfurter, *Canossa: Die Entzauberung der Welt* (Munich, 2007); Jörg Jarnut and Matthias Wemhoff (eds), *Vom Umbruch zur Erneuerung? Das 11. und beginnende 12 Jahrhundert – Positionen der Forschung* (Münich, 2009); Stefan Weinfurter, *1024–1125: Das Jahrhundert der Salier. Kaiser oder Papst?* (Stuttgart, 2004) and Wilfried Hartmann, *Der Investiturstreit* (Münich, 2007).

51 Kluge, *Deutsche Münzgeschichte*, pp. 44, 59 and 63–76.

52 With, for instance, the exceptions of Queen Urraca of León and Castile (1109–26) – see Carlos Castan and Juan R. Cayon, *Las Monedas Hispano Musulmanas y Cristianas 711–1981* (Madrid, 1980), pp. 116–17, and countess Adela of Hamaland – see Peter Ilisch, 'Die Münzprägung im Herzogtum Niederlothringen I: Die Münzprägung in den Räumen Utrecht und Friesland im 10. und 11. Jahrhundert', *Jaarboek voor Munt- en Penningkunde*, 84–5 (1997–98): 43–7.

53 Mehl, *Die Münzen des Stifts Quedlinburg*, nos 14, 17–18, 21–2, 28, 39; Steinbach, *Das Geld der Nonnen und Mönche*, nos 69–75; Dannenberg, *Deutsche Münzen der sächsischen und fränkischen Kaiserzeit*, nos 617, 619, 620–22, 1562 and Kluge, *Deutsche Münzgeschichte*, nos 441–3.

and picture of their own clerical minting lord, their ultimate goal was to create a status symbol of prestige and autonomy befitting a self-confident church.[54]

Erasing the sovereign's name and effigy constituted a violation of a royal privilege, and obviously the perpetrators in question were well aware of that, because they took care to commit this breach ever so gradually. The practice manifested itself primarily in the period of haphazard rule toward the end of the reign of Henry III (1039–56) and after the Investiture Controversy. Whether there have in fact been royal repercussions against it, the sources available do not disclose.

By the end of Salian rule every monastery that still existed had carried through the transition to striking coin with the name and effigy of the abbot in office instead of those of the king. The heyday of monastic coinage came to an end towards the turn of the twelfth into the thirteenth century, when the majority of monastic mints of the Ottonian and Salian era, including those of Werden and Herford, ceased striking coin. They stood little chance against the large episcopal workshops or the financial prowess of the cities, which also strove for the right of coinage.

On its own the coinage of the large imperial abbeys, most notably Corvey and Fulda, lasted through the Middle Ages, in some cases even well into early modern times.[55] Coinage by monasteries and convents on German imperial territory has by and large remained a passing phenomenon of the High Middle Ages. In its intensity and extent, however, it was unique within western Christendom and, as such, of particular significance not only from a numismatic perspective, but also for the economic and ecclesiastical history of the Middle Ages in general.

[54] A good example in this case might be the extensive minting of the archdiocese of Cologne, which commenced with coins struck in the Emperor's name during the Ottonian reign (936–1024), changed to coins struck with both the name of the Emperor and the Archbishop in the early Salian period (1024–56) and then to minting only in the name of the Archbishop in the second half of the eleventh century. For an overview of the types see Kluge, *Deutsche Münzgeschichte*, nos 19 (Otto I, 936–73), 20 (Otto II, 973–83), 21 (Otto III, 983–1002), 66 (Heinrich II, 1002–24), 362–3 (Konrad II, 1024–36, and Archbishop Pilgrim, 1021–36), 364 (Konrad II, 1024–36, and Archbishop Hermann II, 1036–56), 365 (Archbishop Hermann II, 1036–56, alone), 366 (Heinrich IV, 1056–1106, and Archbishop Anno, 1056–75) and 367–72 (only in the name of the Archbishops Anno, 1056–75; Hildolf, 1076–79; Sigwin, 1079–89; and Friedrich, 1100–31). For the minting of Cologne in general Walter Hävernick, *Die Münzen von Köln vom Beginn der Prägung bis 1304* (Cologne, 1935).

[55] Peter Ilisch and Arnold Schwede, *Das Münzwesen im Stift Corvey 1541–1794* (Paderborn, 2007).

Chapter 11

Saints, Dukes and Bishops: Coinage in Ducal Normandy, c. 930–c. 1150

Jens Christian Moesgaard

During the period of the tenth to twelfth/thirteenth centuries, coinage in France was not national, but regional or even local. The Capetian kings did not strike national coins. They struck only local coins in the territories over which they exercised direct control, that of the Ile de France and a few other places. Elsewhere dukes, counts, lords, bishops and monasteries had taken over these responsibilities.

The Duchy of Normandy was no exception to this rule. Very few written sources speak about coin production. To gain knowledge of who was in charge of the coinage, especially in the early period, the only source of evidence is the coins themselves. The suite of Norman coins struck between c. 930 and c. 1150, during the ducal period, comprise an impressive variety of types: some 200 different coin types are recorded. Up until c. 1000 and again from the late eleventh century on, the legends are intelligible. For most of the eleventh century, they are unintelligible or, in numismatic terms, blundered legends, often composed of pseudo-letters.[1]

In the tenth century, most legends on Norman coins carried the name of the duke on the obverse and the name of Rouen on the reverse. The latter refers either to the mint in the town of Rouen or to the territory within which the coins were valid, the jurisdiction of the county of Rouen. In the twelfth century the legends generally state the mint name (Rouen) or the jurisdictional area (Normandy) or the title of the ruler (duke of Normandy). There is also a series including personal names of an enigmatic nature.

There are, however, a few coins with saints' names or other ecclesiastical and religious allusions within this corpus of legends. Alongside theses, monograms on other coins have been interpreted as saints' or archbishops' names. The list comprises both coins with reasonably secure attributions and coins with highly speculative interpretations. The existence of these coins poses a series of questions relating to the church and money, in this case, more precisely, minting.

---

[1] Françoise Dumas, 'Les monnaies normandes', *Revue numismatique*, 6th series, 21 (1979): 84–140.

How these coins should be interpreted, whether the church was involved in their striking, and, if it was, how and to what degree, are all central issues to consider.

Traditionally, these coins have been understood as purely ecclesiastical issues, presumably resulting from a permanent or temporary grant of the full right to minting by the duke who alone held the minting *regalium* in Normandy. Several scholars nevertheless underline that such grants must have been exceptional and in circumstances where they did not substantially threaten the duke's monopoly of coinage.[2] In the following, the coins with ecclesiastical themes and their interpretation in previous research will be presented. An alternative line of argument will then be proposed in order to shed further light on the ducal coinage of Normandy as a whole, especially in the tenth and the beginning of the eleventh centuries.

---

[2] A. Dieudonné, *Monnaies féodales françaises* (*Manuel de numismatique française*, IV) (Paris, 1936), p. 303, see also p. 304; Françoise Dumas, *Le trésor de Fécamp* (Paris, 1971), pp. 51, 91–100; Reinhold Kaiser, 'Münzprivilegien und bischöfliche Münzprägung in Frankreich, Deutschland und Burgund im 9.–12. Jahrhundert', *Vierteljahrschrift für Sozial- und Wirtschaftgeschichte*, 63 (1976) : 289–338, see esp. 315–16; Dumas, *Le trésor*, pp. 90–91; Jacqueline Delaporte, 'La monnaie', in Françoise Debaisieux, Elisabeth Chirol et al. (eds), *Trésors des abbayes normandes* (Rouen-Caen, 1979), p. 40; Jacqueline Pilet-Lemière, 'Ateliers monétaires des abbayes', in *Trésors des abbayes normandes*, pp. 41–7; Jean Lafaurie, 'Trésor de deniers du XIe siècle trouvé à Gaillefontaine (Seine-Maritime)', in Brigitte Beaujard, Nancy Gauthier et al. (eds), *Histoire et numismatique en Haute-Normandie* (Caen, 1980), pp. 117–29, esp. pp. 122–3; Dominique Legros, *Monnaies féodales françaises* (No place of publication, 1984), pp. 183–98; Jacqueline Pilet-Lemière, 'Deniers inédits de Rouen à la legend METROPOLIS', *Bulletin de la Société française de numismatique*, 40 (1985): 639–40; Françoise Dumas and Jacqueline Pilet-Lemière, 'La monnaie normande – Xe–XIIe siècle. Le point de la recherche en 1987', *Les Mondes Normands* (Caen, 1989), pp. 125–31, esp. p. 127; Jacqueline Pilet-Lemière, 'Les monnayages ecclésiastiques', *L'évangélisation de la Normandie, Les dossiers d'archéologie*, 144 (1990): 66–7; Michel Dhénin, 'Les Monnaies normandes', *Le Domfrontais medieval* 7 (*Les conférences d'histoire locale du Lycée de Domfront* IX) (1990): 14–30, see esp. 20–22, 27; Jacqueline Pilet-Lemière, 'Les monnaies de la cathédrale de Rouen', in *Le trésor de la Cathédrale de Rouen* (Rouen-Caen, 1993), pp. 31–2; Jens Christian Moesgaard, [notices 12–16], *Le trésor de la Cathédrale de Rouen*, pp. 35–6; Jacques Le Maho, 'Une monnaie rouennaise aux environs de l'an mil: le denier de 'Saint-Romain'', in Mathieu Arnoux et al. (eds), *La Normandie vers l'an mil*, Société de l'Histoire de Normandie, 73 (Rouen, 2000), pp. 202–5; Jacques Le Maho, 'Autour de la renaissance monastique du Xe siècle en Normandie: les Vies des saints Aycadre et Hugues de Jumièges', Martin Heinzelmann (ed.), *Livrets, collections et texts: études sur la tradition hagiographique latine*, Beihefte der Francia, 63 (Ostfildern, 2006), pp. 285–322, esp. p. 289.

Coins with the Name of Saint-Ouen

Saint-Ouen was bishop of Rouen 641–84. He was buried in the suburban Basilica of Saint-Peter situated just outside the city walls to the north-east of Rouen. His grave soon became the object of veneration and an important pilgrimage destination. A community of monks transformed the basilica into an abbey that took the name of Saint-Ouen. For long periods, the Archbishop of Rouen was also abbot of Saint-Ouen. The abbey was destroyed during the Viking raids, and after the creation of the Duchy of Normandy (county of Rouen) in 911/12, it was the first religious house to be restored by the new Norman-Viking rulers as early as 918.

A coin type with a reasonable standard of literacy carries the obverse legend SA-TE AVDOENI (Dumas XV, 16), which beyond any doubt can be translated as Saint-Ouen (Sanctus Audoenus) (see Plate 13). Its date has been much debated, but has been narrowed down to c. 918/40 recently.[3] The degenerated legend SEADNORTI (Dumas XV, 17) on a coin type dated to the 980s at the latest, has hypothetically been interpreted as a blundered version of Saint-Ouen.[4] Likewise, the letters O S on a coin from the late tenth century (Dumas XV, 18) have tentatively been read as Saint-Ouen.[5] This latter type carries the name of Richard. It is continued well into the eleventh century (Dumas XVII, 8–11, XVIII, 19).[6] The reading of these latter coins from the late tenth century and the eleventh (and by way of consequence, their attribution to Saint-Ouen) is, however, highly insecure.

The coins in the name of Saint-Ouen have quite naturally been seen as an issue from the abbey. Indeed, the abbey had a monetary tradition; coins were struck here in the eighth century.[7] The alleged grant of the minting right, in the ducal period, has been seen in the context of tenth-century politics, perhaps linked to the rivalry between Saint-Ouen and the abbey of Jumièges, further downstream on the Seine. The former was favoured by the first duke Rollo (911–27/32) and the Frankish king Louis IV during his dominion of Normandy 942–45, but on bad terms with William Longsword at the end of his reign c.

3 Jens Christian Moesgaard, 'Les deniers de Saint-Ouen de Rouen (Xe siècle)', *Bulletin de la Société française de numismatique*, 64 (2009): 242–46.

4 Dumas, *Le trésor de Fécamp*, p. 100, n. 2.

5 Dhénin, 'Les monnaies normandes': 20; see also Dumas, 'Les monnaies normandes': 138.

6 Legros, *Monnaies féodales françaises*, pp. 192–5; Dhénin, 'Les Monnaies normandes': 21.

7 Jean Lafaurie, 'Deniers du VIIIe siècle de Saint-Ouen de Rouen', in Brigitte Beaujard, Nancy Gauthier et al. (eds), *Histoire et numismatique en Haute-Normandie* (Caen, 1980), pp. 109–16.

940.[8] Duke Richard I (942/45–96) was also a benefactor of Saint-Ouen.[9] A monetary privilege linked to the restoration in 918 cannot be excluded either as inherently implausible, although not demonstrable.[10] A temporary grant in order to finance a building campaign has been suggested also.[11] Given the close links between the Cathedral and the Abbey, the coinage perhaps may be seen as archiepiscopal rather than monastic.

Coins with the Name of Saint-Romain

Saint Romain (or Romanus) was bishop of Rouen in the 630s. There is no abbey dedicated to him, but he was eventually considered the patron-saint of the city. Several chapels and churches throughout the city carried his name.

A series of coins exist, with the name of Romain qualified either as Saint or bishop, with a good standard of literacy: S-E ROMANE, S-C ROMANC, SC ROMAN, ROMANS EP'S (Dumas XV, 19–22, XVI, 1–2) (see Plates 14 and 15). These coins were struck during the period c. 965/75–1000.[12] The latest of the coins in this sequence carries the name of Duke Richard alongside the name of Saint-Romain (Dumas XVI, 1–2). This suggests ducal involvement, which will be discussed further below.

In her masterly thesis on the Fécamp hoard,[13] which consists of more than 8,578 coins – at least 6,044 from the mint at Rouen – deposited c. 980/985, Françoise Dumas linked this coinage to the private chapel of the ducal palace, which was dedicated to Saint-Romain.[14] However, Jacques Le Maho was not persuaded by this identification.[15] He investigated a series of other possible interpretations with the starting point that the cult of Romain was linked to the Cathedral. Romain was also the patron of the Chapter of the Cathedral. Le Maho rejects the idea that the coinage may have originated from the Saint-Romain chapel at the rear of the Archbishop's palace and adjacent to one of the city gates.[16] He points out that the very important western narthex of the Cathedral, comprising a chapel Saint-Romain, was being rebuilt at the same time as the

8 Le Maho, 'Autour de la renaissance monastique du Xe siècle en Normandie', p. 289, see also Moesgaard 'Les deniers de Saint-Ouen de Rouen': 245.

9 Dumas, *Le trésor de Fécamp*, p. 100, n. 2.

10 See Moesgaard 'Les deniers de Saint-Ouen de Rouen': 245.

11 Lafaurie, 'Trésor de deniers du XIe siècle', pp. 122–3.

12 Dumas, *Le trésor de Fécamp*, pp. 98–100.

13 Dumas, *Le trésor de Fécamp*.

14 Dumas, *Le trésor de Fécamp*, pp. 98–100.

15 Le Maho, 'Une monnaie rouennaise aux environs de l'an mil'.

16 Le Maho, 'Une monnaie rouennaise aux environs de l'an mil'.

striking of the coins,[17] and it would be tempting to link the coinage directly to the Cathedral,[18] either as some sort of commemoration or as an outright grant to the church in order to finance the construction. In fact in this connection Dumas had interpreted the monogram EP'S = episcopus = bishop on the late phase of the Romain-coinage (Dumas XVI, 1–2), not as a qualification of Romain as bishop, but as a reference to a hypothetical minting right of Archbishop Robert (989–1037) who undertook important construction works.[19]

As his final conclusion, however, Le Maho suggests that the coinage might be seen in connection with the suburban church of Saint-Godard, which was originally called Saint-Romain, since, according to the tradition, Romain was buried here. His bones were taken originally to the Cathedral, but in the second half of the tenth century, they were re-translated and deposited in the Saint-Godard church, which was a dependent institution of the Cathedral. The aim was to create a new place of pilgrimage to compete with Saint-Ouen, which had been separated from the Cathedral roughly contemporaneously around the year 960, with the appointment of its own independent abbot, Hildevert. The pilgrimage at Saint-Romain was successful and an important market grew up alongside this on Saint-Romain's feast-day, October 23. This would provide a plausible context for a coinage. Le Maho also drew attention to Duke Richard I's wish to gain goodwill by promoting the cult and veneration of the patron-saint.[20]

Other Coins

A coin type exists which carries an enigmatic monogram seemingly composed by the letters HGT, hypothetically interpreted by Dumas as Hugh, Archbishop of Rouen (942–89) (Dumas XV, 23–24) (see Plate 16). This type was struck c.

---

17 Jacques Le Maho, 'Les fouilles de la cathédrale de Rouen de 1985 à 1993', *Archéologie médiévale*, XXIV, (1994): 1–49, at 36; Jacques Le Maho, 'Nouvelles hypothèses sur l'église Notre-Dame de Rouen au Xe siècle', in Silvette Lemagnen (ed.), *Chapitres et Cathédrales en Normandie* (Caen, 1997), pp. 295–306, esp. p. 301.

18 Jacques Le Maho, 'Les fouilles de la cathédrale de Rouen de 1985 à 1992', *Groupe de recherche archéologique du Pays de Caux, bulletin 1992* (1992): 27–41, at 38. See also Moesgaard, *Le trésor de la Cathédrale de Rouen*; Dumas and Pilet-Lemière, 'La monnaie normande – Xe–XIIe siècle', p. 127.

19 Dumas, 'Les monnaies normandes': 91.

20 Jacques Le Maho, 'Recherches sur les origines de quelques églises de Rouen (VIe–XIe siècles)', *Bulletin de la Commission départementale des antiquités de Seine-Maritime*, 43 (1995/96): 143–205; Le Maho 'Une monnaie rouennaise aux environs de l'an mil'. See also Felice Lifschitz, *The Dossier of Romanus of Rouen: The Political Uses of Hagiographical Texts* (New York, 1988).

980.[21] It was completely unknown until the discovery in 1963 of the Fécamp hoard which included more than 2,782 specimens of this particular coinage. Dumas's hypothesis has generally been accepted. It must, however, be stressed that this type also carries the name of the duke, Richard. Consequently, if the hypothesis of archiepiscopal involvement is correct, this involvement was only partial, in partnership with the duke, who also had his part in the coinage.

There are also one or two coin types of the early eleventh century with a blundered legend composed of corrupted letters (Dumas XVII, 1 and maybe XVI, 19). This legend has been interpreted tentatively in two different ways; neither of them are, however, very likely. The letters have been read as SIMOLAM on some specimens, which could be Saint-Mellon, bishop of Rouen 260–312. There is no Saint-Mellon Abbey, but Mellon was venerated, perhaps linked to the Cathedral or the Saint-Gervais Church where he was buried.[22] The same coin legend has been interpreted as Saint-Maclou (= the Breton Saint-Malo).[23] The Saint-Maclou church just to the east of the Rouen city wall was founded, according to the traditional narrative, as a chapel in the tenth century, but it is only firmly documented from the late eleventh century. The whole neighbourhood was a swamp until the canalisation of the rivers in the later period.[24] Topographically an early eleventh-century coin issue in the name of this church is, therefore, highly unlikely.

A few further examples of coins from the tenth to eleventh centuries have been classified as ecclesiastical, however on very insecure grounds. To take a few examples: one type carries two keys, another type has a vague similarity with the earlier Saint-Romain coins, and yet another type carries the legend RACOI, which, highly speculatively, has been interpreted as RACIO, that is RATIO MONASTERII.[25] More convincing is the interpretation of the much later coin type with the legend ROTOMAGVS / METROPOLIS, struck c. 1130/45 as an issue by Rouen Cathedral.[26]

New Perspectives

From the discussion above, it will be clear that there are many uncertainties about the coins under scrutiny that were issued in Normandy in the period

21 Dumas, *Le trésor de Fécamp*, pp. 91–7.

22 Lafaurie, 'Trésor de deniers du XIe siècle', pp. 122–3 and n. 9.

23 Georges Depeyrot, *Le numéraire carolingien*, 3rd edition (Wetteren, 2008), no. 886.

24 Elisabeth Chirol et al., *Le guide de Rouen* (Besançon, 1991), p. 208; Jérôme Decoux and Guillaume Gaillard, *Le quartier Martainville de Rouen* (Rouen, 2011), p. 11.

25 Legros, *Monnaies féodales françaises*, nos 415–16, 422, 430, 434–40.

26 Pilet-Lemière, 'Deniers inédits de Rouen à la legend METROPOLIS'; Dumas and Pilet-Lemière, 'La monnaie normande – Xe–XIIe siècle', p. 127 and n. 5.

c. 930–c. 1150. These coin series can be interpreted in a number of different ways, some of which are mutually contradictory. Several interpretations can be presented to link these coins to the Cathedral, first in the context of the archbishop as abbot of Saint-Ouen, and then later on, after the separation of Saint-Ouen from the Cathedral, in the context and name of Saint-Romain as the new saint promulgated by the Cathedral. One line of argument might stress the possibilities of coins being used to finance or commemorate important building campaigns, to sustain market activities linked to pilgrimage, to express ducal support to one or another ecclesiastical faction or in the competition between ecclesiastical institutions promoting themselves as places of pilgrimage.

The question remains, however, how certain is the identification of these coinages as ecclesiastical? After all, if uncertain readings of monograms are excluded, then all that remains are saints' names in the inscriptions. These may represent simply an act of homage to the local saint by the coin issuer, in the present case the duke of Normandy, who may very well have held complete control of the coinage without any ecclesiastical involvement.

It is helpful, in this case, to put the Norman examples into a wider context. Eleventh-century coins with the busts and the names of Saint Simon and Saint Judas from Goslar, in the Holy Roman Empire, are not ecclesiastical but royal. On the other hand, the tenth-century coins of Saint Martin of Tours are clearly monastic, as shown by the well-documented grant of the minting right to the Abbey in 919.[27] The complications are greater still in earlier Tours coins bearing the name of the king and of Saint Martin (CARLVS REX / SCI MARTINI MONETA) which date from the early years of Charles the Bald's reign (840–77): are they royal or monastic? Another example might be taken from coins minted at Saint-Denis from the later years (post-864) of the same reign. While their type is the same as in all the royal mints, which was a type clearly controlled by the king, the reverse legend reads SCI DIONVSII M (the coin of Saint-Denis). The question is raised whether Saint-Denis was simply used as the place name for the mint, or whether the Abbey had some kind of control of the coinage. In some places, such as Cambrai, the issue struck from 864 to 877 comprises both coins with the reverse legend SCI GAVGERICI MO (the coin of Saint-Géry) and coins with the reverse legend CAMARACVS CIVIS (the civitas of Cambrai). Both are of the uniform royal coin type, controlled by the king, but there must have been two mints, of which one would have been, to a certain degree, controlled by the Abbey of Saint-Géry.[28]

---

[27] Pierre Crinon, 'Catalogue des monnaies carolingiennes de Tours du VIIIe s. au début de la féodalité, Xe s.', in Jacqueline Pilet-Lemière (ed.), *Tours, études numismatiques* (Paris, 1997), pp. 53–87, see esp. p. 71.

[28] Karl F. Morrison and Henry Grunthal, *Caroligian Coinage* (New York, 1967), nos 919–21 (Tours), 840–7 (St-Denis), 669–77 (Cambrai).

As these cases show, there is considerable diversity in the use of saints' names on coins. The conclusion must be, surely, that there should be no automatic assumptions that a saints' name on a coin indicates an ecclesiastical minting, unless there is good corroborative evidence with which to make the assertion.

Norman coins with saints' names should not be considered in isolation. Fresh insight might be gained through an attempt to see them in the context of the ducal coinage as a whole, as well as with wider comparisons. Most of the evidence dates from the tenth century, and the coinage of this period has been subject recently to a new interpretation.[29] This particularly concerns the well-known system of *renovatio monetae*, which consisted of periodical renewal of the currency. At more or less fixed terms, for instance every second or fourth year, a new coin type was introduced and the old type ceased to be legal tender. The coin holders had to exchange their old coins in order to obtain new, against a fee to the issuing power. Thus, the system was in reality a tax on trade conducted in coins and on monetary fortunes. It required, and this is important to keep in mind, a strong control of the market by the coin issuer. In Normandy, the duke was the issuing authority. It seems that the renewal of the currency was carried out every three or four years. This system generated income to the duke, sometimes substantial money, sometimes probably less.

The idea of replacing the currency by a new issue was not new. It had already been done in the Carolingian Empire in 793/94, 813, c. 816, 822/23 and 864[30] and in Wessex at several occasions during the reign of Alfred (871–99).[31] The novelty was the regularity of the repeated short intervals between the renewals. It may well be the case that the paternity of the *renovatio monetae* belongs to the duchy of Normandy which may have invented it several decades before it was introduced into England c. 973.[32] There are not enough coin hoards to prove this beyond doubt, but the sparse evidence is consistent. This in turn would explain the exceptional number of coin types in Normandy, in sharp contrast to the immobilised coin types in the neighbouring areas, such as the continued issuing in Maine of coins maintaining the name of Charles the Bald for the whole of the tenth century, which was followed by an unchanged type in the name of count Herbert for the next two centuries.[33]

How the alleged ecclesiastical coinages fit into this pattern is a complex question. Table 11.1 provides an overview of Norman coin types of the tenth

[29] Jens Christian Moesgaard, '*Renovatio Monetae* et la chronologie des monnaies de Richard Ier, duc de Normandie 942/945–996', *Bulletin de la Société française de numismatique*, 66 (2011): 125–33.

[30] Simon Coupland, *Carolingian Coinage and the Vikings* (Aldershot, 2007).

[31] Mark Blackburn, 'Alfred's Coinage Reforms in Context', in T. Reuter (ed.), *Alfred the Great* (Aldershot, 2003), pp. 199–217.

[32] Moesgaard, '*Renovatio Monetae*'.

[33] Dumas, *Le trésor de Fécamp*.

century. The approximate dating of most types is given by their occurrence in hoards.[34] The exact date or even the precise order of the types is difficult to ascertain. For a few coin types, no hoard provenances are recorded, and these have been put into the chronological sequence by an estimation of their styles compared to other types.[35]

The sequence of coins and types suggested in Table 11.1 may be used to put forward the case that, on the assumption that *renovatio monetae* was in place, it was a system that was ducally controlled, and which also included the coins with saints' names. Issues with ecclesiastical legends are rare before c. 965. To the contrary, they count for a substantial part of the coinage after that date. However, if one removes all the coinages with definite or possible saints' names and other ecclesiastical allusions from the table, the neat pattern suggesting regular intervals of three to four years for the introduction of new types cannot be maintained. Thus, the ecclesiastic coin types are necessary to claim the existence of the *renovatio monetae* system. This in turn implies that these coins were under firm ducal control: they cannot have been fully independent ecclesiastical issues.

Whether one chooses to see the discussion above as an argument against the existence of the *renovatio* system or against the idea of completely independent ecclesiastic issues is of course a matter of debate. However, several features speak in favour of the duke: the presence of the duke's name on a number of the relevant coin types, and the existence of parallel issues of the same coin type, one with the name of the duke, another with the name of Saint-Romain (and maybe Saint-Ouen). These examples indicate firm ducal control of the coinage.

The coins with saints' names may be simply a manifestation of ducal veneration for the patron-saint without ecclesiastical involvement in the coinage. Indeed, both Saint-Ouen and Saint-Romain were popular saints. The history of coinage contains many examples of secular power issuing with religious motifs and messages. The existence of parallel issues of the same type, one with the duke's name, the other with Saint-Romain (and maybe Saint-Ouen) may indicate that the duke gave part of the mint right to ecclesiastic institutions for short periods (we must remember that each coin type was probably only valid three or four years). It is important to note that, if this is correct, he did not give away the right to decide the coin type, but rather only a portion of the income from coinage. Similar arrangements are documented for later periods in England, Norway and Denmark.[36]

---

[34] For more detail on this subject see Moesgaard '*Renovatio Monetae*'.

[35] Moesgaard '*Renovatio Monetae*'.

[36] For England (St Edmunds and York): J. J.North, *English Hammered Coinage*, vol. 1, 3rd edition (London, 1994); for Norway: Jon Anders Risvaag, 'Ikke-kongelig utmynting i Norge frem til reformasjonen' *Nordisk Numismatisk Årskrift* (1994–96): 157; for Denmark: Gert Posselt, 'Nogle danske mønter med gejstlige fremstillinger før ca. 1150', *Hikuin*, 11 (1985): 207–14; Keld Grinder-Hansen, *Kongemagtens krise* (Copenhagen, 2000).

This debate is far from settled. What this chapter has suggested is that a saint's name in the context of ducal Normandy does not necessarily make a coinage ecclesiastic. Rather the duke of Normandy probably controlled the coin production, fully, even if he may have given the church a part of the revenue from coinage for shorter periods. Coinage in Normandy as elsewhere took advantage of a connection with local saints in promoting their currency to those who would use it in their daily transactions.

Table 11.1 The coinage of Normandy in the tenth century. The datings are approximate and the detail of the precise order of the types is unknown.[37]

Date	Secular	Secular and Ecclesiastic	Ecclesiastic
Before 942	William Longsword		
	No corresponding type	No corresponding type	D XV, 16: 'St-Ouen'
	D XV, 1: 'William'	No corresponding type	No corresponding type
942–45	King Louis IV		
	D XV, 2: 'Louis king'	No corresponding type	No corresponding type
945–c. 965	Richard I		
	D XV, 3: 'Richard'	No corresponding type	No corresponding type
	D XV, 5: 'Richard'	No corresponding type	No corresponding type
	D XV, 6: 'Richard'	No corresponding type	No corresponding type
	D XV, 12: 'Richard'	No corresponding type	No corresponding type
	D XV, 14: 'Richard marquis'	No corresponding type	No corresponding type
	D XV, 4: 'Richard'	No corresponding type	No corresponding type
c. 965–975	Richard I		
	D XV, 7–9: 'Richard'	No corresponding type	D XV, 19: 'St-Romain'
	No corresponding type	No corresponding type	D XV, 20–21: 'St-Romain'

37 For arguments on the datings see Moesgaard, '*Renovatio Monetae*'.

Date	Secular	Secular and Ecclesiastic	Ecclesiastic
	D XV, 15: 'Richard'	No corresponding type	D XV, 17? maybe 'St-Ouen'
	Richard I		
	D XV, 10–11: 'Richard'	No corresponding type	No corresponding type
	D XV, 23–24: 'Richard' and maybe 'Hugh'?		No corresponding type
	BSFN 1997, pp. 124–125: 'Richard'	No corresponding type	No corresponding type
c. 985–990/1000	Richard I and II		
	No corresponding type	No corresponding type	D XV, 22: 'St-Romain'
	D XVI, 3: 'count Richard'	D XVI, 1–2: 'Richard marquis' and 'Romain bishop'	No corresponding type
	D XV, 18: 'Richard' and maybe 'Saint-Ouen'?		No corresponding type

Chapter 12

Saints, Sinners and ... a Cow: Offerings, Alms and Tokens of Memory

Lucia Travaini

Coins are found in ritual contexts throughout western Christendom, and indeed in pre-Christian societies.[1] What this chapter will present is a series of case studies including some of the more extraordinary sources and examples of this practice emerging from an archaeological context, and also as they are recorded in documentary sources. The discussions incorporate Italian sources, not often discussed in wider medieval scholarship. On the basis of the examples some commentary will be offered on ritual practice and the worth and value of the coins deposited. A longer chronological perspective is adopted, from the twelfth and thirteenth centuries up to the later Middle Ages, with earlier examples from the ninth century.[2]

---

[1] My research on ritual use of coins started when preparing a paper for a symposium in Cambridge on *Gods, Graves and Numismatics: Interpreting Early Medieval Coin Finds of Northern Europe in Sacred Contexts*, which was to take place in March 1999: I was invited to talk about coins in medieval Italian graves. The Symposium was organised by Mark Blackburn and Kristin Bornholdt. Mark died on 1 September 2011, after a long and courageous battle against cancer: he made a fundamental contribution to numismatics and especially to the interpretation of coins in archaeological contexts. In that Cambridge symposium I was able to share my Italian evidence and ideas with colleagues from northern Europe which subsequently appeared as 'Saints and Sinners: Coins in Medieval Italian Graves', *Numismatic Chronicle*, 164 (2004): 159–81.

[2] Medieval archaeology in Italy developed only during the 1970s, and medieval numismatics even later. Although there has been great progress in the classification and attribution of the coinages of many mints and States, general overviews only started to appear in the 1970s and 1990s, including the volumes of *MEC* (1 and 14), and a lot remains to be done. For a general survey of Italian coinage in the early Middle Ages, see *MEC* 1 = P. Grierson, M. Blackburn, *Medieval European Coinage with a Catalogue of the Coins in the Fitzwilliam Museum, Cambridge. Vol. 1, The Early Middle Ages (5th –10th Centuries)* (Cambridge, 1986); *MEC* 14 = P. Grierson, L. Travaini, *Medieval European Coinage with a Catalogue of the Coins in the Fitzwilliam Museum, Cambridge. Vol. 14 Italy (III). (South Italy, Sicily, Sardinia)* (Cambridge, 1998); for a history of Italian medieval numismatics see L. Travaini, 'Le zecche italiane', in *Le zecche italiane fino all'Unità*, L. Travaini (ed.) (Rome:

The topic of coins in ritual contexts incorporates a wide range of material and documentary evidence and involves a number of different interpretative approaches. The present discussion will be framed around the notion that coins should be interpreted with a metaphysical dimension. This applies especially to discussion of coins outside their material function and use within worldly exchange, and more precisely to their role as tokens of memory and indicators of the Christian faith, particularly pertaining to the dead. In what follows, attention will be given to the function and meaning of coins in funerary contexts, and as memorial devices.

Traditional engagement with coins involves considering first their metal, weight and images, and then how they were used; in ritual contexts it is important to consider the intentions, honesty, and faith of those who dealt with and deposited them.[3] In this way coins can be thought of as good or bad, as tokens of memory, as signs of identity by provenance, and as indicators of time.

Saints and Sinners: Coins in Funerary Contexts

Of all of the funerary contexts in which to find coins, that of Saint Francis of Assisi might be thought the least likely. Francis is synonymous with poverty and its radical adoption in the mendicant way of religious life.[4] Saint Francis abhorred money and wanted to protect his friars from the 'contamination' of money and coins. In the *Regula bullata* of 1223 he prohibited the friars from

Istituto Poligrafico e Zecca dello Stato, 2011), pp. 31–122, and for South Italy, Sicily and Sardinia, *MEC* 14, pp. 476–518.

[3] Before talking of the ritual use of coins in any given period, it is important to have an idea of how many coins were available at that time; this is not easy to say for the period covered by this volume, but it is at least possible to give an idea of how many mints were active in Italy in the period under scrutiny. In the 1130s the beginning of a formidable increase in the number of mints active in central and northern Italy can be observed: an increase of 185 per cent from 1130 to 1200, jumping from 13 mints in 1101–30, to 37 mints in 1131–1200; the number of mints in the Kingdom of Sicily, created in 1130, was limited due to a very centralised coin production. Also from the 1130s the scale of production increased, and factory mints were certainly in place by the mid-century at Palermo, Messina, Lucca, Milan and Genoa. Such development of factory mints in this period was already hinted at by Peter Spufford in a symposium in 1985: see P. Spufford, 'Mint Organisation in Late Medieval Europe', in N. J. Mayhew and P. Spufford (eds), *Later Medieval Mints: Organisation, Administration and Techniques*, The 8th Oxford Symposium on Coinage and Monetary History, British Archaeological Reports, int. series 389 (Oxford, 1988), pp. 7–30.

[4] For a general introduction to St Francis see M. Robson (ed.), *The Cambridge Companion to Saint Francis of Assisi* (Cambridge, 2011).

accepting coins and money in all forms (*denarios vel pecuniam non recipient)*.[5] However, when his grave was opened, in the course of the survey of 1818, 12 coins were discovered next to the skeleton alongside a silver ring with an ancient gemstone (see Plate 17). Although this may seem surprising, the archaeologists at the time explained their presence by suggesting that the coins had been deposited to indicate the time of burial (*ad indicandum tempus*). In this way the coins acted as a chronological token, and this seems likely to have been the case.[6]

Coins in the graves of saints or of other important people must be distinguished from graves of ordinary people. Coins inside 'privileged' graves can be more easily understood as tokens of memory: they probably show, at least in part, an awareness of the need to leave some form of documentation for posterity. One set of circumstances in which this information would have been useful concerns the relocation of saints' graves on the occasion of building works, or surveys, within church, within the medieval period and beyond. Tombs and graves were often moved from one part to another of a church. In addition, saints' bodies could be dismembered in order to offer parts of them as relics to new churches; and, in a related vein, saints' graves were inspected to make sure that no parts had been taken or that it was really the original grave and not that of an impostor.

The grave of St Geminiano in Modena Cathedral is a particularly interesting case, with a total of 72 billon deniers and two silver crosses discovered during a survey in 1955. Geminiano was the first bishop of Modena, who died in 397, and a basilica *ad corpus* was built around his grave. The grave was surveyed twice in the Middle Ages, in 1109 and 1184, and is documented in written records which survive.[7] In 1109 the sarcophagus had to be moved to a new location in the newly built church which still stands in the present day. A survey of the body took place in the presence of Countess Matilda of Canossa, the bishop, local authorities and others: 18 denarii of Lucca can be dated to this period and must have been offered then. Matilda offered a cloak (*pallium*) decorated with

5 G. G. Merlo, 'Francesco d'Assisi e il denaro', in L. Travaini (ed.), *Valori e disvalori simbolici delle monete. I 30 denari di Giuda*, (Rome, 2009), pp. 145–52.

6 F. Guadagni, *De invento corpore Divi Francisci Ordinis Minorum Parentis* (Rome, 1819), the record of the investigation is not very precise about the position of the coins around the body; I. Gatti, *La tomba di S. Francesco nei secoli* (Assisi,1983), pp. 108–9, 267 and pl. 11; Travaini, 'Saints and Sinners ... ': 171–2; L. Travaini, 'Le monete nella tomba di san Francesco di Assisi', *Cercetări Numismatice*, IX–XI (2003–05): 193–8.

7 The coins are as follows: 18 denarii of Lucca dating to the eleventh century and almost certainly deposited at the moment of the survey of 1109; 54 denarii of Milano, Cremona, Mantova, Venezia, Ferrara and one denarius of Lucca of a later type deposited on the occasion of the survey of 1184: see L. Travaini, 'Le monete', in F. Missere Fontana and L. Travaini (eds), *Monete medievali e materiali nella tomba di San Geminiano di Modena* (Nonantola, 2005), pp. 35–57.

silver crosses of which only two remain today; these had been produced in the Holy Land for pilgrims.[8] In 1184 there was a new survey in the presence of Pope Lucius III who consecrated the new cathedral: 52 coins were deposited at this time. It seems reasonable to believe that coins were deposited to indicate the time of the burial or survey.[9]

Before indications of identity on the exterior of graves became more common, only the inside of a grave bore the occasional token or sign of identity.[10] The funeral ceremony, however rich in candles and offerings, left no physical trace in the long term. How did memory work between the inside of the grave and the outside? A good case-in-point is the account of the death of Emperor Lothar III (1125–37) in the chronicle of Otto of Freising: 'so that they could never be forgotten, the emperor's deeds were inscribed on sheets of lead and buried with him'. A survey of Lothar's grave in 1620 did indeed recover a lead plaque and a lead globe surmounted by a cross, now in the Herzog Anton-Ulrich Museum, Brunswick.[11] Those in charge of Lothar's burial, it can be suggested,

---

[8] A stone mould found in the Holy Land to produce such crosses is illustrated (but not described with dimension or provenance) in the exhibition catalogue, S. Rozenberg (ed.), *Knights of the Holy Land. The Crusader Kingdom of Jerusalem* (Jerusalem, 1999), p. 240. A similar cross was found in a hoard from Alife (Caserta) hoarded at the end of the twelfth century: E. A. Arslan, 'Le trésor de monnaies normandes et françaises d'Allifae (Campanie, XIIe siècle)', *International Numismatic Newsletter*, 30 (1997): 6–7.

[9] New data after Travaini, 'Saints and Sinners'; A. Degasperi, 'La moneta in tomba nella Toscana centro-settentrionale tra alto- e bassomedioevo', *Archeologia Medievale*, XXXIX (2012): 337–54. Other scholars argue that coins might have been offered in saints' graves as an *ex-voto* taken from coins offered by devout people and with no intention of memory; see A. Saccocci, 'Monete rinvenute nell'urna del santo', in S. Lunardon (ed.), *San Secondo. Un santo cavaliere tra le lagune,* Atti della Giornata di studi Venezia, Istituto Veneto di Scienze Lettere e Arti, 22 ottobre 2004, (Venice, 2007), pp. 149–67, 232–45, 274–6; comments also in Travaini, 'Valori e disvalori simbolici delle monete', in *Valori e disvalori simbolici,* pp. 30–33.

[10] St Augustine insisted that funeral offerings, meals and celebrations should be abolished, but they remained in use; the coins offered outside the grave were to be considered as alms if distributed to the poor on the spot, see Travaini, 'Saints and Sinners', p. 164, n. 22, and A. Boureau, 'A Royal Funeral of 1498', in M. Rubin (ed.), *Medieval Christianity in Practice,* (Princeton, 2009), pp. 59–63.

[11] K. F. Morrison, *History as a Visual Art in the Twelfth-Century Renaissance* (Princeton, 1990), p. 214: 'Even taking the very long term into account, it is difficult to imagine circumstances under which those in charge of the Emperor's funeral would have anticipated the exhumation of body and plaque together. A second perplexity arises from the inscription itself, which is far from a comprehensive memoir. In eleven lines, the inscription records Lothar's name and titles, the length of his reign, the date of his death, and a brief eulogy. Perhaps Otto did not know the content of the inscription any more than he knew that there was only one lead plaque. But was there some connection in his mind between the

would have foreseen an exhumation in the future. By the twelfth century, and long before, other tombs had been opened and their bones, particularly those of saints, relocated, thus justifying the function of the plaque as an object of record.

Another German grave relevant to this point is that of Albert the Bear, margrave of Brandenburg (1124–70), whose sarcophagus lies alongside that of his wife Sophie (d. 1160) in the monastery of Ballenstedt. The only coin found inside is a bracteate which bears the image of the standing margrave and his wife, issued in c. 1155/60 (see Plate 18). Albert issued many different coin types from 1134, mainly bracteates, but this particular type is the only one showing him together with his wife and this is the very type that was chosen to accompany him in his grave, once more next to his wife, as depicted on the coin. Whoever was responsible for the selection of this coin must have understood the significance of the iconography to the context of this burial. In this way the bracteate here represented a human relationship after death.

As well as rulers and saints, ordinary people also were buried occasionally with coins: it is difficult to interpret the meaning, as offerings, or objects of a magical nature, or *pars pro toto*. The strong possibility that the coins represented personal memory, a token from the living to the dead, should be considered although it is never possible to know for sure without corroborating evidence.[12] Even monks were occasionally buried with coins, as we know from Guibert of Nogent.[13]

Late medieval graves sometimes contain a small parcel of coins, even precious coins; although the question remains as to whether these were deposited intentionally as offerings by those in charge of the burial. In case of plague many were buried in haste without being touched; a purse containing coins attached to the belt could be a sign of a body untouched for fear of contagion.[14] However, it

---

memorial function of the record in the silence of the tomb and that of his own words in the silences of the codex?'. The original reads: ' ... honorifice sepelitur, [actusque eius, ut nulla possent aboleri oblivione, in plumbeis laminis descripti iuxta eum reconduntur]'. According to the editor (but ignored by Morrison), the words in square brackets were added in the thirteenth century: *Ottonis Episcopi Frisingensis Chronica sive Historia de Duabus Civitatibus*, A. Hofmeister (ed.), Monumenta Germaniae Historica, Scriptores Rerum Germanicarum in Usum Scholarum Separatim Editi (SS rer. Germ), vol. 45 (Hannover, 1912), p. 340. The passage about the lead plaque may have been added in the thirteenth century, but the plaque found in the tomb was presumably deposited at the time of the original burial.

[12] Travaini, 'Saints and Sinners': 165, 176.

[13] Guibert of Nogent, *Monodiae*, 1.22; Guibert of Nogent, *A Monk's Confession* (trans.), Archchambault (University Park, Pennsylvania, 1995), pp. 77–8. For more details on this example see the contribution to this volume by Giles E. M. Gasper.

[14] F. Pigozzo, 'La moneta cucita: i nascondigli per il denaro alla fine del Medioevo', *Bollettino del Museo Civico di Padova*, 94 (2005): pp. 159–62; further bibliography is to be found in Travaini, *Valori e disvalori*, p. 38, and in L. Travaini, 'Il lato buono delle monete:

could also indicate a belief that that the dead person might be in need of money for the journey in the afterlife, plague or no plague, so that the purse would be left with the intention to be useful. The various possibilities of interpretation remain an open issue.

Normally, when graves have one or more coins they are small value ones, and this holds true also for saints' graves: these coins are what may be termed 'good coins', those acceptable because they did not contaminate the soul. In this regard the 'obol' of classical tradition might be recalled; it too was a single, low-value coin, a symbol that death makes rich and poor equal.[15] Official teaching might warn against the deposit of coins in Christian graves, therefore when hoards of coins, including precious coins, are discovered in Christian contexts care needs to be taken. Any late medieval man or woman knew that it was dangerous to have coins on their deathbed, as preachers were so insistent about this point. Evidence for this is to be found in the great *exempla* collections produced from the later twelfth and early thirteenth centuries. The most famous and earliest collection was that of Jacques de Vitry, c. 1200.[16] Many *exempla* did involve coins

devozione, miracoli e reliquie monetali', *Cristianesimo nella storia*, 33 (2012): 475–92. Very different is the case of hoards discovered by human remains with no trace of burial: this could have been an accidental death, like in the case of the Pontremoli hoard: Travaini, 'Saints and Sinners': 178.

15 Placing a coin in the mouth as the Charon's obol of Antiquity is documented within areas of Slavic settlement. For example at Mikulčice in Moravia (Czech Republic) a solidus of Michael III (842–67) was found in one burial's mouth (N. Profantová, 'Byzantine Coins of the 5th–9th Century from the Czech Republic', in Marcin Wołoszyn (ed.), *Byzantine Coins in Central Europe between the 5th and 10th Century*, Proceedings from the conference organised by Polish Academy of Arts and Sciences, Institute of Archaeology University Rzeszów under the patronage of Union Académique Internationale (Programme no. 57 Moravia Magna) Kraków, 23–26 IV 2007, Polish Academy of Arts and Sciences and Institute of Archaeology University Rzeszów, Moravia Magna, Seria Polona, vol. III (Kraków, 2009), pp. 581–98). This tradition is well documented in Dalmatia by the fourteenth century. The obol in the mouth is very rarely documented in medieval Italy, with the exception of a few fourteenth-century cemeteries in the Salento, the heel of Italy, with deniers tournois of Frankish Greece placed in the mouth: the very localised tradition makes it possible to suppose that the cemeteries belonged to communities of immigrants from the Balkans who carried the tradition with them. For the evidence in the Salento see P. Arthur, 'Il cimitero', in P. Arthur (ed.), *Da Apigliano a Martano. Tre anni di archeologia medioevale (1997–1999)* (Martina Franca, 1999), pp. 51–3, and A. Degasperi, 'Le monete', in ibid., pp. 37–9. For the tradition in the Balkans and contacts with the Salento see also P Arthur, 'L'Albania e la Terra d'Otranto nel Medioevo: tre casi studio', in Fondazione Cassamarca (ed.), *Convegno Internazionale di Studi. Gli Illiri e l'Italia* (Treviso, 2005), pp. 77–91. I am most grateful to Paul Arthur for his generous help and exchange of references.

16 See C. Bremond, J. Le Goff and J.-C. Schmitt, *'L'Exemplum'*, Typologie des Sources du Moyen Âge Occidental, 40, (Turnhout, 1982); S. Thompson, *Motif-Index of*

and money as the devil's tools: the stories found in the *exempla* are reflected in medieval visual art, with the clear message that men should not be attached to earthly goods and especially to riches and money. Coins, as symbol of richness, were seen as dangerous to the soul: the 30 pieces of silver sold Christ; the usurers died in Hell, and so on down to the definition of *pecunia stercus diaboli*. A precious hoard in a Christian grave must be looked at with suspicion, for the risk to the soul it implied: the archaeological evidence must be really clear to dismiss the possibility of a secondary deposition as a hoard hidden in a cemetery. They may represent deliberate deposits in the face of church prohibition; they may not. Pots containing coins placed by the head in a few twelfth-century graves in Tuscany seem possibly due to voluntary deposition.[17] They may represent a survival of pagan practice in a formally Christian society. Or they may represent both of these possibilities and many more.

Offerings and Devotion

Saints' graves also attracted considerable monetary gifts in the medieval period, as is well known. Pilgrims travelled at great risk to reach shrines and to pray there; the memory of the journey would always remain with them as a spiritual and physical experience that brought them closer to God, whatever their individual beliefs were. It would seem quite reasonable to imagine that having reached the end of their long journey pilgrims wanted to touch the shrine of the saint to make physical contact with the object of their devotion, and to extend this association by offering something of themselves. Coins proved to be very well suited for this purpose, being small and durable, bearing the images of one's own region, and therefore ideal as tokens of identity and personal memory which could be left behind, attached to the shrine, to a saint's body or icon.[18] An example of this might be a Swedish bracteate of Magnus Eriksson (1319–63) hidden in the hand of the statue of Saint Olaf in the church of Lunner in Oppland (Norway).[19] Coins thus offered by pilgrims were usually of small value, available to all; 'good' coins by virtue of their moral value and for personal memory if identified as an

Folk Literature. A Classification of Narrative Elements in Folktales, Ballads, Myths, Fables, Mediaeval Romances, Exempla, Fabliaux, Jest- Books and Local Legends, revised and enlarged edition, 6 vols (Bloomington-Indianapolis, 1955–58).

17 Degasperi, 'La moneta in tomba nella Toscana centro-settentrionale'. On the subject of 'dead man's treasure' see Travaini, 'Saints and Sinners': 177–8.

18 See also Travaini, 'Saints and Sinners': 172–4; Travaini, 'Valori e disvalori', pp. 35–8.

19 K. Skaare, 'Universitetets Myntkabinett (Annual Report)', *Nordisk Numismatisk Årsskrift*, (1973–74): 154–5.

'everyday coin': the moment of the offering was most likely connected with a prayer or a votive offering.[20]

Another striking example concerns the tomb of St Catervius, in a Roman sarcophagus in the Duomo of Tolentino (Marche), which was surveyed in 1750. Many coins were found along with belts and rosaries, all apparently personal tokens of pilgrims. The tomb had a heavy lid sealed with plaster, but devout people were so determined to enter the sacred space that they broke the lid in order to insert their offering so that it could touch the sacred body.[21] The coins here span a long period of time, meaning that the tomb was accessible for centuries. For many pilgrims making a coin offering, this was an act of devotion, a tactile act and a personal encounter with the saint. The offering was a sacred act, a gift to God.[22]

A question over the quality of coins made in church offerings is indicated in the 'Topography of Ireland' *(Topographia Hibernica)* composed by Gerald of Wales in around 1188. Soon after the Norman incursion into Ireland, after the fall of Dublin (1171), a bowman wanted to offer a penny at the cross, in the Cathedral of the Holy Trinity (Christ Church), but, as he turned, the penny hit him on the back. He took it and offered it again, but the penny came back again on him, leaving everybody astonished. The bowmen, ashamed, had to confess publicly that he had plundered the archbishop palace. He was asked to return all he had taken; once he did that, he offered the penny again, with devotion

---

[20] A modern equivalent is the practice by tourists of casting a coin into the Trevi fountain in Rome, something in which even Theodor Mommsen participated. See L. Travaini, 'Le monete a Fontana di Trevi: storia di un rito', *Rivista Italiana di Numismatica*, 101 (2000): 251–9. Travaini, 'Saints and Sinners': 172.

[21] The text of the survey of 1750 in Tolentino is given by G. Alteri, 'Il sarcofago di Catervio', *Bollettino di Numismatica*, 26–7 (1996): 7. For this and other cases of coins forcedly inserted in a saint's grave, see Travaini, 'Saints and Sinners': 172–3. A distinction must be made between coins offered by individuals during a long period of time at shrines or saints' graves which were accessible to the public, as at Tolentino, and coins offered at the moment of the burial or official survey by those responsible and sealed with no further intrusion of coins or other objects.

[22] In this context the reactions of the English protestant traveller Fynes Moryson are instructive. In 1594 he visited the shrine of Loreto in Italy. Disguised as a Catholic, in the company of two Dutch travellers, once behind the altar where pilgrims were expected to offer coins, he quickly did otherwise and took away some coins (' ... and myself being the last, when my turne was to give alms, did in stead thereof, gather some tenne quatrines of theirs, which lay scattered upon the grate, and got that cleare gain by that Idoll'). In this story there are at least four different potential attitudes to coins as offerings: 1, the priest was interested in getting as much money as possible; 2, some devout pilgrims may have given a coin with intention and devotion and may be asking for a grace; 3, some other pilgrims of less strong faith must have simply just given a coin because they had to; 4, the English traveller as false Catholic wanted to defy the idolatry of saints. F. Moryson, *An Itinerary* (Glasgow, 1907), vol. I, p. 217.

and fear, and the penny remained at the bottom of the cross. The story is a striking reminder that in religious exchanges purity of the metal is not enough; purity of the heart is essential for the efficacy of the religious transaction.[23] This sentiment resonates long after the end of the Middle Ages: the Italian traveller Pietro Della Valle in a letter from Isphahan of 24 August 1619 recorded that the King of Persia used special coins to offer as alms; to each of the poor he gave three sequins but not just ordinary ones. The sequins had been purchased from the Armenians because, so he wrote, their coins were reputed to be earned with justice and hard work, and therefore most appreciated by God.[24]

On a more general point, the size and multitude of offerings in churches are attested for in documentary and archaeological evidence. For the Jubilee year of 1300 Cardinal Jacopo Stefaneschi reported that in that year the altar of St Peter collected 30,000 florins, and that of St Paul 21,000 florins, and this sum was not made of large gifts of gold or silver, but of small coins currently used in all provinces.[25] In the excavations under the altar of St Peter in the Vatican in the 1930s–1940s over 1,500 coins were found, and many of them are foreign coins, from France, Germany, Low Countries, Spain, England, Bohemia, Livonia, Hungary and Slavonia, and at least some of these must have been intentionally offered as personal tokens in the form of coins 'of their own country'.[26]

It is not easy to identify the reasons why coins, which survive today, were offered centuries ago. However, some documents reveal traces of the intention to preserve personal memory in the offering. The nature of numismatic evidence

---

23 Giraldo Cambrense, *Agli estremi confini d'Occidente. Descrizione dell'Irlanda (Topographia Hibernica)*, M. Cataldi (trans.) (Turin, 2002), p. 76. For an English translation: Gerald of Wales, *The History and Topography of Ireland*, John O'Meara (trans.) (London, 1982); the standard edition remains Giraldi Cambresensis, *Opera*, Rolls Series, 21, 8 vols, J. S. Brewer, J. F. Dimock and G. F. Warner (eds) (London, 1861–91).

24 *Viaggi di Pietro Della Valle il pellegrino descritti da lui medesimo in 54 lettere familiari all'erudito suo amico Mario Schipano, divisi in tre libri, cioè: La Turchia, La Persia e L'India, con la vita dell'autore* (Turin, 1843), part II, *La Persia*, vol. II, p. 42. See also L. Travaini, 'Monete e sangue', in *Valori e disvalori*, p. 242.

25 "Quae celeberrima toto terrarum orbe altaria, singulis iamdudum annis, ex peregrinantium oblatis Apostolorum Principis Florinorum auri ... afferebant, milia triginta Principis circiter unum et viginti milia Doctoris hoc centesimo repulere, non ex magnis auri vel argenti donis, sed ex usualis monete provintie cuiusque minutis...': text from A. Frugoni, *Il giubileo di Bonifacio VIII*, Bullettino dell'Istituto Storico Italiano per il Medio Evo e Archivio Muratoriano, 62 (1950): 1–121, quoted also in Travaini, 'Valori e disvalori', p. 37 and Travaini, 'Saints and Sinners': 174.

26 C. Serafini, *Le monete*, in B. M. Apollonj Ghetti, A. Ferrua, E. Josi and E. Kirschbaüm, *Esplorazioni sotto la Confessione della Basilica di San Pietro in Vaticano* (Città del Vaticano, 1951), pp. 225–44. Amongst the finds there was also one gold tremissis of Charles the Great recently published by E. A. Arslan, 'Il dono di re Carlo all'apostolo Pietro: un Tremisse d'oro', *Numismatica e Antichità Classiche. Quaderni Ticinesi*, 37 (2008): 377–406.

does not contain evidence for the moral qualities of a coin, and the body of medieval contemporary evidence on this topic is scarce. Those that do suggest that, when dealing with ritual use of coins, the moral quality of the donor, and the purity of intention, are what distinguished a good from a bad coin. Even though the physical coins were the same, they were made different by the added value of purity of the soul and honesty of trade. This point is clarified in a Latin prayer book of c. 1400 which had a prayer for fevers prescribing as follows: '… and when you have said this oration, kiss your alms and after give it to a poor man or woman': the alms here were certainly in coins, and they were kissed before being given.[27] A kiss leaves no physical trace, similarly to a prayer, but both may have been followed by a miracle.

Coins as Foundation Offerings

Placing coins in the foundation of buildings was in part a propitiatory act, an offering to divinity, but also a sign of memory, varying according to time and context. Well known within Antiquity, this rite was continued for Christian buildings. It is documented by find records for the Constantinian basilica of St Peter's in the Vatican, and such rite would not have been different from the offer of coins in the grave of St Ambrose at Milan (d. 397).[28]

The rite is variously documented in medieval Europe. From the ninth to tenth century the consecration of a church space was an important event and implied offerings. The laying down of the first stones of the Abbey church at St-Denis in 1140 was a grand event in the presence of King Louis VII, as is known from the words of Abbot Suger. Once the stones were laid 'certain persons also deposited gems out of love and reverence for Jesus Christ'.[29] Coins are not mentioned in this case, but it might easily be imagined how they could have served well in the absence of gems; moreover, coins often bear crosses.

There are very few certain archaeological data on foundation deposits in Italy before the thirteenth century and the earliest is probably the one related to the small church of San Damiano in Assisi (1205). When Saint Francis visited the ruined church he had a vision of the Crucifix asking him to restore his church: Francis took it literally and restored the building in 1205, although the hagiographic tradition makes it obvious that Francis was asked to restore the church in the spiritual sense. Under the floor dated to St Francis' time

27 E. Duffy, 'Two Healing Prayers', in *Medieval Christianity in Practice*, pp. 164–70.

28 Travaini, 'Valori e disvalori', p. 40.

29 D. Iogna-Prat, 'The Consecration of Church Space', in *Medieval Christianity in Practice*, pp. 95–9.

archaeologists discovered a niche containing nine deniers of Lucca, making of this a foundation offering according to an existing tradition.[30]

Foundation offerings are better documented from the thirteenth century on.[31] An anonymous chronicle of Siena in the fourteenth century recorded two ceremonies of building foundations in the city. The first one was related to the façade of the Duomo in 1284: 'the laying down of the first stone took place in great solemnity, with the bishop and all clerics chanting hymns and prayers, as homage to the Virgin Mary, with holy water and incense, the sound of bells and of the trumpets of the commune; and in the foundation many coins of various kinds were placed as a sign of offering'.[32] Here the coins were meant as 'offerings' to the Virgin. The second foundation ceremony in the anonymous chronicle is related to the Torre del Mangia in 1325: here too the ceremony was attended by all local authorities, with great participation, and at some point a workman of the commune placed at the bottom of the foundation 'many coins in memory of the tower'. Here the coins were placed for memory of the tower itself, whilst its protection against thunder, lightning, and storm was entrusted to stones inscribed in Hebrew, Latin and Greek placed at each corner of the foundation (these were the three languages of the *titulus Crucis*, the plaque on the Cross of Christ).[33]

---

30 A. Saccocci, 'Le monete', in L. Ermini Pani, M. G. Fichera and M. L. Mancinelli (eds), *Indagini archeologiche nella chiesa di San Damiano in Assisi*, Medioevo francescano, arte 1 (Assisi, 2005), pp. 119–30: the author does not consider the coins as a foundation deposit but rather as personal 'ex-voto' offering by Saint Francis; however, it has been observed that the hagiographic episodes of St Francis' restoration of the small churches of San Damiano and of Santa Maria della Porziuncola have more of a symbolic value than a realistic one, and therefore the saint can hardly be imagined as the material builder (personal communication by Grado Giovanni Merlo); see also comments in Travaini, 'Valori e disvalori', p. 44, n. 90.

31 In the church of San Bartolomeo in the castle of Formigine (Parma) excavations brought to light a parcel of 12 denarii of the mid-thirteenth century in the central nave under the floor (denari of Bologna, Ferrara and Parma): see M. Baldassarri, 'Tra terra e "cielo": i reperti numismatici e devozionali dallo scavo di Formigine', in E. Grandi and M. Librenti (eds), *'In la terra de Formigine'. Archeologia di un abitato* (All'Insegna del Giglio, Borgo San Lorenzo-Firenze, 2013), pp. 131–44. In Alghero (Sardinia) one Roman and two medieval coins were found in the foundation of the house of a Catalan smith (second half of the fourteenth century). In the church of Santumiali (Sardinia) a hoard of 3,500 denari of Genoa was found under the altar: the date before 1330, although these are yet to be studied in full. I am grateful to Monica Baldassarri for supplying these references.

32 'e fu fatto nella prima pietra una grande solennità, e 'l vescovo con tutto el clericato cantando ini e salmi e orazioni, a riverenzia della Vergine Maria, e con aqua benedetta e oncenso, e con suono delle chanpane e delle tronbe del comuno; e fu grande solennità, e fu messo ne' detti fondamenti molta moneta di più ragioni per segnio di donagione', *Cronache senesi*, A. Lisini and F. Iacometti (eds), XV, part VI, 2nd edition (Bologna, 1931–39), p. 68.

33 '... l'operaio del chomuno di Siena mise in fondo di detta torre alquanta moneta per memoria di detta torre. E fuvi messe in ogni chanto una pietra co' lettere ebraice e greche e

In Padua the first purposely produced foundation medals are known for buildings of Francesco I da Carrara, Lord of Padua from 1350 to 1388.[34] However, medals produced for such purpose became more common elsewhere in the second half of the fifteenth century and this in connection with the diffusion of portrait medals.[35] Coins, however, remained still in use as foundation offerings for a long time, for important buildings, for which we have written records, and there were surely many more for more modest structures.[36]

The Cow

It is now time to present the cow referred to in the title of this discussion. It was discovered in a foundation context, in the Chiesa della Purificazione at Caronno Pertusella (Varese), in north-western Lombardy, founded in the mid-fifteenth century (see Plate 19). During the recent excavations a rather extraordinary

latine perché non fusse perchossa ne da tono, ne da saetta, ne da tempesta; e in questo modo fu fondata la detta torre', *Cronache senesi*, pp. 129–30. For the *titulus crucis* see A. Pontani, 'Note sull'esegesi e l'iconografia del *titulus crucis*', *Aevum. Rassegna di scienze storiche linguistiche e filologiche*, LXXVII (2003): 138–86.

34 This particular type of 'tessere murali' of Padua were placed inside clay cases and these were inserted in the walls of new buildings: see L. Rizzoli Jr, 'Teche e medaglie murali carraresi', *Bollettino del Museo Civico di Padova*, II (1899): 56–8; A. Saccocci, 'Teche e "medaglie" murali carraresi (1355–1405)', in A. Verdi (ed.), *Le mura ritrovate* (exhibition catalogue) (Padova, 1987), pp. 154–5; B. Callegher, 'Monete, medaglie e sigilli a Padova tra Duecento e Trecento', in V. Sgarbi (ed.), *Giotto e il suo tempo* (Milan, 2000), pp. 276–82, 415–21.

35 For medals in building foundations see M. Schraven, 'Out of Sight, Yet Still in Place. On the Use of Italian Renaissance Portrait Medals as Building Deposits', *Res: Anthropology and Aesthetics*, 55–6 (2009): 182–93.

36 Many are the written texts referring to coins offered in Italian building foundations in the fourteenth and fifteenth centuries: see bibliography in Travaini, 'Valori e disvalori', pp. 40–45. Many deniers were thrown in the foundation of the restored Ponte Vecchio in Pisa in 1383: *Cronica di Pisa,* in L. A. Muratori, *Rerum Italicarum Scriptores, XV* (Mediolani, 1729), col. 1079. Andrea Saccocci in general excludes for Italy the use of foundation deposits before the fourteenth century, making it a rite totally inspired by classical Antiquity (see A. Saccocci, 'Il ripostiglio di monete', in G. Ciampoltrini and E. Pieri (eds), *Archeologia a Pieve a Nievole: dalla basilica sita in loco Neure alla pieve romanica* (Pisa, 2004), pp. 71–83). On the contrary, I believe that we cannot exclude an earlier existence of the rite (and San Damiano seems to confirm it), especially considering that the creation of fourteenth-century foundation medals in Padua may be seen as a mature development of an existing rite which would have otherwise normally used coins. A synthesis of the different interpretations by Saccocci and Travaini on foundation deposits can be read in A. Bernardelli, 'In defossis locis dispersae, vel muris intus locatae ... Considerazioni su un uso rinascimentale della medaglia, le origini: secoli XIV e XV', *Rivista Italiana di Numismatica,* 111 (2010): 363–402, esp. 383 and n. 77.

discovery was made: in the middle of the central nave, and oriented like other human burials, archaeologists found the skeleton of a young cow (see Plate 20), buried in a kneeling position across the nave but with the head turned toward the main altar; inside its mouth was a denier of Emperor Frederick II of Hohenstaufen (1220–50) struck in Milan[37] (see Plate 21). The floor, which sealed the burial, can be dated 1455.[38] The cow skeleton bears neither trace of slaughtering nor of illness so it might have been jugulated; this must have been a ritual sacrifice for the rite of foundation, a very pagan-looking sacrifice but which could not possibly have happened far from the eyes of the clerics. The question is raised how to judge this kind of ritual offering. Cattle were probably the most valuable property in a rural community such as Caronno Pertusella and this offering was quite likely a generous gift to God from the community.

The evidence of the cow at Caronno Pertusella is much later than the period concerning us here, but it belongs to the topic of ritual contexts and serves as example of how difficult, or impossible, it is to separate pagan and Christian behaviours. The bovine was a valuable and symbolic offer, but the question may be asked as to why the medieval coin was deposited. It may have been placed in the mouth as a remembrance of ancient burial traditions, and the choice of an old coin that did not circulate in the fifteenth century was possibly more appropriate for a rite which might have been considered to be an ancient one.

Conclusion

This discussion has presented coins in a variety of different circumstances all of which relate to ritual offerings. Coins in these contexts can be presented as 'good' or 'bad', tokens of memory, a sign of identity and indicators of chronology. With and without the context of archaeological and written documentation, the numismatic evidence – the coins – offers insight into a wide spectrum of circumstances and occasions. The coins are the physical legacy of the encounter between the human and the divine, on an individual basis, and as such offer a tantalising glimpse into this most personal of activities known to medieval people.

---

[37] A silver denaro piano: see M. Chiaravalle, 'La moneta nella bocca del bovino: un denaro imperiale federiciano per Milano', in P. Colombo, P. Monti and P. Zaffaroni (eds), *Chiesa della Purificazione* (Firenze, 2011), pp. 171–6.

[38] S. Di Martino, 'La sepoltura di bovino: analisi osteologica', in *Chiesa della Purificazione*, pp. 167–9. B. Grassi and G. Ridolfi, 'Le ricerche archeologiche', in *Chiesa della Purificazione*, pp. 141–66. Caronno was a rural 'comune': a fortified village at the bottom of a castle.

Chapter 13

The Church and Money in Norway c. 1050–1250: Salvation and Monetisation

Svein H. Gullbekk

Norwegian coinage was in its infancy at the turn of the first millennium. When the name of the Viking King Olaf Tryggvason (r. 995–1000) appeared in the legend of silver pennies ONLAF REX NO[RMANNORVM] the Norwegians were at the same time in the process of becoming Christianised. According to later tradition, from the late twelfth century onwards, it was King Olaf Haraldsson (r. 1015–28, 1030) who completed the task of forging Norway as a Christian kingdom. Olaf Haraldsson was also the first to organise minting on a scale sufficient to be considered as a first important step in the direction of a national coinage. Nevertheless, the number of coins issued in the 1020s would have been insufficient for a national purpose. According to the thirteenth-century *Heimskringla* and twelfth-century legal texts, Olaf Haraldsson was instrumental in legal reforms carried out at the Mosterthing in 1016. Later texts referring to these laws of Saint Olaf, 'Rex Perpetuus' of Norway, are without reference to coinage or any administrative measures concerning coin circulation, but the legal administrative system became important for the organisation of coinage and a monetary regime on a national level, and law codes implemented in the twelfth and thirteenth centuries contain laws on money and coinage, that is, on counterfeit coinage.[1]

On the eastern and northern borders of eleventh-century Christendom minting was introduced in Bohemia, Hungary, Poland, Kiev, Sweden and Norway, alongside a fresh start to royal coinage in Denmark, followed shortly after official acceptances of Christianity.[2] The most reasonable hypothesis linking coinage and Christianity suggests that the official adoption of Christianity involved the rulers of these newly converted kingdoms including missionaries

---

1 For a discussion on law and money in medieval Norway, see Svein H. Gullbekk, 'Law and Money in Medieval Norway', *Numisamtic Chronicle*, 158 (1998), 173–84; Svein H. Gullbekk, *Pengevesenets fremvekst og fall i Norge i middelalderen* (Copenhagen, 2009), pp. 106–28.

2 Stanislaw Suchodolski, Die Anfänge der Munzprägung in Scandinavien und Polen, *Nordisk Numismtisk Årsskrift* (1971): 20–37; Peter Spufford, *Money and its Use in Medieval Europe* (Cambridge, 1988), pp. 82–3.

in their intimate counsel. These men, from societies in which coinage was an accepted and expected attribute of kingship, advised their new patrons that they too ought to strike coin. Such external influence was presumably crucial for King Harald Sigurdsson, better known by his saga sobriquet Hardrada (r. 1047–66), when he established a national coinage for Norway in the late 1040s with a standard of 240 pennies to a mark. Hardrada had spent some 15 years in the service of Byzantine emperors moving in high circles; the only Viking to be mentioned by name in contemporary Byzantine sources.[3] His years in Constantinople would have given Harald Sigurdsson first-hand insight into how the most sophisticated coinage and money-economy in the Mediterranean at that time was operated.

The contemporary historical evidence for the use of money within Norwegian society pre-1200 limits itself to a few remarks in the *Gesta Hammaburgensis Ecclesiae Pontificum* of Adam of Bremen written in the 1070s, the saga of King Sverre Sigurdsson (r. 1177–1202) begun under the king's supervision in 1185, the Land laws written down from the 1170s, accounts of land-rents from Bergen and Nidaros c. 1200 which have survived only in fragmentary form, and sources within foreign material, primarily papal administrative documents, including letter collections.[4] The use of money is, however, mentioned in a range of different legal contexts, for the payment of fines, for compensation for travel to the Thing, and for payment of tax at the Thing meeting. With no comprehensive or even broadly indicative accounts of the practical or theoretical aspects of the economy or monetary systems modern scholarship has to take a wide perspective, using admittedly patchy evidence but from a range of different disciplines, in many cases dependent on evidence from material culture, predominantly archaeology and numismatics.[5]

---

3 Kolbjørn Skaare, *Coins and Coinage in Viking Age Norway* (Oslo, 1976); Svein H. Gullbekk, 'Myntvesenet som kilde til statsutvikling i Norge ca. 1050–1080', in *Statsutvikling i Skandinavia i middelalderen,* (eds) Sverre Bagge et al. (Oslo, 2011), pp. 76–100; Sverre Bagge, 'Harald Hardråde i bysants. To fortellinger, to kulturer', in *Hellas og Norge: Kontakt, komparasjon, kontrast,* (eds) Øivind Andersen and Thomas Hägg (Bergen, 1990), pp. 169–92.

4 For Norwegian payments of dues to the Papal See, see *Pavelige Nuntiers Regnskabs- og Dagbøger 1282–1334,* (ed.) P. A. Munch (Christiania, 1864), hereafter *PNRD*. The economy of the medieval church is an extensive field of study, one which is outside the scope of this chapter. In Scandinavia the financial organisation of the church to a large extent followed the patterns of the universal church in the Latin West, see Gustav Storm, *Afgifter fra den norske kirkeprovins til det apostoliske kammer og Kardinalkollegiet 1311–1523* (Christiania, 1897); Gunnar Pettersen, *De økonomiske sidene ved provent-institusjonen i Norge ca. 1280–1500* (Oslo, 1992).

5 Viking Age and medieval Norwegian history, general accounts are available in Sverre Bagge, 'The Scandinavian Kingdoms', in *The New Cambridge Medieval History*, V, c.

In eleventh-century Norwegian society, money was not only synonymous with coin. The use of silver and commodities as money was a widespread and established practice, since the arrival of currency starting with Islamic dirhems from the second quarter of the ninth century.[6] Despite Harald Hardrada's introduction of a national coinage that replaced foreign coins in circulation, and his son, King Olaf the Peaceful's (r. 1067–93) institution of recoinage (*renovatio monetae*), commodities were still used commonly as money for payment of tax, land-rent and land transactions well into the fourteenth century and beyond. While money-economy prevailed in urban environments, natural economy continued to dominate significant elements of rural society in large parts of the kingdom. The parallel use of two economic systems created a complex system of values in which the old norse mark-of-silver (c. 214 grams) was used as common denominator; one *kyrlag* (value of a normal cow) would be equal to three lauper of butter (one laup, 16.2 litres) or one-third of a mark of burnt silver. The relationship between values of different commodities and money secured a system of conversion between monetary values and commodities that incorporated a pseudo-monetary system with a high degree of flexibility.[7]

After the introduction of coinage on a national scale by Harald Hardrada severe debasement was introduced for the first time within Scandinavia. Modern analysis provides evidence for the silver content of coins being lowered from c. 90 per cent to c. 33 per cent within a short period of time.[8] This level of debasement suggests that the king took advantage of his royal prerogative for minting, expanding, presumably lucratively, its scope considerably.[9]

The newly adopted church would, as anywhere else in the Latin West, introduce new institutions, customs and value systems based on a prevailing monetary mentalilty. An important turning point in the role of the church in

1198–c. 1300, David Abulafia (ed.) (Cambridge, 1999), pp. 720–42; Knut Helle (ed.), *The Cambridge History of Scandinavia*, vol. 1, *Prehistory to 1520* (Cambridge, 2003).

6 Mark Blackburn, 'The Coin-finds', in *The Means of Exchange*, Dagfinn Skre (ed.) (Kaupang Excavation Project Publication Series, vol. II. Norske Oldfunn XXIII, Aarhus, 2007), pp. 29–74; Christoph Kilger, 'Kaupang from Afar: Aspects of the Interpretation of Dirham Finds in Northern and Eastern Europe between the Late 8th and Early 10th Centuries', in *The Means of Exchange*, pp. 199–252.

7 For an extensive study of the medieval Norwegian commodity-money-system, see Kåre Lunden, *Korn og kaup. Studiar over prisar og jordbruk på Vestlandet i mellomalderen* (Oslo-Bergen-Tromsø, 1978).

8 Metal analysis of pennies from Harald Hardrade's reign has been published in Skaare, *Coins and Coinage*, pp. 79–85 and 191–206.

9 This development is referred to in the Morkinnskinna edition of Harald Hardrade's saga, written down c. 1200 *Morkinnskinna*, (ed.) F. Jónsson, Udgivet for Samfund til Udgivelse af gammel nordisk Litteratur LIII, [København 1932], pp. 149–51. For a discussion of this source in a monetary context, see Skaare, *Coins and Coinage*, pp. 9–11.

the process of monetisation was the creation of the archiepiscopal see in Nidaros, under the guidance of the English papal legate Nicholas Brekespear (later to become Pope Hadrian IV) in 1152/53.[10] From this point the Norwegian church took a first definite step away from its dependence on the monarchy, and adopted the priorities and values of the reform papacy: a church free from secular influence and responsive to the leadership of the papacy. Already from the start the monarchy made concessions in three areas that were considered of major importance: 1) the church should have the decisive say in the election of bishops and the appointment of priests; 2) it should have jurisdiction over its own personnel and in matters of particular concern to the church; 3) it should have financial control of the churches and their property.

Nicholas Brekespear's visit had wide-reaching effects on many aspects of church life. The understanding of how to adminster the economy of an ecclesiastical organisation from an archbishopric to parish churches would be drawn from well-proven models elsewhere within Christendom. Basic elements of the economic situation encountered by Brekespear, such as the combination of natural and money-based payment, would have been familiar. Tithes and land-rents were often paid in the produce of the farms, in commodities rather than money. However, the church propagated money in a different way to other institutions, and in so doing did a great deal to transform part of the medieval economy towards a money-economy. In this process, the demand for coinage and monetary payments from a church organisation that became increasingly more powerful, both politically and financially and not last spiritually, made significant impact on the monetisation of Norway, and Scandinavia in the Middle Ages. These payments were now connected to a super-regional authority, which made occasional and increasing demands for money communicated with each member of the congregation on an individual level.

Managing Money: Saint Peter's Pence, Ecclesiastical Fines and Crusader Taxation

One obligation which, once introduced, would make a direct impact on how the common parishioner encountered the church and its pecuniary mentality, was Saint Peter's Pence, (*Romescot* or *Denarii Sancti Petri*), an annual payment to Rome. The earliest source for Saint Peter's Pence in a Norwegian context is

[10] Originally the Norwegian church was organised under the Archbishop of Hamburg-Bremen, and then from 1102/3, under the Danish Archbishop of Lund. In the twelfth century when papal policy aimed at bringing the smaller provinces on the periphery of Europe into more directly subordinate relationship with Rome, Norway was, as a consequence, established with an archbishopric of its own. On Hadrian IV see Brenda Bolton (ed.), *Adrian IV The English Pope (1154–159): Studies and Texts* (Farnham, 2003).

in King Magnus Erlingsson's coronation oath from 1163/64: 'obseruabo ea que dominus papa adrianus statuit cum legatus esset in regno Norwagie. de censu beati petri [and to observe that which the lord Pope Hadrian adopted when he was legate to the kingdom of Norway, concerning St Peter's money and the state and church affairs]'.[11] The introduction of Saint Peter's Pence has been subject to debate. One line of argument suggests that its introduction predates the establisment of a Norwegian archbishopric in 1152/53 while another aligns its introduction with the making of the archbishopric.[12] From a papal perspective, the earliest reference to Saint Peter's Pence in Norway is in Cardinal Albinus's census from 1188–89.[13] Three years later [1192] this is repeated in the papal chamberlain Cencius Camerarius's (later Pope Honorius III) *Liber censuum*.[14]

The introduction of Saint Peter's Pence exposed Norwegian society to decisions that originated at the papal curia in Rome resulting in the request for

11 *Latinske dokument til norsk historie*, E. Vandvik (ed. and trans.) (Oslo, 1959), no. 10; *Norges Middelalderdokumenter* (*NMD*), Sverre Bagge, Synnøve Holstad Smedsdal and Knut Helle (eds) (Bergen, 1973), no. 7; Olaf Kolsrud, 'Kong Magnus Erlingssons kronings-eid 1163', *Historisk Tidsskrift*, XXXI (1937–40): 465. Cf. Arne Odd Johnsen, *Nicolaus Breakespears legasjon til Norden* (Oslo, 1945) pp. 249. *NMD* no. 7; *Regesta Norvegica* I, no. 110 dates this document to the summer 1163–64. The organisation of the church into dioceses and parishes opened up for ecclesiastical taxation on a broad scale. St Peter's Pence is tentatively recorded in Danish context in a letter from Pope Alexander II (1061–73) to King Svein Estridsen written between 1061 and 1073 (*Diplomatarium Danicum*, series 1, vol. 1, no. 3. The letter is discussed by B. Poulsen in this volume, p. 149). In Sweden the introduction of St Peter's Pence is seen as a driver for the oldest coinage struck in Lödöse in the western part of Sweden c. 1150 (Rune Ekre, *Om den medeltida utmyntingen i Lödöse, in Skärvor och fragment: kring medeltiden i Älvsborg län*, Västgöta-dal 1989–90 (Vänersborg, 1991), pp. 17–25

12 Absalon Taranger, *Den angelsaksiske kirkes indflytelse* (Christiania, 1890), pp. 290–91; Arne Odd Johnsen, *Nicolaus Breakespears legasjon til Norden* (Oslo, 1945), p. 251; Heruf Nielsen, '*Peterspenge*', *KLNM* XIII (1968), sp. 251.

13 *In Norogueia singuli lares i monetam eiusdem terre* (Liber censuum II, 121).

14 'Notandum quod singule domus Norwagie singulos dant denarios monete ipsius terre' (*Liber censuum* I, 228 ff). A letter from Pope Innocent III dated 11 February 1206, gave Archbishop Tore I of Nidaros a mandate to collect St Peter's Pence in his province, and to use clerical punishment for those stubbornly refusing to pay (*Diplomatrium Norvegicum* VII, no. 6). Some 15 years later the Prior of the abbey of St Victor in Paris, in a letter addressed to Pope Honorius III dated before 12 January 1221, stated that Archbishop Guttorm of Nidaros had deposited two arm-rings, 20 marks in new sterlings and 40 marks good silver as payment for St Peter's Pence (DN VI, no. 13). On 3 February of the same year the Pope addressed the Bishops in the archbishopric of Nidaros and told them to assist the archbishop in the collection of St Peter's Pence (DN VI, no. 16 and King Sverre's speech against the Bishops and Sverre's church laws 36; *Norsk gamle love*, II *Fra 1263 til 1280*, R. Keyser and P. A. Munch (ed.) (Christiania 1848 333, 338 and III *Fra 1280 til 1387*, R. Keyser and P. A. Munch (Christiania, 1849), 84, 309).

each and every person to pay one penny annually, normally collected through their local parish church. The demand for this money-payment was imposed upon the whole Norwegian population, rural as well as urban, and, in all probability represented the first form of monetary tax generally, systematically and institutionally imposed. In this way the parish churches were bound into the church universal, and by demanding a coin from every Christian soul in the kingdom a link was established between money and religion, a link that, so far as the evidence allows, was entirely novel for the Norwegian peasantry. The Norwegian church literally and symbolically bought into the papal reform movement in the eleventh and twelfth centuries. Each believer was given, willingly or not, a tangible stake in the church: each penny was to be paid in the name of and to Saint Peter upon whom Christ built his church.[15]

As the church grew more powerful in Norway, and as part of a general cultural shift in the twelfth century, attitudes towards money became more complex, balancing for example moral debates on the one hand, and pragmatic responses on the other. The activity of the secular church in particular was wide-ranging, involving pastoral care and general maintenance and upkeep of the ornaments, lighting and fabric of church buildings. These activities often held spiritual significance as well as and alongside their practical purpose, and required a number of revenue sources to be exploited. In many places, while tithe remained the most important income, payment for services and offerings also would provide important additions, as would land rent and, from the mid-twelfth century, revenue from court fines.

Revenue from fines as a result of legal process is considered the largest source of income for the Norwegian royal treasury in the Middle Ages.[16] As for the Norwegian ecclesiastical law codes, these include the establishment of a money-based fine system codified within twelfth- and thirteenth-century laws.[17] The importance of revenue from church fines is demonstrated in 1162, when, as a consequence of a debasement of the coins in circulation, Archbishop Øystein made an agreement with the peasantry that within his archbishopric all should pay fines based on the value of weighed money rather than money by tale. In

15 The oldest account for collections of St Peter's Pence in Norway is dated 20 September 1305 and details the collections in the Bergen bishopric in the years 1294 to 1300 (DN IV, no. 60). From the fourteenth century there is evidence for collections of St Peter's Pence in the following years: 1317–20, 1323, 1324–26, 1327, 1328, 1329, 1330, 1331, 1332, 1333, 1345, 1346, 1351, 1352–64, 1371, 1395 and 1399. The tradition of collecting Peter's Pence has been reinvented by the Papal State. In 2006 the total sum added up to more than USD 100 million. The money was used in philanthropic engagements.

16 Knut Helle, *Norge blir en stat 1130–1319*, 2nd edition (Oslo-Bergen-Tromsø, 1996), pp. 186–8.

17 Olaf Kolsrud, 'Kong Magnus Erlingssons kronings-eid 1163', *Historisk Tidsskrift*, XXXI (1937–39): 472.

practice this meant that the church received fines double the value of what the king would receive.[18]

This became subject of debate between the king and the archbishop. From the archbishop's point of view the reduction of revenues from fines by 50 per cent, as a result of a series of debasements, was difficult for the church to compensate. The debasements were carried out by the royal authorities able to take pecuniary advantage through the minting process, which was not an option for the church, which only received right to mint at a later stage, in the 1220s.[19] As a net receiver of debased money, the church suffered financially, hence Archbishop Øystein's attempt to insist on the weight of coinage, and thereby maintain the important revenues from fines.

The issue remained contentious. In papal privileges for the Norwegian church dated to 15 June 1194 the question of fines was referred to with support for the position of the church, as might be expected.[20] This was confirmed in an extensive agreement drawn up between the church and the king in the so-called 'Settargjerden' in Tønsberg in 1277.[21] The struggles between the king and church during the twelfth and thirteenth centuries raised a series of important issues, of which several focused upon money and financial arrangements. Not only were the rates for the fines concerning ecclesiastical laws a matter of concern, but so too was the availability of silver.

The climax of the broader struggle between church and king was played out during the 1270s and 1280s, a period in which the debate about silver also quickened. As a consequence of the church's need for good quality silver with which to make payments of papal taxation related to the crusader tax introduced by the Lyon Council in 1274, the demand for quality silver to be exported from Norway reached high, and probably unprecedented, levels. The basic point at issue was the debased silver content and quality of Norwegian coinage. Silver was available in Norway, but the natural deposits were exploited only much later, in the early modern period.[22] Realising the poor silver content of Norwegian coins, the papacy demanded payment not in currency, but in good quality silver. The

---

18 *Heimskringla*, Magnus Erlingsson's saga, chs 16 and 21.

19 Kolsrud, 1937–39: 474–5; Grethe Authén Blom, *Kongemakt og privilegier i Norge inntil 1387* (Oslo-Bergen-Tromsø, 1967), p. 132 ff.

20 'Nulli eciam regi vel principi liceat approbatas patrie leges et scriptas absque consensu episcoporum et sapientum consilio et pecuniarias penas tam in clericis quam in laicis contra antiquam consuetudinem in ecclesiarum seu clericorum dispendium (immutare)' (DN II, no. 3, Kolsrud (trans.), 1937–39: 475).

21 NGL II, 467–8.

22 Minting of locally mined silver is documented at Gimsøy by Skien in Telemark in the years 1543–46 and from 1628 in Christiania (Oslo) and Kongsberg in Buskerud from 1686, where the Royal Mint was established near the large silver deposits, and where the mint producing Norwegian coinage today is still in existence.

debate can be followed in the correspondence of the Norwegian Archbishop Jon the Red with the papacy. In a petition dated 4 December 1276 Raude made the point that the silver quality in the Norwegian coinage was poor and therefore should be exchanged into trade goods and sold for good quality silver abroad.[23]

It is likely that the archbishop tried to exchange as much as possible into good quality silver, for instance English sterlings that were widely available in Norway in this period.[24] In response the king issued a ban on the sale of silver from lay people to clergy in general, and specifying the sale of sterlings. Anyone engaging in such trade would be punished severely. This ban on the purchase of silver by ecclesiastical institutions was acceptable neither to the Papal See that had embarked on plans for the recapture of Jerusalem, nor to the archbishop. In a letter of 4 March 1282 Pope Martin IV demanded that the Norwegian king recall the ban because of the problems it created for the Norwegian church in making their contribution to the holy cause.[25] This demand was restated in a letter of 5 January 1286 signed by Pope Honorius IV.[26] The ban on the sale of silver to the church has been interpreted as an important step in the restriction of the church's financial and political rights by the crown.[27] It certainly provoked contemporary reaction and was considered a serious breach of the church's autonomy.

The need for payments of papal dues and taxes was a continuous affair which again and again posed questions of how and what to export for this purpose. The demand for payments towards the Papal See continued with equal force in the fourteenth century. According to surviving records from the period 1276–1364 the sum collected in ecclesiastical taxes and dues that are recorded from Norway comes to more than 24,272 ½ marks ½ ore in Norwegian coinage.[28] These sums were often recorded by papal nuncios of Italian or French origin, commissioned to collect taxes from the Norwegian bishoprics. In a manner completely different to secular documents, these tax records give detailed information on the number of specific coin types and their values, and are even specific, on occasion, about the silver content. The emphasis on monetary values and coins

---

23 DN VI, no. 39. Jens Arup Seip, *Sættargjerden i Tunsberg og kirkens jurisdiksjon* (Oslo, 1942), p. 152.

24 In recent years the number of medieval English sterlings found as stray finds in Norway has increased significantly. In the Oslo-fjord area the number of sterlings is almost equal with the number of Norwegian medieval coins in stray finds (Anette Sættem and Svein H. Gullbekk, *Norske myntfunn ca. 1050–1319*, work in progress).

25 DN I, no. 73; *PNRD*, p. 154.

26 DN I, no. 76; *PNRD*, p. 163. The Pope advises the Norwegian King to support the liberation of the Holy Land by making sure the tithes can be taken out of his realm (DN I, no. 72; *PNRD*, pp. 153–4).

27 P. A. Munch, *Det Norske Folks Historie*, vol. II, part 4 (Christiania, 1859), p. 4.

28 Gullbekk, *Pengevesenets fremvekst*, p. 245.

in these records provides strong evidence for how the church operated a money-based economy from the third quarter of the thirteenth century, and, it might be presumed, earlier.

The earliest detailed account of tax-collection to have survived from the Norwegian archbishopric is that for the above mentioned tithe in support of the crusades to liberate the Holy Land, announced at the Lateran Council in Lyon in 1274. The tithe was collected from the income of the clergy rather than from the population directly, and it was carried out in the years 1276–82. The records have survived in a papal record in the Vatican Library that provides a detailed insight into the different coinages that the clergymen used to pay this tithe, or, to be more precise, the money that was sent out of Norway for the purpose of payment to the papal treasury.[29] The different sums stated are defined in specific coinages and are described in such detail to allow them to be matched with representative coin types in the numismatic collections of today. For example, 4,400 Roman weight marks were received in bracteates assayed at 25 per cent silver, which in terms of the weight standard for each bracteate from this period implies a total of no less than 3.7 million bracteate coins.[30] In a situation where the papal camerarius had demanded payment in good quality money it is remarkable that such a large sum of money was transported all the way from Norway to Rome in debased Norwegian coin instead of it being replaced with good quality currency at one of the markets in northern Europe, for example, Bruges.[31]

This is one amongst many detailed accounts of ecclesiastical taxation being collected and paid in money, from the thirteenth century. Together with the evidence from the mid-twelfth century of the collection of Saint Peter's Pence, the church can be posited as an important driving force in monetisation in the period c. 1150 onwards.

---

[29] *PNRD*, pp. 1–14, at 12–14. The document has no date, but is dated to 1287 by Asgaut Steinnes, 'Peningar vegnir og peningar svartnir', *Historisk Tidsskrift*, XXVII (1927): 522–32, at 522.

[30] The bracteates in question were issued in the reign of Magnus the Lawmender (r. 1263–80). The assaying carried out at the papal office in Rome has been confirmed by modern analysis of these bracteates. The equivalent in Denmark amounted to 55.203 ½ marks in copper coins, 427 marks silver and 54 skilling 10 pennies sterling (DD II, 3, no. 33, referred to in *De skriftlige kilder til Danmarks middelalderlige møntvæsen. Et udvalg 1085–1500*, Jørgen Steen Jensen (ed.) (Copenhagen, 1989), no. 96).

[31] For a discussion of ecclesiastical payments out of Norway in the fourteenth century, see Sverre Dyrhaug, 'Kjøp, kreditt og kontanter i utenrikshandelen på 1300-tallet', *Collegium Medievale*, 25 (2012): 41–66.

Church and Coin: Money-Offerings and their Material Residue

Another area in which the church sought money from individuals within the period in question was from the practice of *oblationes*, offerings. The action of offering involved a spiritual transaction for the donor; the revenue from offerings would support the pastoral care of the church, as well as building and upkeep. Across Christendom the church encouraged offering in coin. In the case of converted Norway, an important phase of conversion was the transformation of offerings in kind, including food, and with pagan overtones, into money-based offerings in the course of the second half of the eleventh and the twelfth century. The spiritual injunction to make offerings from the mid-eleventh and later imposed with a stronger church organisation from the mid-twelfth century created the first general demand on all inhabitants of the kingdom for a form of monetary payment, if not fully obligatory by decree. The making of offerings became fixed upon the parishioner by custom and Christian teaching and was invested in the doctrine and liturgy of the medieval church.

The earliest references to money-offerings, in a Norwegian, and indeed, Scandinavian context, emerge in a letter from Archbishop Adalbert of Hamburg-Bremen to King Harald Hardrada in the 1050s or 1060s, in which the king was accused of tyrannical harassment of the church. One of the charges was that he had stolen the offerings that believers had presented to the shrine of Saint Olaf and used this for the payment of his soldiers.[32]

The role of Hamburg-Bremen in the new Christian kingdom of Norway and the issue of money-offerings are mentioned also, in more general terms, by Adam of Bremen in the 1070s. In his *Gesta Hammaburgensis Ecclesiae Pontificum* Adam describes the Norwegians as treating their priests and churches with great respect. Those that do not act accordingly, and do not present offerings at mass, are portrayed negatively.[33] Adam's reflections naturally tend to promote the archbishopric which he served, as the successful instigator of Christianity in a society that still was considered partially pagan. That said, the observations are valuable as early confirmation of the practice of offerings in churches in a Scandinavian context. Adam also makes complaints about the greed of the Norwegian clergy: they were greedy for money because they charged for performing the sacraments.[34] In making this allegation, Adam stresses the point that without proper supervision this

---

32 Adam, *Gesta* III, 17; RN I, no. 42.

33 Adam av Bremen, *Historia Norvegiae*, overs. Halvdan Koht, Gamalnorske bokverk IV (Christiania, 1921), p. 79.

34 Adam av Bremen, *Historia Norvegiae*, p. 82.

breach of priestly irresponsibility will go uncorrected, thereby promoting the role of his own church in the development of the Norwegian church.

The practice of charging for clerical services was widespread within eleventh-century Norway as a money-economy was emerging. The *Kristendomsbolken* [*The Christian Law Code*] in the Gulathing law, a regional law for the western part of Norway, one of four major law areas in Norway, states explicitly that 'um nokon vert sjuk og vil han senda etter presten, då skal han senda etter den presten som han kjøper messer hjå. Denne presten skal så ta 2 ører for oljekjøp, 1 ½ øre for liksangkjøp, og en uspesifisert sum for messesang [if someone becomes ill they should call for the priest from whom they normally buy service. This priest should then charge 2 ores for conducting the last rites, 1 ½ ore for singing for the dead and an unspecified sum for singing a mass]'.[35] The same text also insists that a priest must not 'fara i sokni åt ein annan prest for å tena pengar [operate within another priest's parish for the purpose of earning money]'.[36] On one hand this suggests that income from services was limited to the parish, but on the other hand, that income from money-based services seems to have been widespread already during the reigns of Harald Hardrada (1047–66) and Olaf the Peaceful (1067–93), and probably also in the following reigns of Magnus Barefoot (1093–1103) and his sons Olav Magnusson (1103–15) and Sigurd Magnusson, later to receive the sobriquet *Jorsalfar* (1103–30).

Any further written evidence for clergy providing services in return for money is not forthcoming for this early period. However, archaeological finds of coins within churches provide material evidence for parish churches as a location for the reception and distribution of money; from a slow start in the first half of the twelfth century to a radical increase in the latter part of that same century. In the churches which have been subject to archaeological investigations the finds are spread over the whole of the church, in the vestry, nave, transepts and chancel; the transepts and chancel being rather more sparesly supplied than the nave. The concentrations of finds are often to be found around the altar, the entrance and along the west wall where the font was usually placed throughout the Middle Ages. All of this suggests offerings being carried out in relation to the altars and shrines in the church. The numerous finds of coins under the floors in medieval churches are generally understood as accidental losses during offering rituals. In certain cases coins would have been deliberatedly slipped between the floorboards in churches, but these are considered anomalies compared to the regular offerings.[37]

---

35 GT § 23.

36 GT § 23.

37 Fritze Lindahl, 'Om mønter og medailler som bygningsofre', *Nationalmuseets Arbejdsmark* (1956): 93–102; Kirsten Bendixen, 'Middelaldermønter i de sidste 10 års danske kirkefund', *NNÅ* (1972): 63; Kenneth Jonsson and Lars Olof Lagerqvist, *Mynten från Finströms kyrka, Åland, Åländsk Odling* (1974): 5–29; Henrik Klackenberg, *Moneta Nostra.*

From the perspective of monetisation, the coin finds in these churches represent a remarkable body of evidence for the penetration of coinage within rural parish congregations as has been convincingly shown for Sweden by Henrik Klackenberg in his magistral study *Moneta Nostra* (1992). Indeed, some of the largest numbers of coins found in a church are recorded for the churches Alstahaug and Dønnes on the coast of Helgeland in Nordland county, just below the Arctic Circle. The largest number of coins found within a medieval Norwegian church was at the Lom stavechurch, within the vicinity of Jotunheimen, the most mountainous parts of Norway, at the valley-end of Gudbrandsdalen in the county of Oppland. Within this small parish church some 2,400 coins were recorded by archaeologists in 1973.[38]

As the availability of money increased, the rise of a money-economy, fully or partially, provided the means for coins used in offerings.[39] In Norway, as elsewhere in Scandinavia and northern Europe, the availability of coin fluctuated during the course of the medieval period. While silver was abundant in the first three quarters of the eleventh century, the supply dropped quite significantly in the last quarter of the eleventh and the first three quarters of the twelfth century. New discoveries of silver in the Empire (Freiberg, Meissen, Freisach), Bohemia (Kutna Hora) and Italy (Tuscany) secured increased availability of silver from the 1160s and 1170s onwards.[40] Around 1300 more silver was in circulation than ever before in Europe. This is well documented in historical and archaeological sources from northern Europe. In a Norwegian context the fluctuations in silver are mirrored in the hoard material; hoards are a regular feature of this period except for the first three quarters of the twelfth century. An interesting feature of this period is that the drop in minting and availability of coin coincides with significant developments in church organisation across Western Christendom and a profound acceleration in ecclesiastical building.[41]

The mid-twelfth-century surge in silver coincided with the period during which the Norwegian archbishopric was established. From the point when Jon Birgisson, formerly bishop of Stavanger, was installed as the first archbishop in Nidaros in 1152/53, the Norwegian landscape was, as elsewhere in the Latin West, about to be transformed through intensive church building. Within

Monetarisering i medeltidens Sverige (Lund, 1992), pp. 35–40. For arguments in favour of deliberate offerings of coins between the floorboards, see Herleik Baklid, 'Hvad der har bragt dem gjennem gulvet er dessverre efter al sansynlighet en hemmelig ofring […]', *Heimen*, 3 (1995): 181–96.

38 Kolbjørn Skaare, 'Myntene fra Lom kirke', *Ab.* (1978): 113–31.

39 The wafers used as bread in the sacraments of the Eucharist as seen in the light of a coin is discussed in Aden Kumler, 'The Multiplication of the Species. Eucharistic Morphology in the Middle Ages', *RES: Anthropology and Aesthetics*, 59/60 (2011): 179–91.

40 Spufford, *Money and its Use*, pp. 109–31.

41 See James Bolton's discussion in this volume.

decades of the mid-twelfth century several hundred churches were erected, from the southernmost parts to the regions beyond the Arctic Circle. The archaeological harvest from this early period in Norwegian church-building is not rich, either in coins or other material evidence. Of the total of 9,760 coins from the period c. 1130–c. 1320 only some 18 coins have been found from the period c. 1130 to the 1170s. These coins come from 10 different churches: Kaupanger stave church, Sogn and Fjordane (one coin), Hoprekstad stave church, Sogn and Fjordane (six coins), Urnes stave church, Sogn and Fjordane (one coin), Uvdal stave church, Buskerud (two coins), Flå church, Buskerud (one coin), Øyar stave church[tomt], Oppland (one coin), Hvaler church, Østfold (one coin), Sandar church, Vestfold (two coins), Sørbø church, Rogaland (two coins) and Sandeid old church, Rogaland (one coin). By contrast, coin finds in Norwegian churches from the successive period c. 1180–c. 1220, struck in the reign of King Sverre Sigurdsson (r.1177–1202), add up to some 1,222 coin finds from 33 churches.

The number of coins recorded from churches before and after c. 1180 show a remarkable discrepancy: 18 before and 1,222 after. The finds from the Lom stavechurch provide a striking example, where the 472 bracteates from the late twelfth century are by far the most numerous for any church in this period, in contrast to none from the preceeding period, before c. 1177. The oldest parts of the church are dated to 1157/58, and despite several alterations it remained at the same location throughout the Middle Ages. Another example is the Hoprekstad stavechurch in Vik in the county of Sogn and Fjordane, dated after c. 1131. In this church only six coins from the period c. 1130–80 have been found compared to 164 from the following period c. 1180–c. 1220. In the same county, excavation at Kaupanger stavechurch, built some time after c. 1137, produced only a single coin from the early period compared to 165 from the latter. In sum these finds suggest a limited availability of coin before c. 1180, especially in the countryside, to the economy of which the churchfinds are most closely related.

The evidence of coin finds suggests social and economic change. In the 1160s and 1170s extensive church-building was carried out within the Norwegian archbishopric, the physical manifestation of Norwegian parocial organisation, and from a monetary perspective in a period with a significant increase in the availability of silver. The numismatic sources from the reign of King Sverre Sigurdsson (r. 1177–1202) show a considerable increase in the number of issues.[42] This is paralleled in the monetary reform in England under King Henry II (r. 1154–89) in 1180/81 and, more generally, in the extensive output of coinage from mints in Germany during the reign of Frederic Barbarossa (1152–90).

---

[42] Kolbjørn Skaare, 'Kong Sverres utmynting', *NNÅ* (1979–80): 93–109.

The church finds reveal rural Norway as responsive to this general increase in the production of coin across northern Europe, and indeed throughout Christendom, from the third quarter of the twelfth century. What did not happen immediately was any concession in Norway for ecclesiastical minting. This required a more specific set of circumstances. It is hard to see how ecclesiastical minting would have been possible in Norway before the independent church organisation created in 1152/53. The first record we have of ecclesiastical minting in Norway is not numismatic, but historical. In an agreement from 1222, where the Archbishop of Nidaros was granted the right to issue coins, it states, quite clearly, that the coins issued by the archbishop were to follow the royal issues in appearance, design, weight and fineness.[43] This instruction offers an obvious explanation for why ecclesiastical issues are so difficult to distinguish from the royal. An exception is the remarkable issues of Archbishop Jon the Red (r. 1268–81), who, fighting a fierce battle for the rights of the church, issued a coin showing his own portrait, mitre included, in breach of the agreement of 1222.[44] Such a monetary protest proved too much for the baronial government introduced after the death of King Magnus Lawmender in the summer 1280, which put an end to ecclesiastical right to issue coins in a decree dated 1281. The then infant King Eirik Magnusson (r. 1280–99), was, as a result of the anti-clerical actions carried out by his administration, often nicknamed Eirik 'hater of priests/prelates'.

The history of the Norwegian church in the twelfth and thirteenth centuries is intimately connected with money. The practical and political aspects of that connection are evident, as the example of Jon the Red's minting of what was identifiably his own coin shows. What Jon the Red was making plain, however, was the spiritual independence of the church from secular authority. The medium of coin offered him a wide audience: coins reached all social groups, and drew on the powerful connections established in the eleventh and early twelfth centuries between spiritual authority and money. The spiritual power of money was something with which all in Norwegian society would have been familiar, as the coin finds in churches reveal.

---

[43] NGL I, 446, (trans.) NMH, I, 107. The right to coin was given to the Archbishop of Nidaros in a *Rettarbot* in 1222, and was confirmed in the concordat made in Tunsberg in 1277, the so-called *Sættargjerden* (Grethe Authén Blom, *Kongemakt og privilegier i Norge inntil 1387* (Oslo, 1967), p. 132 ff).

[44] Kolbjørn Skaare, 'En ny norsk erkebispemynt'. *Numismatiska Meddelanden*, XXX (1965): 92–102. For a discussion of 'myntrett' or minting rights, see Jon Anders Risvaag, *Erkebiskopens i Nidaros' utmynting i middelalderen. Med særlig vekt på erkebiskopens myntrett* unpubl. Magistral thesis, University of Oslo, 1995, pp. 54–9; Jon Anders Risvaag, 'Ikke-kongelige utmynting i Norge frem til reformasjonen', *NNÅ* (1994–96): 130–61, at 143–7.

Spiritual Money: Ritual, Offerings and Salvation

From Lom in Gudbrandsdalen, to Mære in Northern Trøndelag, in Torpo within the valleys and forests of Buskerud, in the further reaches of the Sognefjord on the West coast, and in the congregations belonging to the churches in Kaupanger and Hoprekstad, all would have attended mass according to the church calendar in the twelfth and thirteenth century, and there, as everywhere else in the Latin West, collections were made during regular services as well as at major feasts or on special occasions.[45] These acts of devotion have left tens of thousands of material indicators below the church floors, indicators that are consequent on intimate religious acts: namely the coins lost, accidentally discarded, or pehaps deliberatly dropped, when money-offerings were made, which found their way between the floorboards. Money-offerings were made to saints at their shrines, but also within the round of services, within the mass, at the heart of the medieval communion service.

Monetary offerings would have been presented on the main altar of the church, or one of the saints' shrines, or in money-boxes and offering-purses or offering-bags. The use of money in this spiritual context reflects, presumably, a spiritual transaction. Money offered becomes money transformed; from means of exchange to spiritual objects. Within the spiritual transaction whereby money was offered an enormous degree of trust in each coin is implied. Coins are deemed to be an acceptable medium for such a transaction, and in the ritual of offering the coin became a token of trust bearing an ideological value beyond its normal value. It might even be suggested that the coin offered became transubstantiated: currency still, but in the cosmic exchange of sin, penance and salvation, between God and his creation mediated through Christ, the community of saints and the church.[46]

The potential spiritual revenue from monetary offerings was significant: money-offerings constituted a material sacrificial bond between man and God in the act of personal devotion. These were a universal feature of medieval Western Christian thought and practice and gifts given on earth had, potentially, eternal effects, reinforced by the architectural, artistic and liturgical settings in which offerings were made. In high medieval Europe the coin, every bit as much as it did in the worldly economy, became a universal token in an economy of

[45] For a general introduction to revenues for medieval parish churches, see Brigitte Resl, 'Material Support I: Parishes' in *The Cambridge History of Christianity*, vol. 4, *Christianity in Western Europe c.1100–c.1500*, Miri Rubin and Walter Simons (eds) (Cambridge, 2009), pp. 99-106.

[46] The doctrine of transubstantiation received formal expression in the first canon of the Fourth Lateran Council, *Decrees of the Ecumenical Councils*, 2 vols, N. Tanner (ed.) (London, 1990), vol. 1, pp. 230–71, text available online at http://www.ewtn.com/library/councils/lateran4.htm.

salvation. This was not an economy in which normal parameters of economic attitudes prevailed; the value of each individual offering was less significant than the ritual performance. In what must have been millions of cases every year, small denominations of currency, and in small amounts, were used as trusted material mediation between man and God. In providing the guarantee of salvation mediated between heaven and earth, the church acted as spiritual and financial broker in contemporary society. In the rise of a money-economy a commodification of religion, monetisation of vocabulary, and an increasing awareness of financial matters from an ecclesiastical and vernacular perspective can all be observed.[47]

The worth of the coin-offerings was seldom based on monetary value. In this context the New Testament parable of the poor widow's mite should be recalled: her two small coins [duo minuta], were more valuable than all of the coins offered by the rich.[48] The emphasis on ritual rather than value is indicated clearly in the archaeological evidence from the Norwegian stavechurches. The numerous finds provide a rare insight into the practice rather than the theory on the matter. In the period between 1263 and 1320, pennies, halfpennies, farthings and bracteates (the smallest coins produced) were issued; 3,661 individual finds of these coins have been found in 110 churches in the following denominational ratios: 62 per cent bracteates, 19 per cent quarter pennies, 12 per cent half pennies, and only 8 per cent pennies.[49] The breakdown reveals that 81 per cent of the coins weighed less than 0.25 grams. The relation between the bracteates and the pennies remains imprecise, but it might very well have been in the range of 1/10 of a penny, that is to say, an amount of money which a farmer or wage earner could have afforded. All of this suggests a situation in which the size of the offering was less significant than the ritual exercise of the liturgical drama. Coins of the lowest value were consistently offered, not high-value denominations, on which subject ecclesiastical administrators responsible for the church's financial dealings often held different opinions.

The church, its doctrine and its liturgy was embedded into the lives of people and society.[50] In this context, however, the local nature of the liturgical experience is worth emphasising as much as the universal. The medieval church did not strive for liturgical uniformity, and liturgical change could respond to a wide variety of factors: the reinterpretation of doctrine, increase in the church's wealth, new religious orders, ecclesiastical hierarchy, social, political and

47 See Greti Dinkova-Brun, Giles Gasper and Rory Naismith in this volume.

48 Mark 12:41–4 and Luke 21:1–4. On this subject see Lucia Travaini, 'Saints and Sinners: Coins in Medieval Italian Graves', *NC* (2004): 173.

49 Bracteate = 2,259, 1/4 penning = 697, 1/2 penning = 422, penning = 283; sum = 3,661.

50 S. J. P. van Dijk, *The Myth of the Aumbry: Notes on Medieval Reservation Practice and Eucharistic Devotion* (London, 1957), p. 14.

economic development within the secular part of society, all together creating the basis for increased liturgical complexity.[51] Money-offerings as stated above were an integral part of liturgical acts, whose particular rhythms are difficult to assesss, however much they participated in general patterns. In this case the material record of the offerings, as it is shown in the archaeological evidence, might provide evidence through which to extrapolate some of the patterns of the accompanying rituals.[52]

The interpretation of this evidence is not straightforward. The complexity of the sites is increased by post-reformation activity affecting the archaeological environment beneath the floors, for example burials, especially from the seventeenth and eighteenth century. Another issue that complicates interpretation in some cases is that of the poor methods used to document artefactual finds.[53] This is especially the case with reference to excavations carried out prior to the 1970s when the focus was primarily on the architectural remains and the building structures of the church rather than the artefacts *in situ*.[54] However, within the compound of this rich body of evidence patterns of coin-use are possible to distinguish. In considering the question of how people made their offerings in church, the complexity of behavior of the members of the congregation during service is, of course, related to regional and local

---

[51] Sven Helander, 'The Liturgical Profile of the Parish Church in Medieval Sweden', in *The Liturgy of the Medieval Church*, Thomas J. Heffernan and E. Ann Matter (eds) (Kalamazoo, 2001), p. 148. Thomas J. Heffernan, 'The Liturgy and Literature of Saint's Lives', in *The Liturgy of the Medieval Church*, p. 73.

[52] For this material, Scandinavian evidence in general is by far the most significant compared to similar sites elsewhere, in terms of the quantity and breadth of the material. In total, archaeological investigation has revealed nearly 60,000 medieval coins in churches from the medieval Nordic region. These finds represent individual losses and donations, not hoards where hundreds or even thousands of coins could be deposited together. A significant part of this archaeological record provides evidence for a broad distribution of artefacts, and notably coins within the sacred space of the church. The fact that all these coins have been found within the church building not only places them, potentially, within the Christian liturgical framework of the medieval church, it also suggests that offerings were as common and widespread in the periphery of medieval Europe as in the heart of the Latin West.

[53] Cf. 'Harpecirkulæret' issued by the National Museum in Copenhagen, ref. Olaf Olsen, 'Kirkegulvet som arkaeologisk arbejdsmark', *Nationalmuseets Arbejdsmark* (1958): 17–30; Klackenberg, *Moneta Nostra*, p. 34.

[54] Antiquarian interest in Scandinavian churches and their archaeology goes back to the seventeenth century. The importance of the church buildings as great monuments of the past created interest in church architecture that in some cases would lead to studies of the building construction as it was laid out on the ground. The need for modernisation of these churches, combined with an increasing awareness of the church as an archaeological site, paved the way for the record of finds of artefacts as church floors were removed in increasing numbers from the 1950s onwards.

variation of habit and mores, as well as subject to change over time. There are, nevertheless, features of the coin finds and the pattern of coin spoils which allow a more detailed analysis.

One of the preconditions for the vast number of coin finds within Scandinavian churches is the environment in which many of these churches were built. In comparison with most churches elsewhere in Christendom, wood was a common building material, not only for the construction of the building, but also as flooring. Wooden floors dry up and leave cracks between the boards, often of significant size, through which coins occassionally would fall, whether at the act of offering or simply accidentally, but either way leaving an indicator of the use of money within the church, including in liturgical practices widespread among members of congregations throughout western Europe. By comparison, most surviving religious buildings elsewhere incorporate stone floors that would not allow coins to disappear in the same way, and, more importantly, in similar numbers. In this way, churches in northern Scandinavia provide a useful and unusual laboratory for the investigations of the money-offering institute in the Middle Ages.[55] That single finds of coins appear in their thousands, in an archaeological context within strictly defined spaces, spread throughout a landscape encompassing the whole of society, and a geographical compass that includes towns, rural society, coastal areas, valleys, mountains and plains, and islands, in a region with kingdoms (not always friendly to each other), is remarkable. In spite of similar finds in parts of Central Europe, nowhere within Western Christendom are finds of medieval coins within the strict definition of the church more telling than in Scandinavia.[56]

While these finds are recorded in large numbers, it is likely that these records reflect only a small proportion of what would be available if a full survey of medieval Scandinavian churches were undertaken. In Norway finds from 110 churches add up to more than 15,000 coins in total. A chronological breakdown provides a figure for the period c. 1180–c. 1320 of some 9,760 coins from a period of 150 years.[57] A quantitative analysis of coin finds from churches is in

---

[55] On the subject of floors in medieval churches, see Henriette Rensbro, *Spor i kirkegulve. De siste 50 års arkæologiske undersøgelser i kirkegulve som kilde til sognekirkernes indretning og brug i middelalder og renæssance* (Doctoral thesis, Aarhus University, 2007), p. 129 ff; N-K. Liebgott, *Dansk Middelalderarkeologi* (Copenhagen, 1989), p. 142 ff; M. Ullén, *Medeltida träkyrkor*, vol. I, *Sveriges Kyrkor* (1983), p. 240.

[56] For similar finds from churches in Central Europe, see *Trouvailles monétaires d'églises*, O. F. Dubuis and S. Frey-Kupper (eds), Études de numismatique et d'histoire monétaire 1 (Lausanne, 1995).

[57] In addition, new finds have appeared from five churches in recent years (Håkon Roland and Svein H. Gullbekk, unpublished manuscript). A large portion of the Norwegian finds were discovered in the period from the beginning of the 1950s to 1984 when a significant number of medieval churches underwent refurbishment that involved new heating systems.

nature a very complex exercise involving a large number of factors, such as the size of coins, churches and congregations, humidity creating cracks between the floorboards, how often people participated in service, how often people were likely to have lost coins and so forth.[58]

The excavations in the Fjære church in Aust-Agder county in Norway provide an insightful example. The floorboards in the apse of a wooden medieval parish church were partly lifted in the 1930s and the local archaeologist found 91 coins.[59] A full survey of the church would have yielded, presumably, a far larger number; a survey with modern archaeological methods would almost certainly have uncovered more finds and provided better contextual information. How many more coins is, of course, difficult to assess, but taking the space of the church from the nave and the choir, several hundred more coin finds might easily have been recorded, from what is known from similar excavations. An extrapolation of these estimates onto the 1,200 to 1,500 medieval churches where clergy conducted services on regular basis suggests that large numbers of coins await discovery within the context of medieval churches, possibly as many as 100,000 to 200,000. Moreover, this would represent the surviving examples. The numbers of coins brought into services and used for offerings would have been far greater. The large numbers of coins being lost in Norwegian churches constitute only a small share of the coins being brought into the church but provide solid evidence for a circulation of coins in sacred contexts within medieval Norway.[60]

The reformed church of the High Middle Ages managed to make the money-offerings a universal feature of Christian society. References to oblationes are

---

This was a process that involved floors being removed either from the whole or part of the church area.

[58] An example of such an analysis is provided in Christian Simensen, 'Hvilken informasjon gir myntfunn gjort i norske kirker', *NNUM* (1986): 42–53; a comment and critical assessment is provided by Bjørn Poulsen, 'Hvilke informationer giver kirkefund ikke?' *NNUM* (1986): 150–51.

[59] Carsten Svarstad, 'Myntfunnet fra Fjære kirke', *NNÅ* (1957): 106–9. In the vicinity, at Vig in Fjære in Aust-Agder a rather famous find was made in 1876: two Anglo-Saxon coins of Eanred of Northumbria, c. 810–35, each mounted on a lead weight, two weights, weapons, and smith's equipment including a soapstone mould for making silver bars (Skaare (1976), no. 67; *Sylloge of Coins of the British Isles, Norway*, vol. I, Elina Screen (ed.) (Oxford, 2013), no. 54).

[60] The number of coins found in hoards still dwarves the numbers of coins found in churches. In Denmark, coins from hoards (up until c. 1998) total c. 316,000 coins from the period c. 1050–c. 1500. For Sweden and Norway the equivalent numbers are c. 216,000 and c. 18,000, respectively. In addition to coins, the total numbers of finds from the churches add up to hundreds of thousands of recorded artefacts, encompassing everything from vast numbers of broken pieces of glass, pieces of leather, pieces of broken combs and clay pipes, needles and nails, to some precious items such as gold jewellery, seals and manuscripts.

abundant and in a wide variety of sources from scholastic writing, saints lives, vernacular literature, account records, legal records and so on. Perhaps the best surviving records of offerings on a grand scale are those from the great Jubilee of 1300 in Rome where the altars of St Peter's and St Paul's provided offerings valued at 30,000 and 20,000 gold florins, respectively, all made in large numbers of petty local coins of all provinces that numbered in the millions.61 In Bergen a few years later, in 1308, money-offerings were accounted for from the altar of Saint Olaf in St John's church, near to the monastery of St John. As a result of internal conflicts within the monastery, King Håkon V decided to move the collected money-offerings. As a consequence, a detailed account of the currency was made, of which only the parts that contain foreign currencies has survived. The detailed accounts provide evidence for 346 marks in foreign currency, English, French, Swedish and Gotlandic.[62] To place this sum in context, it represented about 5 per cent of the total estimated value of the crown's annual income from taxes at that time.[63] This example accounts only for the foreign coins; it is highly likely that substantial sums of greater value were presented to the same shrine in Norwegian coins. Adding this revenue would certainly raise the total value of these offerings; by how much is a matter for speculation. The only explicit historical record of offerings to a Norwegian shrine from the twelfth century dates to 2 April at some point between 1189 and 1194.[64] An announcement from Pål, Bishop of Bergen, mentions offerings and gifts to the shrine of Saint Sunniva, the patron saint of Bergen, of which the canons at Christ Church should receive half.[65] It is reasonable to assume that the revenues from this shrine were significant, but, whether extensive or not, the example attests to the universal nature of offerings, and their significance both for the ecclesiastical institutions and individual church-goers in Bergen at the time. Danish pilgrims who visited the town in 1191 attested the custom of offerings: the Norwegians were generous when offering alms, but they were heavy drinkers.[66]

---

61 P. Fedele, *Il giublieo del 1300, Gli Anni Santi* (Rome, 1934), pp. 7–25, cited by Lucia Travaini, 'Saints and Sinners: Coins in Medieval Italian Graves', *NC* (2004): 174.

62 DN II, no. 96; see also Svein H. Gullbekk, 'Svensk og gotlandsk mynt ofret til St. Olav i Bergen', *Myntstudier* (vol. 1, 2009): 16–21.

63 Asgaut Steinnes, *Gamal skatteskipnad i Norge*, vol. II (Oslo, 1933), p. 207. Even though later research builds on Steinnes's studies, more recent research suggest larger estimates of royal income, both from tax and other revenues, see Ole Georg Moseng, Erik Opsahl and Gunnar I. Pettersen, *Norsk Historie 750–1537* (Oslo, 1999), p. 209.

64 For dating see RN I, no. 225.

65 DN VIII, no. 4.

66 *Historien om danenes ferd til Jerusalem*, trans. Astrid Salvesen (Oslo,1969), ch. xi.

Conclusion

Money-offerings occurred in the context of a world in which sin and the meditation of saints were pervasive features. In the case of the Norwegian church finds, and the physical and documentary evidence for coin collection, the strong suggestion is that, with respect to offerings, it was not so much the monetary value that mattered, but the ritual.

That the *oblationes* provided a tangible point of contact with the spiritual realm from the perspective of individual souls may be posited with confidence. Tactility is a common aspect of Christian ritual practice across the Middle Ages and this activity speaks to a similar response. Moreover, money in these contexts was offered in the same environment in which the host was received and confession heard and absolution given, and all other liturgical and pastoral activities connected to the church as building took place. Money, like bread, could be transformed, as a material contribution using their *pecuniae* to create good, in the service of Christ. Just as the coin has two sides, the *oblationes* fulfilled a practical and spiritual mission.

In providing the hope for salvation mediated between heaven and earth, the church acted as spiritual and financial broker in contemporary society. In the rise of a money-economy a commodification of religion, monetisation of vocabulary, and an increasing awareness of financial matters from an ecclesiastical and vernacular perspective can all be observed.[67] This provided an opportunity for each and every church-goer to offer a material gift to the saints and to Christ, and in that way consecrating their belief through the symbol of faith that was offered. As sacremental, an offering became an important part of the liturgical act where man and God came together through a material transfer.

This process of spiritual and financial brokerage is central to the way in which the church became a driving force in the monetisation of society both among town dwellers and the rural population, in Norway, Scandinavia and more universally throughout the Latin West. The use of money-offerings as an institutional part of the ecclesiastical organisation made it possible to finance pastoral care, religious duties and to some extent building programs in an increasingly effective way that would otherwise have been difficult, if not impossible, to impose.

---

[67] See Greti Dinkova-Brun, Giles Gasper and Rory Naismith in this volume.

Plate 1 Coin issued from the Danish Slagelse mint, 1020s. Photo courtesy of the National Museum of Denmark, Copenhagen.

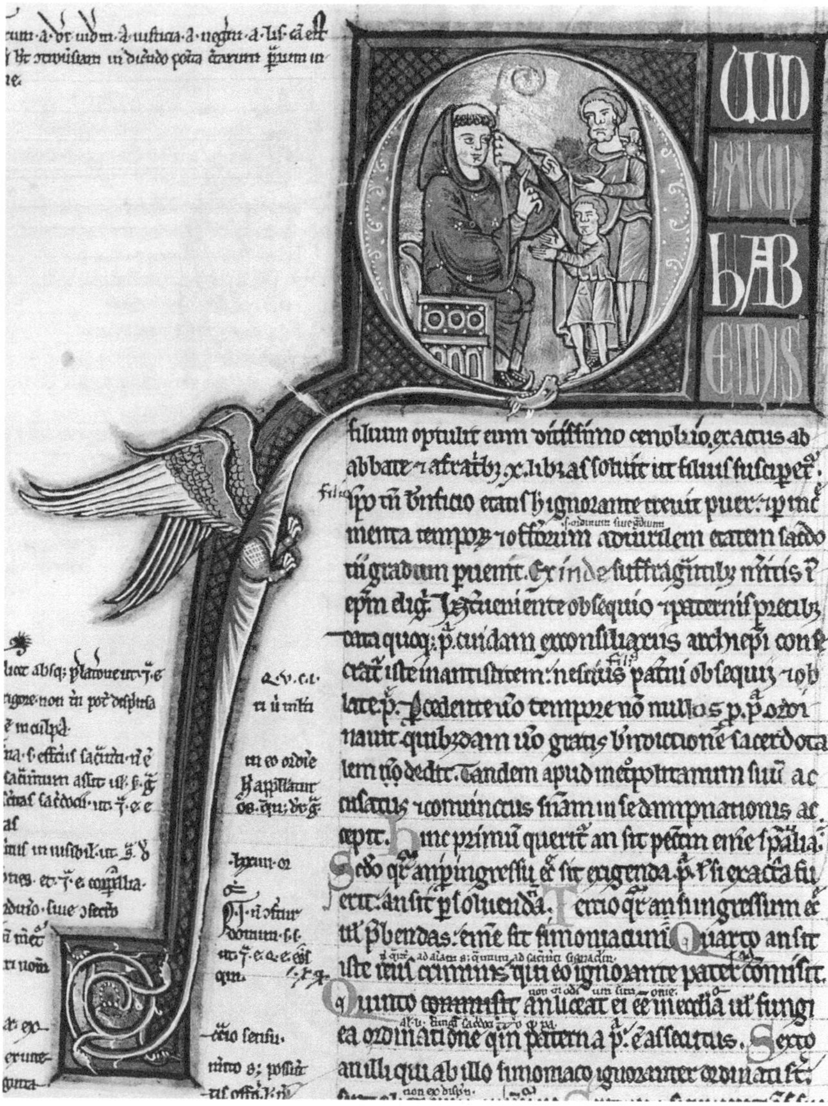

Plate 2 Detail from the prologue to Causa 1 of Gratian's *Decretum*, featuring a money-offering for a monastic oblate. Durham Cathedral Library C.I.7. f. 60r. Photo courtesy of the Dean and Chapter, Durham Cathedral.

Plate 3
Fresco in the church of Fjenneslev, Sjælland, c. 1125–50. The magnate Asser Rig is depicted giving God a church while his wife, Inger, gives a golden ring.

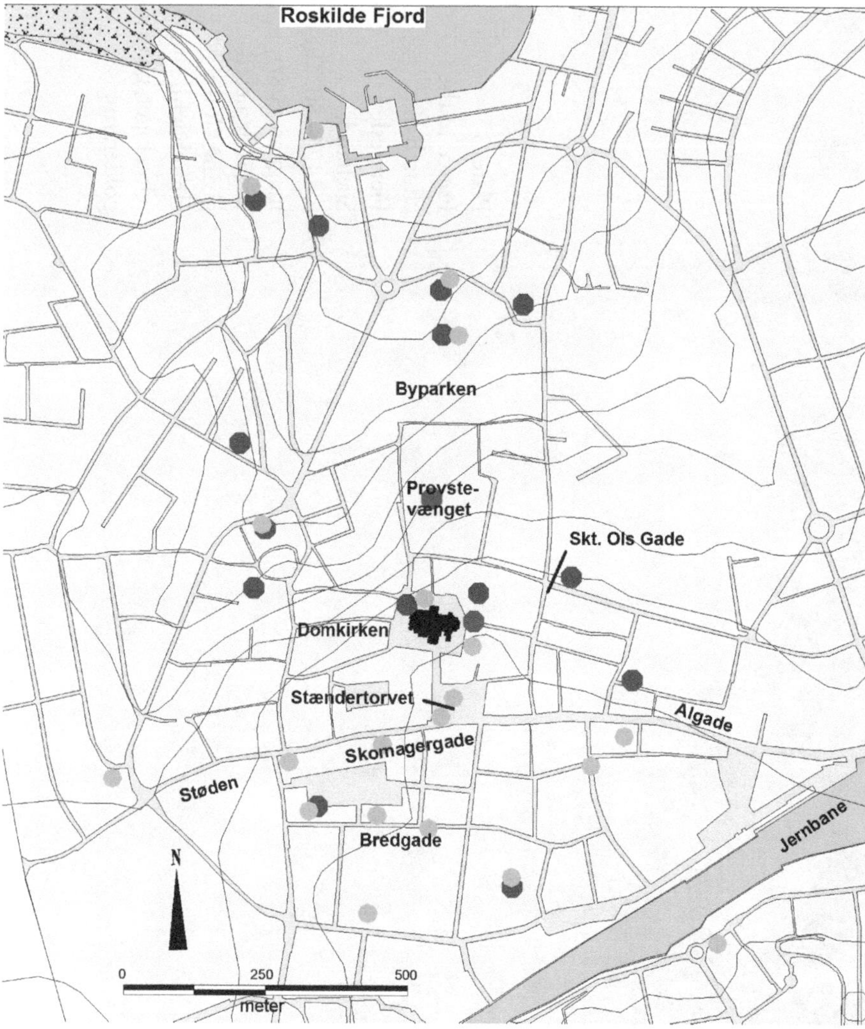

Plate 4 Map of the distribution of early coin stray finds inside the medieval area of Roskilde. The red dots on the map are from the tenth century (1 arabic 'cufic' dirhem from the 'Provstevænget' and the an Æthelred penny), the blue are from the eleventh century, and the green ones from the twelfth century. Map kindly supplied by Jens Ulriksen, Roskilde Museum.

Plate 5
Penny minted in Emden, Hermann (Billunger), c. 1045–60. Found near the cathedral of Ribe. Photo: Ribe Museum.

Plate 6 Map of monastic mints in the Ottonian-Salian Empire (919–1125) considering the numismatic material.

Plate 7
(Av and Rv) Hersfeld, Abbey. Adelmann (1114–27). Penny. 0.84 g. +ANDERENANCO Cross with one pellet in each angle//+HEREVELDIA Building with three towers. Source: Auction Fritz Rudolf Künker 130, Osnabrück 2007, no. 2186.

Plate 8
(Av and Rv) Hersfeld, Abbey. Anonymous, eleventh century. Penny. 0.71 g. +KAROLVS IMP Bust of Emperor Charlemagne with cross-staff//+SCS LVLLVS Bust of Saint Lullus with crosier. Source: Auction Fritz Rudolf Künker 130, Osnabrück 2007, no. 2185.

Plate 9
(Av and Rv) Quedlinburg, Abbey. Mathilde (966–99) or Adelheid (999–1044). Penny. 1.55 g. +DGRA+REX Cross, O-D-D-O in the angles//SCS SERVACIVS Church-Building (*Holzkirche*), T-T at sides. Source: Auction Fritz Rudolf Künker 130, Osnabrück 2007, no. 1799.

Plate 10
(Av and Rv) *Otto-Adelheid-Pfennig*, around 1000. Penny. 1.55 g. +DIGRA+REX Cross, O-D-D-O in the angles//ATEAHEHT Church-Building (*Holzkirche*). Source: Auction Fritz Rudolf Künker 130, Osnabrück 2007, no. 1541.

Plate 11
(Av and Rv) Stavelot, Abbey. Anonymous, eleventh century. Penny. 1.03 g. S REMACLVS EPS Bust of Saint Remaclus r. with crosier// STABVLAVS Building. Source: Auction Fritz Rudolf Künker 205, Osnabrück 2012, no. 2435.

Plate 12
(Av and Rv) Marsberg, Mint of the Corvey Abbey. Saracho (1065–71). Penny. 1.38 g. +SCS PETRVS Bust of Saint Petrus//+HERESBVRG Wall with three towers. Source: Auction Fritz Rudolf Künker 152, Osnabrück 2009, no. 6235.

Plate 13
(Av and Rv) Normandy, penny, Rouen, c. 940, 1.24 g, type Dumas XV, 16, with the name of Saint-Ouen. Source: Musée départemental des Antiquités de la Seine-Maritime, inv. 93.4.1 (Ó cg76 – Musée départemental des Antiquités – Rouen, cliché Yohann Deslandes).

Plate 14
(Av and Rv) Normandy, penny, Rouen, c. 965/975, 1.24 g, type Dumas XV, 19/Fécamp 6042 with the name of Saint-Romain. Maybe from the Fécamp hoard. Source: Musée départemental des Antiquités de la Seine-Maritime, inv. 92.13.2 (Ó cg76 – Musée départemental des Antiquités – Rouen, cliché Yohann Deslandes).

Plate 15
(Av and Rv) Normandy, penny, Rouen, c. 965/975, 1.14 g, type Dumas XV, 20/Fécamp 6044, with the name of Saint-Romain. Probably found Place du Vieux-Marché, Rouen, 1867. Source: Musée départemental des Antiquités de la Seine-Maritime, inv. R.93.104.1 (Ó cg76 – Musée départemental des Antiquités – Rouen, cliché Yohann Deslandes).

Plate 16
(Av and Rv) Normandy, penny, Rouen, c. 980, 1.02 g, type Dumas XV, 23–24/ Fécamp 4147, with a monogram HGT that has been interpreted as Hugh, archbishop of Rouen. Probably from the Fécamp hoard. Source: Musée départemental des Antiquités de la Seine-Maritime, inv. 79.1.2 (Ó cg76 – Musée départemental des Antiquités – Rouen, cliché Yohann Deslandes).

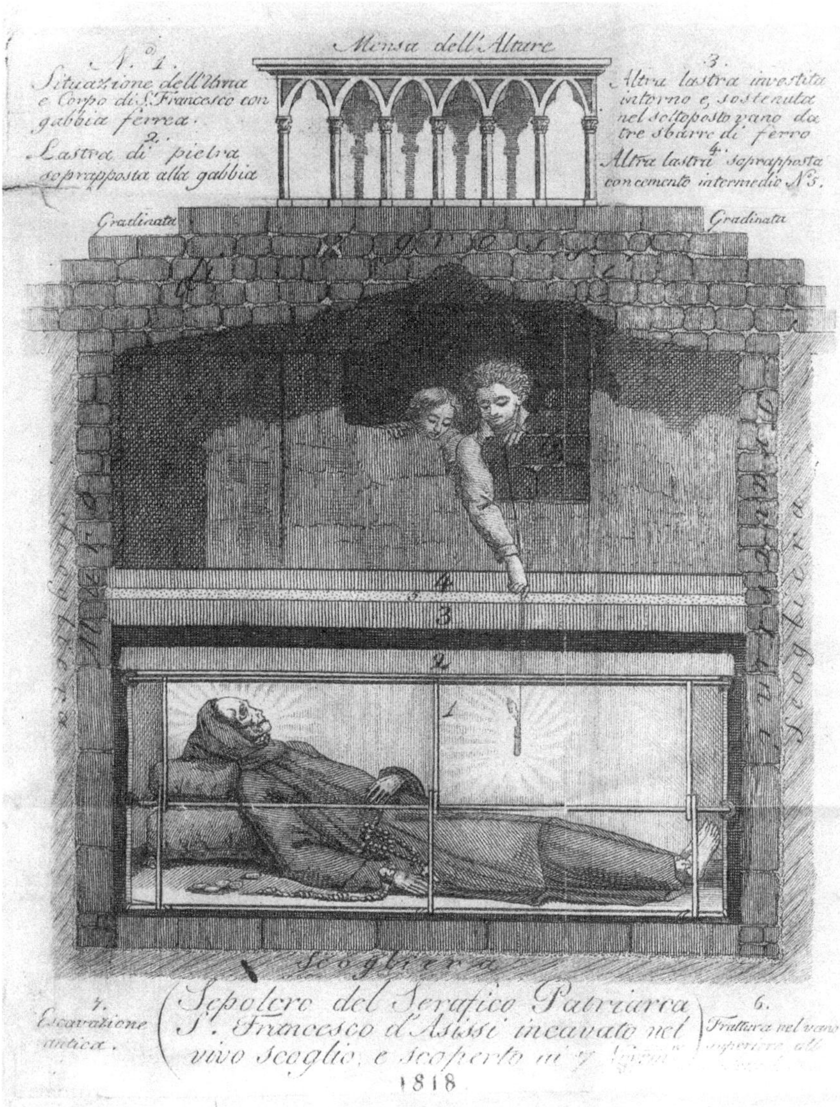

Plate 17 Engraving showing (with some imagination) the grave of St Francis of Assisi at the moment of its discovery in 1818; coins are visible under the right arm. Image from *Compendio della vita del serafico Patriarca Francesco di Assisi con un distinto ragguaglio sul reperimento e verificazione delle sue sagre spoglie rinvenute sotto l'altar maggiore della Chiesa Patriarcale dei MM.RR. PP. Minori Conventuali della stessa Città l'anno 1818,* Assisi 1820 (anastatic reprint, no date).

Plate 18 County of Anhalt, Albert the Bear margrave of Brandenburg (1157–70); bracteate (silver, 0.74 g). ADELBERTS MARCHI O; the margrave and his wife Sophie, standing. Image courtesy of Jean Elsen & ses Fils sa, Bruxelles, auction 76 no. 968.

Plate 19 Caronno Pertusella (Varese), Chiesa della Purificazione. Photo courtesy of Soprintendenza per i Beni Archeologici della Lombardia, Milano.

Plate 20 Caronno Pertusella (Varese), Chiesa della Purificazione, skeleton of the young cow discovered under the foundations. Photo courtesy of Soprintendenza per i Beni Archeologici della Lombardia, Milano.

Plate 21 Caronno Pertusella (Varese), Chiesa della Purificazione, the head of the cow with the coin. Photo courtesy of Soprintendenza per i Beni Archeologici della Lombardia, Milano.

Bibliography

Manuscripts

Domesday Book, II (National Archives, UK)

Primary Sources

Acta Processus Litium inter regem danorum et archiepiscopum Lundensem, A. Krarup and W. Norwin (eds) (Copenhagen, 1932)
Adam av Bremen, *Historia Norvegiae*, overs. Halvdan Koht, Gamalnorske bokverk, IV (Christiania, 1921)
Adam von Bremen. Hamburgische Kirchengeschichte, Bernhard Schmeidler (ed.), 3rd edition (Hannover and Leipzig, 1917)
Aelredus Rieuallensis, *De spiritali amicitia*, A. Hoste (ed.), Corpus Christianorum Continuatio Mediaevalis, 1 (Turnhout, 1971)
Ailred of Rievaulx, *Genealogia regum anglorum*, J.-P. Migne (ed.), PL, 195 (Paris, 1853), cols 711–36
Ailred of Rievaulx, *The Historical Works*, M. Dutton (ed.) and J. P. Freeland (trans.) (Kalamazoo, 2005)
Ailred of Rievaulx, *Spiritual Friendship*, M. Dutton (ed.) and L. C. Braceland (trans.) (Kalamazoo, 2010)
Ailred of Rievaulx, *Vita S. Edwardi regis et confessoris*, J.-P. Migne (ed.), PL, 195 (Paris, 1853), cols 737–88
Alan of Lille, *Anticlaudianus*, R. Bossuat (ed.) (Paris, 1955)
Alan of Lille, *Anticlaudianus or the Good and Perfect Man*, J. J. Sheridan (trans.) (Toronto, 1973)
Alan of Lille, *De virtutibus et de vitiis et de donis spiritus sancti*, O. Lottin (ed.), in O. Lottin, *Psychologie et morale aux XIIe et XIIIe siècles*, vol. 6 (Gembloux, 1960), pp. 27–92
Alan of Lille, *Liber poenitentialis*, J. Longère (ed.), Analecta Mediaevalia Namurcensia, 17–18, 2 vols (Louvain, 1965)
Alan of Lille, *Opera*, J.-P. Migne (ed.), PL, 210 (Paris, 1855)
Alan of Lille, *Opera*, Charles de Visch (ed.) (Antwerp, 1654)
Alan of Lille, *The Plaint of Nature*, J. J. Sheridan (trans.) (Toronto, 1980)
Alanus de Insulis, *Textes inédits*, Marie Thérèse d'Alverny (ed.) (Paris, 1965)

Ambrosius, *Hexemaron, De paradiso, De Cain, De Noe, De Abraham, De Isaac, De bono mortis*, C. Schenkl (ed.), Corpus Scriptorum Ecclesiasticorum Latinorum, 32/1 (Vienna, 1896)

Anglo-Saxon Chronicle, Abingdon Manuscript, AD 1055/6, M. Swanton (trans.) (London, 1996)

Anselm of Canterbury, *The Letters of Anselm of Canterbury*, trans. W. Fröhlich, 3 vols (Kalamazoo, 1990–94)

Anselm of Canterbury, *Memorials of Anselm*, Richard W. Southern and Franciscus S. Schmitt (eds) (London, 1969)

Anselm of Canterbury, *Opera omnia S. Anselmi Cantuariensis archiepiscopi*, ed. F. S. Schmitt, 6 vols [vol. 1 printed at Seckau, 1938; vol. 2 at Rome 1940, all reset for the Nelson edition] (Edinburgh, 1946–61)

Anselm of Canterbury, *Prayers and Meditation of Saint Anselm*, B. Ward (trans.) (London, 1973)

Anselm of Liège, *Gesta episcoporum Leodiensium*, MGH SS, 7 (Hannover, 1846)

Atto of Villambrosa, *Vita sancti Iohannis Gualberti*, J.-P. Migne (ed.), PL, 146 (Paris, 1884), cols 667–706

Augustine, *The City of God*, W. Babcock (trans.) (New York, 2012)

Augustine, *De civitate Dei*, Bernard Dombart and Alfons Kalb, (ed.), Corpus Christianorum Series Latina, 47–8 (Turnhout, 1955)

[Augustine] Augustinus, *Enarrationes in Psalmos I-L*, E. Dekkers and J. Fraipoint (eds), Corpus Christianorum Series Latina, 38 (Turnhout, 1956 [repr. 1990])

Augustine, *Sermo* C. Lambot (ed.), Corpus Christianorum Series Latina, 41 (Turnhout, 1961)

Bede, *Ecclesiastical History of the English People*, Bertram Colgrave and R. A. B. Mynors (eds and trans) (Oxford, 1969)

Benedict's Rule: A Translation and Commentary, T. Kardong (ed. and trans.) (Collegeville, MN, 1996)

Bernard of Angers, *Liber miraculorum sanctae Fidis* II .5 (*Liber miraculorum sancte Fidis*), L. Robertini (ed.) (Spoleto, 1994)

Bernard of Clairvaux, *Apologia ad Guillelmum Sancti-Theoderici abbatem*, J.-P. Migne (ed.), PL, 182 (Paris, 1859)

Bernard of Clairvaux, *An Apology to Abbot William*, M. Casey (trans.) (Kalamazoo, 1970)

Bernard of Clairvaux, *De consideratione*, J.-P. Migne (ed.), PL, 182 (Paris, 1859)

Bernard of Clairvaux, *Epistolae*, in *Sancti Bernardi Opera,* vii–viii, J. Leclerq and H.-M. Rochais (eds), Editiones Cisterciones (Rome, 1974 and 1977)

Bernard of Clairvaux, *The Letters of St Bernard of Clairvaux*, B. S. James (trans.) (Stroud, 1998, orig. pub. 1953)

Boethius, *De consolatione philosophiae*, H. F. Stewart, E. K. Rand and S. J. Tester (trans), Loeb Classical Library (Cambridge, MA, 1973)

The Book of Sainte Foy, P. Sheingorn and R. L. A. Clark (trans) (Philadelphia, 1995)
Chronicon Abbatiae de Evesham, W. D. Macray (ed.), Rolls Series, 29 (London, 1863)
Chronicon Roskildense, M. Cl. Gertz (ed.), *Scriptores Minores Historiæ Danicæ Medii Ævi*, vol. 1 (Copenhagen, 1917)
La chronique de Saint-Hubert, dite Cantatorium, K. Hanquet (ed.) (Brussels, 1906)
Conradi I., Heinrici I. et Ottonis I. Diplomata, Theodor von Sickel (ed.), MGH, Diplomata (Berlin, 1956)
Cronache senesi, A. Lisini and F. Iacometti (eds), XV, part VI, 2nd edition (Bologna, 1931–39)
Cronica de Pisa, in L. A. Muratori, *Rerum Italicarum Scriptores*, 15 (Mediolani, 1729)
The Cult of St Swithun, M. Lapidge (ed. and trans.) (Oxford, 2003)
Danmarks gamle Landskabslove med Kirkelovene, Johannes Brøndum-Nielsen and Poul Johannes Jørgensen (eds), vols 1–8 (Copenhagen, 1933–61)
De pontificibus et sanctis Ecclesiae Eboracensis, The Bishops, Kings, and Saints of York, P. Godman (ed. and trans.) (Oxford, 1982)
Decrees of the Ecumenical Councils, N. P. Tanner (ed. and trans.) (2 vols, London and Washington, DC, 1990), http://www.ewtn.com/library/councils/lateran4.htm
Diplomatarium Danicum, series 1, vol. 2 (Copenhagen, 1938ff)
Douglas, D. C. (ed.), *Feudal Documents from the Abbey of Bury St Edmunds* (London, 1932)
Drogo of Saint-Winnoc, *Historia translationis sancta Lewinnae* (AA SS Jul V)
Eadmer of Canterbury, *Eadmer's History of Recent Events in England*, G. Bosanquet (trans.) (London, 1964)
Eadmer of Canterbury, *Historia novorum in Anglia*, M. Rule (ed.), Rolls Series, 81 (London, 1884; repr. 1965)
Eadmer of Canterbury, *Vita Anselmi*, R. W. Southern (ed. and trans.) (London, 1962)
The Early Lives of St Dunstan, M. Winterbottom and M. Lapidge (eds and trans) (Oxford, 2012)
Flodoard, *Historia Remensis ecclesiae*, MGH SS, 36 (Hannover, 1998)
Galbertus notarius, *Vita Caroli boni comitis Flandriae* (AA SS Mar. I D. 2)
La 'Garcineida': estudio y edición crítica con traducción, M. Pérez González (ed. and trans.) (León, 2001)
[Gerald of Wales] Giraldo Cambrense, *Agli estremi confini d'Occidente: Descrizione dell'Irlanda (Topographia Hibernica)*, M. Cataldi (trans.) (Turin, 2002)

Gerald of Wales, *The History and Topography of Ireland*, John O'Meara (trans.) (London, 1982)
Gerald of Wales, *The Journey through Wales and The Description of Wales*, Lewis Thorpe (trans.) (London, 1988)
[Gerald of Wales] Giraldi Cambresensis, *Opera*, J. S. Brewer, J. F. Dimock and G. F. Warner (eds), Rolls Series, 21, 8 vols (London, 1861–91)
Die Gesetze der Angelsachsen, F. Liebermann (ed.), 3 vols (Halle, 1903–16)
Gilbert Crispin, *The Works of Gilbert Crispin*, A. S. Abulafia and G. R. Evans (eds) (Oxford, 1986)
Gratian, *Decretum Gratiani*, A. Winroth (ed.): https://sites.google.com/a/yale.edu/decretumgratiani/
Gratian, *Decretum Magistri Gratiani*, Emil Friedberg (ed.), 2 vols (Leipzig, 1879 [repr. Graz, 1959])
Gregory the Great, *Homeliae in evangelia*, R. Étaix (ed.), Corpus Christianorum Series Latina, 141 (Turnhout, 1999)
Gregory the Great, *Moralia in Job*, M. Adriaen (ed.), Corpus Christianorum Series Latina, 143, 3 vols (Turnhout, 1979–85)
Gregory the Great, *Morals on the Book of Job*, James Bliss and Charles Marriott (trans), 3 vols in 4 (Oxford, 1844–50)
Guibert de Nogent: Autobiographie, E.-R. Labande (ed. and trans.) (Paris, 1981)
Guibert of Nogent, *A Monk's Confession*, Paul J. Archchambault (trans.) (University Park, 1995)
Guibert of Nogent, *Monodies* and *On the Relics of Saints*, J. Rubenstein and J. McAlhaney (trans) (London, 2011)
Guigo, *Meditationes*, M. Laporte (ed. and trans.), Sources chrétiennes, 308 (Paris, 1983)
Guigo, *The Meditations of Guigo*, A. Gorden Mursell (trans.) (Kalamazoo, 1995)
Guigues Ier, Prieur de Chartreuse, *Coutumes de Chartreuse. Introduction, texte critique, traduction et notes par un chartreux*, M. Laporte (ed.), Sources chrétiennes, 313 (Paris, 1984)
Haymo of Halberstadt, *In Epistolam ad Ephesios*, cap. 5, PL 117, cols 699B–734D
Helgaud of Fleury, *Vie de Robert le Pieux*, R. H. Bautier and G. Labory (eds and trans) (Paris, 1965)
Herman of Laon, *Miracula S. Mariae Laudunensis*, J.-P. Migne (ed.), PL 156 (Paris, 1853)
Hieronymus, *Commentarii in IV epistulas Paulinas*: Ad *Ephesios*, J.-P. Migne (ed.), PL 26 (Paris, 1903)
Hildebert of Le Mans, *Vita S. Hugonis abbatis Cluniacensis*, J.-P. Migne (ed.), PL, 159 (Paris, 1845)
Humberti Cardinalis Libri III adversus Simoniacos, Friedrich Thaner (ed.), MGH, Libelli de Lite, 3 vols (Hannover, 1891–7; repr. 1956)

Isadorus Hispalensis, *Sententiae*, P. Cazier (ed.), Corpus Christianorum Series Latina, 111 (Turnhout, 1998)

[John Cassian] Iohannes Cassianus, *Collationes XXIIII*, M. Petschenig (ed.), Corpus Scriptorum Ecclesiasticorum Latinorum, 13 (Vienna, 1886; repr. curante Gottfried Kreuz, Vienna, 2004)

John Cassian: The Conferences, Boniface Ramsey (trans. and ann.), Ancient Christian Writers, 57 (Mahwah, NJ, 1997)

John Cassian, *Opera Omnia*, J.-P. Migne (ed.), PL, 49 (Paris, 1874)

John of Salisbury, *Frivolities of Courtiers and Footprints of Philosophers*, J.B. Pike (trans.) (New York, 1972, orig. publ. 1938)

John of Salisbury, *Policraticus*, C. C. J. Webb (ed.) (Oxford, 1909)

John of Worcester, *The Chronicle of John of Worcester*, vol. 3, P. McGurk (ed. and trans.) (Oxford, 1998)

Kong Valdemars Jordebog, Svend Aakjær (ed.), vols 1–3 (Copenhagen, 1926–45, repr. Copenhagen, 1980)

Landulf of Milan, *Historia Mediolanensis*, MGH SS, 8 (Hannover, 1848)

Lanfranc of Canterbury, *Letters*, H. Clover and M. Gibson (eds and trans) (Oxford, 1979)

Lanfranc of Canterbury, *Monastic Constitutions*, M. D. Knowles (trans.) (Oxford, 1951)

Latinske dokument til norsk historie, E. Vandvik (ed. and trans.) (Oslo, 1959)

Lees, B. A. (ed.), *Records of the Templars in England in the Twelfth Century: The Inquest of 1185 with Illustrative Charters and Documents*, Records of the Social and Economic History of England and Wales, vol. 9 (Oxford, 1935)

Lewes Historic Character Assessment Report, www.lewes.gov.uk/Files/ plan_Lewes_EU S_reportpg28to36.pdf

Lives and Miracles of Saints Oda, Dunstan, and Oswald, A. J. Turner and B. J. Muir (eds and trans) (Oxford, 2006)

Marie de France, *Les lais de Marie de France*, J. Rychner (ed.) (Paris: Éditions Champion, 1966)

Marie de France, *The Lais of Marie de France*, G. Burgess and K. Busby (trans), 2nd edition (London, 1999)

Memorials of Saint Dunstan, Archbishop of Canterbury, W. Stubbs (ed.) (London, 1874)

Miracula S. Ursmari in itinere per Flandriam facta, MGH SS, 15.2 (Hannover, 1881)

Morkinnskinna, F. Jónsson (ed.), Udgivet for Samfund til Udgivelse af gammel nordisk Litteratur 53 (København, 1932)

Mortet, Victor, and Paul Deschamps, *Recueil de textes relatifs à l'histoire de l'architecture et à la condition des architectes en France au Moyen* Âge, *XIe–XIIIe siècles*, préface de Léon Pressouyre, 2 vols, single binding (Paris, 1995, first edition 1911 and 1929)

Necrologium Lundense. Lunds Domkyrkas Nekrologium, Lauritz Weibull (ed.) (Lund, 1923)

Norges Middelalderdokumenter (*NMD*), Sverre Bagge, Synnøve Holstad Smedsdal and Knut Helle (eds) (Bergen, 1973)

Nortbert, *Vita Bennonis II episcopi Osnaburgensis*, MGH SS, 30.ii (Leipzig, 1934)

Odo of Cluny, *Vita s. Geraldi comitis Auriliacensis* I.2, J.-P. Migne (ed.), PL, 133 (Paris, 1881)

Orderic Vitalis, *The Ecclesiastical History*, M. Chibnall (ed. and trans.), 6 vols (Oxford, 1969–80)

Ottonis III. Diplomata, Theodor von Sickel (ed.), MGH, Diplomata, II.2 (Berlin, 1957)

Ottonis Episcopi Frisingensis Chronica sive Historia de Duabus Civitatibus, A. Hofmeister (ed.), MGH SS rer. Germ, 45 (Hannover, 1912)

Pavelige Nuntiers Regnskabs- og Dagbøger 1282–1334, P. A. Munch (ed.) (Christiania, 1864)

Peter Damian, *Die Briefe des Petrus Damiani*, Kurt Reindel (ed.), MGH Epistolae, 2.4, 4 vols (Munich, 1983–93)

Peter Damian, *De patientia in insectatione improborum*, J.-P. Migne (ed.), PL 145 (Paris, 1853)

Peter Damian, *Epistolae*, MGH Briefe d. dt. Kaiserzeit, 4 vols (Munich, 1983–93)

Peter Damian, *Liber gratissimus*, MGH LdL, 1 (Hannover, 1891)

Les plus anciens texts de Cîteaux: sources, textes et notes historiques, J. de la C. Bouton and J. B. Van Damme (eds) (Achel, 1974)

Primasius Episcopus Hadrumetinus, *Commentarius in Apocalypsin*, A. W. Adams (ed.), Corpus Christianorum Series Latina, 92 (Turnhout, 1985)

Prou, M. (ed.), *Receuil des actes de Phillipe Ier roi de France* (Paris, 1908)

Recueil des actes de Robert Ier et de Raoul, rois de France, R. H. Bautier and J. Dufour (eds) (Paris, 1978)

Recueil des chartes de l'abbaye de Cluny, A. Bruel (ed.), 6 vols (Paris, 1876–1903)

Regula Venerabilis Viri Stephani Muretensis, in *Scriptores Ordinis Grandimontensis*, J. Becquet (ed.), Corpus Christianorum Continuatio Medievalis, 8 (Turnhout, 1968)

Robertson, A. J. (ed.), *Anglo-Saxon Charters* (Cambridge, 1956)

Robinson, Elaine, 'Humbertus de Silua Candida, *Libri tres aduersus simoniacos:* A Critical Edition with an Introductory Essay and Notes', unpubl. PhD Dissertation, Princeton University (1972)

Rodulfi Glabri, *Historiarum libri quinque* / Rodulfus Glaber, *The Five Books of the Histories*, J. France, N. Bulst and P. Reynolds (eds and trans) (Oxford, 1989)

Saxo Grammaticus, *Gesta Danorum*, J. Olrik and H. Rader (eds) (Copenhagen, 1931)

Scott, A. B., Deirdre F. Baker and A. G. Rigg (eds), 'The *Biblical Epigrams* of Hildebert of Le Mans: A Critical Edition', *Mediaeval Studies*, 47 (1985): 272–316

Seneca, *Epistulae morales*, R. Gummere (trans.), Loeb Classical Library, 75 (Cambridge, MA, 1917)

Stephen of Muret, *Maxims*, D. van Doel (trans.) (Kalamazoo, 2002)

Taxatio Ecclesiastica Database, Humanities Research Institute, University of Sheffield, http://www.hrionline.ac.uk/taxatio/

Thomas Aquinas, *Sancti Thomae Aquinatis Opera Omnia* (Parma, 1852–73), vol. 16 (1865)

Tractatus Garsiae (*Tractatus Garsiae, or the Translation of the Relics of SS. Gold and Silver*, R. M. Thompson (ed. and trans.) (Leiden, 1973)

Transcript of Sussex Wills, R. Garraway Rice and Walter H. Godfrey (eds), vol. 1, Sussex Record Society (Lewes, 1935)

Twiss, T. (ed.), *Monumenta Juridica, or the Black Book of the Admiralty*, vol. 2 (London, 1875)

Two Compotus Rolls of Saint Augustine's Abbey, Bristol, for 1491–2, Gwen Beechcroft and Arthur Sabin (eds), Bristol Record Society ([Bristol], 1938)

Viage literario á las iglesias de España, J. L. Villanueva (ed.), 22 vols (Madrid, 1803–52)

Viaggi di Pietro Della Valle il pellegrino descritti da lui medesimo in 54 lettere familiari all'erudito suo amico Mario Schipano, divisi in tre libri, cioè: La Turchia, La Persia e L'India, con la vita dell'autore (Turin, 1843), part II, *La Persia*, vol. II

Vita Aedwardi regis qui apud Westmonasterium requiescit, F. Barlow (ed. and trans.) (London, 1962)

Vita venerabilis viri Stephani Muretensis, in *Scriptores Ordinis Grandimontensis*, J. Becquet (ed.), Corpus Christianorum Continuatio Medievalis, 8 (Turnhout: 1968)

Vitae Sanctorum Danorum, M. Gertz (ed.) (Copenhagen, 1908)

Walter Daniel, *The Life of Ailred of Rievaulx*, F. M. Powicke (ed. and trans.) (London, 1950)

Whitelock, D. (ed.), *Anglo-Saxon Wills* (Cambridge, 1930)

Widukini monachi Corbiensis rerum gestarum Saxonicarum libri tres, Paul Hirsch (ed.), MGH Scriptores rer. Germ, 60 (Hannover, 1935)

William of Malmesbury, *The Deeds of the Bishops of England* (Woodbridge, 2002)

William of Malmesbury, *Gesta Pontificum Anglorum*, M. Winterbottom (ed. and trans.), 2 vols (Oxford, 2007)

William of St Thierry, *The Golden Epistle*, XXXVI , 147–9, Theodore Berkley (trans.), pp. 59–60, *Epistola ad Fratres de Monte-Dei*, R. Thomas (ed.), 2 vols (Chambarand, 1968)

Secondary Sources

Ainonen, Tuija, 'Manuscripts, Editions and Textual Interpretation: Alan of Lille's Distinction Collection *Summa "Quot modis"* and the Meaning of Words', in Marko Lamberg, Jesse Keskiaho, Elina Rasanen and Olga Timofeeva (eds), with Leila Virtanen, *Methods and the Medievalist: Current Approaches in Medieval Studies* (Newcastle, 2008), pp. 12–37

Albrecht, Gunther, *Das Münzwesen im niederlothringischen und friesischen Raum vom 10. bis zum beginnenden 12. Jahrhundert* (Hamburg, 1959)

Alfonso, I., 'Cistercians and Feudalism', *Past & Present*, 133 (1991): 3–30

Allen, Martin, *Mints and Money in Medieval England* (Cambridge, 2012)

Allen, Martin, *The Durham Mint*, British Numismatic Society Special Publication, 4 (London, 2003)

Allerton et al., J., *Norwich: Cathedral, Church, City, Diocese 1096–1996* (London and Rio Grande, 1996)

Alteri, G., 'Il sarcofago di Catervio', *Bollettino di Numismatica*, 26–7 (1996): 7

Amandry et al., Michel, *Dictionaire de Numismatique* (Paris, 2006)

Andersen, Michael, 'Ærkebiskop Absalons testamente – historie og kulturhistorie', in Frank Birkebæk, Tom Christensen and Inge Skovgaard-Petersen (eds), *Absalon. Fædrelandets fader* (Roskilde, 1996), pp. 209–27

Arslan, E. A., 'Il dono di re Carlo all'apostolo Pietro: un Tremisse d'oro', *Numismatica e Antichità Classiche. Quaderni Ticinesi*, 37 (2008): 377–406

Arslan, E. A., 'Le trésor de monnaies normandes et françaises d'Allifae (Campanie, XIIe siècle)', *International Numismatic Newsletter*, 30 (1997): 6–7

Arthur, P., 'L'Albania e la Terra d'Otranto nel Medioevo: tre casi studio', in Fondazione Cassamarca (ed.), *Convegno Internazionale di Studi. Gli Illiri e l'Italia* (Treviso, 2005), pp. 77–91

Arthur, P., 'Il cimitero', in P. Arthur (ed.), *Da Apigliano a Martano. Tre anni di archeologia medioevale (1997–1999)* (Martina Franca, 1999), pp. 51–3

Aston, G., 'The Towns of Berkshire', in J. Haslam et al., *Anglo-Saxon Towns of Southern England* (Stroud, 1984), pp. 53–86

An Atlas of Anglo-Saxon and Norman Coin Finds, c. 973–1086 (London, 1998)

Attenborough, F., *The Laws of the Earliest English Kings* (Cambridge, 1922)

Bagge, Sverre, 'The Scandinavian Kingdoms', in *The New Cambridge Medieval History*, V, *c. 1198–c. 1300*, David Abulafia (ed.) (Cambridge, 1999), pp. 720–42

Bagge, Sverre, 'Harald Hardråde i bysants. To fortellinger, to kulturer', in *Hellas og Norge: Kontakt, komparasjon, kontrast*, Øivind Andersen and Thomas Hägg (eds) (Bergen, 1990), pp. 169–92

Bain, E., 'Les marchands chassés du temple, entre commentaires et usages sociaux', *Médiévales*, 55 (Autumn 2008): 53–74

Baklid, Herleik, 'Hvad der har bragt dem gjennem gulvet er dessverre efter al sansynlighet en hemmelig ofring [...]', *Heimen*, 3 (1995): 181–96

Baldassarri, M., 'Tra terra e "cielo": i reperti numismatici e devozionali dallo scavo di Formigine', in E. Grandi and M. Librenti (eds), *'In la terra de Formigine'. Archeologia di un abitato* (Borgo San Lorenzo-Firenze, 2013), pp. 131–44

Barber, M., *The New Knighthood: A History of the Order of the Temple* (Cambridge, 1994)

Barlow, F., *William Rufus* (London, 1983)

Baron, Alain, *Die Münzprägung der Bischöfe, Kaiser und Könige in Straßburg (751–1123)*, unpubl. Dissertation am Institut für Numismatik der Universität Wien (1987)

Barral i Altet, Xavier, 'Les moines, les évêques et l'art', in Dominque Iogna-Prat and Charles Picard (eds), *Religion et culture autour de l'an mil, Actes du colloque 'Hugues Capet 987–1987, la France de l'an mil'* (Paris, 1990)

Barral i Altet, Xavier, *Le paysage monumental de la France autour de l'an mil, colloque international C.N.R.S. Hugues Capet 987–1987. La France en l'an Mil, juin–septembre 1987* (Paris, 1987)

Barrow, G. W. S., 'David I (c. 1085–1153)', *Oxford Dictionary of National Biography*, Oxford University Press, 2004; online edition, Jan 2006, http://www.oxforddnb.com/view/article/7208

Barrow, J., 'Churches, Education and Literacy in Towns 600–1300', in D. M. Palliser (ed.), *The Cambridge Urban History of Britain* (Cambridge, 2000), vol. 1, pp. 127–52

Barrow, J., 'German Cathedrals and the Monetary Economy in the Twelfth Century', *Journal of Medieval History*, 16 (1990): 13–38

Bartel, Heike, 'Das Münzprivileg Ludwigs des Frommen für Corvey (BM2 922)', *Archiv für Diplomatik. Schriftsgeschichte, Siegel- und Wappenkunde*, 58 (2012): 147–68

Bartels, Christoph, Michael Fessner, Lothar Klappauf and Friedrich Albert Linke, *Kupfer, Blei und Silber aus dem Goslarer Rammelsberg von den Anfängen bis 1620* (Bochum, 2007)

Bartlett, Robert, *England under the Norman and Angevin Kings: 1075–1225* (Oxford, 2000)

Bartlett, R., *The Making of Europe: Conquest, Colonization and Cultural Change 950–1350* (London, 1993)

Barton, R. E., *Lordship in the County of Maine, c. 890–1160* (Woodbridge, 2004)

Baxter, S., 'The Making of Domesday Book and the Languages of Lordship', in *Conceptualizing Multilingualism in England, c. 800–c. 1250* (Turnhout, 2011), pp. 271–308

Becquet, Jean, *Recherches sur les institutions religieuses de l'Ordre de Grandmont au Moyen Âge*, École practiques des hautes études (Paris, 1951)

Bell, D. N., 'The Carthusian Connection: Guigo I of La Chartreuse and the Origins of Cisterican Spirituality', *Cistercian Studies Quarterly*, 27 (1992): pp. 51–62

Bendixen, Kirsten, *Skatten fra Lundby Krat. Et himmerlandsk skattefund fra Erik Ejegods tid. De danske mønter* (Copenhagen, 1993)

Bendixen, Kirsten, 'Middelaldermønter i de sidste 10 års danske kirkefund', *Nordisk Numismatisk* Årsskrift (1972): 47–70

Bentsen, Lars C., 'Udgravningerne ved Gl. Jacobi Skole', *Opdatering: Museet for Varde og Omegns Årbog* (2008): 32–46

Bercea, Brighita, Robert B. Ekelund Jr and Robert D. Tollison, 'Cathedral Building as an Entry-Deterring Device', *Kyklo*, 58 (2005): 453–65

Beresford, M. W., and H. P. R. Finberg, *English Medieval Boroughs: A Handlist* (Newton Abbot, 1973)

Berghaus, Peter, *Münzgeschichte Herfords* (Herford, 1971)

Bernardelli, A., 'In defossis locis dispersae, vel muris intus locatae ... Considerazioni su un uso rinascimentale della medaglia, le origini: secoli XIV e XV', *Rivista Italiana di Numismatica*, 111 (2010): 363–402

Biddle, M. (ed.), *Winchester in the Eleventh and Twelfth Centuries* (Oxford, 1976)

Binding, Günther, and Susanne Linscheid-Burdich, *Planen und Bauen im frühen und hohen Mittelalter nach den Schriftquellen bis 1250* (Darmstadt, 2010)

Bisson, T. N., *The Crisis of the Twelfth Century: Power, Lordship and the Origins of European Government* (Princeton, 2009)

Bisson, T. N., *Conservation of Coinage: Monetary Exploitation and its Restraint in France, Catalonia, and Aragon (c. A.D. 1000–c. 1225)* (Oxford, 1979)

Blackburn, Mark, 'The Coin-finds', in Dagfinn Skre (ed.), *The Means of Exchange*, Kaupang Excavation Project Publication Series, vol. 2, Norske Oldfunn, 23 (Aarhus, 2007), pp. 29–74

Blackburn, Mark, 'Alfred's Coinage Reforms in Context', in T. Reuter (ed.), *Alfred the Great* (Aldershot, 2003), pp. 199–217

Blackburn, M., '"Productive" Sites and the Pattern of Coin Loss in England, 600–1180', in T. Pestell and K. Ulmschneider (eds), *Markets in Early Medieval Europe: Trading and 'Productive' Sites, 650–850* (Macclesfield, 2003), pp. 20–36

Blackburn, Mark, 'Coinage and Currency', in E. King (ed.), *The Anarchy of Stephen's Reign* (Oxford, 1994), pp. 145–205

Blair, John, *The Church in Anglo-Saxon Society* (Oxford, 2005)

Blair, W. J., and N. L. Ramsay, *English Medieval Industries: Craftsmen, Techniques, Products* (Hambledon, 1991)
Bloch, M., 'La Vie de S. Edouard le Confesseur par Osbert de Clare', *Analecta Bollandiana*, 41 (1923): 5–131
Blumenthal, Ute-Renate, *The Investiture Controversy: Church and Monarchy from the Ninth to the Twelfth Century* (Philadelphia, 1988)
Bois, G., *The Transformation of the Year One Thousand*, J. Birrell (trans.) (Manchester, 1992)
Blom, Grethe Authén, *Kongemakt og privilegier i Norge inntil 1387* (Oslo-Bergen-Tromsø, 1967)
Bolton, Brenda (ed.), *Adrian IV The English Pope (1154–159): Studies and Texts* (Farnham, 2003)
Bolton, J. L., *Money in the Medieval English Economy: 973–1489* (Manchester, 2012)
Bolton, T., *The Empire of Cnut the Great: Conquest and Consolidation of Power in Northern Europe in the Early Eleventh Century* (Leiden, 2009)
Bompaire, M., A. Clairand and R. Prot, 'La monnaie de Corbie (XIe–XII e siècles)', *Revue numismatique*, 153 (1998): 297–325
Botet y Sisó, J., *Les monedes catalanes*, 3 vols (Barcelona, 1908–11)
Bouchard, C. B., *Holy Entrepreneurs: Cistercians, Knights, and Economic Exchange in Twelfth-Century Burgundy* (Ithaca, 1991)
Bougard, F., 'Le crédit dans l'occident du haut Moyen Âge: documentation et pratique', in J. P. Devroey, L. Feller and R. Le Jan (eds), *Les élites et la richesse au haut Moyen Âge* (Turnhout, 2010), pp. 439–77
Boureau, A., 'A Royal Funeral of 1498', in M. Rubin (ed.), *Medieval Christianity in Practice* (Princeton, 2009), pp. 59–63
Brand, P. A., 'The Control of Mortmain Alienation in England, 1200–1300', in J. H. Baker (ed.), *Legal Records and the Historian* (London, 1978), pp. 29–40
Bremond, C., J. Le Goff and J.-C. Schmitt, *L'Exemplum'*, Typologie des Sources du Moyen Âge Occidental, 40 (Turnhout, 1982)
Britnell, R. H., *The Commercialistion of English Society 1000–1500* (Cambridge, 2009)
Britnell, R., *The Winchester Pipe Rolls and Medieval English Society* (Woodbridge, 2003)
Britnell, R., 'The Economy of British Towns 600–1300', in D. M. Palliser (ed.), *The Cambridge Urban History of Britain*, vol. 1 (Cambridge, 2000), pp. 105–26
Britnell, R., 'Markets and Fairs in Britain and Ireland before 1216', https://sites.google.com/site/feanbeast/miscellaneous-papers/markets-and-fairs
Brooke, Christopher, *The Medieval Idea of Marriage* (Oxford, 1989)
Brown, Peter, *Through the Eye of a Needle: Wealth, the Fall of Rome, and the Making of Christianity in the West, 350–550 AD* (Princeton, 2012)

Buchenau, Heinrich, 'Ein Essener Denar des XI. Jahrhunderts', *Blätter für Münzfreunde*, 7 (1901): 207

Burton, J. E., 'The Cistercians in England', in J. Burton and J. Kerr (eds), *The Cistercians in the Middle Ages* (Woodbridge, 2011), pp. 149–88

Burton, J. E., *The Monastic Orders in Yorkshire, 1069–1215* (Cambridge, 1999)

Burton, J E., *Monastic and Religious Orders in Britain 1000–1300* (Cambridge, 1994)

Bysted, Ane L., *Ringsted Kloster og Skt. Bendts Kirke* (Ringsted, 2010)

Bøgh, Anders, 'Bundones regis. Selvejerbøndernes antal og funktion – især i senmiddelalderen', in Agnes Arnórsdóttir, Per Ingesman and Bjørn Poulsen (eds), *Konge, kirke og samfund. De to* øvrighedsmagter *i senmiddelalderen* (Aarhus, 2007), pp. 117–49

Callegher, B., 'Monete, medaglie e sigilli a Padova tra Duecento e Trecento', in V. Sgarbi (ed.), *Giotto e il suo tempo* (Milan, 2000), pp. 276–82, 415–21

The Cambridge History of Christianity Volume 3: Early Medieval Christianities c. 600– c. 1100, Thomas F. X. Noble and Julia M. H. Smith (eds) (Cambridge, 2008)

The Cambridge History of Christianity Volume 4: Christianity in Western Europe c. 1100–c. 1500, Miri Rubin and W. Simons (eds) (Cambridge, 2009)

Cameron, G., 'Purgatory and Modernity', in *Bridging the Medieval-Modern Divide: Medieval Themes in the World of the Reformation*, James Muldoon and Paul Monod (eds) (Farnham, 2013), pp. 87–106

Campbell, B. M. S., 'Benchmarking Medieval Economic Development: England, Wales, Scotland, and Ireland, c. 1290', *Economic History Review*, 2nd series, 61 (2008): 896–945

Campbell, James, 'Production and Distribution in Early and Middle Anglo-Saxon England', in Tim Pestell and Katharina Ulmschneider (eds), *Markets in Early Medieval Europe: Trading and 'Productive' Sites, 650–850* (Macclesfield, 2003), pp. 12–19

Cantor, N., 'The Crisis of Western Monasticism, 1050–1130', *American Historical Review*, 66 (1960): 57–67

Carelli, Peter, *En kapitalistisk anda. Kulturella förändringar i 1100-tallets Danmark* (Stockholm, 2001)

Carelli, Peter, 'Varubytet i medeltidens Lund. Uttryck för handel eller konsumtion?', *Meta. Medeltidsarkeologisk tidskrift*, 3 (1998): 3–27

Cartlidge, Neil, *Medieval Marriage: Literary Approaches 1100–1300* (Bury St Edmunds, 1997)

Castan, Carlos, and Juan R. Cayon, *Las Monedas Hispano Musulmanas Cristianas 711–1981* (Madrid, 1980)

The Cathedral of Anagni: Art, History, Legend (Anagni, 1998)

Cavalié, E., 'Le type numismatique de Saint-Gilles', *Revue numismatique*, 162 (2005): 417–42

Chadwick, Henry, *East and West: The Making of a Rift in the Church from Apostolic Times until the Council of Florence* (Oxford, 2003)
Chiaravalle, M., 'La moneta nella bocca del bovino: un denaro imperiale federiciano per Milano', in P. Colombo, P. Monti and P. Zaffaroni (eds), *Chiesa della Purificazione* (Firenze, 2011), pp. 171–6
Chibnall, M., *Piety, Power and History in Medieval England and Normandy* (Farnham, 2000)
Chibnall, M., 'The English Possessions of Bec in the Time of Anselm', in Raymonde Foreville (ed.), *Les mutations socio-culturelles au tournant des Xe–XIIe siècles*, Spicilegium Beccense, 2 (Paris, 1984), pp. 273–82
Chibnall, M., *The World of Orderic Vitalis* (Oxford, 1984)
Chibnall, M., 'The Relations of Saint Anselm with the English Dependencies of the Abbey of Bec, 1079–93', *Spicilegium Beccense*, 1 (Paris, 1959), pp. 521–30
Chirol, Elisabeth, et al., *Le guide de Rouen* (Besançon, 1991)
Christensen, Aksel E., 'Tiden 1042–1241', in Aksel E. Christensen et al. (eds), *Danmarks historie*, vol. 1 (Copenhagen, 1977), pp. 213–399
Christensen, C. A., 'Roskildekirkens jordegods før år 1200. Fra skibengods til bispegods', *Historisk Tidsskrift*, 14, series 1 (1980): 30–39
Clark, J., *The Benedictines in the Middle Ages* (Woodbridge, 2011)
Constable, G., *The Abbey of Cluny: A Collection of Essays to Mark the Eleven-Hundredth Anniversary of its Foundation* (Münster, 2010)
Coppack, G., and M. Aston, *Christ's Poor Men: The Carthusians in Britain* (Stroud, 2002)
Coss, P. R., and T. John (eds), *The Early Records of Medieval Coventry* (Oxford, 1986)
Coupland, Simon, *Carolingian Coinage and the Vikings* (Aldershot, 2007)
Cowdrey, H. E. J., 'The Gregorian Papacy and Eremitical Monasticism', in P. De Leo (ed.), *San Bruno e la Certosa di Calabria: Atti del convegno internazionale di studi per il IX centenario della Certosa di Serra S. Bruno, Squillace, Serra S. Bruno 15–18 settembre 1991* (Messina, 1991), pp. 33–54
Cowdrey, J., *Pope Gregory VII, 1073–1085* (Oxford, 1998)
Crinon, Pierre, 'Catalogue des monnaies carolingiennes de Tours du VIIIe s. au début de la féodalite, Xe s.', in Jacqueline Pilet-Lemière (ed.), *Tours,* études *numismatiques* (Paris, 1997), pp. 53–87
Cushing, K. G., *Reform and Papacy in the Eleventh Century: Spirituality and Social Change* (Manchester, 2005)
D'Avray, David, *Medieval Marriage: Symbolism and Society* (Oxford, 2008)
Dahan, Gilbert, 'Alain de Lille et l'exégèse de la Bible', in J.-L. Solère, A. Vasiliu and A. Galonnier (eds), *Alain de Lille, le docteur universel, philosophie, théologie et littérature au XIIe siècle* (Turnhout, 2005)

Danmarks Gilde- og Lavsskraaer fra middelalderen, C. Nyrop (ed.), vol. 1 (Copenhagen, 1899–1900)

Dannenberg, Hermann, *Die deutschen Münzen der sächsischen und fränkischen Kaiserzeit*, 4 vols (Berlin, 1876–1905)

Dannenberg, Hermann, *Die Münzen der deutschen Schweiz zur Zeit der sächsischen und fränkischen Kaiser* (Genf, 1903)

Darby, H. C., *Domesday England* (Cambridge, 1977)

De skriftlige kilder til Danmarks middelalderlige møntvæsen. Et udvalg 1085–1500, Jørgen Steen Jensen (ed.) (Copenhagen, 1989)

Decoux, Jérôme, and Guillaume Gaillard, *Le quartier Martainville de Rouen* (Rouen, 2011)

Degasperi, A., 'La moneta in tomba nella Toscana centro-settentrionale tra alto-e bassomedioevo', *Archeologia Medievale*, 39 (2012): 337–54

Delaporte, Jacqueline, 'La monnaie', in Françoise Debaisieux, Elisabeth Chirol et al. (eds), *Trésors des abbayes normandes* (Rouen-Caen, 1979), p. 40

Delivré, Fabrice, 'Les diocèses méridionaux d'après le *Provinciale Romanum* (XIIe–XVe siècle)', in *Lieux sacrés et espace ecclésial (IXe–XV siècle)*, Cahiers de Fanjeaux, 46 (Toulouse, 2011), pp. 395–419

Depeyrot, Georges, *Le numéraire carolingien*, 3rd edition (Wetteren, 2008)

Dereine, C., 'Odon de Tournai et la crise de cénobitisme au XIe siècle', *Revue du Moyen Âge latin*, 4 (1948): 137–54

Devroey, J. P., *Puissants et misérables: système social et monde paysan dans l'Europe des Francs (VIe–IXe siècles)* (Brussels, 2006)

Dhénin, Michel, 'Les Monnaies normandes', *Le Domfrontais medieval* 7 (*Les conférences d'histoire locale du Lycée de Domfront* IX) (1990): 14–30

Di Martino, S., 'La sepoltura di bovino: analisi osteologica', in P. Colombo, P. Monti and P. Zaffaroni (eds), *Chiesa della Purificazione* (Firenze, 2011), pp. 167–9

Dieudonné, A., *Les monnaies féodales*, Manuel de la numismatique française, vol. 4 (Paris, 1936)

Donkin, R. A., 'The Cistercian Order and the Settlement of Northern England', *Geographical Review*, 59 (1969): 403–16

Doubleday, H. (ed.), *The Victoria County History of Bedfordshire*, vol. 1 (London, 1900)

Douglas, D. C., *The Social Structure of Medieval East Anglia*, Oxford Studies in Social and Legal History, vol. 9, Sir Paul Vinogradoff (ed.) (Oxford, 1927, repr. New York, 1974)

Dubuis, O. F., and S. Frey- Kupper (eds), *Trouvailles monétaires d'églises*, Études de numismatique et d'histoire monétaire, 1 (Lausanne, 1995)

Duby, G., *The Early Growth of the European Economy: Warriors and Peasants from the Seventh to Twelfth Century*, Howard B. Clarke (trans.) (London, 1974)

Duby, G., *Hommes et structures du Moyen Âge* (Paris, 1973)

Duby, G., 'Économie domaniale et économie monétaire: Le budget de l'abbaye de Cluny entre 1080 et 1155', *Annales*, 7 (1952): 155–71

Dugdale, W., *Monasticon Anglicanum*, vol. 1 (London, 1817)

Dumas, Françoise, 'Les monnaies normandes', *Revue numismatique*, 6th series, 21 (1979): 84–140

Dumas, Françoise, *Le trésor de Fécamp et le monnayage en Francie occidentale pendant la seconde moitié du Xe siècle* (Paris, 1971)

Dumas, Françoise, and Jacqueline Pilet-Lemiere, 'La monnaie normande – Xe–XII siècle: Le point de la recherche en 1987', *Les Mondes Normands* (Caen, 1989), pp. 125–31

Dumville, D. N., 'Anglo-Saxon Books: Treasure in Norman Hands?', *Anglo-Norman Studies*, 16 (1993): 83–99

Dutton, M., 'Aelred, Historian: Two Portraits in Plantagenet Myth', *Cistercian Studies Quarterly*, 28 (1993): 112–44

Dyer, C., 'The Hidden Trade of the Middle Ages: Evidence from the West Midlands of England', *Journal of Historical Geography*, 18 (1992): 141–57

Dyer, C., and T. R. Slater, 'The Midlands', in D. M. Palliser (ed.), *The Cambridge Urban History of Britain*, vol. 1 (Cambridge, 2000), pp. 609–38

Dyrhaug, Sverre, 'Kjøp, kreditt og kontanter i utenrikshandelen pa 1300-tallet', *Collegium Medievale*, 25 (2012): 41–66

Dyson, T., 'Two Saxon Land Grants for Queenhithe', in J. Bird, H. Chapman and J. Clark (eds), *Collectanea Londoniensia: Studies Presented to Ralph Merrifield* (London, 1978)

Ehrend, Helfried, *Speyrer Münzgeschichte, Teil I: Speyrer Münzgeschichte, Teil I: Münzen und Medaillen (um 650–1900)* (Speyer, 2005)

Ekre, Rune, *Om den medeltida utmyntingen i Lödöse*, in *Skärvor och fragment: kring medeltiden i Älvsborg län,* Västgöta-dal 1989–90 (Vänersborg, 1991), pp. 17–25

Emmerich, Bettina, *Geiz und Gerechtigkeit.* Ökonomisches *Denken im frühen Mittelalter*, Vierteljahrschrift für Sozial- und Wirtschaftsgeschichte, Beihefte, 168 (Stuttgart, 2004)

Engel, Arthur, and Ernest Lehr, *Numismatique Alsace* (Paris, 1887)

Erlande-Brandenburg, Alain, 'Le grand dessein de Maurice de Sully (1160)', in Michel Lemoine (ed.), *Notre-Dame de Paris, un manifeste chrétien (1160–1230), colloque organisé à l'Institut de France le vendredi 12 décembre 2003* (Turnhout, 2004), pp. 70–92

Études *documents pour l'histoire des Chartreux*, Dom Augustin Devaulx (ed.), *Analecta Cartusiana*, 208 (Salzburg, 2003)

Faith, R. J., 'Demesne Resources and Labour Rent on the Manors of St Paul's Cathedral, 1066–1222', *Economic History Review*, 2nd series, 47 (1994): 657–78

Faith, R. J., *The English Peasantry and the Growth of Lordship* (London, 1997)
Fauroux, M., *Recueil des actes des ducs de Normandie de 911 à 1066 complété d'un index rerum par Lucien Musset* (Paris, 1961)
Favreau, Robert, 'Commanditaire, auteur, artiste dans les inscriptions médiévales', in Michel Zimmermann (ed.), *Auctor et auctoritas, invention et confirmisme dans l'écriture médiévale, actes du colloque tenu à l'Université de Versailles-Saint-Quentin-en-Yvelines (14–16 juin 1999)* (Paris, 2001), pp. 40–43
Fedele, P., *Il giublieo del 1300, Gli Anni Santi* (Rome, 1934)
Fell, C. E., 'Edward King and Martyr and the Anglo-Saxon Hagiographic Tradition', in D. Hill (ed.), *Ethelred the Unready*, British Archaeological Reports (London, 1978), pp. 1–15
Feller, L., 'Sur la formation des prix dans l'économie du haut Moyen Âge', *Annales*, 66 (2011): 627–61
Feller, L., 'Accumuler, redistribuer et échanger durant le haut moyen âge', *Settimane di studio del centro italiano di studi sull'alto medioevo*, 56 (2009): 81–110
Feveille, Claus, and Morten Søvsø, 'Ribe genopstår', in Søren Bitsch Christensen (ed.), *Ribe Bys Historie*, vol. 1, *700–1520* (Ribe, 2010), pp. 38–45
Fichtenau, H., *Living in the Tenth Century: Mentalities and Social Orders*, P. Geary (trans.) (Chicago, 1991)
Finberg, H. P. R., *Early Charters of Wessex* (Leicester, 1964)
Finlay, M., *The Ancient Economy*, 2nd edition (London, 1985)
Frassetto, M., 'The Sermons of Ademar of Chabannes and the Letter of Heribert: New Sources concerning the Origins of Medieval Heresy', *Revue bénédictine*, 109 (1999): 324–40
Fröhlich, W., 'St Anselm's Special Relationship with William the Conqueror', *Anglo-Norman Studies*, 10 (1987): 101–10
Frugoni, A., *Il giubileo di Bonifacio VIII*, Bullettino dell'Istituto Storico Italiano per il Medio Evo e Archivio Muratoriano, 62 (1950): 1–121
Gaettens, Richard, *Das Geld- und Münzwesen der Abtei Fulda im Hochmittelalter unter Auswertung der Münzen als Quelle der Geschichte und Kunstgeschichte, der Wirtschaftsgeschichte und des Staatsrechts* (Fulda, 1957)
Gasper, Giles E. M., and Svein H. Gullbekk, 'An Intimate Encounter with English Coinage in the High Middle Ages: The Case of Wulfric of Haselbury', *British Numismatic Journal*, 83 (2013): 112–19
Gasper, Giles E. M., and Svein H. Gullbekk, 'Money and its Use in the Thought and Experience of Anselm, Archbishop of Canterbury (1093–1109)', *Journal of Medieval History*, 38 (2012): 155–82
Gasper, Giles E. M., and Ian Logan (eds), *Saint Anselm of Canterbury and his Legacy* (Toronto, 2012)
Gatti, I., *La tomba di S. Francesco nei secoli* (Assisi,1983)

Gazeau, V., 'The Effect of the Conquest of 1066 on Monasticism in Normandy: The Abbeys of the Risle Valley', in D. Bates and A. Curry (eds), *England and Normandy in the Middle Ages* (London, 1994), pp. 131–42

Gazeau, V., 'Le domaine continental du Bec; aristocratie et monachisme au temps d'anselme', in Raymonde Foreville (ed.), *Les mutations socio-culturelles au tournant des Xe–XIIe siècles*, Spicilegium Beccense, 2 (Paris, 1984), pp. 259–71

Geary, P., *Phantoms of Remembrance: Memory and Oblivion at the End of the First Millennium* (Princeton, 1994)

Geary, P., *Furta Sacra: Thefts of Relics in the Central Middle Ages* (Princeton, 1990)

Geiger, Hans-Ulrich, 'Moneta Sancti Galli. Die Münzprägung St. Gallens im Mittelalter', *Schriften des Vereins für Geschichte des Bodensees und seiner Umgebung*, 106 (1988): 131–41

Giles, J.A., *Bede the Venerable, Saint, 673–735, also, the Anglo-Saxon Chronicle* (London, 1903)

Goddard, R., *Lordship and Medieval Urbanization: Coventry 1043–1355* (Woodbridge, 2004)

Goez, Werner, *Kirchenreform und Investiturstreit 910–1122* (Stuttgart, 2008)

Grassi, B., and G. Ridolfi, 'Le ricerche archeologiche', in P. Colombo, P. Monti and P. Zaffaroni (eds), *Chiesa della Purificazione* (Firenze, 2011), pp. 141–66

Gray, H., 'Moneylending in Twelfth-Century England', unpubl. PhD thesis, University of London (2007)

Green, J. A., *The Government of England under Henry I* (Cambridge, 1989)

Grierson, Philip, 'The Volume of Anglo-Saxon Coinage', *Economic History Review*, 20 (1967): 153–60

Grierson, P., and M. Blackburn, *Medieval European Coinage with a Catalogue of the Coins in the Fitzwilliam Museum, Cambridge. Vol. 1, The Early Middle Ages (5th –10th Centuries)* (Cambridge, 1986)

Grierson, P., and L. Travaini, *Medieval European Coinage with a Catalogue of the Coins in the Fitzwilliam Museum, Cambridge. Vol. 14 Italy (III). (South Italy, Sicily, Sardinia)* (Cambridge, 1998)

Grinder-Hansen, Keld, *Kongemagtens krise. Det danske møntvæsen 1241–1340* (Copenhagen, 2000)

Grinder-Hansen, Keld, 'Mønter som kilde til middelalterens økonomiske historie – en presentation af et kildemateriale', *Fortid og Nutid*, 2 (1994): 101–33

Guadagni, F., *De invento corpore Divi Francisci Ordinis Minorum Parentis* (Rome, 1819)

Gullbekk, Svein H.,'Money and its Use in the Saga Society: Silver, Coins and Commodity Money', in Svavar Sigmundsson (ed.), *Viking Settlements and Viking Society* (Reykjavik, 2011), pp. 176–88

Gullbekk, Svein H., 'Myntenes omløpshastighet i norsk middelalder', *Historisk Tidsskrift*, 90 (2011): 511–29

Gullbekk, Svein H., 'Myntvesenet som kilde til statsutvikling i Norge ca. 1050–1080', in Sverre Bagge et al. (eds), *Statsuvikling i Skandinavia i middelalderen* (Oslo, 2011), pp. 76–100

Gullbekk, Svein H., *Pengevesenets fremvekst og fall i Norge i middelalderen* (Copenhagen, 2009)

Gullbekk, Svein H., 'Svensk og gotlandsk mynt ofret til St. Olav i Bergen', *Myntstudier*, 1 (2009): 16–21

Gullbekk, Svein H., 'Lite eller mye mynt i Norge i middelalderen?', *Historisk Tidsskrift*, 84 (2005): 551–72

Gullbekk, Svein H.,'Natural or Money Economy in Medieval Norway', *Scandinavian Journal of History*, 30 (2005): 3–19

Gullbekk, Svein H., 'Myntforringelse i Danmark og innføring av monopolmynt under Sven Estridsen (1047–74)', *Nordisk Numismatisk* Årsskrift, *1994–96* (2000): 111–29

Gullbekk, Svein H., 'Law and Money in Medieval Norway', *Numisamtic Chronicle*, 158 (1998): 173–84

Gurevich, A. J., *Categories of Medieval Culture*, G. L. Campbell (trans.) (London, 1985)

Hahn, Wolfgang, *Moneta Radasponensis. Bayerns Münzprägung im 9., 10. und 11. Jahrhundert* (Braunschweig, 1976)

Haines, Dorothy (ed.), *Sunday Observance and the Sunday Letter in Anglo-Saxon England* (Cambridge, 2010)

Hallam, E., 'Henry II as a Founder of Monasteries', *Journal of Ecclesiastical History*, 28 (1977): 113–32

Hallam, E., 'Henry II , Richard I and the Order of Grandmont', *Journal of Medieval History*, 1 (1975): 165–86

Haring, Nikolaus M., 'Alan of Lille, *De planctu naturae*', *Studi medievali*, series 3, 19 (1978): 797–879

Harper-Bill, C., 'Herluin, Abbot of Bec and His Biographer', in D. Baker (ed.), *Studies in Church History*, 15 (1978): 15–25

Hartmann, Wilfried, *Der Investiturstreit* (Munich, 2007)

Harvey, P. D. A., 'The Manorial Reeve in Twelfth-Century England', in R. Evans (ed.), *Lordship and Learning: Studies in Memory of Trevor Aston* (Woodbridge, 2004), pp. 125–38

Harwood, T., *The History and Antiquities of the Church and City of Lichfield* (London, 1806)

Haseldine, Julian, 'Monastic Friendship in Theory and in Action in the Twelfth Century', in A. Classen and M. Sandidge (eds), *Friendship in the Middle Ages and Early Modern Age: Explorations of a Fundamental Ethical Discourse* (Berlin, 2010), pp. 349–93

Haslam, J. (ed.), *Anglo-Saxon Towns* (Chichester, 1984)
Hatz, Gert, Vera Hatz, Ulrich Zwicker, Noel Gale and Zofia Gale, *Otto-Adelheid-Pfennige. Untersuchungen zu Münzen des 10./11. Jahrhunderts* (Stockholm, 1991)
Hauberg, P., *Danmarks Møntvæsen i Tidsrummet 1146–1241* (Copenhagen, 1906)
Hauberg, P., *Møntforhold og udmyntninger i Danmark indtil 1146*, Det kgl. Danske Videnskabernes Selskabs Skrifter, 6. Rakke, historisk og filosofisk afdeling, vol. 1 (Copenhagen, 1900)
Hävernick, Walter, *Die Münzen von Köln vom Beginn der Prägung bis 1304* (Cologne, 1935)
Heffernan, Thomas J., 'The Liturgy and Literature of Saint's Lives', in Thomas J. Heffernan and E. Ann Matter (eds), *The Liturgy of the Medieval Church* (Kalamazoo, 2001), pp. 73–105
Helander, Sven, 'The Liturgical Profile of the Parish Church in Medieval Sweden', Thomas J. Heffernan and E. Ann Matter (eds), in *The Liturgy of the Medieval Church* (Kalamazoo, 2001), pp. 146–86
Helle, Knut (ed.), *The Cambridge History of Scandinavia*, vol. 1, *Prehistory to 1520* (Cambridge, 2003)
Helle, Knut, *Norge blir en stat 1130–1319*, 2nd edition (Oslo-Bergen-Tromsø, 1996)
Hess, W., 'Pfennigwährungen und Geldumlauf im Reichsgebiet zur Zeit der Ottonen und Salier', in B. Kluge (ed.), *Fernhandel und Geldwirtschaft. Beiträge zum deutschen Münzwesen in sächsicher und salischer Zeit. Ergebnisse des Dannenberg-Kolloquiums 1990* (Sigmaringen, 1993), pp. 17–35
Hess, W., 'Münzstatten, Geldverkehr und Handel am Rhein in ottonischer und salischer Zeit', in B. Diestelkamp (ed.), *Beiträge zum hochmittelalterlichen Städtwesen* (Cologne and Vienna, 1981), pp. 111–33
Hill, D., *An Atlas of Anglo-Saxon England* (London, 1981)
Hodges, R., *Dark Age Economics* (London, 1982, 1989)
Hollister, C. W., *Henry I* (New Haven and London, 2001)
Holt, Richard, and Nigel Baker, *Urban Growth and the Medieval Church: Gloucester and Worcester* (Aldershot, 2004)
Hooke, D., and P. Sawyer, *Worcester Anglo-Saxon Charter Bounds* (Woodbridge, 1990)
Hopkins, K., 'Taxes and Trade in the Roman Empire (200 B.C.–A.D. 400)', *Journal of Roman Studies*, 70 (1980): 101–24
Hudson, John, *The Oxford History of the Laws of England, II, 871–1216* (Oxford, 2012)
Hürlimann, Hans, *Zürcher Münzgeschichte* (Zürich, 1966)
Hutchison, C., *The Hermit Monks of Grandmont* (Kalamazoo, 1989)

Hybel, Niels, and Bjørn Poulsen, *The Danish Resources c. 1000–1550: Growth and Recession* (Leiden, 2007)

Ilisch, Peter, *Kleine Corveyer Münzgeschichte* (Paderborn, 1999)

Ilisch, Peter, 'Die Münzprägung im Herzogtum Niederlothringen I: Die Münzprägung in den Räumen Utrecht und Friesland im 10. und 11. Jahrhundert', *Jaarboek voor Munt- en Penningkunde*, 84–5 (1997–98): 43–7

Ilisch, Peter, and Arnold Schwede, *Das Münzwesen im Stift Corvey 1541–1794* (Paderborn, 2007)

Ingvardson, Gitte Tarnow, *Møntbrug. Fra vikingetid til vendertogter* (Aarhus, 2010)

Iogna-Prat, D., *Ordonner et exclure: Cluny et la société chrétienne face à l'hérésie, au judaisme et à l'islam, 1000–1150* (Paris, 2004)

Iversen, Tore, 'Jordeie og jordleie: Eiendomsbegrepet i norske middelalderlover', *Collegium Medievale*, 14 (2002): 79–113

Jacquemart, Ludolphe, Pacome de Falconnet, Bernard-Marie Dubosquet and Gerard Hulsbosch, *Maisons de l'ordre des Chartreux: Vues et notices*, 4 vols (Montreuil-sur-Mer, 1913–19)

James, John, *In Search of the Unknown in Medieval Architecture* (London, 2007)

Jammer, Vera, *Die Anfänge der Münzprägung im Herzogtum Sachsen. 10./11. Jahrhundert*, Numismatische Studien 3–4 (Hamburg, 1952)

Jarnut, Jörg, and Matthias Wemhoff (eds), *Vom Umbruch zur Erneuerung? Das 11. und beginnende 12 Jahrhundert – Positionen der Forschung* (Munich, 2009)

Jasper, K. L., 'The Economics of Reform in the Middle Ages', *History Compass*, 10 (2012): 440–54

Jensen, J., et al., *Danish Coins from the 11th Century in the Royal Collection of Coins and Medals* [*Tusindtallets Danske Mønter fra Den Kongelige Mønt- og Medaillesamling*] (Copenhagen, 1995)

Jensen, Jørgen Steen, 'Møntfornyelse (renovatio monetae) i Danmark indtil år 1200', *Nordisk Numismatisk Unions Medlemsblad*, 8 (1996): 130–6

Jensen, Jørgen Steen, 'En mindemønt for Assers opnåelse af arkebispevardigheden i Lund 1104?', *Nordisk Numismatisk Unions Medlemsblad* (1993): 2–8

Jensen, Jørgen Steen, *Danmarks middelalderlige skattefund fra c. 1050–c. 1550, Denmarks mediaeval treasure-hoards c. 1050–c. 1550* (Copenhagen, 1992)

Jensen, Jørgen Steen, 'Bårarp-fundet 1932. Et hallandsk møntfund fra Svend Grathes tid', *Numismatiska Meddelanden*, 32 (1983): 101–24

Jensen, Jørgen Steen, 'Hvor stor var udmøntningen i Danmark i 1000–og 1100-tallet?', *Fortid og Nutid*, 30 (1983): 19–25

Jeppesen, Jens, 'Magnate Farms and Lordship from the Viking Age to the Medieval Period in Eastern Jutland: The Excavations at Lisbjerg and Haldum Churches' in Bjørn Poulsen and Søren Michael Sindbæk (eds), *Settlement and Lordship in Viking and Early Medieval Scandinavia* (Turnhout, 2011), pp. 137–46

Jesse, Wilhelm, *Quellenbuch zur Münz- und Geldgeschichte des Mittelalters* (Halle/ Saale, 1924)

Jestice, P. G., 'A New Fashion in Imitating Christ: Changing Spiritual Perspectives around the Year 1000', in M. Frassetto (ed.), *The Year 1000: Religious and Social Response to the Turning of the First Millennium* (New York, 2002), pp. 165–85

Jestice, P. G., *Wayward Monks and the Religious Revolution of the Eleventh Century* (Leiden, 1997)

Jevon, W. S., *Money and the Mechanism of Exchange* (London, 1875)

Johnsen, Arne Odd, *Nicolaus Breakespears legasjon til Norden* (Oslo, 1945)

Jones, S. R. H., 'Transaction Costs, Institutional Change, and the Emergence of a Market Economy in Later Anglo-Saxon England', *Economic History Review*, New Series, 46 (1993): 658–78

Jonsson, Kenneth, and Lars Olof Lagerqvist, 'Mynten från Finströms kyrka, Åland', Åländsk Odling (1974): 5–29

Jørgensen, Ellen, *Fremmed indflydelse under den danske Kirkes tidligste Udvikling* (Copenhagen, 1908)

Kaboub, Fadhel, 'Money', in *Encyclopedia of World Trade from Ancient Times to the Present*, vol. 3 of 4, Cynthia Clark Northrup (ed.) (New York, 2005), p. 670

Kaiser, R., 'Quêtes itinérantes avec des reliques pour financer la construction des églises (XIe–XIIe siècles)', *Le Moyen Âge*, 101 (1995): 205–25

Kaiser, R., *Bischofsherrschaft zwischen Königtum und Fürstenmacht. Studien zur bischöflichen Stadtherrschaft im westfranzösischen Reich im frühen und hohen Mittelalter* (Bonn, 1981)

Kaiser, R., 'Münzprivilegien und bischöfliche Münzpragung in Frankreich, Deutschland und Burgund im 9.–12. Jahrhundert', *Vierteljahrschrift für Sozial- und Wirtschaftgeschichte*, 63 (1976): 289–338

Kamp, N., *Moneta regis: königliche Münzstätten und königliche Münzpolitik in der Stauferzeit* (Hannover, 2006)

Kamp, N., 'Probleme des Münzrechts und der Münzpragung in salischer Zeit', in B. Diestelkamp (ed.), *Beiträge zum hochmittelalterlichen Städtwesen* (Cologne and Vienna, 1981), pp. 94–110

Keynes, S. D., and R. Naismith, 'The *Agnus Dei* Pennies of King Athelred the Unready', *Anglo-Saxon England*, 40 (2012): 175–223

Kilger, Christoph, 'Kaupang from Afar: Aspects of the Interpretation of Dirham Finds in Northern and Eastern Europe between the Late 8th and Early 10th Centuries', in Dagfinn Skre (ed.), *The Means of Exchange*, Kaupang Excavation Project Publication Series, vol. 2, Norske Oldfunn, 23 (Aarhus, 2007), pp. 199–252

King, E., *King Stephen* (New Haven and London, 2011)
Klackenberg, Henrik, *Moneta Nostra: Monetarisering i medeltidens* (Lund, 1992)
Klein, Ulrich, and Albert Raff, *Die Münzen und Medaillen von Esslingen* (Stuttgart, 1997)
Kleineke, H., *Borough Market Privileges: The Hinterland of Medieval London, c. 1400* (2006), www.british-history.ac.uk/source.aspx?pubid=345
Kluge, Bernd, 'ALTHALHET, ATEAHLHT und ADELDEIDA. Das Rätsel der Otto-Adelheid-Pfennige', in Franz Staab and Thorsten Unger (eds), *Kaiserin Adelheid und ihre Klostergründung in Selz* (Speyer, 2005), pp. 91–114
Kluge, Bernd, *Otto Rex / Otto Imp. Zur Bestandsaufnahme der ottonischen Münzprägung*, in Bernd Schneidmuller and Stefan Weinfurter (eds), *Ottonische Neuanfänge* (Mainz, 2001), pp. 91–114
Kluge, Bernd (ed.), *Fernhandel und Geldwirtschaft. Beiträge zum deutschen Münzwesen in sächsischer und salischer Zeit* (Sigmaringen, 1993)
Kluge, Bernd, *Deutsche Münzgeschichte von der späten Karolingerzeit bis zum Ende der Salier (ca. 900 bis 1125)* (Sigmaringen, 1991)
Klukas, A. W. 'The Architectural Implications of the *Decreta Lanfanci*', *Anglo-Norman Studies*, 6 (1984): 136–71
Knoop, D., and G. P. Jones, *The Medieval Mason* (Manchester, 1967)
Knowles, D., *The Monastic Order in England*, 2nd edition (Cambridge, 1963)
Kolsrud, Olaf, 'Kong Magnus Erlingssons kronings-eid 1163', *Historisk Tidsskrift*, 31 (1937–40): 453–88
Kosminsky, E. A., *Studies in the Agrarian History of England in the Thirteenth Century* (Oxford, 1956)
Kramer, Heinz Josef, *Das Stift Essen. Münzen und Medaillen. Königliche und stiftische Prägungen in und für Essen* (Münster, 1993)
Kristiansen, Anne Mette, 'Enner-skatten – ny viden om et gammelt fund', *Nordisk Numismatisk Unions Medlemsblad* (2006): 63–71
Kumler, Aden, 'The Multiplication of the Species: Eucharistic Morphology in the Middle Ages', *RES: Anthropology and Aesthetics*, 59/60 (2011): 179–91
Lackner, B. K., *The Eleventh-Century Background of Cîteaux* (Washington, DC, 1972)
Lafaurie, Jean, 'Deniers du VIIIe siècle de Saint-Ouen de Rouen', in Brigitte Beaujard, Nancy Gauthier et al. (eds), *Histoire et numismatique en Haute-Normandie* (Caen, 1980), pp. 109–16
Lafaurie, Jean, 'Trésor de deniers du XIe siècle trouvé à Gaillefontaine (Seine-Maritime)', in Brigitte Beaujard, Nancy Gauthier et al. (eds), *Histoire et numismatique en Haute-Normandie* (Caen, 1980), pp. 117–29

Landes, R., 'Economic Development and Demotic Religiosity', in R. Fulton and B. W. Holsinger (eds), *History in the Comic Mode: Medieval Communities and the Matter of Person* (New York, 2007), pp. 101–16

Langholm, Odd, *Economics in Medieval Schools: Wealth, Exchange, Value, Money and Usury according to the Paris Theological Tradition, 1200–1350* (Leiden, 1992)

Langholm, Odd, *Price and Value in the Aristotelian Tradition: A Study in Scholastic Economic Sources* (Bergen, 1979)

Lannby, Monica Golabiewski, 'Unikt gravfynd med 1100-talsmynt i Skänninge', *Svensk numismatisk tidskrift*, 5 (2009): 110

Lawrence, C. H., *Medieval Monasticism: Forms of Religious Life in Western Europe in the Middle Ages*, 3rd edition (Harlow, 2001)

Le Goff, Jacques, *La naissance du purgatoire* (Paris, 1981), translated into English as *The Birth of Purgatory*, A. Goldhammer (trans.) (Chicago, 1986)

Le Maho, Jacques, 'Autour de la renaissance monastique du Xe siècle en Normandie: les Vies des saints Aycadre et Hugues de Jumièges', Martin Heinzelmann (ed.), *Livrets, collections et texts:* études *sur la tradition hagiographique latine*, Beihefte der Francia, 63 (Ostfildern, 2006), pp. 285–322

Le Maho, Jacques, 'Une monnaie rouennaise aux environs de l'an mil: le denier de "Saint- Romain"', in Mathieu Arnoux et al. (eds), *La Normandie vers l'an mil*, Société de l'Histoire de Normandie, 73 (Rouen, 2000), pp. 202–5

Le Maho, Jacques, 'Nouvelles hypothèses sur l'église Notre-Dame de Rouen au Xe siècle', in Silvette Lemagnen (ed.), *Chapitres et Cathédrales en Normandie* (Caen, 1997), pp. 295–306

Le Maho, Jacques, 'Recherches sur les origines de quelques églises de Rouen (VIe–XIe siècles)', *Bulletin de la Commission départementale des antiquités de Seine-Maritime*, 43 (1995/96): 143–205

Le Maho, Jacques, 'Les fouilles de la cathedrale de Rouen de 1985 a 1993', *Archéologie médiévale*, 24 (1994): 1–49

Le Maho, Jacques, 'Les fouilles de la cathedrale de Rouen de 1985 a 1992', *Groupe recherche archéologique de Pays de Caen, bulletin 1992* (1992): 27–41

Leclercq, J., 'The Monastic Crisis of the Eleventh and Twelfth Centuries', in N. Hunt (ed.), *Cluniac Monasticism in the Central Middle Ages* (London, 1971), pp. 217–37

Legros, Dominique, *Monnaies féodales françaises* (n.p., 1984)

Lehmann-Brockhaus, Otto, *Lateinische Schriftquellen zur Kunst in England, Wales und Schottland vom Jahre 901 bis zum Jahre 1305*, 5 vols (Munich, 1955–60)

Lehmann-Brockhaus, Otto, *Schriftquellen zur Kunstgeschichte des 11. und 12. Jahrhunderts für Deutschland, Lothringen und Italien*, 2 vols (Berlin, 1938)

Lemarignier, J. F., E. Lamon and V. Gazeau, 'Monachisme et aristocratie autour de St Taurin d'Evreux et du Bec' in L. Musset (ed.), *Aspects du monachisme* (Paris, 1982), pp. 100–107
Leyser, H., *Hermits and the New Monasticism: A Study of Religious Communities in Western Europe, 1000–1150* (New York, 1984)
Licence, T., *Hermits and Recluses in English Society, 950–1200* (Oxford, 2011)
Liebgott, N.-K., *Dansk Middelalderarkeologi* (Copenhagen, 1989)
Lifschitz, Felice, *The Dossier of Romanus of Rouen: The Political Uses of Hagiographical Texts* (New York, 1988)
Lindahl, Fritze, 'Om mønter og medailler som bygningsofre', *Nationalmuseets Arbejdsmark* (1956): 93–102
Lindkvist, Thomas, *Landborna i Norden under äldre medeltid* (Stockholm, 1979)
Little, L. K., *Religious Poverty and the Profit Economy* (London, 1978)
Little, L. K., 'Price Goes before Avarice: Social Change and the Vices in Latin Christendom', *American Historical Review*, 76 (1971): 16–59
Lobrichon, G., 'The Chiaroscuro of Heresy: Early Eleventh-Century Aquitaine as Seen from Auxerre', in T. F. Head and R. A. Landes (eds), *The Peace of God: Social Violence and Religious Response in France around the Year 1000* (Ithaca, 1992), pp. 80–103
Lopez, R. S., *The Commercial Revolution of the Middle Ages* (Englewood Cliffs, NJ, 1971)
Lopez, R. S., 'Économie et architecture médiévale: cela aurait-il tué ceci?', in *Annales,* économies, *sociétés, civilisations*, 7 (1952): 433–9
Loyn, H. R., *Anglo-Saxon England and the Norman Conquest* (Oxford, 1962)
Lund, Niels, *Lid, leding og landeværn* (Roskilde, 1996)
Lunden, Kåre, 'Mynt, andre pengar og politisk-økonomisk system i mellomalderen', *Historisk Tidsskrift*, 86 (2007): 7–34
Lunden, Kåre, 'Money Economy in Medieval Norway', *Scandinavian Journal of History*, 24 (1999): 245–65
Lunden, Kåre, *Korn og kaup. Studiar over prisar og jordbruk på Vestlandet i mellomalderen* (Oslo-Bergen-Tromso, 1978)
Lunt, W. E., *Financial Relations of the Papacy with England to 1327* (Cambridge, MA, 1939)
Lynch, Joseph H., *Simoniacal Entry into Religious Life from 1000 to 1260: A Social, Economic and Legal Study* (Columbus, 1976)
Lynch, Joseph H., 'Monastic Recruitment in the Eleventh and Twelfth Centuries: Some Social and Economic Considerations', *American Benedictine Review*, 26 (1975): 425–47
McGuire, B. P., *Friendship and Community: The Monastic Experience, 350–1250* (Kalamazoo, 2000)

Markus, R. A., *Saeculum: History and Society in the Theology of St Augustine* (Cambridge, 1970)

Mason, Emma, 'Lawrence (d. 1173)', *Oxford Dictionary of National Biography*, Oxford University Press, 2004, http://www.oxforddnb.com/view/article/16168

Masters, R., *The History of the College of Corpus Christi, Cambridge* (Cambridge, 1753)

Mate, M., 'The Indebtedness of Canterbury Cathedral Priory 1215–1295', *Economic History Review*, 2nd series, 26 (1973): 183–97

Mayhew, N. J., 'Modelling Medieval Monetisation', in R. H. Britnell and B. M. S. Campbell (eds), *A Commercialising Economy: England 1085 to c. 1300* (Manchester, 1995), pp. 55–77

Mayhew, N. J., Presidential Addresses to the Royal Numismatic Society on 'The Quantity Theory of Money': 1, 'The Money Supply' *Numismatic Chronicle*, 170 (2010): 525–31; 2, 'Prices', *Numismatic Chronicle*, 171 (2011): 519–24; 3, 'Velocity', *Numismatic Chronicle*, 172 (2012): 397–403

Mayr-Harting, H., 'Functions of a Twelfth-Century Recluse', *History*, 60 (1975) 337–52

Mehl, Manfred, *Die Münzen des Stiftes Quedlinburg* (Hamburg, 2006)

Menadier, Julius, 'Ein Adelheidspfennig der Abtei Selz im Elsass', *Berliner Münzblätter*, 110/111 (1889): 985–90

Menadier, Dorothea, 'Die Münzen und das Münzwesen der deutschen Reichsäbtissinnen im Mittelalter', *Zeitschrift für Numismatik*, 32 (1920): 185–293

Merlo, G. G., 'Francesco d'Assisi e il denaro', in L. Travaini (ed.), *Valori e disvalori simbolici delle monete. I 30 denari di Giuda* (Rome, 2009), pp. 145–52

Metcalf, D. M., 'Viking-Age Numismatics, 5, Denmark', *Numismatic Chronicle*, 159 (1999): 395-430

Metcalf, D. M., *Thrymsas and Sceattas in the Ashmolean Museum Oxford, I* (London, 1993)

Metcalf, D. M., 'Continuity and Change in English Monetary History', *British Numismatic Journal*, 50 (1980): 20–49

Metcalf, D. M., *Coinage in South-Eastern Europe 820–1396* (London, 1979)

Metcalf, D. M., 'The Prosperity of North-Western Europe in the Eighth and Ninth Centuries', *Economic History Review*, 20 (1967): 344–57

Metcalf, D. M., 'How Large was the Anglo-Saxon Currency?', *Economic History Review*, 18 (1965): 475–82

Miller, E., 'England in the Twelfth and Thirteenth Centuries: An Economic Contrast', *Economic History Review*, 2nd series, 24 (1971): 1–14

Miller, E., and J. Hatcher, *Medieval England: Rural Society and Economic Change, 1066–1348* (Harlow, 1978)

Millward, R., and A. Robinson, *The Peak District* (London, 1975)

Moesgaard, Jens Christian, '*Renovatio Monetae* et la chronologie des monnaies de Richard Ier, duc de Normandie 942/945–996', *Bulletin de la Société française de numismatique*, 66 (2011): 125–33

Moesgaard, Jens Christian, 'Les deniers de Saint-Ouen de Rouen (Xe siècle)', *Bulletin de la Société française de numismatique*, 64 (2009): 242–6

Moesgaard, Jens Christian, 'Møntpragning i Ringsted og Slagelse i 1000-tallet', *Årbog for Historisk Samfund for Sorø Amt*, 87 (2000): 40–9

Moesgaard, Jens Christian, 'Enkeltfundne mønter fra vikingetiden', in Gillian Fellows-Jensen and Niels Lund (eds), *Beretning fra attende tværfaglige vikingesymposium* (Aarhus,1999), pp. 17–34

Mollat, M., 'Les moines et les pauvres, XIe–XIIe siècles', in *Il monachesimo e la riforma ecclesiastica (1049–1122)* (Milan, 1971), pp. 193–213

Moore, R. I., 'Property, Marriage, and the Eleventh-Century Revolution: A Context for Early Medieval Communism', in M. Frassetto (ed.), *Medieval Purity and Piety: Essays on Medieval Clerical Celibacy and Religious Reform* (New York, 1998), pp. 179–208

Moore, R. I., 'Family, Community and Cult on the Eve of the Gregorian Reform', *Transactions of the Royal Historical Society*, 30 (1980): 49–69

Morgan (Chibnall), M., *The English Lands of the Abbey of Bec* (Oxford, 1968)

Morrison, K. F., *History as a Visual Art in the Twelfth-Century Renaissance* (Princeton, 1990)

Morrison, K. F., and Henry Grunthal, *Caroligian Coinage* (New York, 1967)

Moryson, F., *An Itinerary* (Glasgow, 1907)

Moseng, Ole Georg, Erik Opsahl and Gunnar I. Pettersen, *Norsk Historie 750–1537* (Oslo, 1999)

Müller-Mertens, Eckhard, *Verfassung des Reiches, Reichsstruktur und Herrschaftspraxis unter Otto dem Großen*, in Matthias Puhle (ed.), *Otto der Große. Magdeburg und Europa*, vol. 1 (Mainz, 2001), pp. 189–98

Müller-Mertens, Eckhard, *Die Reichsstruktur im Spiegel der Herrschaftspraxis Ottos des Großen* (Berlin, 1980)

Munch, P. A., *Det Norske Folks Historie*, vol. II , part 4 (Christiania, 1859)

Murray, Alexander, 'Confession before 1215', *Transactions of the Royal Historical Society*, sixth series, 3 (1993): 51–81

Murray, Alexander, *Reason and Society in the Middle Ages* (Oxford, 1978)

Myrdal, Janken, *Jordbruket under feodalismen 1000–1700*, Det svenska jordbrukets historia, 2 (Stockholm, 1999)

Naismith, R., 'The English Monetary Economy c. 973–1100: The Contribution of Single-Finds', *Economic History Review*, 66 (2013): 198–225

Naismith, R., *Money and Power in Anglo-Saxon England: The Southern English Kingdoms 757–865* (Cambridge, 2012)

Neel, Carol (ed.), *Medieval Families, Perspectives on Marriage, Household and Children* (Toronto, 2004)

Nelson, J. L., 'Society, Theodicy and the Origins of Heresy: Towards a Reassessment of the Medieval Evidence', in D. Baker (ed.), *Schism, Heresy and Religious Protest* (Cambridge, 1972), pp. 65–77

Nessel, Franz Xaver, 'Die Münzen der Abtei Selz', *Frankfurter Munzzeitung*, 9 (1909): 421–39, 449–59

Newhauser, Richard, 'Avarice and the Apocalypse', in R. A. Landes, A. C. Gow and D. C. van Meter (eds), *The Apocalyptic Year 1000: Religious Expectation and Social Chance, 950–1050* (Oxford, 2003), pp. 109–19

Nicholson, H., *The Knights Hospitaller* (Woodbridge, 2001)

Nicholson, H., *The Knights Templar: A New History* (Stroud, 2001)

Nielsen, Herluf, 'Peterspenge', *Kulturhistorisk Leksikon for Nordisk Middelalder*, 13 (1968), cols 249–52

Noell, B., 'Cistercian Monks in the Market: Legal Study, Economic Statutes, and Institutional Evolution in the Twelfth Century', *Cîteaux*, 59 (2008): 169–92

North, J. J., *English Hammered Coinage*, vol. 1, 3rd edition (London, 1994)

Notre Dame de Paris, la grâce d'une cathédrale (Strasburg, 2012)

Nyborg, Ebbe, 'Kirke og sogn i højmiddelalderens by', in Søren Bitsch Christensen (ed.), *Middelalderbyen* (Aarhus, 2004)

Nørlund, Poul, *Gyldne Altre. Jysk Metalkunst fra Valdemarstiden* (Copenhagen, 1968)

Ohler, Norbert, *Reisen im Mittelalter* (Zürich/München, 2004)

Olsen, Olaf, 'Kirkegulvet som arkaeologisk arbejdsmark', *Nationalmuseets Arbejdsmark* (1958): 17–30

Oram, R., *The King who Made Scotland* (Stroud, 2004)

Owen, Virginia Lee, 'The Economic Legacy of Gothic Cathedral Building: France and England Compared', *Journal of Cultural Economics*, 13 (1989): 89–100

Page, W. (ed.), *The Victoria County History of the County of York, vol. III* (London, 1913)

Palliser, D. M., T. R. Slater and E. Patricia Dennison, 'The Topography of Towns 600–1300', in D. M. Palliser (ed.), *The Cambridge Urban History of Britain*, vol. 1, pp. 153–86

Paxton, F., *A Medieval Latin Death Ritual: The Monastic Customaries of Bernard and Ulrich of Cluny* (Missoula, Montana, 1993)

Paxton, F., and I. Cochelin, *The Death Ritual at Cluny in the Central Middle Ages* (Turnhout, 2013)

Pease, J. G., and H. Chitty, *A Treatise on the Law Of Markets and Fairs With The Principal Statutes Relating Thereto* (London, 1899), archive.org/details/treatiseonlawofm00peasiala

Pestell, T., and K. Ulmschneider (eds), *Markets in Early Medieval Europe: Trading and 'Productive' Sites, 650–850* (Macclesfield, 2003)

Petersen, Henry, 'St. Kelds Helgenskrin i Viborg Domkirke', *Aarbøger for Nordisk Oldkyndighed og Historie* (1888): 110–14

Pettersen, Gunnar, *De økonomiske sidene ved provent-institusjonen i Norge ca. 1280–1500* (Oslo, 1992)

Pigozzo, F., 'La moneta cucita: i nascondigli per il denaro alla fine del Medioevo', *Bollettino del Museo Civico di Padova*, 94 (2005): pp. 159–62

Pilet-Lemiere, Jacqueline, 'Les monnaies de la cathedrale de Rouen', in *Le trésor de la Cathédrale de Rouen* (Rouen-Caen, 1993), pp. 31–2

Pilet-Lemière, Jacqueline, 'Les monnayages ecclesiastiques', *L'évangélisation de la Normandie, Les dossiers d'archéologie*, 144 (1990): 66–7

Pilet-Lemière, Jacqueline, 'Deniers inédits de Rouen à la legend METROPOLIS', *Bulletin de la Société française de numismatique*, 40 (1985): 639–40

Platt, C., *The Architecture of Medieval Britain* (London and New Haven, 1990)

Poey d'Avant, F., *Les monnaies féodales de France*, 3 vols (Paris, 1858–62)

Poly, J.-P., and E. Bournazel, *The Feudal Transformation 900–1200*, C. Higgitt (trans.) (New York and London, 1991)

Pontoni, A., 'Note sull'esegesi e l'iconografia del *titulus crucis*', *Aevum. Rassegna di scienze storiche linguistiche e filologiche*, 77 (2003): 138–86

Posselt, Gert, 'Nogle danske mønter med gejstelige fremstillinger før ca. 1150', *Hikuin*, 11 *Festschrift to Brita Malmer* (1985): 207–14

Poulsen, Bjørn, *Bondens penge. Studier i sønderjyske regnskaber 1400–1650* (Odense, 1990)

Poulsen, Bjørn, 'Hvilke informationer giver kirkefund ikke?, *NNUM* (1986): 150–1

Pound, N. J. G., *An Economic History of Medieval Europe*, 2nd edition (London, 1994)

Pratt, C., *The Political Thought of King Alfred the Great* (Cambridge, 2007)

Profantová, N. 'Byzantine Coins of the 5th–9th Century from the Czech Republic', in Marcin Wołoszyn (ed.), *Byzantine Coins in Central Europe between the 5th and 10th Century*, Proceedings from the conference organised by Polish Academy of Arts and Sciences, Institute of Archaeology University Rzeszów under the patronage of Union Académique Internationale (Programme no. 57 Moravia Magna) Krákow, 23–26 IV 2007, Polish Academy of Arts and Sciences and Institute of Archaeology University Rzeszów via Magna, Seria Polona, vol. III (Krakow, 2009), pp. 581–98

Raban, S., *Mortmain Legislation and the English Church, 1279–1500* (Cambridge, 1982)

Radtke, Christian, 'Schleswig c. 1000–1250: System Theory Sketches for Profiling Urbanization', in Nils Engberg, Anne Norgaard Jorgensen, Jakob Kieffer-Olsen, Per Kristian Madsen and Christian Radtke (eds), *Archaeology of Medieval Towns in the Baltic and North Sea Area* (Copenhagen, 2009), pp. 51–63

Von Reden, S., *Money in Classical Antiquity* (Cambridge, 2010)
Reed, C. G., and T. L. Anderson, 'An Economic Explanation of English Agricultural Organization in the Twelfth and Thirteenth Centuries' *Economic History Review*, 2nd series, 26 (1973): 134–7
Rensbro, Henriette, *Spor i kirkegulve. De siste 50 års arkæologiske undersøgelser i kirkegulve som kilde til sognekirkernes indretning og brug i middelalder og renæssance* (Doctoral thesis, Aarhus University, 2007)
Resl, Brigitte, 'Material Support I: Parishes', in *Christianity in Western Europe c. 1100–c. 1500*, Miri Rubin and Walter Simons (eds), *The Cambridge History of Christianity*, vol. 4 (Cambridge, 2009), pp. 99–106
Resnick, I. M., 'Odo of Tournai and Peter Damian: Poverty and Crisis in the Eleventh Century', *Revue bénédictine*, 98 (1988): 114–40
Riley-Smith, J., *The History of the Order of St John* (London, 1999)
Risvaag, Jon Anders, *Erkebiskopens i Nidaros' utmynting i middelalderen. Med særlig vekt på erkebiskopens myntrett* (Magistral thesis, University of Oslo, 1995)
Risvaag, Jon Anders, 'Ikke-kongelige utmynting i Norge frem til reformasjonen', *Nordisk Numismatisk Årsskrift* (1994–96): 130–61
Rizzoli, jr, L., 'Teche e medaglie murali carraresi', *Bollettino del Museo Civico di Padova*, II (1899): 56–8
Robertson, A. J., *The Laws of the Kings of England from Edmund to Henry I* (Cambridge, 1925)
Robinson, Ian Stewart, *Authority and Resistance in the Church Investiture Contest: The Polemical Literature of the Late Eleventh Century* (Manchester, 1978)
Robson, M. (ed.), *The Cambridge Companion to Saint Francis of Assisi* (Cambridge, 2011)
Roesdahl, Else, 'Walrus Ivory – Demand, Supply and Workshops, and Greenland', in A. Mortensen and S. Arge (eds), *Viking and Norse in the North Atlantic: Select Papers from the Proceedings of the Fourteenth Viking Congress Tórshavn 19–30 July 2001* (Tórshavn, 2005), pp. 182–91
Roffe, D., *Decoding Domesday* (Woodbridge, 2007)
Rollason, D., *Saints and Relics in Anglo-Saxon England* (Oxford, 1989)
Rollason, D., 'Relic-Cults as an Instrument of Royal Policy c. 900–c. 1050', *Anglo-Saxon England*, 15 (1986): 91–103
Rosenwein, B. H., and L. K. Little, 'Social Meaning in the Monastic and Mendicant Spiritualities', *Past & Present*, 63 (1974): 4–32
Rouen, La Grâce d'une cathédrale (Strasbourg, 2012)
Royal Historical Bibliography of British and Irish History, Brepolis, online, http://www.history.ac.uk/projects/bbih
Rozenberg, S. (ed.), *Knights of the Holy Land: The Crusader Kingdom of Jerusalem* (Jerusalem, 1999)

Rubenstein, J., *Guibert of Nogent: Portrait of a Medieval Mind* (New York, 2002)
Rüffer, Jens, *Die Kathedrale von Santiago de Compostella (1075–1211), eine Quellenstudie* (Bern, 2010)
Runciman, Steven, *The Eastern Schism: A Study of the Papacy and the Eastern Churches during the XIth and XIIth Centuries* (Oxford, 1955)
Russell, J. C., *British Medieval Population* (Albuquerque, 1948)
Ryland, W., D. Adkins and R. M. Serjeantson (eds), *Victoria County History Northampton*: vol. 2 (1906)
Saccocci, A., 'Monete rinvenute nell'urna del santo', in S. Lunardon (ed.), *San Secondo. Un santo cavaliere tra la lagune*, Atti della Giornata di studi Venezia, Istituto Veneto di Scienze Lettere e Arti, 22 ottobre 2004 (Venice, 2007): pp. 149–67, 232–45, 274–6
Saccocci, A., 'Le monete', in L. Ermini Pani, M. G. Fichera and M. L. Mancinelli (eds), *Indagini archeologiche nella chiesa di San Damiano in Assisi*, Medioevo francescano, arte 1 (Assisi, 2005), pp. 119–30
Saccocci, A., 'Il ripostiglio di monete', in G. Ciampoltrini and E. Pieri (eds), *Archeologia a Pieve a Nievole: dalla basilica sita in loco Neure alla pieve romanica* (Pisa, 2004), pp. 71–83
Saccocci, A., 'Teche e "medaglie" murali carraresi (1355–1405)', in A. Verdi (ed.), *Le mura ritrovate* (exhibition catalogue) (Padova, 1987), pp. 154–5
Sættem, Anette, and Svein H. Gullbekk, *Norske myntfunn ca.1050–1319*, work in progress
Salter, H. E., 'Two Deeds about the Abbey of Bec', *English Historical Review*, 40 (1925): 74–6
Salzman, L. F., *Building in England down to 1540* (Oxford, 1967)
Salzman, L. F., (ed.), *Victorian County History Cambridge and the Isle of Ely*: vol. 2 (1948)
Sargent, Thomas J., and Francois Velde, *The Big Problem of Small Change* (Princeton, 2002)
Sauer, Eberhard, 'In Search of the Port-way', www.oxoniensia.org/volumes/1998/sauer.pdf
Sawyer, P., *The Wealth of Anglo-Saxon England* (Oxford, 2013)
Sawyer, P., *Anglo-Saxon Charters: An Annotated List and Bibliography* (London, 1968) http://www.esawyer.org.uk
Sawyer, P., 'The Wealth of England in the Eleventh Century', *Transactions of the Royal Historical Society*, 5th series, 15 (1965): 145–64
Schlegel, Gerhard, and James Hogg (eds), *Monasticon Cartusiense*, 4 vols in 10, *Analecta Cartusiana* 185, 1–4 (Salzburg, 2004–12)
Schmitt, J.-C., *Ghosts in the Middle Ages: The Living and the Dead in Medieval Society* (Chicago, 1998)

Schöller, Wolfgang, 'Funding the Construction of Gothic Cathedrals: Financial and Legal Realities of the Middle Ages', *Athena Review, Quarterly Journal of Archaeology, History and Exploration*, 4 (2005): 48–52

Schraven, M., 'Out of Sight, Yet Still in Place: On the Use of Italian Renaissance Portrait Medals as Building Deposits', *Res: Anthropology and Aesthetics*, 55–6 (2009): 182–93

Schwarz, Dietrich W. H., *Münz- und Geldgeschichte Zürich im Mittelalter* (Aarau, 1940)

Seip, Jens Arup, *Sættargjerden i Tunsberg og kirkens jurisdiksjon* (Oslo, 1942)

Serafini, C., *Le monete*, in B. M. Apollonj Ghetti, A. Ferrua, E. Josi and E. Kirschbaum, *Esplorazioni sotto la Confessione della Basilica di San Pietro in Vaticano* (Città del Vaticano, 1951), pp. 225–44

Simensen, Christian, 'Hvilken informasjon gir myntfunn gjort i norske kirker', *NNUM* (1986): 42–53

Simmel, Georg, *The Philosophy of Money* (London and New York, 1978)

Skaare, Kolbjørn, 'Kong Sverres utmynting', *NNÅ* (1979–80): 93–109

Skaare, Kolbjørn, 'Myntene fra Lom kirke', *Ab.* (1978): 113–31

Skaare, Kolbjørn, *Coins and Coinage in Viking Age Norway* (Oslo, 1976)

Skaare, Kolbjørn, 'Universitets Myntkabinett (Annual Report)', *Nordisk Numismatisk Årsskrift* (1973–74): 154–5

Skaare, Kolbjørn, 'En ny norsk erkebispemynt', *Numismatiska Meddelanden*, 30 (1965): 92–102

Skyum-Nielsen, Niels, *Kvinde og slave* (Copenhagen, 1971)

Sørensen, Anne Birgitte, Østergaard. *Vikingetid og middelalder* (Haderslev, 2011)

Southern, R. W., *Western Society and the Church in the Middle Ages* (Harmondsworth, 1970)

Southern, R. W., 'The Place of England in the Twelfth-Century Renaissance', *History*, 45 (1960): 201–16

Søvsø, Morten, 'Et møntstempel fra Ribe', *Nordisk Numismatisk Unions Medlemsblad* (2007): 117–23

Spufford, P., 'Mint Organisation in Late Medieval Europe', in N. J. Mayhew and P. Spufford (eds), *Later Medieval Mints: Organisation, Administration and Techniques*, The 8th Oxford Symposium on Coinage and Monetary History, British Archaeological Reports, int. series 389 (Oxford, 1988), pp. 7–30

Spufford, P., *Money and its Use in Medieval Europe* (Cambridge, 1988)

Steinbach, Sebastian, *Das Geld der Nonnen und Mönche. Münzrecht, Münzprägung und Geldumlauf der ostfränkisch-deutschen Klöster in ottonisch-salischer Zeit (ca. 911–1125)* (Berlin, 2007)

Steinnes, Asgaut, 'Mål, vekt og verderekning i Noreg i millomalderen og ei tid etter', in Sven Aakjær (ed.), *Mål og Vekt* (Oslo-Stockholm-København, 1936)

Steinnes, Asgaut, *Gamal skatteskipnad i Norge*, vol. II (Oslo, 1933)

Steinnes, Asgaut, 'Peningar vegnir og peningar svartnir', *Historisk Tidsskrift*, 27 (1927): 522–32

Stephenson, C., 'The Anglo-Saxon Borough', *English Historical Review*, 178 (1930): 177–207

Storm, Gustav, *Afgifter fra den norske kirkeprovins til det apostoliske kammer og Kardinalkollegiet 1311–1523* (Christiania, 1897)

Strasbourg, La grâce d'une cathédrale (Strasburg, 2007)

Suchodolski, Stanislaw, 'Die Anfänge der Munzprägung in Scandinavien und Polen', *Nordisk Numismatisk Årsskrift* (1971): 20–37

Svarstad, Carsten, 'Myntfunnet fra Fjære kirke', *Nordisk Numismatisk Årsskrift* (1957): 106–9

Swanson, R. N., *The Twelfth-Century Renaissance* (Manchester, 1999)

Sweeney, Eileen C., *Anselm of Canterbury and the Desire for the Word* (Washington, DC, 2012)

Sylloge of Coins of the British Isles, Norway, Elina Screen (ed.) vol. 1 (Oxford, 2013)

Tabacco, G., *Spiritualità e cultura nel Medioevo: dodici percosi nei territori del potere e della fede* (Naples, 1993), pp. 267–85

Taeuber, Walter, *Geld und Kredit im Mittelalter* (Berlin, 1933)

Taranger, Absalon, *Den angelsaksiske kirkes indflytelse* (Christiania, 1890)

Tellenbach, G., *The Church in Western Europe from the Tenth to the Early Twelfth Century*, T. Reuter (trans.) (Cambridge, 1993)

Tellenbach, G., *Church, State and Christian Society at the Time of the Investiture Contest*, R. F. Bennett (trans.) (Toronto, 1991), orig. pub. as *Libertas: Kirche und Weltordnung im Zeitalter des Investiturstreites* (Stuttgart, 1936)

Thomas, G., *The Later Anglo-Saxon Settlement at Bishopstone: A Downland Manor in the Making* (York, 2010)

Thomas, Kate, *The Meaning, Practice and Context of Private Prayer in Late Anglo-Saxon England* (unpublished PhD thesis, University of York, 2011)

Thompson, S., *Motif-Index of Folk Literature: A Classification of Narrative Elements in Folktales, Ballads, Myths, Fables, Mediaeval Romances, Exempla, Fabliaux, Jest- Books and Local Legends*, revised and enlarged edition, 6 vols (Bloomington-Indianapolis, 1955–58)

Tobin, James, 'Money', in *The New Palgrave Dictionary of Money and Finance* (London, 1992), pp. 770–78

Todeschini, G., *Ricchezza francescana: dalla povertà volontaria alla società di mercato* (Bologna, 2004)

Todeschini, G., *Il prezzo della salvezza: lessici medievali del pensiero economico* (Rome, 1994)

Travaini, L., 'Il lato buono delle monete: devozione, miracoli e reliquie monetali', *Cristianesimo nella storia*, 33 (2012): 475–92

Travaini, L., 'Le zecche italiane', in L. Travaini (ed.), *Le zecche italiane fino all'Unità* (Rome: 2011)

Travaini, L., 'Le monete', in F. Missere Fontana and L. Travaini (eds), *Monete medievali e materiali nella tomba di San Geminiano di Modena* (Nonantola, 2005), pp. 35–57

Travaini, Lucia, 'Saints and Sinners: Coins in Medieval Italian Graves', *Numismatic Chronicle*, 164 (2004): 159–81

Travaini, L., 'Le monete nella tomba di san Francesco di Assisi', *Cercetări Numismatice*, 9–11 (2003–5): 193–8

Travaini, L., 'Le monete a Fontana di Trevi: storia di un rito', *Rivista Italiana di Numismatica*, 101 (2000): 251–9

Tyerman, C. J., *England and the Crusades 1095–1588* (Chicago, 1988)

Ullén, M., *Medeltida träkyrkor*, vol. I, *Sveriges Kyrkor* (Stockholm, 1983)

Ulmschneider, K., 'Settlement, Economy and the "Productive" Site: Middle Anglo-Saxon Lincolnshire 650–780', *Medieval Archaeology*, 44 (2000): 53–79

Ulriksen, Jens, *Anløbspladser. Besejling og bebyggelse i Danmark mellem 200 og 1100 e. Kr* (Roskilde, 1997)

Ulsig, Erik, 'Landboer og bryder, skat og landgilde. De danske fastebønder og deres afgifter i det 12. og 13. Århundrede', in Karsten Fledelius, Niels Lund and Herluf Nielsen (eds), *Middelalder, metode og medier. Festskrift til Niels Skyum-Nielsen på 60-årsdagen den 17. oktober 1981* (Viborg, 1981)

van Dijk, S. J. P., *The Myth of the Aumbry: Notes on Medieval Reservation Practice and Eucharistic Devotion* (London, 1957)

Van Engen, J. H., 'The "Crisis of Cenobitism" Reconsidered: Benedictine Monasticism in the Years 1050–1150', *Speculum*, 61 (1986): 269–304

Vanderputten, S., 'Crises of Cenobitism: Abbatial Leadership and Monastic Competition in Late Eleventh-Century Flanders,' *English Historical Review*, 127 (2012): 259–84

Vincent, Catherine, and Jacques Pycke (eds), *Cathédrale et pèlerinage aux époques médiévales et moderne: reliques, processions et dévotions à l'église-mère du diocese* (Louvain-la-Neuve, 2010)

Vroom, Wim, *Financing Cathedral Building in the Middle Ages: The Generosity of the Faithful* (Amsterdam, 2010)

Walcott, Mackenzie E. C., 'Bowing to the Altar', *Notes and Queries*, 5th series, 10 (1978): 437–8

Warnke, Martin, *Bau und* Überbau*: Soziologie der mittelalterlichen Architektur nach den Schriftquellen* (Frankfurt am Main, 1979)

Weinfurter, Stefan, *Canossa: Die Entzauberung der Welt* (Munich, 2007)

Weinfurter, Stefan, *1024–1125: Das Jahrhundert der Salier. Kaiser oder Papst?* (Stuttgart, 2004)

West, C., *Reframing the Feudal Revolution: Political and Social Transformation between Marne and Moselle, c. 800–c. 1100* (Cambridge, 2013)
Whitelock, D., *The Beginnings of English Society* (Harmondsworth, 1954)
Wickham, C., 'Mutations et révolutions aux environs de l'an mil', *Médiévales*, 21 (1991): 27–38
Williams, A., 'An Introduction to the Gloucester Domesday', in *The Gloucestershire Domesday*, Alecto (London, 1989)
Witters, D. W., 'Pauvres et pauvreté dans les coutumiers monastiques du Moyen Âge', in M. Mollat (ed.), Études sur l'histoire *de la pauvreté (Moyen Âge–XVI siècle)*, 2 vols (Paris, 1974), vol. 1, pp. 177–215
Wood, D., *Medieval Economic Thought* (Cambridge, 2002)
Yarrow, Simon, *Saints and Their Communities: Miracle Stories in Twelfth-Century England* (Oxford, 2006)
Ziegler, Ernst, 'Zur Münzgeschichte des Klosters St. Gallen von den Anfängen bis zu Abt Ulrich Rösch (1463–1491)', *Rorschacher Neujahrsblatt*, 77 (1987): 37–52

Index

For Product Safety Concerns and Information please contact our EU representative GPSR@taylorandfrancis.com Taylor & Francis Verlag GmbH, Kaufingerstraße 24, 80331 München, Germany